MAYA POLITICAL SCIENCE

D1605840

The Linda Schele Series in Maya and Pre-Columbian Studies

This series was made possible through the generosity of
William C. Nowlin, Jr., and Bettye H. Nowlin,
the National Endowment for the Humanities, and various
individual donors.

Maya Political Science

Time, Astronomy, and the Cosmos

BY PRUDENCE M. RICE

UNIVERSITY OF TEXAS PRESS, AUSTIN

Requests for permission to reproduce material from this work should be sent to Permissions, University of Texas Press, P.O. Box 7819, Austin, TX 78713–7819.

♾ The paper used in this book meets the minimum requirements of ANSI/NISO Z39.48–1992 (R1997) (Permanence of Paper).

LIBRARY OF CONGRESS CATALOGING-IN-PUBLICATION DATA

Rice, Prudence M.
    Maya political science : time, astronomy, and the cosmos / by Prudence M. Rice. — 1st ed.
        p.   cm. — (The Linda Schele series in Maya and pre-Columbian studies)
    Includes bibliographical references and index.
    ISBN 0-292-70261-2 (cl.:/alk. paper)—ISBN 0-292-70569-7 (pbk. : alk. paper)
    1. Mayas—Politics and government.   2. Mayas—History.   3. Mayas—Antiquities.   4. Mexico—Antiquities.   5. Guatemala—Antiquities.
I. Title.   II. Series.
F1435.3.P7R5   2004
320.97281—dc22
                                                                2004005735

In memory of Oliver,
my handsome, tuxedoed, little
ek' b'alam kalomte'

[T]he distinction between past, present, and future is only a stubbornly persistent illusion.

—Albert Einstein, 1955, Letter of condolence
to the Family of Michele Besso

Who controls the past controls the future. Who controls the present controls the past.

—George Orwell, *1984* (1949)

[T]he pattern of Mayan history is strongly suggestive of a continuous tradition of major cultural and political changes at the recurrences of the folding of the *may* every time 8 *Ahau* comes around.

—Munro S. Edmonson, "Some Postclassic
Questions about the Classic Maya" (1979)

Whoever put in order this computation of katuns, if it was the devil, he did it, as he usually does, ordaining it for his own glory, or, if it was a man, he must have been a good idolater, for with these katuns of theirs, he increased all the principal trickeries, divinations and delusions with which these people, besides their miseries, were entirely deluded, and thus this was the science to which they gave the most credit.

—Bishop Diego de Landa, *Relación de las cosas de Yucatan* (1566)

CONTENTS

Figures

Tables

PREFACE

I propose here that Classic Maya political organization is best understood by means of the direct-historical approach, that is, by retrodicting elements of Postclassic and early Colonial period organization back
into the Classic period. I hypothesize that Classic (and also Preclassic)
Maya geopolitico-religious organization was structured by Maya calendrical science, particularly the intervals of approximately twenty years
(k'atun) and 256 years, or thirteen k'atuns (may 'cycle'). By analogy with
Postclassic and early Colonial period Yucatán, Mexico, Classic sites
hosting the may for 256-year periods were capitals of territories in
which k'atun seats rotated among other dependent sites. Portions of the
elaborate ceremonies carried out when the Postclassic calendrical cycles
ended and began anew can be recognized in the images and inscriptions
on Classic-period carved monuments at Tikal, Guatemala, and other
southern lowland sites. May and k'atun seats can be identified archaeologically by the erection of stelae commemorating k'atun endings and
shared distinctive architectural complexes associated with the celebration of these calendrical observations. In addition, the may hypothesis
provides insights into the nature of rulership, ballgame ritual, and warfare among the Classic lowland Maya.

My interpretation of the role of the 256-year k'atun round, or may, in
Classic Maya political history had its origins in several circumstances—
most of them outgrowths of my own history in the field of Maya archaeology—in which I found myself in the mid-1990s. The immediate
impetus for writing this book was a need to incorporate textual and
iconographic information from the carved monuments around the central Petén lakes into an understanding of the Terminal Classic period in
the region. This began as a fairly easily delimited effort to establish the
Terminal Classic terminus post quem of Proyecto Maya-Colonial's investigation of the Postclassic and Colonial period histories of the Maya
in this area. As I inventoried the relatively few and poorly known late
stelae and altars at sites around the lake basins, I realized the impor-

tance of comparing them to the better-known corpus of late monuments at Tikal.

I embarked on this task during a time of rampant arguments about so-called segmentary states and endemic warfare in the southern lowlands. Having spent most of my professional archaeological career working at sites in the shadow of Tikal, I found the hypothesized existence of scores of small, warring, weakly independent polities and segmentary states utterly improbable. I was convinced there had to be a better explanation of Maya political organization. At the same time, I began to question whether the "evidence" for endemic warfare could be as much a matter of epigraphers' interpretations as empirical fact. And I also realized that direct-historical analogy has never been fully exploited as a basis for explaining Classic Maya political geography, particularly in Petén. So I challenged myself to come up with something that seemed more reasonable. The result is this book.

The past seven years have seen an unending series of revisions and expansions of my earlier thinking, and I have had to review literature I last read as a graduate student one and a half k'atuns ago. During this same period, stunning advances in Maya hieroglyphic decipherments have provided desperately needed insights into Maya dynasties and dynastic politics while at the same time also—thankfully—"failing to disconfirm" my thesis, in the neutral terminology of statistical hypothesis testing. Continuing in this Popperian vein, and using the principle of Occam's razor, I believe the *may* model of Maya political organization is the simplest theory that accounts for all the evidence, and none of the evidence currently available to me contradicts it. In particular, I have been gratified to see increasing evidence for, and archaeologists' acceptance of, centralized and regional-state models.

Numerous colleagues have generously read and commented on earlier drafts of these ideas about the *may*, and their reactions were variations of the following: "interesting idea, but calendrical ceremony was merely one device in a much larger toolkit that Maya kings could manipulate to achieve their ends." Maybe. I suspect, however, that the lingering reluctance to embrace calendrical models of political organization, such as the *may* model, is a legacy of reaction against much earlier reconstructions of Maya society. These reconstructions, advanced during the early twentieth century by Spinden, Morley, Thompson, and others, simplistically characterized the Maya as gentle philosophers and astronomer-priests, living in "vacant cities" and "obsessed with time."

But the Maya *were* obsessed with time. How else to explain Long Count calendrical inscriptions, which might consist of more than a dozen glyphs, laboriously carved in stone, all of which firmly anchor events of a particular day in the present by tying them to cosmic history:

precise counts of elapsed days, painstakingly calculated via multiple calendars based on an origin point several thousand years in the past? Of some 34,000 inscriptions in the CD-ROM database compiled by Martha Macri (n.d.), 11,000—nearly one-third—are dedicated to celebrating the completion of specific time periods (Hofling, pers. comm., November 24, 2001). Does this not qualify as "obsession"—generally defined by dictionaries as abnormal or unreasonable preoccupation, fixation, fascination, ruling passion, and so on?

It is unfortunate that the role of time and the calendar for the ancient Maya has so long languished in disrepute among Mayanist archaeologists. Numerous scholarly and popular overviews of the history of time (e.g., Hawking 1996; Krupp 1997; Waugh 1999) have celebrated the degree to which astronomy, celestial cycles, and calendrical precisioning have been major concerns of ancient kings and civilizations throughout history. As Waugh (1999:131) comments, "All the major calendar reforms of the past have been put in place by emperors, popes or potentates." With respect to our current Western calendar, centuries of intensely debated modifications, from Roman times up to the mid-eighteenth century, led to the (re)naming of the months and the eventual switch from the Julian to the Gregorian calendar. In addition, resolution of questions of time and calendrics often requires convening representatives from many political units: the present system of world time zones, for example, was established at a conference of twenty-seven nations in Washington, D.C., in 1884 (Waugh 1999:71). Given the complex history of some sixty calendars in Mesoamerica (Edmonson 1988) and the ancient Maya's demonstrable dedication to (if not "obsession" with) situating events within broader cycles of time, there is every reason to assume that such debates and reforms and conferences would have taken place among the Maya as well. Maya archaeologists, art historians, and epigraphers regularly pay lip service to the concept of Maya kings as "lords of time," yet they have disdained to examine the deeper import of this trope in an "if-then" experimental sense: if Maya kings were indeed lords of time, then what would we expect to find as evidence of this in the archaeological, iconographic, and epigraphic records?

In arguing the importance of calendrical cycling to the Maya, I anticipate criticism for appearing to ignore other aspects of Classic kingship or for cramming everything but the kitchen batea into these cycles. However, scientific parsimony, Occam's razor, and many other points of philosophy of science suggest that the goal of a theory, model, or explanation should be to arrive at the simplest explanation that accounts for the most facts. It is clear that diverse phenomena and events of Maya history can be explained by the model. In addition, to postulate that

Maya political organization was based in calendrical cycling does not negate any components of a Maya king's rich administrative arsenal of statecraft, including warfare, ballgames, and agriculture. It does not deny the salience of individual agency and decision making, or imply that Maya rulers were witless slaves to the turning of metaphorical pages of a calendar. Rather, the *may* model acknowledges that cosmic cycling and quadripartition were not mere ideological furbelows of the Maya but rather fundamental principles that established and operationalized the "deep structure" of their material (terrestrial, sociopolitical) world.

As I completed the final revisions for this book, I found myself experiencing a bizarre sense of channeling parallel universes. I have been struggling for the past seven years or so to interrelate Maya ideology and cosmology with what we ethnocentrically call "the real world," the normal, pragmatic, temporal interactions and concerns of humans and Western civilizations: politics, government, social organization, materiality, and so on. Meanwhile, I recently finished reading an eerie science fiction novel[1] premised on many of the same data discussed herein: That is, the current "creation" of the Maya cosmos occurred on a day 8 Ajaw 4 Kumk'u in 3114 B.C., and this creation will end in less than ten years, on December 21, 2012, with completion of the thirteenth *b'ak'tun* (a b'ak'tun is a period of nearly four hundred years), unless it is saved by a modern incarnation of Hun Hunahpu of the K'iche' Maya myth, *Popol Vuh.* At the same time, I was reading articles in *Science, Scientific American,* and other scholarly publications that have reopened discussions about Einstein's general theory of relativity and the "rubbery" relationships between time and space, or "spacetime."[2] A new scientific theory of the cosmos envisions giant, flexible, parallel multidimensional "membranes" existing only millimeters apart; when they collide the universe is destroyed and then re-created again. This model of the origin of the universe is called "ekpyrotic," or born of fire. And this is also the name of Tikal's mysterious central Mexican visitor, Siyaj K'ak', who arrived at the site in A.D. 378 . . .

Notes

1. Steve Alten, *Domain* (New York: TOR, 2001).

2. Ian Osborne, Linda Rowan, and Robert Coontz, *Spacetime, Warped Branes, and Hidden Dimensions,* introduction to a thematic section on "Spacetime" in *Science* 396:1417–1439 (May 24, 2002). Richard Monastersky, Recycling the Universe, New Theory Posits That Time Has No Beginning or End, *Chronicle of Higher Education,* June 7, 2002, pp. A19–A21.

NOTE ON ORTHOGRAPHY AND DATES

Aside from card-carrying epigraphers, most readers of specialized or even general publications about the Maya have experienced the confusion and frustration of trying to remain current with the rapidly changing readings, interpretations, and orthography of Classic glyphs, kings' names, and so forth (see Montgomery 2001:13). My decisions on how to handle these matters are outlined below.

In general, I try to employ the orthography for Maya words that has been accepted by the Academía de Lenguas Mayas in Guatemala, because the research on which it was based and the primary site discussed (Tikal) are in Guatemala. However, Guatemalan archaeologists also have eliminated, in national publications, Spanish diacritical marks on the names of sites, cultural phases, and ceramic units drawn from indigenous languages. I have chosen to retain these markings and spellings and use the spellings of site names as they customarily appear (or have appeared) on maps produced in the United States by the National Geographic Society.

The above principles do not provide a solid basis for selecting Yukatekan versus Ch'olan Mayan orthography. The western and southern parts of the southern lowlands seem to have spoken and written Ch'olan during the Late Classic period, while the northern lowlands used Yukatekan (although this too is a matter of argument). The central area, from just south of the Petén lakes chain northward to perhaps the Río Bec zone, might have been bilingual in Yukatekan and Ch'olan. Indeed, the whole lowlands might have been bilingual. But given the likelihood that (1) Classic Maya inscriptions might have been written using a combination of Yukatekan and Ch'olan and (2) the south-central and particularly the Tikal zones were not primarily Ch'olan-speaking, I have opted to use Yukatekan spellings. In general, those of us working in the Petén lakes area accept continuities in Yukatekan and Itzaj Maya dialects for the region.

What all this means is that, for example, I spell certain words with the Yukatekan *k* rather than the Ch'olan *ch* (e.g., *kan* rather than *chan*). In addition, I have chosen to use *j* for both the hard and soft *h* sound. I do not incorporate hypothesized long vowels except as such spellings occur in direct quotations.

Finally, in Yukatekan Mayan plurals are expressed with an *ob* ending, for example *k'atunob* to mean multiple k'atuns. Purists will shudder, but, for greater ease of reading, I use the English convention of *s* to denote plurals.

Numerous words in the Maya languages are used in the text. In general, they are italicized when first used and in roman type thereafter. Important exceptions are *may* (pronounced "my"), the Maya 256-year cycle, which is always italicized to avoid confusion with the English auxiliary verb *may;* and *way* (pronounced "wye"), meaning spirit companion, which is always italicized to avoid confusion with the English word.

Finally, as much as possible, Maya dates reported here have been correlated to the Gregorian calendar using the Goodman-Martínez-Thompson correlation and the 584,283 correlation constant.

ACKNOWLEDGMENTS

This monograph had its origins in about 1995 as an effort to synthesize data on the Late and Terminal Classic monuments of the Petén lakes area of Guatemala. I first presented my tentative thoughts about the role of *may* cycles in the Tikal region at the annual meeting of the American Anthropological Association in San Francisco in 1996, in a paper prepared with skeptical coauthors, Don S. Rice and Grant D. Jones. About three years later, I sent out an intermediate but still preliminary article-length version of these ideas to colleagues, and I am grateful to Will Andrews, Arthur Demarest, David Freidel, Norman Hammond, Joyce Marcus, and David Webster for their helpful suggestions and encouragement to pursue this line of reasoning. In the course of finalizing this manuscript, numerous other individuals shared useful data with me, including Tony Andrews, Clemency Coggins, and Kitty Emery. I am especially grateful to Bill Fash, Joyce Marcus, John Montgomery, and David Stuart for generously providing me with copies of illustrations to be reprinted in this book.

I find myself particularly indebted to my Southern Illinois University Carbondale (SIUC), departmental colleague C. Andrew Hofling. Andy was extremely generous in sharing his Maya linguistic and epigraphic expertise, gently but insistently nudging me to dig deeper for substantiating data and suffering my contrarian presence in his Maya hieroglyphs class. He also arranged, through the kind generosity of Martha Macri, to whom I am extremely grateful, to make a copy of her Maya hieroglyphic database available to me and students working with me. Andy's heroism extended to reading the entire manuscript not once but twice! Without Andy's encouragement and support, this book would not have been written. (I quickly add that any errors are entirely my own responsibility.)

I am also extremely grateful to Don Rice for his critiques, insights, and suggestions for clarification. In addition, I was privileged to count on his computer expertise—and patience through many dreary winter weekends—for many of the illustrations. Our four-footed "children"—

Duner, Pee, Boz, and the late, great *Yum* Oliver—provided much-needed fuzz therapy 24/7.

This project began as a matter of organizing background data for the continuing archaeological and historical research project, which I co-directed with Don Rice and Grant Jones, funded by the National Science Foundation (grants DBS-9222373, SBR-9515443). Field research was carried out under permit from the Instituto de Antropología e Historia of Guatemala, and I appreciate their official support for the project. I especially acknowledge the codirectors of this project, Don S. Rice, for his encouragement and assistance, and José Rómulo Sánchez Polo, our Guatemalan field director, for his diplomacy and skills in making sure the project continued on course from year to year. Much of this book was written during a half-time sabbatical from my administrative duties, and I am grateful to John Koropchak and SUIC for providing me with this essential research leave. Last but most certainly not least, I thank an absolutely terrific group of current and former graduate students at SIUC, particularly (in the case of this text) Tim Pugh and Phil Wanyerka, as well as undergraduates Bethany Myers and Amber Napton, all of whom, through seminars, field seasons, and frequent conversations, provided important insights that forced me to sharpen my thinking.

I say again: any errors that appear are, of course, entirely my own responsibility.

MAYA POLITICAL SCIENCE

CHAPTER I

Introduction

APPROACHES TO MAYA
POLITICAL ORGANIZATION

The political organization of the Classic period (A.D. 179–948) lowland Maya civilization of northern Guatemala, Belize, and the Yucatán peninsula of Mexico (Fig. 1.1) has defied explication. Proposed models debate centralized versus decentralized, stable versus unstable, and chiefly versus state systems, often with far-flung analogies: Mediterranean city-states, medieval feudal systems, African segmentary "states," Aegean peer-polities, Thai galactic polities, and Bali theater states. All lack compelling goodness of fit and insight into process.

A more productive avenue for investigating Maya political organization begins with the "direct-historical approach," which integrates modern ethnography and indigenous lowland Maya and Spanish commentary from the contact, conquest, and Colonial periods (roughly A.D. 1500–1800) with Classic period inscriptions. Together, these sources reveal that Maya political organization was structured by short- and long-term temporal cycles recorded in their calendars, particularly recurring intervals of approximately twenty years (the k'atun) and 256 years (the *may*). Maya calendrical science, in other words, was not only a system of precise and predictive astronomical calculations and record keeping but also the foundation or "deep structure" of their political science. The key is deceptively simple: the Maya are "the people of the cycle, the people of the *may*."

Explanation, Analogy, and the Direct-Historical Approach

Archaeological epistemology—how we know what we know—is a complex intermingling of theory and empiricism, generalizing and particularizing, and deduction and induction, just as archaeology itself is an intricate blend of scientific and humanities scholarship. Archaeologists are interested in *explaining* the prehistoric past, particularly the dynamic but elusive processes contributing to social and cultural change (Fritz and Plog 1970; Watson, LeBlanc, and Redman 1971; Ren-

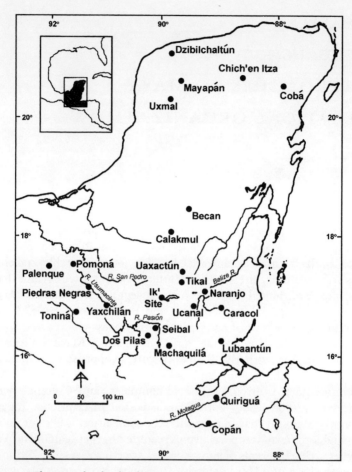

FIGURE 1.1 The Maya lowlands, showing major sites.

frew 1973; Hill 1977). Ultimately, what archaeologists seek are syntheses of descriptive and chronological data with causal mechanisms that
result in satisfyingly conclusive—or at least minimally plausible—
explanations of the events and processes of change in prehistory.

Archaeologists' interpretations of the past have their conceptual basis in analogy and analogical reasoning. An analogy is a similarity that
permits comparison, a relationship between the familiar and the unfa-
miliar that increases understanding of the latter. Analogical reasoning is
a type of inferential argument used in logic, linguistics, mathematics,
biology, and many social science fields, in which "one thing is inferred
to be similar to another thing in a *certain respect* on the basis of the

known similarity in *other respects"* (*Random House Dictionary*; emphasis added). Simultaneously objective, subjective, deductive, inductive, and abductive, analogical reasoning invokes comparisons between the unknown and the known on the basis of recognition of shared similarities or homologies in the *relations* between things, not in the things themselves.

For archaeologists, the relations of interest are those between the form of artifacts or patterns of their occurrence and the human behavior underlying their use or associations. As a simple example, a sharp, straight edge on an ancient stone tool that is similar to the sharp, straight edge on a modern knife prompts extensions to other similarities, leading to the interpretation that the stone tool would have had cutting and slicing functions like modern knives. Therefore, the archaeologist calls it a "stone knife."

Analogical reasoning is far less straightforward when it comes to human behavior because of the inconveniently intervening variables of human motivations, beliefs, preferences, social constraints, decision making, and so forth. Consequently, archaeologists employ two kinds of analogies, general comparative and direct-historical (see Lyman and O'Brien 2001). "General comparative analogy" refers to broad cross-cultural correlations among artifacts, their functions, and human behavior that may be observed widely throughout prehistory as well as in the modern world. The knife example, above, represents such a general comparative analogy. A direct-historical analogy draws specific parallels with historical or living peoples, particularly those occupying the same area, where there might be continuities from the past into the present.

From the 1960s through the mid-1980s, the proper use of analogy was debated in Americanist archaeology (e.g., Ascher 1961; Gould and Watson 1982; Wylie 1985) and the role of analogical reasoning—what one archaeologist dubbed "the tyranny of the ethnographic record" (Wobst 1978)—was subject to methodological and philosophical scrutiny. This debate largely could be attributed to investigators playing fast and loose with the data and selecting analogues that were inappropriate. What emerged from these discussions was dubbed "the New Analogy" and called for careful review of criteria for appropriate and inappropriate analogies. "Appropriateness," it was widely agreed, is a matter of scientific parsimony, justifiability, reliability, validity, and especially continuity.

Continuity is key. The success of the direct-historical approach varies with the degree of continuity between groups, including cultural (technology and subsistence related), linguistic, temporal, and geographic comparisons. To illustrate, in general, it is more appropriate to draw

analogies between the culture and behavior of the prehistoric Pueblo Indians of the American Southwest and the modern Pueblos than between
the prehistoric Pueblos and, say, the ancient Etruscans, because of the
considerable differences in cultural, temporal, and geographic circumstances of the latter. Analogies become increasingly inappropriate—
or, perhaps better said, are decreasingly credible as explanations—the
greater the separation in time, distance, societal complexity, and so on.
In general, the more spatiotemporally removed and culturally generalized, the less useful the analogy.

The most appropriate, credible, and enlightening kinds of analogies
in archaeology, then, are specific rather than general, and are drawn from
known continuities through the direct-historical approach. This process
for investigating culture (pre-)histories involves "working back into prehistoric time from the documented historical horizon" (Willey and
Sabloff 1974:108). Its advantage is the greater "prior probability" that a
given analogy is correct because of known continuities in the compared
cultures (Salmon 1982).

What is the best or most appropriate source of analogy for explaining
Classic lowland Maya political organization? My position favors the direct-historical approach (see also Marcus 1993:115), and thus I seek similarities between the Classic lowland Maya and their Postclassic, early
Colonial period, and modern descendants in the lowlands. "Most appropriate" does not mean perfect isomorphism, freedom from error, absolute "truth," or proof of a theory. Clearly circumstances differ between the Maya in Petén (the modern political unit encompassing
northern Guatemala) in A.D. 750 and the Maya in northern Yucatán in
A.D. 1500–1950. And by adopting the direct-historical approach as the
methodological armature of my study, I am neither negating nor ignoring the usefulness of insights gained from analogies to behavior, events,
and phenomena drawn from farther afield. Nevertheless, I maintain that
we can learn more about Classic Maya political organization by working back from the Postclassic lowland Maya than we can by beginning
with African chiefdoms or feudal Europe. (See Table 1.1.)

What do the terms "political" and "political organization" mean?
Anthropologists have grappled with this question for many decades, because what constitutes politics or a political system in modern Western
society may be more elusive or opaque in non-Western ones. For archaeologists, the problems of comprehending political arrangements are
exacerbated, being restricted to aspects deducible from the fragmentary
material record of prehistoric societies.

Much anthropological thinking on political systems in prehistory
dates from early British functionalism and structural-functionalism of

Table 1.1. Chronological periods in northeastern Petén.

Period	Gregorian Years	Long Count Ending Date*	
Colonial	A.D. 1697–present		
Contact	1524–1697	12.4.0.0.0	10 Ajaw 18 Wo
Late Postclassic	1461–1524	11.15.4.0.0	12 Ajaw 8 Yax
Middle Postclassic	1204–1461	11.12.0.0.0	8 Ajaw 3 Mol
Early Postclassic	948–1204	10.19.0.0.0	8 Ajaw 8 Kumk'u
Terminal Classic	830–948	10.6.0.0.0	8 Ajaw 8 Yax
Late Classic	692–830	10.0.0.0.0	7 Ajaw 18 Sip
Middle Classic	435–692	9.13.0.0.0	8 Ajaw 8 Wo
Early Classic	179–435	9.0.0.0.0	8 Ajaw 13 Kej
Late Preclassic	334 B.C.–A.D. 179	8.7.0.0.0	8 Ajaw 13 Sotz'
Middle Preclassic	591–334 B.C.	7.1.0.0.0	8 Ajaw 18 Xul
Late Early Preclassic	846–591 B.C.	6.8.0.0.0	8 Ajaw 3 K'ayab'

*See Chapter 3.

the 1940s. Theorists such as A. R. Radcliffe-Brown (1940), M. G. Smith (1960, 1968), and others (see Cohen and Middleton 1967; de Montmollin 1989; Kurtz 2001:68–80) defined "the political" in a complex society by

1. its *structures:*
   a. an administrative or organizational sector, usually hierarchical, of policy- or decision-making roles, and
   b. a "political" sector where decisions are made and competition for power takes place; and also
2. its *functions:* rules and sanctions that implement policy, maintain societal order, and safeguard territorial sovereignty.

Modern political anthropology has strayed little from this structural-functional milieu (Kurtz 2001; cf. Roscoe 1993), and this is also true for studies of the Classic Maya civilization, although the latter have been amplified by analogy to modern Maya and readings of contemporaneous texts. These texts consist of Classic period hieroglyphic inscriptions, which can be found carved in stone, particularly on upright monoliths (pl. stelae; sing. stela), wall panels, and benches, as well as on wooden lintels over doorways and painted on the walls of tombs and on polychrome pottery. These reveal some of the administrative structures and functions, including elite titles and mythico-religious charters, rituals, and sanctions, that maintained societal and cosmological order. But despite a high level of detail, these texts have yielded little information thus far about processes in the "political" sector, about how and why the system "works." In the succeeding chapters I describe Maya political organization as it developed and was both structured by and practiced through celebration of calendrical cycles. In advancing this argument, I bring certain biases, viewpoints, and assumptions about the Maya, which are identified here.

"Political organization," as I use the term, refers to the hierarchically structured offices (or roles) of power and authority existing within, between, and among polities and their elites, whereby decisions about internal and external relations (including those with the supernatural realm) and allocation of resources (human, material, and ideational) are made and implemented (see Kurtz 2001:22–23, 31–38). In part because the present discussion, like most of those in archaeology, has a temporal dimension, I find Roscoe's (1993) essay on political evolution and practice theory particularly illuminating. Roscoe articulates the recursive relations between, on the one hand, agency (of leaders or rulers), increasing centralization of political power, and demographic nucleation and, on the other, relations of autonomy and dependence among subordinates that are mediated by time and distance. He also departs from traditional thinking by highlighting the role of ideology and "nonmaterial circumstances" in political systems, an approach that is especially useful for my arguments about the role of calendrical cycles. The Maya represent an unusually lucid example of these complex relations among individuals, institutions, and time—or, stated differently, between practice, agency, structure, and cosmos.

I believe the Classic Maya represent a state (rather than chiefdom) level of organization and share many cross-cultural similarities with other archaic states (see Marcus 1993, 1998; Feinman and Marcus 1998), such as four-tiered (rather than three-tiered) settlement hierarchies. There is, however, little consensus on what to call individual Maya "political" units. The terms "state," "city-state," "nation," "hegemon," "kingdom," "civilization," "empire," and so on have been applied at various times, but they carry considerable theoretical baggage that intensifies confusion. One alternative term is "regional state," a spatially large and socially complex political unit having one or more major population centers (Culbert 1991a:xvii). Another is "polity" (from Latin *polis*), a relatively neutral designator of an autonomous sociopolitical unit. "Polity" does not translate directly into Spanish, however, and some Spanish-speaking archaeologists (Lacadena and Ciudad Ruíz 1998) have advocated use of the Maya's own term, *ajawlel* or *ajawlil* 'rule, reign' (and perhaps by extension, the territory?) of an *ajaw* 'lord, king'. But given the accumulating evidence that the Classic Maya had a higher-order position above an ajaw, even this term is inadequate.

The Classic Maya had a complex social organization with an elite stratum at the top. An "elite" may be defined as a "small group within the upper echelon of a society that exerts ideological, political, social, or economic power or any combination of these" (Culbert 1991a:xvii) or, more simply, as "those who run society's institutions" (Chase and Chase 1992; see also Yoffee 1991). Maya kings were divinely sanctioned and sacred; rulership was hereditary in certain royal matrilines and patrilines, or *ch'ib'als* (or perhaps through the *naj* 'house, lineage'; see Gillespie 2000b); and female as well as male rulers (i.e., "queens" as well as "kings") were recognized.

Sources for a Direct-Historical Approach: A Critical Review

Five sources of direct, historical, analogical information can be used to reconstruct Classic period lowland Maya political organization. Of these, the most direct and historical, yet enigmatic, are the Classic Maya's own writings, the hieroglyphic inscriptions. The remaining four sources—later indigenous Maya texts, Spanish ethnohistoric documents, dictionaries, and modern ethnographic accounts—are more abundant and approachable to modern readers but represent decreasing continuities with the Maya in the heartland of Classic civilization, the Department of El Petén. Discontinuities are both spatial and temporal, as these writings come from or refer primarily to the northern Yucatán peninsula or the Maya highlands and are Postclassic or later in date.

Classic Period Hieroglyphic Inscriptions

The Classic period Maya of the southern lowlands chronicled their "politics"—the internal and external accomplishments of their royal dynasties—in abundant and flamboyant, albeit cryptic, style. Maya hieroglyphic writing is a combination of systems, phonetic and logographic, with signs representing whole words and syllables. Of perhaps more than one thousand "glyphic components," three hundred to five hundred glyphs or signs were regularly used, approximately 60 percent of them now deciphered (Martin and Grube 2000:11). Recently it was suggested that Classic texts were written not in Ch'olan and/or Yukatekan Mayan, as long assumed, but in a "prestige" or "high" language called Classic Ch'olti'an, related to the now extinct Ch'olti' language of the Eastern Ch'olan Maya language family (Houston, Robertson, and Stuart 2000). This language, if in fact it existed, is thought to have originated in western and south-central Petén, and would have been used in the inscriptions and perhaps also spoken by elites and priests (Houston 2000:162).

Virtually the only surviving examples of Maya hieroglyphic texts are those inscribed and sometimes painted narratives on stelae (see Stuart 1996) and carved elements of buildings, such as stone panels, tomb walls, benches, or wooden lintels over temple doorways. Some texts appear on painted pottery, but many are the so-called Primary Standard Sequence (Coe 1978:13; Grube 1991; Reents-Budet 1994) consisting of brief pro forma statements about ownership of the vessel. No Classic period painted codices ("books" of sized bark "paper") are known to have survived.

With advances in decipherment, archaeologists are increasingly able to study Classic Maya civilization as the Maya themselves wrote about it (Stuart 1995), with the result that Maya archaeology is moving toward the subfield of historical or "text-aided" archaeology (Little 1992). Historical archaeology is a multi- and interdisciplinary endeavor in which written and material records are evaluated, one against the other, to illuminate events and circumstances of the past. But as historians and historical archaeologists have long known—and the past decade of postmodern, critical, and reflexive approaches in anthropology has emphasized—dangers abound in placing too much reliance on written records for reconstructing political organization and history. No written texts are unbiased records of historical "reality": all histories were written with a purpose and can be consciously manipulated and revised as those purposes change.

Maya monuments are sometimes considered public propaganda displays—stone billboards, in effect—proclaiming the supernatural power of divine kings. This viewpoint has been critiqued (Stuart 1996:153) with the observation that stelae often have a "strong self-referential quality" that almost approaches personification of the monument itself. But the monuments *are* about the rulers, and their texts record royal dynasties, royal ancestors, royal genealogies, and royal triumphs vis-à-vis kings of other cities. Quotidian matters such as internal decision making and intercourt squabbles, crop yields, pottery production quotas, corvée labor assignments, and so forth were not recorded in this way. Classic Maya inscriptions largely convey "winners' history" (Hammond 1991:2) or "heroic history" (Sahlins 1983:522) and should be interpreted with due diligence. The events they record may be little more than dynastic chest thumping or claims to fulfillment of quasi-historical prophetic mandates. Rulers could put their own rhetorical "spin" on events by commissioning texts to proclaim what they *wanted* present and future generations to believe about themselves and their royal dynasties. We must remain alert to the possible tyranny of the epigraphic record.

There is another danger in relying on dated, carved stelae to explore the *may* hypothesis, as I must do here, because key monuments may be missing from key sites (see Coggins 1970; Robertson 1972). We know that early monuments, in particular, were often moved, defaced, or buried by later occupants of the sites; in more recent times looting and other activities such as logging and agriculture have exacerbated the losses. Dates and imagery on the monuments might have been removed by the erosive forces of nature. Plain stelae might have had commemorative dates and glyphs recorded in perishable media, such as paint over stucco, rather than carved on them. In addition, some important lowland cities lack stelae entirely. However, certain elements of politico-ritual organization are mirrored in architectural and stylistic components, often shared widely throughout the lowlands.

Native Texts of the Postclassic and Colonial Periods

A direct-historical approach to Classic period lowland political organization may be effected by cautiously working backward in time from extant, indigenous texts written in the Postclassic and Colonial periods. Several kinds of documents have survived the centuries and are useful today.

One category of native Mesoamerican text is the codex. Codices are known from highland Mexico and the Maya area, date from the Postclassic and Colonial periods, and probably are, at least in part, copies of earlier versions. Providing extensive treatment of astronomical and divinatory affairs, these books "shaped practically every aspect of individual and community behavior" (Boone 1992:197). In the Maya lowlands codices were made of long strips of the beaten bark of the fig tree (*Ficus cotonifolia; copo* in Yukatekan Maya), sized with a lime wash and folded accordion style. Each "page" (Fig. 1.2) had hieroglyphic texts, tables, and illustrations written in black pigment, with red, blue, and other color highlights.

Sadly, only four of these codices from the Maya lowlands are known

FIGURE I.2 Page 25 of the Dresden Codex (after Villacorta and Villacorta [1930] 1989:50).

today, all dating to the Postclassic period and written primarily in Yukatekan Maya; as noted, no Classic period codices survive. The Franciscan friar Diego de Landa, writing in the sixteenth century, tells us why:

> We found a large number of books in these [hieroglyphic] characters and, as they contained nothing in which there were not to be seen superstition and lies of the devil, we burned them all, which they regretted to an amazing degree, and which caused them much affliction. (Tozzer 1941:169)

Small wonder! The major book-burning episode in the northern low-lands is thought to have accompanied the Inquisition at Maní on July 12, 1562 (Tozzer 1941:77–78n340).

The surviving Maya codices are named for the places where they were found or now reside: Dresdensis (Vienna), Tro-Cortesianus or Madrid (three fragments owned by separate families in Spain), Pérez or Pere-sianus (Paris), and Grolier (the Grolier Club in New York). All treat "pre-dictive astronomy," that is, tables by which to predict the astronomical events and cycles governing ritual. The dates and origins of all three are subject to debate, although prototype astronomical tables may go back to the mid-eighth century (Justeson 1989:76).

The Dresden Codex, which treats Venus, Mars, and eclipse cycles, has glyphic and iconographic associations with eastern Yucatán, espe-cially Chich'en Itza, and Sir J. Eric S. Thompson (1972) dated it to the early thirteenth century. More recent studies (e.g., Paxton 1986) note iconographic similarities to the western Terminal Classic Puuc site of Kabah and date the Dresden to the Late Postclassic. The surviving work may be the product of eight different scribes (Sharer 1994:603).

The Madrid Codex (Bricker and Vail 1997), the longest of the codices (6.7 m, 112 pp.), has been described as being "concerned with the ritual aspects of everyday life rather than cosmic themes" (Graff 1997:167n2). Thompson thought the codex originated in western Yucatán sometime between A.D. 1250 and 1450. Victoria Bricker's (1997a:25; 1997b:180) intensive studies suggest that some sections date to A.D. 925 but point to "the one-hundred-year span between A.D. 1350 and 1450 as the most likely period" of the codex's composition. Later studies have revived Thompson's (1972) earlier suggestion that it might have come from Tayasal, the Itza capital, and date as late as the seventeenth century because of incorporated fragments of European paper (Coe and Kerr 1998:181; Schuster 1999). Stylistically, the Madrid Codex is similar to the murals of eastern coastal sites such as Tulum and Tancah (see Miller 1982).

The Paris Codex, consisting of twenty-two pages, treats the k'atun, the important Maya calendrical interval of approximately twenty years. It also depicts the constellations, or zodiac. Bruce Love (1994:13) be-lieves the document was produced at Mayapán in northern Yucatán in the late fourteenth or early fifteenth century, citing iconographic paral-lels to that site's stelae.

The fourth surviving codex, the Grolier (Coe 1973:150–154), con-sists of fragments of eleven pages including part of a Venus table. The Grolier's authenticity was originally debated: although the bark paper is pre-Columbian in date, its tables add little to what is available in the

Dresden, and it is sometimes considered a forgery (Sharer 1994:604; Milbrath 2002).

Other important Postclassic native documents that inform Classic Maya political organization are the so-called prophetic histories, collectively known as the books of the *chilam b'alams* from northern Yucatán. These books are much-reworked compilations of oral and codical traditions originally delivered by the spokesman or speaker (*chilan, chilam*) of the jaguar priest (*b'alam*) who ruled over the k'atun. An analysis of these texts in the late nineteenth century indicated that they recorded astrological and prophetic matters, medical recipes and directions, postconquest history and Christian teachings, and ancient chronology and history (Morley 1917:196, citing Brinton [1885] 1969). With respect to the last of these subjects, the books can be deemed part origin myth and part reconfigured mythocyclical histories, referring to events of the Postclassic and Colonial periods and doubtless having Classic antecedents in the codices burned by Fray Landa (Morley and Brainerd 1956:255; Thompson 1972:27). Only approximately sixteen manuscripts of the chilam b'alams have survived to modern times; many remain untranslated. They are known today by the names of the towns in which the manuscripts—none originals but rather all later copies—were found, for example, the *Chilam Balam of Chumayel*, of Tizimin, of Mani, Kaua, Navula, Tusik. The extant versions of nearly all these books date between 1824 and 1837 (Edmonson 1979:9).

Great care is required in reading directly from these texts to the archaeological and historical records of Postclassic and especially Classic times. The contents were committed to writing during the Colonial period by educated Maya who had been trained to write their own (Yukatekan) language, using characters of the Spanish alphabet, as part of their religious instruction. There are two sets of k'atun prophecies in these books (Roys [1933] 1967:185): an earlier one, which has more symbolic language and few references to postconquest events, and a slightly later one, which includes references to Europeans and Christianity. In addition, the language of the books of the chilam b'alams is not prose but poetry, "a highly charged and allusive language that stresses the *quality* of time over its factual content" (Farriss 1987:577; emphasis added). Perhaps this is because some of these books are compilations of oral dramatic performances. At the same time, Edmonson (1979:12–13) believes the richly metaphorical language may have been intentionally obfuscating to ensure that Maya traditions would remain secret from the Spanish authorities.

More significantly, these books have heavy ethnocentric loading: they are ethnopoetic charters of ethnomythic history and identity, as well as ethnic propaganda tracts for the two major elite lineages of the

Postclassic northern lowlands. *The Book of Chilam Balam of Chumayel* (Roys [1933] 1967; Edmonson 1986a), for example, is a self-aggrandizing historical chronicle of the people known as the Tutul Xiw in western Yucatán and makes repeated reference to symbolically significant defeats of their rivals, the Itza/Kokom. Similarly, *The Book of Chilam Balam of Tizimin* (Edmonson 1982) is an idealized and mythologized reconstruction of Itza/Kokom Maya history, and as such presents an accounting favorable to the Itza.

It is readily evident, then, why in the intellectual annals of Maya scholarship the credibility of the books of the chilam b'alams for reconstructing Classic Maya history has waxed and waned. Some of the reported events appear to date to the Late Classic period, and Sylvanus G. Morley, one of the great pioneers in Maya archaeology, thought there was "in fact little doubt" that the temporal cycles presented in these documents were "literal translations of Maya historical codices" (Morley and Brainerd 1956:255). Morley (1915) was aware, however, of the peculiar problem posed by the occasional failure of the k'atuns to follow in proper numerical sequence in parallel texts of different books and concluded that some were omitted and others repeated. While this casts a shadow on the chronicles' reliability as event histories, he concluded that the texts "exhibit a similarity of detail which is little short of remarkable, and it is highly indicative of their reliability that . . . [over] a period of about eleven hundred years, there is always at least one of the chronicles which carries on the sequence of the katuns unbroken" (Morley 1915:199).

Modern researchers are more skeptical. Edmonson (1982:xvi) believes these books are "essentially mythological as they relate to the Classic period" but reasonably trustworthy from the tenth century onward. His perusal of these documents led him to pose a series of provocative questions concerning what they might tell us about the Classic period, including the suggestion that Classic Maya recognized certain cities as "seats" of the *may*, the thirteen-k'atun, or 256-year, calendrical interval (Edmonson 1979). My reconstruction of Classic political organization here is heavily based on the books of the chilam b'alams, particularly on Edmonson's interpretation of the *may* as elucidated from these texts.

Native Maya literature is also known from elsewhere in the lowlands, for example, the *Paxbolon Papers* from the Chontal region (Scholes and Roys 1968), and from the Maya highlands, for example, the *Annals of the Cakchiquels* (Brinton 1969; Recinos and Goetz 1953), a history of Kaqchikel Maya speakers in the central highlands of Guatemala. The *Popol Vuh* (lit. "Book of the Mat"; Marcus 1992a:85), or "Council Book" (Tedlock 1985:23; 1992), is a sixteenth-century account of the origins, history, and cosmogony of the K'iche' Maya in the western highlands. There is considerable evidence that these myths and beliefs were widely shared among highland and lowland Maya from Preclassic times onward. Preclassic stelae from the Pacific coast site of Izapa, in Chiapas, Mexico, near the border with Guatemala, display scenes that closely parallel events in the *Popol Vuh* (Smith 1984; Kerr 1992), as do polychrome plates from the Late Classic southern lowlands of Petén (Coe 1978, 1989).

Another potential source of inferences about territorial boundaries and organization are postconquest land treaties and rare native-drawn maps. Many if not most of these documents, in the Maya area as elsewhere in the Spanish Colonial world, were prepared as justifications for native claims to particular lands and jurisdictions on the basis of prior occupation (Farriss 1987:571). Two of the known Maya maps, one in *The Chilam Balam of Chumayel* and the other in the *Land Treaty of Maní* (Fig. 1.3), are circular, showing the main town in the center and west at the top, and are divided into four quadrants with subject towns in each. According to a 1600 document, the Yukatekan term for map is *pepet dz'ibil* 'circular painting, drawing' (Roys [1943] 1972:184; Mundy 1998:195, 210). These representations reveal Maya concepts relating to land and space—quadripartition and boundaries of realms (Marcus 1993:126–128; see also Restall 1997:200–203).

Spanish Colonial Documents

A third category of sources on Classic Maya political organization consists of ethnohistoric documents: records of various sorts kept by Colonial Spanish administrators and priests about their observations and experiences in the northern lowlands. The first European occupants of the Yucatán peninsula struggled to gain control over the area and the Maya by both military means and heavy-handed proselytizing. Instruction in the Catholic religion was carried out principally by the Franciscan order, which established a string of missions throughout the northern peninsula (Hanson 1995; Perry and Perry 1988) and left substantial records of their activities among the Maya.

Here again, one must be cautious in reconstructing Classic affairs from these documents, which often divulge little more than what the Spaniards *thought* the Maya were doing. Archaeologists in the late twentieth century have emphasized the dangers of uncritically generalizing from Spanish administrators' observations about the northern lowland Maya—who had suffered conquest, religious indoctrination, massive population losses and dislocations from disease and warfare,

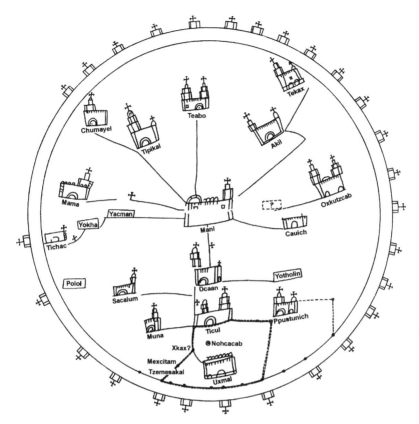

FIGURE 1.3 Colonial period map of the Yucatán town of Maní (after Roys [1943] 1972:Map 6 and Andrews 1984:Fig. 1).

economic servitude, and worse, all at the hands of the Spaniards—and projecting them back eight centuries or more to the southern lowland Maya of the Classic period:

> The early chroniclers were unfamiliar with the ways of the native inhabitants of the New World and, thus, frequently did not understand what they were witnessing. . . . Often, European-based [sociopolitical] models—specifically those pertaining to a society such as existed in [post-]medieval Europe of the time—were applied to New World societies and indigenous forms of organization were ignored or contorted to fit a Western mindframe. . . . Ethnohistoric accounts are also generally transcribed, translated, and published . . . [which] . . . can lead to nearly imperceptible changes—such as in

wording—that nevertheless can greatly alter documentary interpretation. . . . [T]he descriptions of the lowland Maya in the early European documents tended to refer to the Yucatec Maya . . . [who may not be] representative of the various other parts of the Maya realm. Finally, . . . the degree to which historical accounts have embodied ideal as opposed to real distinctions in the social order can be questioned. (Chase 1992:118–119)

An example of these problems can be seen in the most detailed and frequently used of the ethnohistoric accounts for the Maya, the 1566 *Relación de las cosas de Yucatan* written by Fray Diego de Landa (see Tozzer 1941 for an annotated English translation). Landa, later the second bishop of Yucatán, recorded prodigious amounts of information abut the Maya, including their daily life, religion, and calendrics and a phonetic transliteration of the Spanish alphabet into Maya glyphs. Much of his material came from two informants who were members of politically powerful rival lineages, Gaspar Antonio Chi, a Xiw from Maní, and Juan Nachi Kokom, a Kokom from Sotuta. Landa compiled his observations after he was ordered before an ecclesiastical court in Spain in 1562 to justify his harsh treatment of the Maya. Thus he might have exaggerated certain aspects of Maya culture, such as "idolatry" and human sacrifice, which the Spaniards found abhorrent, in the hope of being accorded more sympathetic treatment (Thompson 1970:457). Moreover, he was known as a plagiarist (Tozzer 1941:vii).

Despite these disturbing biases, many archaeologists and anthropologists continue to find Colonial documents useful for suggesting what the past *might* have been like, with full recognition that the insights they provide do not necessarily represent historical fact.

Dictionaries

Another category of evidence about political organization, one that overlaps ethnohistory and ethnography, comes from various Maya-Spanish and Maya-English dictionaries. Some of these vocabularies were compiled in the Colonial period, most notably the late-sixteenth-century *Diccionario de Motul: Maya-Español* (Martínez Hernández [1585] 1929), which gives a wealth of information on Yukatekan Maya. Others date from as late as the nineteenth and twentieth centuries, such as the compilation of previous vocabularies in the *Diccionario maya cordemex: Maya-español, español-maya* (Barrera Vásquez et al. 1980) and the *Diccionario español-maya* (Solís Alcalá 1949a). Most recently, the trilingual *Itzaj Maya-Spanish-English Dictionary* (Hofling and Tesucún 1998) records the language of the last speakers of Itzaj Maya in San José, Petén, Guatemala.

Dictionaries offer insights into native categorizations of polities through the presence, absence, quantities, varieties, and etymologies of words that denote territorial units and decision-making personnel. Generally, the richer the vocabulary for some phenomenon in a language, the more significant that phenomenon is for its speakers. Fortunately, the Maya had a rich but little analyzed vocabulary for their polities and authority structures. In principle, the most significant or valid of these terms, from the point of view of analogical reasoning, are those recorded during the Colonial period in dictionaries and later documents such as the *Relaciones de Yucatán* (1898–1900). Many words survived into modern times, and some can be traced back to titles recorded in Classic period hieroglyphic inscriptions (see Roys 1957, [1943] 1972; Marcus 1993:128–130; Restall 1997:24–29). However, study of these terms in Classic period inscriptions reveals that some titles were more common in certain sites or regions, and their roles and responsibilities might have varied as well (Houston 2000:175).

Modern Ethnography

Anthropological studies of Mesoamerican peoples began in the late nineteenth century and have continued with little interruption (see Vogt 1969 for a historical summary through the mid-twentieth century). During the first half of the twentieth century, anthropologists undertook considerable ethnographic research throughout the Maya area, lowlands and highlands, and their observations have greatly illuminated the social and political institutions, as well as the daily lives, of the Maya. Relating modern political organization to that of the pre-Hispanic past poses special challenges, however. Twentieth-century Maya are separated from their Classic and Postclassic forebears by some five hundred years of religious, linguistic, economic, political, demographic, agricultural, and other disruptions imposed by the Spanish conquerors and modern national administrative structures. Beginning with the 1552 *ordenanzas* (ordinances) issued by the Spanish governing authority in the region, the Real Audiencia de Guatemala, the Maya, like prehistoric peoples throughout the hemisphere, were subject to the Spanish Colonial administrative policy of resettlement known as *reducción, congregación,* or *agrupación.* This policy forced the Maya to leave their small, dispersed agricultural villages and settle in larger, nucleated towns, whereby the Spaniards could better tax, catechize, and indenture them while at the same time guard against apostasy. The legacy of this alien settlement pattern can still be seen in highlands and low-lands alike.

Relatively little information is available on the geographically closest analogue to the Classic Maya, the Lacandon, in the lowland forests of Chiapas, west of Petén (McGee 1990; Borremanse 1998). Descendants of refugee groups who fled both Spaniards and hostile Maya neighbors, the Lacandon Maya have lived in near-isolation for centuries, with the result that they are the least acculturated to the modern world. This suggests that, in principle, they would provide the most appropriate analogies to their ancestors. However, the Lacandon have dwindled to a handful of families in two groups, northern and southern, and any-thing resembling "political organization" is virtually nonexistent: "The northern group, scattered over a large territory, lost all political or reli-gious organization and system of leadership so long ago that they can-not remember ever having had it. The Jatate and Cedro-Lacanha groups used to have leaders and priests, but their number is now so reduced that the system has collapsed" (Duby and Blom 1969:290).

In the early twentieth century, the primary sociopolitical unit of ad-ministration throughout much of Mesoamerica was the *municipio*. In the highlands of Guatemala, a municipio is something like the U.S. county, each having "its own religious and political organization, its pa-tron saint, its distinctive costume. . . . The Indian municipio undoubt-edly has considerable time depth and might be a continuation of the basic societal unit of preconquest society" (Wagley 1969:55; see also Tax and Hinshaw 1969:88). Wagley's statement is of dubious veracity, however, and might represent a tendency of early ethnographers to cor-roborate Thompson's views (see Chap. 2; see also Becker 1979).

Throughout Colonial Mesoamerica, the Catholic religion, with its multiplicity of saints and saints' days, was easily grasped by the indige-nous inhabitants and readily integrated with native calendars, patron deities, and ritual practices (e.g., Nash 1958; Bricker 1989). An impor-tant politico-religious system of the Maya highlands is the *cofradía*, a brotherhood charged with caring for a patron saint and arranging ceremonies according to the religious calendar. Such systems might have had ancient roots in deity cults and their priests in Mesoamerican prehistory.

All five of these sources of information about Maya political organiza-tion provide, with varying emphases, combinations, and degrees of suc-cess, analogies to reconstructions of Classic lowland Maya political re-lations. As discussed in the next chapter, early-twentieth-century archaeologists and anthropologists relied on all but the first, because until the 1960s little was understood of the hieroglyphic writing system beyond calendrics. But while the past decades' accelerating decipherment of glyphic texts has made it increasingly possible to read Classic period history as the Maya themselves wrote it, one consequence has been the creation of a highly fragmented and particularized reconstruction of Classic period history based on details of a few individual lords and dynastic lines at a small number of sites. It may be true that "all politics is local," to use an old cliché, but in narrowly focusing on individual trees we have been "losing sight of the forest," to paraphrase another. An integrative synthesis of Classic lowland Maya political history is sorely needed.

Maya Cosmology and Worldview

Understanding Maya cosmology broadly is an important first step in producing a synthesis of Classic lowland Maya political history, because political organization, at least in the sense the term is used here, has a spatial and territorial component. How did the Classic Maya conceptualize their world? To those trained in occidental, "rational" scientific thought, the ancient Maya worldview and cosmology seem like a baffling stew of mysticism, astrology, geomancy, and numerology, with some fairy tales, *feng shui,* and puppy dogs' tails tossed in for good measure. For anthropologists, however, science, religion, cosmology, and politics are all examples of different but interrelated belief systems that "work" for those who partake of them. For example, the U.S. Constitution articulates the founding fathers' belief system that included a "separation of church and state." Such separation of religious belief and political policy tends to be the exception rather than the rule, however, especially in prehistory. And so it was with the ancient Maya: their political and territorial organization was deeply interwoven with their religion and cosmology.

Ancient Maya worldview and cosmology (see, e.g., León-Portilla 1988) have been retrodicted from the sources just reviewed, in addition to similar sources from central Mexico, all of which show a great deal of agreement. The Maya, like most Mesoamerican peoples, believed that there had been numerous episodes of cosmic creation, the present one being the fourth (or fifth). The Maya cosmos had three vertical domains with multiple levels: the heavens (thirteen levels), the natural earthly world, and the Underworld (nine levels). Each level or plane was the dwelling of a particular deity, hence thirteen benign celestial gods and nine malevolent gods of the Underworld.

In all levels, the Maya cosmos was, above all, divided horizontally into four parts. According to the *Popol Vuh*, the highland Maya book of creation, the first act by the gods was to "set up the *kan xuk kan tzuk*, 'four corners, four partitions'" (Schele and Mathews 1998:345n2):

> ... THE MAKER, MODELER, MOTHER-FATHER OF LIFE
> [proceeded]
> to complete the emergence of all the sky-earth:
> the four-fold siding, four-fold cornering,
> measuring, four-fold staking, halving the cord,
> stretching the cord
> in the sky, on the earth,
> the four sides, the four corners.
>
> (Tedlock 1985:72)

This quadripartite cosmovision, roughly based on the four cardinal (or intercardinal) directions, was shared throughout Mesoamerica in ancient times and modern (Gossen and Leventhal 1993). The cardinal directions were simultaneously connected to the cosmic levels, and each had multiple associations (see the "Ritual of the Four World-Quarters" in *The Chilam Balam of Chumayel*; Roys [1933] 1967:63–66).

However, Maya quadripartite organization of horizontal space is not strictly based on the four fixed cardinal directions recognized in the modern world. Instead, the divisions seem to invoke the solstice-equinox positions and movements of the sun as it rises on the eastern horizon and sets on the western; there is also the element of personification of the sun or Sun God as it proceeds on its journey from east to west (Brotherston 1976; Gossen 1974; Bricker 1983; B. Tedlock 1992: 173–178). Among the lowland Maya, this solar basis for naming directions is evident by incorporating *k'in*, 'sun', into the term. East (*lak'in*) was associated with sunrise, birth, and the color red (*chak*), while West (*chik'in, ochk'in*) was associated with sunset, death, and the color black (*ek'*). By contrast, *xaman* (North) was associated with "up" (as in the sun at zenith), the Sun God's "right" side on his journey, heavens, the number 13, the place of ancestors, and the color white (*sak*). *Nojol* (South) was associated with "down" or the sun's nadir, the sun's "left," the Underworld, the number 9, night ("death" of the sun and its Underworld journey back to the east), and the color yellow (*k'an*).

A fifth "direction" is center, an *axis mundi* extending through all levels; metaphorically, it is a ceiba tree (the Maya "World Tree"; *Ceiba pentandra*, kapok tree) growing from the center of the earth and reaching up into the heavens. Center is associated with the three hearthstones of creation and with the color blue-green-turquoise (*ya'ax*), which is also used to represent a variety of precious substances such as water, jade, and corn.

The quadripartition of the Mesoamerican world is a common feature of prehistoric cosmologies worldwide, and the earthly domain or built world typically mimics that four-part structure (Eliade 1954; Coe 1965; Marcus 1973; Marcus, Flannery, and Spores 1983:38–39; Carlson 1981; Tichy 1981). Mesoamerican cities, architectural complexes, and individual buildings are thus often cosmograms, earthly representations of the sacred cosmic domain (Coggins 1980; Guillemin 1968; Ashmore 1989), and thus constitute sacred landscapes. Eduardo Matos Moctezuma observed that the site for the founding of a city

> is always "discovered" by humans through certain symbols laden with mystic meaning, among which frequently occurs the presence of some animal. . . . As Eliade (1979:335) says: "The foundation of the new city repeats the creation of the world; indeed, once the place has been ritually validated, a fence is erected in the form of a circle or a square broken by four doors which correspond to the four cardinal directions." (1987:191)

In Mesoamerica and among the Maya, buildings were arranged in the four directions around plazas and towns may have been divided physically and administratively into four quarters or wards. Further, as noted previously, the few surviving Maya maps show the landscape divided into four quarters.

In addition, many Mesoamerican gods, for example, the rain gods, had four aspects or existed in groups of four, each with an associated color, direction, and augury. Maya rain or lightning gods were known as Chaks: the eastern Chak brought "red" and good rains (prevailing trade winds in Mesoamerica typically bring rainy season storms from the east); the northern Chak, "white" good rains (usually winter rains from cold fronts moving south from North America); the western Chak, "black" poor rains; and the southern Chak, "yellow" poor rains (meteorologically, rain rarely moves into the lowlands from the west or south). Each directional god aspect also had an associated priest, tree, and other elements.

The following chapters explore these concepts and additional information relating to Maya cosmology and worldview in terms of their implications for understanding political organization and process.

CHAPTER 2

Previous Reconstructions of Classic Maya Political Organization

The Classic period (A.D. 179–948; see Table 1.1) political organization of the lowland Maya has been the subject of endless theorizing, modeling, and debate throughout the twentieth century (see reviews by Becker 1971:28–105, 1979; Willey 1986; Hammond 1991:14–18; Culbert 1991b; Marcus 1993; Lucero 1999; McAnany 2001; Iannone 2002; Webster 2002:Chap. 5). Early reconstructions have fallen into disfavor and then reemerged as more data are accumulated and intellectual currents shift. Debates have crystallized around polar positions on interrelated and generally scalar issues of size, centralization, hierarchy, autonomy, and stability of Maya polities in the Late Classic and through time. Lurking behind these arguments is the awareness that the Maya lowlands encompasses an area of some 250,000 to 300,000 square kilometers and intersite political relations, whether friendly or hostile, could have been maintained only by means of travel on foot or by watercraft through dense tropical forest and often difficult terrain.

Early Thoughts

Through the first quarter of the twentieth century, attempts to understand Classic Maya civilization broadly—political, social, economic, religious, and material aspects—consisted of descriptive syntheses of travelers' reports, ethnographic analogies, and British structural-functionalism. During what Becker (1971) identified as an "Early Period" of this endeavor, from 1838 to 1923, explorers such as Edward H. Thompson, Alfred Percival Maudslay, Teobert Maler, Cyrus Thomas, Alfred M. Tozzer, and Sylvanus Griswold Morley viewed Maya sites as complex "cities" characterized by grandiose palace and temple architecture and large, socially differentiated resident populations. An analogy was drawn between the Maya and the Greeks, based on the inference that they were both "artistic and intellectual people" and that, politically, "both were divided into communities or states that bickered and quarreled. There were temporary leagues between certain cities, but real unity only against a common enemy" (Spinden 1917:177).

The end of this early interval corresponds roughly to the initiation of major projects in Maya archaeology by the Division of Historical Research of the Carnegie Institution of Washington, which dominated the field for nearly half a century (see Special Section in *Ancient Meso-america* 1[2], 1990). The first of these Carnegie projects was Morley's effort to record Maya inscriptions, which led him to the following enormously influential conclusion:

> The Maya inscriptions treat primarily of chronology, astronomy— perhaps one might better say astrology—and religious matters. They are in no sense records of personal glorification and self-laudation. . . . They tell no story of kingly conquests, recount no deeds of imperial achievement; . . . they are so utterly impersonal, so completely nonindividualistic, that it is probable that the name-glyphs of specific men and women were never recorded upon the Maya monuments. (Morley 1946:262)

The anthropomorphic figures on the monuments bearing these inscriptions were judged to be peaceful gods, priest-astrologers, or calendar priests.

Morley's investigations led him to propose (1915, 1946) a highly centralized, even imperial, model of Maya civilization flourishing in two phases, an Old Empire (comprising sites in the southern lowlands; see also Gann and Thompson 1935:29–66) and a New Empire (comprising the later sites in the northern Maya lowlands). The Old Empire, now known as the Classic period, was regarded as exhibiting a high degree of homogeneity for roughly six hundred years, which at the time suggested "the presence of one supreme ruler over the area" (Bell 1956:437). Morley acknowledged the difficulties of explaining the consolidation and maintenance of such a unified political structure, because there seemed to be "no evidence of warfare as a nationalizing force" (Morley and Brainerd 1956:45).

It is noteworthy that in his early synthetic work, *The Ancient Maya* (Morley 1946; Morley and Brainerd 1956:144), Morley noted that in the central and southern lowlands during the Classic period there may have been at least four "archaeological sub-provinces [that] corresponded roughly to a political unit of some sort." These included central and northern Petén, Guatemala, plus adjacent Belize; the Usumacinta valley in the west; the southeastern area (centered on Copán); and the southwestern area (Río Pasión). In addition, "eastern Campeche and southern Yucatan formed a region apart." Morley (1946:316–319; Morley and

Brainerd 1956:267–270) also created a four-tiered hierarchy to classify Maya "religious centers according to their relative importance" based on areal size, architecture, and "number and excellence of their sculptured monuments." On this basis, Morley (1946:160–161) proposed four regional polities within the southern lowland empire: Tikal controlled north-central Petén and Belize; Copán ruled the southeastern region; Palenque, Piedras Negras, or Yaxchilán headed the Usumacinta area; and Toniná dominated the northwestern zone. Morley and Brainerd (1956:Plate 19, Table VII) identified four Class 1 "metropolises" (Tikal, Copán, Chich'en Itza, and Uxmal), nineteen Class 2 "cities," including Calakmul (whose 103 known monuments were "for the most part of little esthetic merit"), thirty-nine Class 3 sites ("large towns"), and fifty-four Class 4 sites ("small towns").

Another authoritative Maya archaeologist of the time, J. Eric Thompson, agreed with Morley that Maya political organization was essentially peaceful and controlled by priests, with religion the basis of power. Thompson (1970:94) supported his theocratic view of Maya society by noting the lack of evidence for warfare, such as fortifications; in addition, the seemingly continuous pace of building construction argued for "prevailing peace during the Classic period." The collapse of Classic Maya culture was, in his view, a consequence of "peasant revolt" against priestly rule. Further, he suspected that "the provinces into which Yucatán relapsed after the fall of Mayapán were in existence long before the rise of Mayapán and continued to reflect more or less the set-up of the 'districts' controlled by each major ceremonial center" in earlier periods (Thompson 1970:90).

Unlike Morley, however, Thompson (e.g., 1942) saw Maya political organization as highly decentralized. He believed that Maya society consisted of two classes, priests and peasants. The peasants lived in small agricultural villages and hamlets surrounding the large sites, which, in his view, were not populated cities but vacant ceremonial centers, sacred precincts of temples and palaces that were uninhabited except for priests and had only intermittent ceremonial functions. These sites, together with the villages in the surrounding hinterlands, constituted autonomous city-states, and Classic Maya political organization consisted of a "loose federation" of them, with government "largely in the hands of a small caste of priests and nobles" (Thompson 1970:97). He went on to characterize that government by suggesting, "It is quite likely that, as in [Aztec] central Mexico, the rulership of each city state was dual."

Thompson's highly popularized interpretations of Maya civilization led to a series of superficially supportive but often circular and sometimes specious claims on the part of ethnographers working in both the

Guatemalan highlands and the Yucatán peninsula (Becker 1979:9–10). Although influential, his views were based on little empirical evidence and indeed reflected many of the biases of his personal upbringing as well as the anticommunist tenor of the times (Becker 1971:67, 1979: 12–14; Kremer 1994).

The views of both Morley and Thompson were at least partly shaped by then-current understandings of Maya subsistence. The prevailing concept was that the Maya, like most tropical peoples, practiced slash-and-burn (or swidden) agriculture—cutting down a patch of forest near the end of the dry season, burning it, and planting corn and beans in the nutrient-rich, ashy soils just as the rains began to fall. Because slash-and-burn agriculture is land-extensive, it is generally associated with dispersed settlement, low population density, and decentralized socio-political organization.

In sum, from the 1930s through the 1950s, two closely related yet distinct positions dominated scholarly thinking about Classic lowland Maya political organization. There was concurrence that the civilization was largely theocratic and peaceful, with the human figures depicted on stelae being astrologer-priests, or "calendar priests." There was disagreement about whether or not there was some hierarchy of centralized power among the Maya, with Morley taking an affirmative view and Thompson advocating a model of decentralized authority vested in numerous city-states. Both positions were based largely on the same evidence: archaeological site maps, excavations, and artifacts; assumptions about the subsistence system; limited understanding of iconography and epigraphy (primarily calendrical information); and direct-historical analogy to Landa's *Relación* and other native and Spanish texts.

The Political Geography of the Yucatan Maya

One of the earliest discussions of lowland political organization that provides analogies for the Classic Maya is Ralph L. Roys's 1957 monograph, *The Political Geography of the Yucatan Maya.* This is a province-by-province review of the sixteen "native states" in the Yucatán peninsula in the early sixteenth century after the collapse of the Mayapán "confederacy." Mayapán is a large Late Postclassic archaeological site lying southeast of Mérida. According to Roys's ([1933] 1967) readings of the books of the chilam b'alams, from its ceremonial founding in the early thirteenth century until its "collapse" in 1450, Mayapán was identified as the centralized seat of *multepal,* which he translated as "joint government" by lineage leaders. This joint government resulted from an agreement between the two major elite lineages of the Yucatán peninsula, the Xiw in the west and the Kokom in the east. It fell apart after a Xiw-led uprising against the Kokom, at which point Mayapán was abandoned and the lineage leaders returned to their home territories. This was the situation encountered by the Spaniards some fifty years later: a strong historical memory of the centralized Mayapán confederacy but a realpolitik of sixteen or so postbreakup provinces throughout the peninsula.

Roys (1957:6–7; see also Marcus 1993:118–120) organized the variability in administrative and territorial organization of these provinces into three categories (Fig. 2.1):

A. Provinces, or *kuchkab'als,* are centralized territories ruled by a hereditary *jalach winik* with the title *ajaw.* There is a capital or large town *(noj kaj)* where the jalach winik resided; a hierarchy of other towns (kaj) heading smaller dependent polities *(b'atab'il)* ruled by a *b'atab';* and numerous small towns *(chan kaj).* Examples of these centralized polities in post-Mayapán times include Cochuah, Maní (Xiw), Hocaba, Sotuta (Kokom), Cehpech (Cumkal and Mutul), Champoton, Cozumel Island, and probably also Ah K'in Chel and Tases, plus Tayasal in Petén (Roys [1943] 1972: 59). These provinces are equivalent to what some anthropologists might call complex, or "maximal," chiefdoms (e.g., Marcus 1993:157).

B. This category of province lacks a single territorial ruler (jalach winik). Instead, administration is in the hands of related b'atab's who are usually members of the same lineage. Examples include the sixteenth-century Aj Kanul (Calkini) and Kupul provinces; these would fall into the anthropological category of simple, or "minimal," chiefdoms (Marcus 1993).

C. Polities in this category were small and highly decentralized, consisting of loosely allied groups of towns or slightly larger units but lacking a jalach winik and clear territorial organization. They tended to be found on the outskirts of more centralized systems and included the sixteenth-century Ecab, Uaymil, Chakan, and Chikinchel provinces.

Roys's study was based on the "tax list of 1549," which itemizes 180 grants of *encomienda* (stewardship; labor and tribute rights) to the early Spanish settlers of Yucatán and lists nearly 57,000 tributaries, suggesting a total population of some 256,200 Maya (Roys 1957:10). His use of this document avoids the problem of relying on late-sixteenth-century sources, which would have been influenced by midcentury ordinances requiring the Maya in scattered rural villages to resettle in compact

FIGURE 2.1 Early Colonial period (post-Mayapán) polities in the Yucatán peninsula (after Roys 1957:Map 1).

towns with a plaza, church, and other administrative buildings after the Spanish pattern. In Yucatán, many small settlements were abandoned as a result of this order, but it was gradually forgotten, and by the mid-eighteenth century more than half the tribute payers were again living close to their lands (Villa Rojas 1969:247). Spanish personnel policies had more long-lasting effects, however, as the power and influence of territorial rulers, or jalach winiks, was eroded to the level of former b'atab's (see Thompson 1999:38–49).

Several recent documentary and historical studies have provided support for, as well as challenges to, Roys's model. Sergio Quezada (1993), for example, identified two rather than three types of political units in the sixteenth century. One type consisted of polities based on subordination, kuchkab'als headed by powerful jalach winiks with combined military, political, religious, and judicial roles. These polities centered on powerful ruling dynasties, with succession passed on to a male relative. The second type had a less centralized organization, in which military, religious, and politico-judicial functions were administered by three individuals. In many details, however, Quezada's model differs little from Roys's.

Matthew Restall's (1997) study of Colonial Yucatán's sociopolitical organization focused on the community level in the period 1550–1850 and noted the lack of sound evidence for indigenous "macro-units," or provinces of the type that Roys discussed. Restall's conclusions are based on varying interpretations of the term "kuchkab'al" as well as his conclusion that the title jalach winik is primarily honorific. Here it is important to remember that Roys's analysis was based on a document dated 1549, less than a decade after the Spanish capital of Mérida was established, whereas Restall's covers the subsequent centuries of imposition of colonial authority.

A third recent study, by Philip C. Thompson (1999), is a "documentary ethnography" of the town of Tekanto, in north-central Yucatán (the former Aj K'in Chel kuchkab'al), in the eighteenth century. Thompson (1999:311–312; emphasis mine) concluded that "fundamental preconquest concepts about the relationship between time and space and political power, *concepts ultimately based in Maya calendrics*," had survived despite two centuries of Spanish domination. Among the concepts and principles Thompson cites are the quadripartite rotation of town leaders, the basis for selecting each b'atab' (alternating matrilines), and the twenty-year term of office of the b'atab'.

Twentieth-Century Ethnography

Alfonso Villa Rojas's (1969) synthesis of the ethnography of the Maya of Yucatán highlights the imposition of Catholic religious and modern Mexican political structure in the region but also reveals strong continuities of precontact practices (see also Redfield and Villa Rojas 1934; Steggerda 1941). For example, the Yucatán Maya had two types of religious specialists: one to take care of matters of the church and another (the *j-men* 'one who knows') to handle rituals of the indigenous gods. The most frequently observed ceremonies were *ch'a chak* (to bring rain), *u janli kol* (dinner of the milpa), *u janli kab'* (dinner of the bees), and *loj kaj* (purification of the town) (Villa Rojas 1969:269).

Of particular interest is a group of Krusob' Maya in X-Cacal, Quintana Roo, ruled by a "military theocracy" headed by a high priest and a military chief (Villa Rojas 1945, 1969:269–270). Religious ceremonies were performed in the town's two-room, thatched-roofed Templo Mayor. Native rituals such as *tup k'ak'* (fire-quenching; see Chap. 8) and ch'a chak were carried out in the front room while Catholic services took place in the back, where there was an oracle-like "cross that speaks" (see Bennett 1970). Villa Rojas describes his experience:

> During my stay among the tribe, the cross restricted its speaking to dialogues and messages given in private to its immediate interpreters: the scribes. This contrasts with its habit of three or four decades ago when it used to deliver sermons of great transcendence during special sessions . . . in the middle of the night and in which, among other things, it announced forthcoming calamities. (1969:270)

Ethnographic research suggested that many towns in the Maya highlands were primarily politico-economic and religious centers, without a large resident population. Most of the population lived and worked on their farmsteads or in dispersed hamlets in the countryside, close to their fields. Visits to the city, where they often also had homes, took place primarily on market days or for religious festivals. Chichicastenango (Tax 1937:430; Tax and Hinshaw 1969:72–73) along with other communities in the western highlands (Wagley 1969:55–56) were examples of this kind of dispersed hamlet.

These virtually empty central places in the highlands provided the "vacant-town" model (Tax 1937) that was widely applied to the ancient lowland Maya and was readily accommodated by the prevailing theocracy interpretation. In Wagley's (1941:8) ethnography of the Maya of Chimaltenango, for example, he pointed out that "[t]he majority of Guatemala Indians . . . live near their fields, as did their ancient ancestors; the Spanish pueblo with its church and market center had supplanted the aboriginal *ceremonial centers*" (emphasis added; see also Becker 1971:49–64), the latter term apparently taken from Thompson (1931). In the municipio of Zinacantán, Chiapas, Mexico, which itself housed only 6 percent of the population, farmers living in small, scattered hamlets worked in the lowland piedmont, or "Tierra Caliente, some 12 or more hours distant on foot, where most of the maize feeding the population is grown" (Vogt 1961:134). The vacant town–ceremonial center phenomenon was probably a vestige of the 1552 policy of congregación. Because of the isolation and difficulty of travel in the rugged highlands, it was even easier here for the decrees to be ignored over time, as they were in Yucatán, and the Maya returned to their former dispersed settlement pattern.

In many if not most of these highland communities, ethnographic studies uncovered a synthesis of indigenous Maya politico-religious belief and ritual with modern administrative units. These combined into a shadow system of native administration, unacknowledged by the national government, consisting of numerous officials with primarily traditional ritual obligations. In Mam-speaking Todos Santos, Guatemala, for example, the *principales*, mostly former town mayors, are the ultimate authorities on all civil and ritual matters. One of the principales is the Chiman Nam, also known as "El Rey," a shaman-priest whose office is hereditary and who "has the final word on all public ritual, knowledge of the Maya calendar, and divination on public matters" (Wagley 1969:59).

The Tzotzil of Zinacantán (Vogt 1961, 1969, 1981) preserved numerous pre-Columbian traditions syncretized with Catholicism, for example, rotating men from field labor into town to carry out the important *cargo* (charge, burden, responsibility) of religious ceremonies, including pilgrimages of saints to and from larger communities with churches. Vogt (1964:35) was impressed with the way the Zinacantecos maintained "their successive turns in order on a waiting list for priestly duties for which they applied sometimes as many as twenty years in advance." Small hamlets of patrilineal households clustered together around sacred water holes and commemorated ancestors and sacred spots in the environment by erecting crosses or trees (e.g., *k'in krus* celebrations in May and October).

A new generation of more systematic approaches to Classic Maya political organization—integrating data from modern ethnography, Roys's studies, early Spanish documents, particularly Landa's *Relación,* and other sources—began to appear in the last half of the twentieth century. One of the most important of these was Michael Coe's (1965) model of ancient Maya community structure, which took as its starting point the descriptions of cyclical rotations of Wayeb' year-ending rites (see Chap. 3). His idealized model proposed that each community consisted of four wards (*tzukuls*), each associated with a cardinal direction, a color, and a series of ranked offices. Ritual and political leadership of the community rotated through the four wards in a four-year counterclockwise cycle. Higher levels of politico-ritual administration, including large cities like Mayapán and entire territories, could also be accommodated in this model, with a jalach winik or ajaw ruling from the territorial capital and a b'atab' in each of the four divisions. Temple-pyramids and perhaps entire sectors of cities and towns might have been identified with specific lineages (Coe 1965:111).

Coe noted that use of "calendrical permutations to rotate power among equal segments of a community" seemed "uniquely Maya" and solved the widespread theoretical and practical problem of legitimate succession of kingship. Furthermore, the "suggestion of some kind of regular transfer of ascendancy, perhaps purely ritual" in northern Yucatán gains further credence through analysis of the twenty-year cycles of the k'atun. As conveyed in the chilam b'alams, these "present an ideal model of 13 territories" (Coe 1965:109–110).

Site Size and Size-Hierarchy Models

Archaeological investigations of Classic lowland Maya sociopolitical organization received new impetus in the early 1960s when settlement pattern studies came into vogue (e.g., Ashmore 1981; Bullard 1960; Willey et al. 1965). By that time, there was some consensus that the large Classic sites served as "the religious, political, and probably, commercial nucleus of Maya society and that these nuclei held some sort of sovereignty over specified territories" (Willey et al. 1965:13). But an old question reemerged: Can these sites—often referred to as central places or civic-ceremonial centers—also be called "cities"? Are they "urban" centers?

Standard sociological definitions of cities emphasize population size, density, and nucleation, along with heterogeneous and often concentric zonation of largely secular functions in the case of urban centers. In theory, at least, cities and urbanization—that is, large populations concentrated in multifunctional centers—are a requisite of civilizational development: nucleated populations are more readily subject to political, economic, and social regulation by a state administrative apparatus. But, increasingly, archaeologists are arguing that large, non-Western, preindustrial centers also constitute cities, even though they fail to match the ethnocentric definition of modern, Western sociology (see Marcus 1983). Many Maya archaeologists (e.g., Sanders and Webster 1988; Ball and Taschek 1991) have adopted Richard G. Fox's broader categorization of cities as central places within a state where certain *kinds* of functions are concentrated. Of particular interest to Mayanists is Fox's (1977:41) definition of "regal-ritual cities" as settlements whose "primary urban role is ideological." He continues, "This cultural role emerges from the prestige and status of the state ruler or the cohesive power of state religion." The political power of the rulers of such states and cities rests in ideological control.

Some investigations of Classic political organization—particularly of centralization and hierarchical structure—compared sites by their sizes, assuming a linear relationship between size and power. Site sizes were estimated by total population, total area of settlement, number of plazas surrounded by civic-ceremonial buildings, or volume (cubic meters) of construction. In this way, sites were rank-ordered into size hierarchies, proxy scales for relative political power and importance.

Estimating prehistoric population sizes is a notoriously difficult task. The bases for such estimates have included models of agricultural carrying capacity, numbers of residents per household (using ethnohistoric or ethnographic census data), counts of structures, determination of site boundaries, and other projections and data (see Rice and Culbert 1990; Culbert and Rice 1990). Estimates are also based on evidence of intensive agriculture plus new models of carrying capacity of corn-based swidden, as well as extensive settlement surveys producing counts of housemounds that reflect the presence of populations well above the assumed carrying capacity for swidden. Comparisons of Late Classic populations are further confounded by the varying spatial units researchers use: some base their estimates on the "central core"; others, on the "habitable urban zone," "periphery," "rural zone," "whole site," and so on. It is probably safe to say, however, that population sizes for "central cores" ranged from about 1,500 (Quiriguá, Aguateca) to 10,000 to 15,000 (Copán) to 40,000 or more (Tikal, Calakmul, Caracol), while total populations including rural zones, "sustaining areas," and larger territories may have ranged in the hundreds of thousands (Rice n.d.:Table 1).

A related basis for estimating site size is population or mound densities rather than total counts. At Tikal, for example, the initial site map (Carr and Hazard 1961) revealed 235 mounds per square kilometer (km^2) in the central core, but a subsequent survey suggested something closer to 635 per km^2, with a total population of approximately 40,000 (Haviland 1970:193; 1972:138). Densities fall off with distance from the centers but still can be as high as 100 per km^2.

The validity of rank-ordering Maya centers using construction volume (Turner, Turner, and Adams 1981) is based on the relationship between construction volume and the "fossilized energy" represented by the labor investment of planners, architects, stonemasons, plasterers, and so on, devoted to the construction effort (Abrams 1994). The techniques of using courtyards (Table 2.1) and acropolises (Adams 1981, 1995; Adams and Jones 1981) are complementary, with the volumetric system more precise and data-sensitive than the courtyard counts (Turner, Turner, and Adams 1981:85; Abrams 1994), and both are more sensitive than Morley's monument counts (Adams 1981:Table 9.6).

Several geographic techniques of locational or spatial analysis have been applied to Classic Maya sites as an aid to reconstructing political and economic relationships. These include central place theory (CPT), nearest neighbor analysis, trend surface analysis, and Thiessen poly-

Table 2.1. Courtyard counts at Classic period sites in the southern lowlands.

Tikal	85
Naranjo	42
Uaxactún	23
Yaxhá	20
Caracol	17
Nakum	16
Tayasal	10
Ixlú	5
Xunantunich	5

Source: Adams and Jones 1981.

gons. Reconstructions are based on variations between "real-world" site dispositions and those of an idealized model. According to CPT, for example, an idealized distribution in such a situation is a lattice of equal-sized, often nested hexagons consisting of sites or cities surrounding central places (Haggett 1966:49). Such spacing facilitates economic interaction and political control through levels of administrative hierarchies that are more or less equally accessible in a day's travel. The stipulations of this model—a level, featureless plain—are clearly quite unrealistic, as past and present cities throughout the world are dispersed over heterogeneous landscapes characterized by differences in topography, surface water features, soils and mineral resources, vegetation, and weather. Nonetheless, the kinds and degrees of departure from the ideal can be revealing. How much do Maya cities depart from this idealized hexagonal lattice? Very little, according to Marcus (1993:154), who notes that the sites forming a hexagonal lattice around Calakmul are equidistantly spaced at intervals of 30 kilometers, or a day's travel (Fig. 2.2a).

Thiessen polygons have been used (Hammond 1972, 1974; Flannery 1977; Mathews 1985) to define site territories by marking midpoint distances between capitals and then drawing and linking perpendicular lines between them, creating a lattice of polygons over the lowlands (Fig. 2.2b). This approach has provided de facto support for a decentralized model, because it treats all sites as equal rather than as components

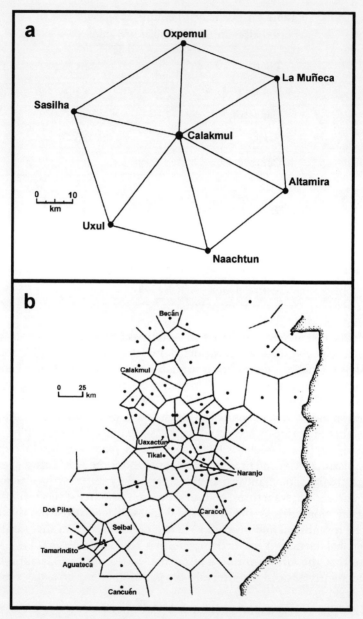

FIGURE 2.2 Defining lowland Maya political boundaries by geographic techniques: (a) hexagonal lattice created by application of central place theory to the site of Calakmul and its satellites (after Marcus 1976:Fig. 1.15); (b) territories of lowland sites identified by Thiessen polygons (after Hammond 1974:Fig. 3).

of a hierarchy (although the sizes of larger territories can be similarly computed). At the same time, however, by equalizing all sites and ignoring hierarchies, this technique makes Tikal one of the smallest of all lowland political territories (Marcus 1993:155). In any case, the usefulness of these polygons lies in estimating total territory within a site's domain or realm. Estimates of site territories have varied considerably, ranging from roughly 1,000 km^2 at the low end to 3,000 km^2 at the upper end. Obviously, territory sizes increase dramatically in centralized models, ranging from about 30,000 to 100,000 km^2.

Trend surface analysis, a form of regression analysis of the distribution of points (i.e., sites) over a surface (landscape), was used in an effort to gain insights into the Maya "collapse" (Bove 1981). That study, which used dates on forty-seven Late Classic stelae, supported the idea of large regional states in the lowlands. Five regional zones were interpreted from the data for A.D. 849: these were centered on Calakmul, Tikal, Motul de San José, Seibal, and Chinkultic. Two other earlier zones, Palenque and Copán, were excluded because they were probably abandoned by this date.

Analysis of spatial distances between Classic centers does not qualify as creating "models" of political organization, but it can reveal hierarchies of sites. Many authors have commented on the geographic spacing between Classic centers and its implications for political organization and administration. The distances between sites in the lowlands generally range from 20 to 32 kilometers (Morley, Brainerd, and Sharer 1983:211; Houston 1992:68), or 12 to 20 miles, roughly the distance that could be walked in a day. Similar spacing of archaeological sites has been noted in other regions of the world, such as Europe and the Near East, and may represent a common logistical factor that facilitates administration in early states lacking vehicular or animal transport systems.

A different view of site sizes and spacing draws from archaeological and epigraphic interpretations of widespread conflict in the lowlands during the Late Classic period (Chase and Chase 1998). Distances between sites would have been limited by the logistics of defending territory; thus sites should ideally be located some 120 kilometers apart, as 60 kilometers is an average "military marching distance" (Hassig 1992). The mean size of territories would have been restricted to the area that could be defended within those limits, roughly 8,000 to 9,000 km^2, with a maximum territorial size of some 11,333 km^2. This approach led to the proposal of fourteen "primary capitals" in the lowlands, plus another seven "border centers" (Chase and Chase 1998).

In any event, after four decades of survey and spatial analyses following William R. Bullard's (1960) proposal of a three-tiered settlement hierarchy, it is now evident that a four-tiered hierarchy is more appropriate for the Late Classic lowland Maya (recall Morley and Brainerd 1956:Plate 19, Table VII). At the apex is a large primary site with scores of plazas and a population in the tens of thousands, which dominated a territory of tens of thousands of square kilometers. These primary cities interacted with smaller secondary sites through royal marital ties and other alliances, perhaps economic, ritual, or military. Secondary sites were, in turn, surrounded by even smaller tertiary- and quaternary-level sites, perhaps dower houses (Haviland 1981), and tiny farming homesteads were interspersed around all of these.

Inscription-based Models

While information on site sizes, populations, and geographic spacing is essential for understanding the broader Classic Maya political landscape, such data are static and descriptive. They fail to illuminate "the political" itself, the arenas in which power is negotiated, with whom and by whom, and on what basis decision making takes place. Information on these aspects of political organization has flowed—indeed, it has been gushing since the 1990s—from readings of Classic Maya inscriptions. As decipherments have proliferated (for a history, see Houston, Chinchilla Mazariegos, and Stuart 2001; Stuart 1992), so too has our knowledge of the elements that constituted Maya political formations. These, combined with the interpretations drawn from earlier studies of Maya art and iconography, have illuminated the world of Maya sovereigns, their vassals, and their dynasties in ways that were unimaginable half a century ago. This growing body of knowledge has by no means quieted debates on the particulars, however.

Below I outline some of the titles and terms for polities and political roles and responsibilities derived from Classic period inscriptions and Colonial dictionaries (see Fig. 2.3 for some glyphic signs). These titles yield insights into how the Maya might have conceptualized what we would call their "sociopolitical" world. Their use varied regionally during the Classic period (Harrison 1999:79; Houston 2000:175). For example, *kalomte'* is especially prominent at Tikal, and, while other titles such as ajaw, b'atab', and *sajal* were also known and used in central Petén, they seem to be more common elsewhere in the lowlands.

I. At the highest levels:
- *Kalomte'* (overlord; formerly read *chakte'*, and before that, b'atab'; see glyph T1030): The highest political rank at Classic period Tikal and other sites, indicating a ruler over a large domain, with ajaws under him. Harrison (1999:79) suggests the translation

FIGURE 2.3 Glyphs for Classic period political titles and events (after Montgomery 2002): a–e, *kalomte'*, (a, b) formerly *makuch* or *batab'*; (c, d) formerly T1030, now 1125 and 1124, respectively (Ringle and Smith-Stark 1996:331): c, note axe in left hand; d, note "brass knuckles" in left hand; possibly "bled penis" (Montgomery 2002:236); (e) *k'uhun*; (f) *chilam*; (g) accede (*joy*) to rulership; (h) accede (be seated, *chum*) in rulership.

"emperor." One version shows the head of Chak with an ax (Stuart 1995:406n15) (see Fig. 2.3a–e).

- *Jalach winik* 'true man' (great lord): The highest leadership office in a territory, or kuchkab'al, hereditary through the eldest son in noble patrilineages. The jalach winik formulated "foreign" (e.g., military) and domestic (political and judicial) policy and was also a religious leader. The town in which a jalach winik resided was usually considered the capital of the territory in Colonial times.
- *Ajaw* 'lord', 'king': The top-level hereditary ruler of a territorial polity (kuchkab'al), or perhaps simply the highest social stratum in Maya society (Montgomery 2001a:201). This title is recognized in Classic inscriptions via glyphs T168, T747a, T1000d. The word comes from *aw* 'shout' with the agentive prefix *aj* (A. Hofling, pers. com., June 20, 2002) and can be read as "he who shouts or proclaims" (Stuart 1995:190–191). According to David A. Freidel and Linda Schele (1988a; Freidel 1992), the lowland Maya institution of ajaw originated in the first century B.C. (Late Preclassic period), and by A.D. 199 ajaws had divine or supernatural powers (*k'ul* or *k'ujul ajaw* 'holy lord'). More recent opinion suggests that divine status was achieved around A.D. 400 (Grube and Martin 2000:149). The institution of ajawship established rules for stable succession, transitioning from earlier individualized, charismatic leadership to formal, dynastically based rule; its membership included ancestors, gods, and live humans; ajaws were incarnations of the ancestral Hero Twins; and they held contractual, ritual obligations as intermediaries between the human-natural and divine realms of the cosmos to ensure their continuity.
- *Ajawlil* (Yukatekan), *Ajawlel* (Ch'olan): lordship, rule, or reign.
- *Kuchkab'al* (*kuch* 'burden, office'; *kab'* or *kaj* 'town'): The large territory, jurisdiction, province, or region ruled by a jalach winik or an ajaw; used primarily [only?] in Yucatán?
- *Nakom:* The same word is used to refer to two different offices and individuals. One nakom is a war chief, elected for a three-year period, during which he must remain celibate; the people "burned incense to him as an idol" (Morley and Brainerd 1956:154, quoting Landa). The other nakom is a priest of sorts who was in charge of human sacrifices.

II. Second-ranking political titles and units
- *B'atab':* A town governor or local chief with administrative, judicial, and military (war leader) duties; drawn from members of the noble patrilines and sometimes appointed by a jalach winik.

- *B'atab'il:* Dependent territories of a kuchkab'al, overseen by a b'atab'.
- *Sajal* (formerly *kajal* 'governor'): In Classic times, a noble ruler of a small, dependent site within a larger polity, appointed by the k'ul ajaw, and apparently a war leader. According to Schele and Mathews (1991:251n1), sajal was the next rank below ajaw. The title is found primarily in the Usumacinta and Pasión valleys (Montgomery 2001a:209) and also at a few sites in the northern peninsula (Suhler et al. 2004).
- *Aj k'uhun:* A title known glyphically by the God C glyph, recently translated as "one who keeps" and "he of the holy paper" (Jackson and Stuart 2001) or bookkeeper (Montgomery 2001b:49). This might be a record keeper, one who maintained the codices.
- *Chilam* (*chi* 'mouth'): In the Classic period, perhaps a special type of *aj k'uhun* 'interpreter' (Coe and Kerr 1998:95). In the Postclassic, "speaker, spokesman," perhaps "interpreter" of the *b'alam'*s (jaguar priest) prophecies.

III. Local-level political titles and units

- *Aj kuchkab':* Head of one of the four sudivisions or wards (kuchteel) of a town; member of a town council who assisted the b'atab' in decision making, tax and tribute collection, and other civil affairs. Appointed by the b'atab', the aj kuchkabs were usually wealthy men and heads of important lineages and held office for one year. Thompson (1999:243–244) views the etymology of the term as *aj kuch ka ja'ab',* or Yearbearer.
- *Kuchte'el* 'barrio', 'ward', 'jurisdiction', 'neighborhood') (Sp. *parcialidad*): A division of a b'atab'il, or town, often endogamous, headed by the aj kuchkab', often with its own patron saint, officials, and temple or church.
- *Aj k'ul* (also *Aj k'ujul*): deputies, assistants to the aj kuchkab's in judicial affairs; apparently commoners rather than nobility.
- *Jolpop* (*jol* 'head; *pop* 'mat'): He or those at "the head of the mat," a woven mat being a highland and lowland Maya symbol for the seat of authority. Among the highland K'iche', the mat is a "metonym for a council (whose members sat on a mat or mats) and probably, at the same time, a metaphor for a council (whose members might have been thought of as being interwoven like a mat or as serving to interweave those whom they represented)" (Tedlock 1985:345). Jolpops may have been approximately equal to b'atab's as second-level officials, perhaps heads of small towns or patrilines. They were in charge of festivals, singing, chanting,

and music, and may be analogous to the "Great Toastmasters" and "Keepers of the Reception House Mat" among the K'iche' (Tedlock 1985:61, 345–346). Jolpops may have been selected annually during the Wayeb' rites (Coe 1965:105); another translation of jolpop is "beginning of the month of Pop," or the leader seated in office on the first day of the new year (Thompson 1999:243).

- *Popol naj* (*popol* 'council'; *naj* 'house'): A public house used for receptions and feasting, apparently headed by jolpops. Two popol najs have been excavated at Copán (Fash et al. 1992; Cheek 2003). *Naj* 'house' also could be interpreted not as a structure but rather as a lineage or in the sense of a "house society" (e.g., "House" of Windsor). This might be related to the Tzotzil Maya of Zinacantan, for whom *sna* refers to a physical house or home and *na* refers to an extended family and its land and possessions (Vogt, cited in Gillespie 2000a; see also Gillespie 2000b). *Na* in Classic hieroglyphic inscriptions is often translated as "woman."

The Importance of Emblem Glyphs

The basis for much of what is known about Classic Maya political organization came from two stunning advances in glyphic decipherments half a century ago, which revealed the historical content of Maya texts. One of these was Tatiana Proskouriakoff's (1960) analysis of monuments at Piedras Negras. She discovered a pattern of glyphs that recorded events occurring five years apart, leading her to conclude that the personages portrayed on Maya monuments were humans rather than deities and that the texts recorded significant events in an individual's life. Hers was a pioneering breakthrough because previously it was believed, following Morley, that Maya inscriptions were impersonal and ahistorical.

The other crucial breakthrough at about the same time was Heinrich Berlin's recognition that certain glyphs were names or "emblems" of specific places or groups (1958) and others were names of rulers (1959). Later he (Berlin 1968; see also Stuart 1995:202–205) pointed out two different glyphs of accession marking "effective rulership over a Maya town." One, the earlier of the two, was *joy* (Fig. 2.3g), the so-called toothache glyph (T684b); the other, later glyph was the "seating" glyph (Fig. 2.3h), read *chum* (T644a, T644b). Still later, another important contribution was Berthold Riese's (1984) recognition of the *hel* (now read *tzak*) glyph and counts of succession of rulers in a particular dynasty.

Numerous reconstructions of Classic lowland Maya political organization have been based on sites' display of Emblem Glyphs, although

FIGURE 2.4 The Tikal Emblem Glyph and variants. (a) Emblem Glyph components; (b) the Tikal Emblem Glyph; (c) *tan kun mutul* 'in the seat of mutul'; (d) *aj mu- mutul.* (c and d after Schele and Mathews 1998:65).

archaeologists disagree on how to interpret them. It is generally ac- cepted that Emblem Glyphs have both dynastic meaning (designating a dynasty, its tutelary deity, or rulers' titles) and geographic significance as a toponym referencing a site or territory. This principle is similar to that of naming Maya territorial provinces, which may come from the title of the ruler, the resident ethnic or lineage group, the capital, or a prominent geographic landmark (Marcus 1993:128; Stuart and Hous- ton 1994).

Emblem Glyphs have three parts (Fig. 2.4). The large main sign varies from site to site and is specific to a place and/or its regnant dynasty. A two-part superfix, T168, first read *ben-ich* by Thompson (1960:281– 282), then *aj-po, aj-pop,* or *ajaw* (Lounsbury 1973), is now read with the T130 subfix (*-wa*) as ajaw, 'ruler, lord.' Finally, there is a prefix from Thompson's "water group" of glyphs, which is usually read *k'ul* or *k'u- jul* in Yukatekan Maya (*ch'ul* or *chu'hul* in Ch'olan): 'divine, holy.' This

FIGURE 2.5 Emblem Glyphs of some Classic Maya sites mentioned in text.

"divine prefix" typically has two parts: parallel lines of dots or droplets (blood?) topped by a tiny cartouche that may contain a ya'ax (first, green, water), k'an cross (yellow, precious), U-shaped shell (moon, water), inverted ajaw, or other element. In the context of Emblem Glyphs, Thomas S. Barthel (1968:165–170) interpreted them as symbolizing "preciosity" along the lines of primogeniture and descent in the ruling lineage, or ch'ib'al.

When all elements are present, the Emblem is read in nonstandard order: prefix-main sign-super/subfix: 'divine [site] lord.' When the affixes are missing, the main sign serves primarily as a toponym (Barthel 1968:184). Archaeologists and epigraphers have generally agreed that a site's display of an Emblem (Fig. 2.5) signals its political importance and "independence" in some sense. Not all sites had Emblems, and some sites displayed their Emblems earlier than others. The first site in the lowlands to display an Emblem Glyph—actually, only its main sign—was Tikal in A.D. 292.

Discoveries illuminating the historical content of Maya inscriptions and their Emblems have raised more questions than they have answered. In particular, the rapid advances in decipherment in the 1980s and 1990s brought increasing evidence of Maya warfare at a time when science fiction star-wars movies were wildly popular. It has not gone unnoticed that at the same time models of Maya political organization and intersite affairs became oriented toward incorporating relations of hostility and warfare among sites. All this resulted in a series of intriguing—but often diametrically opposed—models of political organization based on differing interpretations of the same data. The major unresolved issue has been the degree of political centralization versus decentralization in the Classic period, from site to site and region to region.

Emblem Glyph–based (and Other) Decentralized Models

Some analyses of the distribution of Emblem Glyphs supported decentralized—or city-state or "weak state"—models, which already existed in several variants. Advocates of this position argued that there was little inscriptional basis for inferring hierarchical dependency relations among polities and that the known Classic emphasis on documenting royal genealogies supported lineage-based organizations. According to this view, the Classic Maya political landscape was one of many small, unstable, independent polities constantly jockeying for power, all of them having essentially equivalent or redundant political, economic, and ritual systems.

Peter Mathews (1985; 1991:29), for example, presented a highly decentralized picture of Maya political organization that echoed Thompson's views in some ways. He believed that the Emblem Glyph was the hereditary title for the ruler of a specific polity. Because the title given in all Emblem Glyphs is the same—ajaw—and because all the sites have the same political rank, there could be no hierarchical relations among them. Mathews's early study (1985) of the temporal distribution of sites displaying their own Emblem Glyphs revealed that the number increased through the Classic period (Fig. 2.6). Because twenty-three Late Classic polities displayed their own Emblem Glyphs just before the "collapse," he argued that there were at least twenty-three independent lowland Maya polities at the close of the Late Classic. Another sixty to seventy sizable sites lacking Emblems constituted "autonomous city-states," each with a territory of about 2,500 km². Many new Emblem Glyphs have been discovered since Mathews's original study, suggesting

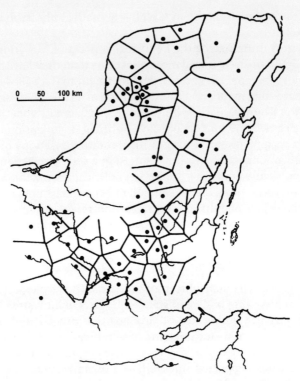

FIGURE 2.6 Decentralized model of the geopolitical organization of the Classic Maya lowlands based on sites displaying Emblem Glyphs (after Mathews 1991: Fig. 2.6).

that more than forty autonomous polities could have existed in the Late Classic.

Like Mathews, Stephen D. Houston (1992, 1993; Houston and Mathews 1985; see also Stuart 1995:272) favored a decentralized and largely nonhierarchical model of Classic Maya political organization, in which city-states or polities identified by Emblems were politically autonomous and spaced approximately 60 kilometers apart. Houston (1992: 67) believed they independently conducted "foreign policy," warfare, and royal intermarriages, and relations of subordination were rare and brief, though strong. Acknowledging that some territories or polities incorporated more than one large site, Houston (1992:68) reminded us that sites and polities are not synonymous.

These political reconstructions based on Emblem Glyph distributions supported other models of decentralized lowland political organization, many of them drawn from outside the Maya lowlands, that emphasized the fragility and instability of Maya polities. Analogies have been drawn from sources so distant temporally, geographically, and culturally, however, that their appropriateness and explanatory power are suspect.

One example is the European feudal system: according to this model, Classic Maya societal organization—the social, economic, and political relations between rulers and the lower classes—was similar to that of feudal overlords and their vassals, with land worked by serfs (Adams and Smith 1977, 1981; Grube and Martin 2000:150). Furthermore, the Terminal Classic "collapse" is explained by causes similar to Malthusian crises affecting medieval Europe, including population growth, worsening climatic conditions, crop failure, famine, and plague. The primary difficulties with the feudal analogy are that feudal societies were not state-level formations and the crucial element of feudalism—ownership of land—is not clearly understood among the Classic Maya.

Another external analogy is the "segmentary state" model of political organization, which several archaeologists (Houston 1993; Dunham 1990; Ball and Taschek 1991; Laporte 1996; Mejía, Quezada, and Chocón 1998; see also Fox et al. 1996) have applied to the lowland Maya. The model, drawn from Aidan W. Southall's (1956, 1988) studies of the Alur in Africa, draws attention to patterns of instability and fissioning of their segmentary lineages. This initially led Southall to characterize the Alur as a "segmentary state," even though they represented little more than a ranked society and not a state at all. Coe's (1965:112) model anticipates some factors that appear to support application of the segmentary state concept to the lowlands: powerful lineages and a dispersed settlement pattern might contribute to conflict among centers and ruling lineages, resulting in cities asserting independence and/or shifting allegiance to other centers. And Fox's (1977) regal-ritual city concept is closely tied to the idea of segmentary states. But there is no evidence that the lowland Maya had segmentary lineages.

Several other decentralized scenarios have been popular in Maya studies, many of which are variants of a city-state model. The city-state model was, of course, employed in both Morley's and Thompson's writings and draws analogies to Greek city-states: small, autonomous polities with a large, powerful city at their center. Others who have used this model include some archaeologists working at Copán (e.g., Webster 1997; but cf. Webster 2002:164; Abrams 1994) and some epigraphers (Grube 2000a). This model has been criticized in part because of a lack of consensus as to whether city-states among the Greeks and elsewhere in the Mediterranean region actually constituted state-level polities (Marcus 1998:89; Marcus and Feinman 1998:8–10). In addition, such polities frequently seemed to postdate the breakdown of large, unitary territorial states, such as that of Mayapán (see also Roys 1957).

Somewhat related is the "peer-polity interaction" approach or model (Renfrew and Cherry 1986), drawn from study of the development of early states in the Aegean. This analytic perspective suggests that to understand the emergence of states, we must first consider the kinds of interactions—warfare, exchange, and so on—that took place among smaller polities that are essentially "peers." These small, autonomous, densely clustered "peer polities," or statelets, exist in a circumstance of uneasy competition against each other without any one able to achieve clear dominance (see Freidel 1986; Sabloff 1986). They may either precede states or follow their breakup, as in the city-state model.

Other decentralized analogues are the "galactic polities" from Stanley Tambiah's (1977) analysis of Thai kingdoms as well as Clifford Geertz's (1980) "theater state" in nineteenth-century Bali (see Demarest 1992; Scarborough 1998). The key element in these systems is the institution of kingship, particularly divine kingship: "The driving aim of higher politics was to construct a state by constructing a king. The more consummate the king, the more exemplary the center. The more exemplary the center, the more actual the realm" (Geertz 1980:124). These Asian polities shared numerous features with the Classic lowland Maya, including cosmologically and ideologically based physical organization of the states and their centers; political unity vested in the personal, charismatic qualities of the ruler, especially through the conduct of ritual performances; loose, decentralized control over labor and production among a "galaxy" of satellites or subordinate centers; and a dynamic, unstable political situation characterized by shifting alliances, territorial expansions and contractions, and elite warfare (Demarest 1992: 150–151). The parallels that Demarest outlines between Asian and Maya polities are striking, and the Classic Maya may indeed be an example of a theater state; moreover, the theater state model writ large has some parallels with Fox's (1977) regal-ritual city concept.

As a final note on decentralized models and analogies to Classic lowland Maya political organization, the advocates of such models have tended to work at smaller sites on the fringes of the domains of the great Late Classic sites such as Tikal, Calakmul, and Caracol. They tend to stress the role of warfare in maintaining political independence—or in obstructing political unification—and favor non-Maya analogues that emphasize shifting and unstable polities (e.g., Pohl and Pohl 1994). These models approximate Roys's (1957) third category of sixteenth-century polities in the Yucatán peninsula: loosely allied groups of towns or unrelated small polities lacking both a powerful lord (jalach winik) and incorporation into larger polities and lying on the peripheries of more centralized systems. This circumstance certainly describes the situation for much of what is now Belize during the Late Classic period but not the core area of central Petén.

Emblem Glyph–based Centralized Models

Just as analyses of the distribution of Emblem Glyphs supported decentralized, weak-state models of lowland Maya political organization, they can also support centralized models. Emblems, plus other recently deciphered glyphs, have yielded evidence of political hierarchies, and there is now a tendency among archaeologists to favor the existence of centralized states among the Classic Maya. By analogy with Roys's Yucatán models (1957; Marcus 1993), these hypothesized states most closely represent Category A, the kuchkab'als or large territorial polities or maximal chiefdoms that survived and flourished after the breakup of the Mayapán confederacy, and also Mayapán in its heyday. The main point of contention is the size of the state.

One of the first Emblem Glyph–based models of political organization was that of Barthel (1968), who recognized the hierarchical and directional significance of Emblems. His observations were later expanded by Joyce Marcus (1973, 1976, 1993:149–150), who analyzed the patterns of occurrence of Emblems on monuments throughout the lowlands. Postulating the existence of a quadripartite division of the Late Classic southern lowlands with four regional capitals, she noted that "although the four capitals apparently could mention each other by name, no secondary center ever mentions a primary center except that to which it is subsidiary" (1973:913). The lack of such patterning during the early Early and Middle Classic periods suggested there were no regional capitals or four-tiered site hierarchies during those periods (Marcus 1976:35). In succeeding centuries (Cycle 9), however, the four-tiered hierarchy developed with four regional capitals, as indicated by Emblem Glyphs.

The occurrence of four sites' Emblem Glyphs on Stela A at Copán (see Fig. 6.2) indicated to Barthel and Marcus that by A.D. 731 the Maya recognized four "capitals" of four large territories that encompassed the entire central and southern lowlands. These capitals were Tikal, Copán, Palenque, and—as suggested by Marcus—Calakmul, each associated with a cardinal direction: west, south, north, and east, respectively. Within each territory was a hierarchy of sites—secondary and tertiary centers—that recorded the primary site's Emblem Glyph (Fig. 2.7). Some politico-ritual unity among these territories is indicated by a Late Classic "Period of Uniformity," from A.D. 687 to 756, in which the Maya adopted a standard lunar calendar; as Barthel (1968:187) commented,

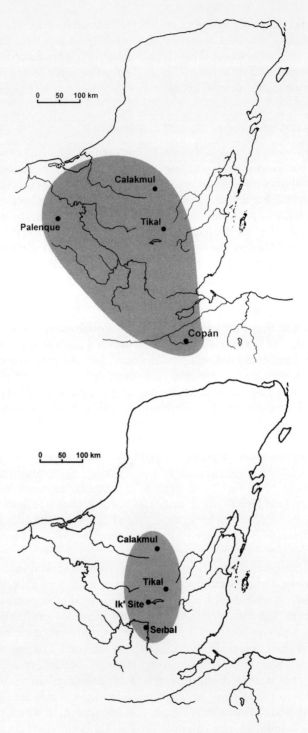

FIGURE 2.7 Centralized model of geopolitical organization of the southern Maya lowlands: four capitals identified by textual mention of Emblem Glyphs. (a) capitals in A.D. 731 (after Marcus 1976:Fig. 1.10; (b) capitals in A.D. 849 (after Marcus 1976:Fig. 1.11).

that cosmic "uniformity" was no doubt established by representatives of the sites mentioned on Stela A. By the Terminal Classic, the total geographic sphere comprising the lowland capitals had diminished, as indicated by the shorter distances between the named capitals on Seibal Stela 10, dated A.D. 849 (see Table 2.2; Fig. 7.4): Tikal, Calakmul, Seibal, and possibly Motul de San José. The Barthel-Marcus postulate of four major capitals is one of the more centralized models of Maya political organization.

In light of this influential model, it is useful to recall that Morley (1946) had earlier suggested four regional divisions of the Maya lowlands. The Barthel-Marcus model, however, was based on textual evidence from Late Classic monuments (Barthel also referred to glyphs on bones from Burial 116 at Tikal), particularly the display of Emblem Glyphs. Barthel (1968:192–193) noted that similar identifications of four named centers with cardinal directions could be found in the chilam b'alams. This raised the possibility that a *sistema cosmosociológico*, a cosmologically based system or quadripartite geopolitical model, was the basis of lowland Maya political organization at least from the Late Classic—and probably much earlier—through Postclassic and Colonial times. It has been noted that the directional identification of these capitals does not correspond to geographic reality, but that may be irrelevant. What might be more important is the order in which they are listed, with east—the direction of sunrise—first, since this corresponds to the cosmological and mythological significance of dawn (as in the *Popol Vuh*; Tedlock 1985) and the counterclockwise order of movement in ritual processions.

Subsequently, Norman Hammond used a framework of four regions—western, Pasión, northeast Petén, and southeastern—for orga-

Table 2.2. The four "capitals" of the Late and Terminal Classic southern lowlands, with associated directions and colors.

Quarter	Color	A.D. 731 (at Copán)	A.D. 889 (at Seibal)
East (*lik'in*)	Red (*chak*)	Copán	Seibal
West (*chik'in*)	Black (*ek'*)	Tikal	Tikal
South (*nojol*)	Yellow (*kan*)	Calakmul	Calakmul
North (*xaman*)	White (*zak*)	Palenque	Motul de San José (?)

Source: Barthel 1968:185–191; Marcus 1976:16–17.

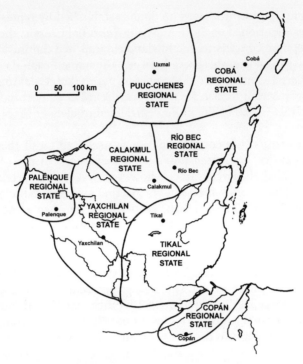

FIGURE 2.8 Centralized model of geopolitical organization of the Classic Maya low-lands: eight regional states (after Adams 1990).

nizing his preface to Culbert's (1991b) edited volume on Maya political history. As Hammond (1991 : 5) explained, "That only these four regions are taken for detailed scrutiny is due to the restricted distribution of Emblem Glyphs."

Richard E. W. Adams (Adams and Jones 1981; Adams 1986, 1990) proposed the existence of eight large "regional states" in the Late Classic lowlands: Puuc-Chenes, Cobá, Calakmul, Río Bec, Palenque, Yaxchilán, Tikal, and Copán (Fig. 2.8). These constituted large territories averaging roughly 30,000 km^2, which were organized around "state capitals" and had a hierarchy of dependent centers. Adams and Jones (1981:318) commented that at one point in the Late Classic period, Tikal could possibly have dominated a much larger territory incorporating the Pasión, Calakmul, and Río Bec zones to the north and west, as well as parts of Belize to the east, a total area of more than 100,000 km^2.

Apart from this notion, arguments favoring models of large, hegemonic Late Classic polities reached their pinnacle in Simon Martin and Nikolai Grube's (1995) hypothesis that two Maya "superstates," Tikal and Calakmul, dominated affairs throughout the lowlands during the

Classic period. These sites are, of course, among those that have long been identified by Maya archaeologists as dominant, centralized polities. More recently, Martin and Grube (2000:19–20) have described Classic lowland Maya political organization in terms of a "pervasive and enduring system of 'overkingship'" and hierarchical relationships. They base their interpretation in part on the phrase u-kab'iy that occurs with the name of a foreign ruler at a particular site. This phrase, "he supervised it," refers to a higher overlord, or "overking," whose superordinate status is acknowledged by a local king. Such statements are used in the contexts of certain rituals, such as the installation of a new king, which took place under the aegis of, and/or were supervised by, the overlord. In addition, they note that certain titles, such as sajal and ajaw, may have prefixes—for example, usajal, yajaw—which they interpret as indicating subordination ("his ajaw") to those of higher rank.

Many other archaeologists have advocated the existence of large, powerful, hierarchically organized, centralized Classic Maya states, among them Arlen F. Chase and Diane Z. Chase for Caracol (1996), T. Patrick Culbert for Tikal (1988, 1991b), and William Folan and colleagues for Calakmul (1995). In general, the archaeologists who most strongly support centralized state models have themselves worked at large sites such as Tikal and Calakmul.

Time and Its Cycles

Two critical elements—process and time—are largely missing from all these reconstructions of Maya political organization, whether centralized or decentralized, direct-historical or drawn from afar. The models reviewed here provide intriguing glimpses into possible structures of the Classic lowland Maya system of political organization, but they have failed to provide an understanding of how that organization "worked," that is, the role of individual and institutional agency in how decisions were made, how power was negotiated, how resources were deployed, how successions were effected, how sites interacted.

Three recent discussions have attempted to interject a dynamic element and recognition of temporal change into lowland Maya political organization. One is Marcus's (1993, 1995) "dynamic model" of oscillating rise and fall, or centralization-consolidation versus decentralization, of Classic period states. It is not entirely clear, however, why these rise-and-fall scenarios exist. Textual sources imply that "treachery" is involved (Marcus 1993:134–135) and that the "lords at secondary centers . . . were the weak link" in the hierarchy of primary, secondary, and tertiary centers (Marcus 1993:164). This observation echoes Arthur A. Demarest's (1992:151) discussion of the similarity between the Classic Maya and Southeast Asian galactic polities, in which subordinate polities and their rulers represented a "large potential pool of usurpers . . . [with] . . . their own claims to divine authority, which created circumstances conducive to rebellion by satellites." Also, Coe's (1965) model calls attention to rotation of offices as resolving such problems of succession.

Another contribution to these discussions is the neoevolutionary "dual-processual theory" offered by Richard E. Blanton and his colleagues (1996), based on the relative dominance of one of two political-economic strategies in a particular society. An "exclusionary" strategy is based on elite monopolization of power sources, whether material-objective or symbolic (knowledge, ritual), through networks of interaction and "patrimonial rhetoric." The "corporate" strategy, based on sharing of power and sources of power across various social sectors, "emphasizes collective representations and the accompanying ritual based on broad themes such as fertility and renewal in society and cosmos" (Blanton et al. 1996:6). In applying their theory to the lowland Maya, these authors see a Late Preclassic corporate strategy (see also Becker 1983) leading to the development of the ajaw kingship office, followed by a Classic period exclusionary network strategy, with the reemergence of corporate strategies in the Postclassic period (Blanton et al. 1996:12). They fail to account for why these shifts in strategies occurred, however.

Gyles Iannone (2002) attempts to resolve the unanswered question, why? by means of the dialectic between kinship and kingship through the temporal concepts of the Annales school (Braudel 1972): *longue durée, moyenne durée (conjonctures)*, and *événement* (event). The first two of these concepts postulate long-term structures and medium-term cycles of change within which events occur. Iannone has interpreted these in terms of kinship and kingship, respectively, and suggests they account for the shifts between centralized and decentralized political organization in Classic Maya states.

But what has been lacking in virtually all these models is the dynamic component of *process* to explain how lowland Maya political organization functioned in strategies of negotiating power, providing adjustments and checks and balances to changing circumstances over generations, regardless of scale. Such a dynamic can be recognized only when the quintessence of Maya cosmology—cyclical time—is integrated into these otherwise static descriptions. Recording, predicting, and retrodicting events in time was, for the Maya, a matter of virtually obsessive import. As seen on their public portrayals, Maya kings were "rulers of time" (Miller 1986; Stuart 1996:165). They were also ruled by it.

Temporal cycles have deep meaning for all of Mesoamerica, where cyclical creations and cyclical time modeled history. The Maya provide an example of a more general Mesoamerican belief system that closely interrelates political power, time, space, and the notion of kingly duty as a sacred "burden." This idea is embodied in the Yukatekan and Cholan Maya word *kuch* (glyph T601), seen in the titles of numerous political offices and jurisdictions as *kuchkab'al* or *kuchte'el: kuch* (also *ikatz;* Stross 1988) means burden, office, charge, responsibility, or prophecy. Not only do humans have the burden of official duties, so does each day, year, k'atun, and other unit of time. Each temporal unit is personified as a divine bearer or porter with responsibility for shouldering a minuscule fraction of the cosmos (a period of time) and its augury, such as drought or war or pestilence. These periods in turn are portrayed as a bundle carried on the bearer's back with a tumpline.

But many of the so-called cycles highlighted in Maya prehistory are not true cycles in a dictionary sense, that is, regularly recurring periods of time "in which certain events repeat themselves in the same order and intervals" (*Random House Dictionary*). Rather, they are two-dimensional pseudocycles, linear sine-wave patterns on X-Y coordinates (Fig. 2.9) charting the peaks and valleys—the beginning, middle, and end—of cultural rise and fall (e.g., Marcus's [1992b, 1993, 1995] "dynamic model"; also Sharer 1992; Demarest 1992; Pohl and Pohl 1994). The role that truly cyclical concepts of time (see Chap. 3) might have played in Maya political activities and histories has by no means been ignored by Maya archaeologists, art historians, epigraphers, and ethnographers, but neither has its salience been fully apprehended.

While many Mesoamerican peoples believed that there was a series of creations and destructions of the world, among the Maya this concept of cyclical time, particularly cycles of the k'atun, seems to have been revered even more profoundly. The historian Nancy M. Farriss (1987:577), for example, believes that the cycling of cosmic time, particularly through the k'atuns, provided a charter for the Maya political system. Claude F. Baudez (1991) suggests that the completion of annual and k'atun cycles was celebrated at Copán and elsewhere by ritual processions through the quadripartite divisions of the city. Arlen Chase (1991) looked at "cycles of time" in relation to the development of Caracol, in west-central Belize, calling attention to events occurring in K'atuns 8 Ajaw, the *"k'atun of change."*

In "Cycles of Growth at Tikal," Christopher Jones (1991:121–124) noted that beginning around 400 B.C., major building programs and changes in the ceramic complexes seem to evidence two-hundred-year cycles. Jones linked the Tikal architectural cycles to halves of Maya four-hundred-year b'ak'tun units and remarked that they also could mark multiples of the fifty-two-year unit known as the Calendar Round. William Haviland (1992), in an article subtitled "Dynastic Troubles and

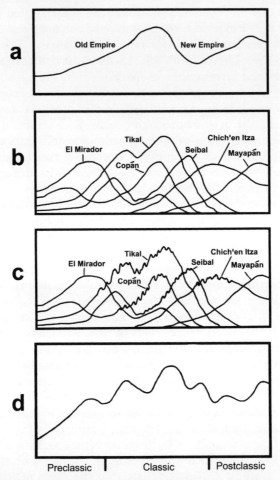

FIGURE 2.9 Schematic, linear models of the history of Maya civilization. (a) Early-twentieth-century old and new empires; (b) Differential histories of individual sites; (c) Detailed histories of individual sites informed by epigraphy; (d) a "dynamic model" of the rise and fall of polities and their sizes through time. (a–c after Sharer 1991:Fig. 8.1; d after Marcus 1998:Fig. 3.1).

the Cycle of Katuns at Tikal, Guatemala," considered similar themes. Citing Roys's ([1933] 1967:184) observation that Maya belief in cyclical time "was so strong at times as to actually influence the course of history," Haviland (1992:79) called attention to the inaugurations of two of Tikal's rulers in successive K'atuns 8 Ajaw, roughly 256 years apart, noting the possibility that the later king saw himself as a reincarnation of the earlier one.

The timing of these two inaugurations had been explored earlier in a portentous article by the late Dennis E. Puleston (1979). Puleston's observations were based on the 256-year span between two periods of cultural decline in the lowlands: the beginning of the so-called hiatus around A.D. 534 and the beginning of the Late Classic collapse around A.D. 790. He also noted the 256-year interval between what were at the time thought to be the accession dates of two of Tikal's most powerful rulers, Siyaj Kan K'awil and Jasaw Kan K'awil. As he (1979:67) commented, because this timing is far too extraordinary to have been mere coincidence, "it seems undeniable that a thirteen-katun historical cycle was recognized and was of great significance during the Classic period." Precisely the same suggestion was published in the same year by Munro Edmonson.

Despite the insights of Puleston, Haviland, Edmonson, and others, Maya archaeologists have failed to recognize the profound implications of the thirteen-k'atun, 256-year interval—the *may*—for Classic period politico-religious hegemony (cf. Lowe, Lee, and Martínez Espinosa 1982; Ball 1986; Rice, Rice, and Jones 1996). While some scholars might prefer to view time and calendrical cycling merely as one of many tools manipulated by Classic Maya rulers to achieve their political ends, such machinations are never "mere," as revealed in comparative histories of time and cosmological thinking (Hawking 1996; Waugh 1999). The *may* analogy, drawn from historically known Postclassic lowland Maya practices, provides a more parsimonious foundation for understanding Classic Maya political geography than the ill-fitting exogenous models with which archaeologists have long struggled. Since first postulated in 1979, the *may* model for the Classic Maya has been supported and strengthened by the burgeoning corpus of textual data pertaining to dynasties, dynastic interrelations, and political centralization. Most important, as described in the following chapters, it injects process and dynamics into the heretofore static structural and classificatory models of Classic lowland Maya political organization.

CHAPTER 3

Maya Politico-Religious Calendrics

A direct-historical approach to Classic lowland Maya political organization begins with proximate groups—close in time, location, language, and culture—for which there is ample information about not only political structures and functions but also their archaeological correlates. Such groups are the Postclassic and Colonial period Maya of the northern Yucatán peninsula, whose geopolitical organization was ordered through a complex web of calendrical cycles and their regular celebration. This chapter focuses on the nature of Maya calendrical science, on the calendrics of the Postclassic Maya of the northern lowlands, and on the principal Maya textual sources for information on ritual surrounding 256-year *may* cycles, the books of the chilam b'alams.

Maya Cosmology and Calendrical Science

Maya political organization was rooted in cosmology, religion, and temporal cycling, themselves inextricably bound: "time is cosmic order," asserts Farriss (1987:574). And Barbara Tedlock (1992:1) notes, "The ancient Maya were great horologists, students of time[,] . . . interested not only in the quantities of time but also in its qualities, especially its meaning for human affairs." The Maya viewed time as both linear (the familiar western conception of historical time) and cyclical. Cyclical time seems peculiar—even prelogical—in the modern world, casually dismissible by the epigram "History repeats itself." But belief in cyclical time, and its integration with linear time, is widespread in prehistory and among modern non-Western peoples (Eliade 1954; Geertz 1973:389–398). In fact, the Maya view of time and a quadripartite universe is not too distant from that of today's physicists, who see the relatively undifferentiated past, present, and future "laid out in a four-dimensional block composed of time and the three spatial dimensions" (Davies 2002:43).

Still, the Maya transcended the familiar recurrence of day and night, and rainy and dry seasons, to calculate and commensurate the infinitely interlocking periodicities of months, years, eclipses, and movements of astral bodies, simultaneously retrodicting them thousands of years into the past and predicting them thousands of years into the future (see Lounsbury 1978; Aveni 1981; Milbrath 1999). Maya skills in predictive astronomy allowed them to foreknow upcoming celestial events, which provided a justification for scheduling important rituals and a "sacred mandate for elite decision-making" (Justeson 1989:104). In addition, astronomers' calculation tables permitted them to project events backward in time, thereby manufacturing "precursors" and "precedents" for the timing of ritual and other activities in the present and future (Justeson 1989:104). This is how the Maya created and re-created their calendars, their histories, their elite affairs, and even their verbal arts (Fought 1985), an unceasingly recursive process that permitted them to "remember their future and anticipate their past" (Farriss 1987:589; see also Bloch 1977).

Ancient Mesoamerican peoples from Mexico through Costa Rica shared a basic native calendrical system. According to Edmonson (1988: 4), "[D]espite its employment by nearly 100 ethnic groups speaking almost as many different languages, it has retained . . . [its] unity over a period of more than 2600 years. This is not just a matter of pattern similarity but of precise mathematical accuracy in the measurement of time." Irrespective of this essential unity, there were sufficient differences in the basic Mesoamerican calendars that at least sixty variants are known (Edmonson 1988:Fig. 3). The ancient Maya, *primus inter pares* of this system, also maintained numerous calendars based on alignments, visibilities, and movements of the sun, moon, Venus, Mars, and other celestial bodies, as well as occurrences of eclipses and other phenomena. Precise records tracked both linear and cyclical time, but temporal cycling was paramount.

The intricacies of Maya calendrics, including correlations with modern calendars, need not be pursued here, but certain points are crucial to understanding Maya concepts of time and the temporal units incorporated into the *may* (for a fuller discussion of Maya calendrics, see Thompson 1960; Edmonson 1988; Sharer 1994:513–629; Marcus 1992a: 132–140; B. Tedlock 1992; Lounsbury 1978; Aveni 1981; Milbrath 1999).

Maya Calendars

The fundamental unit of Maya time was the day, or k'in. The k'in interrelated and embodied notions of sun, day, and time and became "not an abstract entity but a reality enmeshed in the world of myths, a divine being, origin of the cycles which govern all existing things" (León-

Table 3.1. Differences between Western decimal and Maya vigesimal-positional systems of recording time: the day July 2, A.D. 1957.

Modern (Gregorian) Decimal	versus	Maya Vigesimal, Positional: Count of Elapsed Days*
1 unit of 1,000 years		12 units of 144,000 days
9 units of 100 years		17 units of 7,200 days
5 units of 10 years		3 units of 360 days
7 units of 1 year		12 units of 20 days
6 units of 1 month		19 units of 1 day
2 units of 1 day in the seventh month		

Elapsed days since a starting date in August 3114 B.C.

Portilla 1988:33; B. Tedlock 1992:2–3). The Maya kept track of the passage of linear time by counting each elapsed day since a mythical event—their zero point or datum—that occurred in 3114 B.C. in the modern (Gregorian) calendar. The succession of days in the Maya calendars was recorded by means of cycles and epicycles of numbers and names, each having sacred patron deities who bore the burden, or kuch, of that day's auguries and ceremonies and of time itself. Thus the Maya days, and indeed all units of time, were not mere abstractions but living—albeit supernatural—beings.

Counts of days, like all counts, were recorded by the Maya in their "bar-dot" system of numerical notation. This made use of three symbols: a "shell" to represent 0, a dot for 1, and a bar for 5; bars and dots were combined to represent numbers from 1 to 20. Above 20, a position-value notation system was used, increasing vertically from smaller to larger numbers. This can be compared to the Western horizontal positional system, by which we read numbers decreasing by powers of ten, moving from left to right (Table 3.1). Our system is decimal, or base 10; the Maya system, like all Mesoamerican counting systems, is conceptually vigesimal, or base 20, with numbers increasing by powers of 20 from bottom to top. If there were no counts within one of the 20-unit positions, then the shell symbol was placed, signifying null or completion. Not surprisingly, then, the Maya recorded specific dates with reference to a hierarchy of units of elapsed days that were mostly (though not entirely) multiples of 20 (Table 3.2).

Like all peoples of Mesoamerica, the Maya accounted for time's passage in two simultaneously running calendars. One of these is a calendar of 260 days, which archaeologists call the *tzolk'in* (count of days), the "sacred round" or "sacred almanac." It is not clear what the Maya called it, although it may have been referred to as *sak ja'ab'* ("white" or "magnificent" year) (Justeson 1989:77). The basic units of this calendar were a numerical count from 1 to 13 preceding a succession of twenty day-names (read down columns):

Imix	Chikchan	Muluk	B'en	Kab'an
Ik'	Kimi	Ok	Ix	Etznab'
Akb'al	Manik'	Chuwen	Men	Kawak
K'an	Lamat	Eb'	Kib'	Ajaw

The result was a calendar that proceeded for 260 days before the same number-day name combination recurred. This almanac had primary importance in prognostication and in tracking mythoritual time.

The second calendar, *jab'* or *ja'ab'* (year), was based on a "vague year," or solar year, of 365 days. It had 360 days (a period called a *tun*) grouped into eighteen *winals*, or months.

Table 3.2. Maya tun-based temporal units. Note that these units are primarily vigesimal (base-20).

Unit Term	Constituents	Days (K'ins)
1 alawtun	20 k'inchiltuns	23,040,000,000
1 k'inchiltun	20 k'alab'tuns	1,152,000,000
1 k'alab'tun	20 pik'tuns	57,600,000
1 pik'tun	20 b'ak'tuns	2,880,000
1 ('era, creation'?)	13 b'aktuns; 20 mays	1,872,000
1 b'ak'tun	20 k'atuns	144,000
1 *may*	13 k'atuns	93,600
1 k'atun	20 tuns	7,200
1 tun	18 winals	360
1 winal	20 k'ins	20
1 k'in	1 k'in	1

Source: Sharer 1994:560.

Pop	Sek	Ch'en	Mak	K'ayab'
Wo	Xul	Yax	K'ank'in	Kumk'u
Sip	Yaxk'in	Sak	Muwan	Wayeb'
Sotz'	Mol	Kej	Pax	

Each of the eighteen winals comprised twenty numbered days starting with o, to which were added five unlucky days in a wee winal or nineteenth "month" named Wayeb' ("nameless days"). Wayeb' days preceded the first day of the New Year, always o Pop in the Maya ja'ab'. The ja'ab' closely approximated the solar or seasonal year and governed secular events.

A total of 18,980 days, or 52 of the 365-day years, elapsed before any particular number and day in one calendar—say, 4 Ajaw in the 260-day almanac—coincided again with a particular day and month—say, 3 Kank'in—in the solar calendar (Fig. 3.1). This 52-year permutational cycle of the Mesoamerican calendars is called the Calendar Round, or *junab'*. Because Calendar Rounds ended and began only once every 52 years (probably once in most humans' lifetimes), this renewal event at the end of the dangerous Wayeb' days (known as Nemontemi among the Aztec) was grandly celebrated, and the celebrations were accompanied by dedication of new or refurbished temples and lighting new fires. The earliest recorded Calendar Round date may be on an ear ornament from Cuicuilco, which Edmonson (1988:20) dates to 679 B.C. The Calendar Round and the notion of cyclical time are still integral to cosmology, ritual, and administrative life in portions of Mesoamerica and the Maya area, particularly in fairly remote parts of the highlands (Girard 1962; Vogt 1964, 1969; Gossen and Leventhal 1993).

Because the Maya solar year, or ja'ab', consisted of eighteen winals ("months" of twenty days each) *plus five additional days* (Wayeb'), the name of the first day of the year in the tzolk'in annually shifted five places ahead of that of the current year. Over the long term, then, only four of the twenty day names in the 260-day tzolk'in could occupy this starting position. In the Classic period, these were Ak'b'al, Lamat, B'en, and Etz'nab'. These four days in the sacred almanac were referred to as "yearbearers" because they had the responsibility of bearing the burden of the years. In the Postclassic period, the calendars were revised and the year-bearing days changed to K'an, Muluk, Ix, and Kawak.

The most evocative discussion of Maya concepts of time is Thompson's (1960:59): "The Maya conceived of the divisions of time as burdens which were carried through all eternity by relays of bearers . . . [not] the journey of one bearer and his load, but of many bearers, each with his own division of time on his back." Copán Stela D (Fig. 3.2) and its

FIGURE 3.1 The Maya 365-day calendar (ja'ab') and 260-day calendar (tzolk'in), depicted as interlocking, cycling wheels.

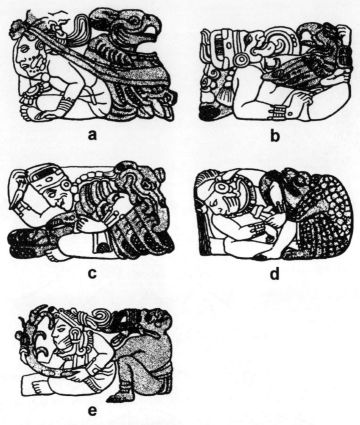

FIGURE 3.2 Full-figure glyphs from Copán Stela D, Initial Series date of 9.15.5.0.0
(10 Ajaw 8 Ch'en), showing time as burdens carried by tumpline on the backs of the
gods. (a) 9 b'ak'tuns; (b) 15 k'atuns; (c) 5 tuns; (d) 0 winals; (e) 0 k'ins (from Thompson 1960:Fig. 28.3, 28.4, 28.14, 29.3, 29.7, respectively). As Thompson (1952:59) interprets the glyphs, "[T]he weary bearers [begin] their rest. For the gods of the numbers 9 and 15 this is a momentary respite; for the others it is the end of the journey.
The 9 and 15 must carry their burdens more stages on the journey, for the current
baktun and katun have still considerable distances to travel before the *lubay* [destination] is reached. The god of number 5 will be immediately replaced by the god
of number 6 as bearer of the tun. . . . The combination pictures feelingly the never-ceasing journey of time. True, there was not in the Maya concept of time a measurable period of repose with the burdens fallen to the ground, for it was a relay race; as
soon as one bearer set down his burden, his successor hoisted it on his back."

full-figure Initial Series (IS) dating glyphs dramatically illustrate this concept:

> The glyphs depict the moment when the period comes to an end, symbolized by the arrival of the procession [of bearers of time] at the *lub*[,] . . . the place where porters set down their burdens, and also the distance between one resting place and another. . . . The glyphs of the IS of this Copán stela depict the weary bearers starting their rest. . . . In the hieroglyphic pictures the resting gods hold the periods or support them in their laps. The god of number 9, the bearer of the baktun, still has his load on his back, held there by the tumpline. . . . His hand is raised as though to slip off the load. (Thompson 1960:59)

Of particular interest in discussions of Classic political organization are longer intervals of time, which the Maya celebrated on their ending dates. These were multiples of the 360-day "years," or tuns. Tun (glyph T548; a hollow log-drum pictograph) may be read as *ja'ab'* and is often read "year," but it also refers to both "stone" (including stelae) and "finalization, ending, completion" (see Fox and Justeson 1984:51–52, 53n32; Justeson 1989:77; Stuart 1996:149–150). Perhaps the most important of the tun periods is the k'atun, probably originally *k'al-tun*, or as on glyph T28:548, *k'a-tun* (Fig. 3.3), although we do not know what the Classic Maya actually called it. While it is typically read as "20 tun endings" or "closing stone," celebrating completion of the count of 7,200 days, Stuart (1996:156) offers another interpretation, "stone binding," suggesting that stelae were wrapped or enclosed. The longest tun-based interval commonly recorded by the Maya is 400 tuns, a tally of 144,000 days or 394.5 solar years. No Maya word for this period is certain; although the glyph is read *pi* or *pi-ya*, scholars call it the *b'ak'tun*, from *b'ak'* (400) plus *tun*.

On rare occasions the Maya recorded units of time larger than the b'ak'tun (see Table 3.2). These longer intervals are recorded on the side of Tikal Stela 10 (Fig. 3.4), which dates to A.D. 527. The upper portion of the glyph for *k'alab'tun* depicts a hand holding a pen with a tassel at the end of it (A-B8). A slightly modified version of this hand with a pointing finger and tassel was a widely used glyph to symbolize "completion" in calendrical texts.

Archaeologists employ a positional notation convention to indicate Maya dates recorded in this system, reading counts of elapsed units of time from left to right, that is, the count of elapsed b'ak'tuns, k'atuns, tuns, winals, and k'ins. For example, a Maya date recorded as 9.13.0.0.0 8 Ajaw 8 Wo (March 16, 692) indicates that nine b'ak'tuns had passed

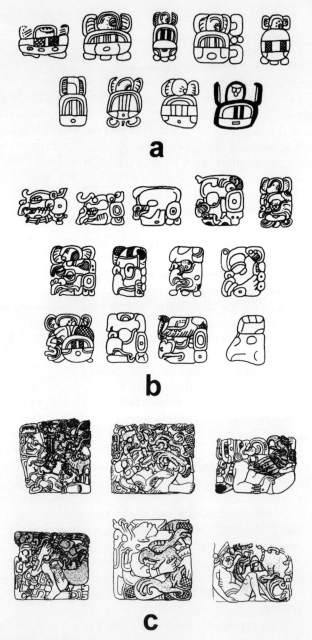

FIGURE 3.3 Glyphs for the k'atun: (a) phonetic variants; (b) head variants; (c) full-figure variants (from Thompson 1960: Figs. 26–28).

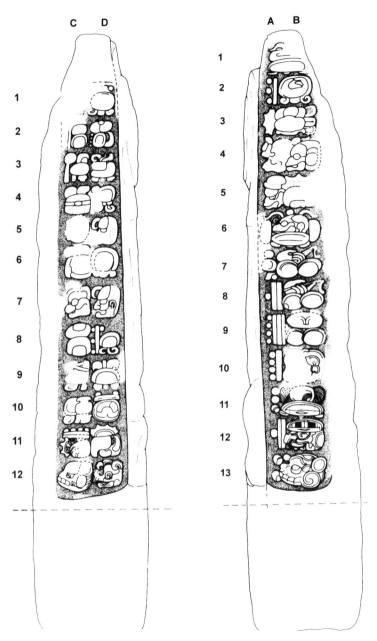

FIGURE 3.4 Tikal Stela 10, left and right sides. Right side shows units of time larger than the b'ak'tun: AB7 reads one k'inchiltun; AB8 is 11 k'alab'tuns; AB9 is 19 pictuns; and AB10 is 9 b'ak'tuns (Jones and Satterthwaite 1982:25; drawing by William R. Coe, courtesy of University of Pennsylvania Museum, Philadelphia, neg. # Tikal 69-5-9b).

(the date is thus in the tenth b'ak'tun), thirteen k'atuns had ended, and no winals, tuns, or k'ins had yet been completed. The specific day in question is named 8 Ajaw in the 260-day calendar and 8 Wo in the 365-day calendar. Furthermore, this date is a "period-ending date," marking the completion of 13 k'atuns within b'ak'tun 9, as indicated by zeros in the places for tuns, winals, and k'ins.

Commemoration of period endings by the erection of carved stelae was crucially important to the Classic Maya. While completions of k'atuns, such as 9.13.0.0.0, were most commonly celebrated, five-year intervals within k'atuns were also recorded at some sites. Such intervals include the first five tuns, known as the *jotun* (e.g., 9.13.5.0.0), the tenth tun or half-k'atun interval, called the *lajuntun* (e.g., 9.13.10.0.0), and three quarters of the k'atun, or *jolajuntun* (e.g., 9.13.15.0.0), read as "five tuns lacking" (until completion of 20 tuns).

This system of recording time by counts of elapsed days in units of b'ak'tuns, k'atuns, tuns, and so on, is known as the Long Count, and, for archaeologists, the beginning and ending of the Classic period is marked by the initiation and cessation of Long Count dating. That the Maya Long Count is truly "long" can be seen in inscriptions at Yaxchilán, Palenque, Quiriguá, and Cobá, for example, which project time forward to the fifth millennium (A.D. 4772) and retrodict site histories, creations, and births of deities in calculations of hundreds of millions of years into the past (Schele and Miller 1986:320–321; Martin and Grube 2000:70; Sharer 1994:571; Montgomery 2001a:299).

Toward the end of the Late Classic, the Maya began to simplify their accounting of time from the typical Long Count and Initial Series format. Instead, they recorded only the k'atun and day-month names and numbers in the two calendars, as, for example, K'atun 18, 11 Ajaw 18 Mak. By the Postclassic and Colonial periods, after about A.D. 950, dating was abbreviated even further to the Short Count, referencing only the passing of k'atuns along with the Ajaw ending day, as, for example, K'atun 8 Ajaw.

Importantly for the argument developed here, the passage of k'atuns in the Postclassic period was recorded through the k'atun cycle or round (*u kajlay k'atunob'*). A k'atun cycle is a count of thirteen k'atuns of 7,200 k'ins per k'atun, or 93,600 days; this is 160 days short of 256 of our solar years (Edmonson 1986a:9). Thus approximately 256 years must elapse between one k'atun and the next having exactly the same combination of day name and number in the Maya 260-day calendar. This is the *may* cycle.

An important if esoteric point, given that we know the Maya were capable of calculations of nearly unfathomable periods of time based on counts of days, is the role of the *may* in such larger periods. As noted, the Maya believed in multiple creations of the cosmos and that the one they were living in, as marked by the initiation point of their calendrical records, began in August 3114 B.C. The present "creation" consisted of thirteen b'ak'tuns of 144,000 days each, or 1,872,000 days; it also would have consisted of twenty *may* cycles of 93,600 days each.

The Maya always named their k'atuns for a day Ajaw (Lord), which was the last of the twenty day names in the tzolk'in. According to Stuart (1996:166), "The day Ahaw was thus the 'face' or 'lord' of the Period Ending . . . [and] the day-name 'Lord' appears only in the Maya area . . . [where it] could 'rule' over a Period Ending" (in other Mesoamerican 260-day calendars, the last day is usually Flower). Because of the permutations of the cycling of the two calendars, the k'atuns' numerical coefficients moved in retrograde order such that each was numbered two less than the preceding (Table 3.3). K'atun 8 Ajaw ended the cycle, at which point the cycle began again with K'atun 6 Ajaw (the significance of an 8 Ajaw ending date will become apparent later). In sixteenth-century Yucatán, the cycle of thirteen k'atuns was represented as a wheel divided into thirteen sections (Fig. 3.5); at the Postclassic site of Mayapán the carapace of a carved stone turtle had thirteen Ajaw glyphs (Proskouriakoff 1962a:Fig. 1.g).

Calendrical Origins

What was the origin of these Maya calendars? The Maya themselves say little if anything about this, although the *Book of Chilam Balam of Chumayel* has a chapter on "the birth of the winal" (Roys [1933] 1967:116–119; Edmonson 1986a:120–126). Edmonson (1988:12, 119), who has studied calendrical systems and their historical development throughout Mesoamerica, argues that the marked similarities of all Mesoamerican calendars suggest a single common origin and that they were probably "altered rarely, grudgingly, and minimally" through time.

The Maya recorded dates in their system as a calculation of elapsed days since 0.0.0.0.0 (or 13.0.0.0.0), 4 Ajaw 8 Kumk'u (August 11, 3114 B.C.). This date lies back in mythohistorical time, as few Mesoamerican peoples in the late fourth millennium B.C. were fully sedentary agricultural villagers, and none are presently known to have used permanent written, numerical, or calendrical recording systems. This date would have marked the beginning of the present Fourth (or Fifth) Creation of the cosmos, the beginning of time itself.

An interesting device in the context of Mesoamerican calendrical computations is the "pecked cross" or "cross-in-circle" symbol

Table 3.3. Retrograde order of naming K'atuns Ajaw within the 256-year cycle. Note that lajuntuns end on a day Ajaw that fits the descending numerical order.

K'atun	Maya Date	Tzolk'in	Ja'ab'	Gregorian
6 Ajaw	9.1.0.0.0	6 Ajaw	13 Yaxk'in	August 26, 455
	9.1.10.0.0	5 Ajaw	3 Sek	July 4, 465
4 Ajaw	9.2.0.0.0	4 Ajaw	13 Wo	May 13, 475
	9.2.10.0.0	3 Ajaw	8 Kumk'u	March 21, 485
2 Ajaw	9.3.0.0.0	2 Ajaw	18 Muwan	January 28, 495
	9.3.10.0.0	1 Ajaw	8 Mak	December 7, 504
13 Ajaw	9.4.0.0.0	13 Ajaw	18 Yax	October 16, 514
	9.4.10.0.0	12 Ajaw	8 Mol	August 24, 524
11 Ajaw	9.5.0.0.0	11 Ajaw	18 Sek	July 3, 534
	9.5.10.0.0	10 Ajaw	8 Sip	May 11, 544
9 Ajaw	9.6.0.0.0	9 Ajaw	3 Wayeb'	March 20, 554
	9.6.10.0.0	8 Ajaw	13 Pax	January 27, 564
7 Ajaw	9.7.0.0.0	7 Ajaw	3 Kank'in	December 5, 573
	9.7.10.0.0	6 Ajaw	13 Sak	October 14, 583
5 Ajaw	9.8.0.0.0	5 Ajaw	3 Ch'en	August 22, 593
	9.8.10.0.0	4 Ajaw	13 Xul	July 2, 603
3 Ajaw	9.9.0.0.0	3 Ajaw	3 Sotz'	May 10, 613
	9.9.10.0.0	2 Ajaw	13 Pop	March 19, 623
1 Ajaw	9.10.0.0.0	Ajaw	8 K'ayab'	January 25, 633
	9.10.10.0.0	13 Ajaw	18 Kank'in	December 4, 642
12 Ajaw	9.11.0.0.0	12 Ajaw	8 Kej	October 12, 652
	9.11.10.0.0	11 Ajaw	18 Ch'en	August 21, 662
10 Ajaw	9.12.0.0.0	10 Ajaw	8 Yaxk'in	June 29, 672
	9.12.10.0.0	9 Ajaw	18 Sotz'	May 8, 682
8 Ajaw	9.13.0.0.0	8 Ajaw	8 Wo	March 16, 692
	9.13.10.0.0	7 Ajaw	3 Kumk'u	January 24, 702
6 Ajaw	9.14.0.0.0	6 Ajaw	13 Muwan	December 3, 711

Source: Sharer 1994:Table A.3.

FIGURE 3.5 Bishop Diego de Landa's drawing of a k'atun wheel (after Tozzer 1941:167).

(Fig. 3.6a). This symbol is typically composed of double (sometimes triple) concentric circles (rarely squares) divided into four quarters by a centered set of generally orthogonal axes. The shapes are created by lines of small (approx. 1 cm dia.) depressions pecked by percussion into plaster floors of ceremonial buildings or on stone outcrops, often on elevations or areas providing unobstructed views of the horizon. These devices are found most commonly in central Mexico but also have been noted in the Maya lowlands at Uaxactún (Smith 1950) and Seibal (Aveni, Hartung, and Buckingham 1978) and in Belize (Wanyerka 1999), as well as in western North America (Aveni, Hartung, and Buckingham 1978:275).

The common functional interpretation of these devices is calendrical, as the number of pecked holes typically totals 260, providing a material connection to the 260-day sacred Mesoamerican calendar. The "outer circle consists of 25 holes per quadrant, totaling 100; the inner circle consists of 20 holes per quadrant, totaling 80" (Aveni, Hartung,

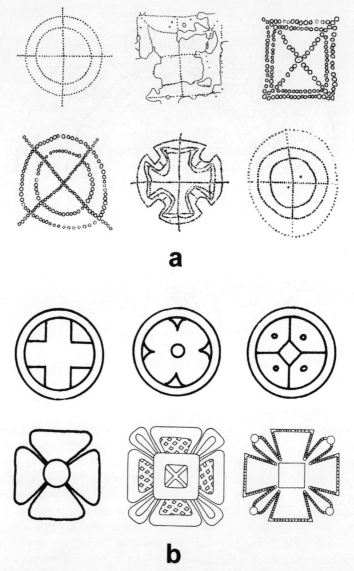

a

b

FIGURE 3.6 (a) Pecked cross or cross-in-circle devices (after Aveni, Hartung, and Buckingham 1978; Grazioso Sierra 1995); (b) Maya quadripartite glyphs for "completion" (after Coggins 1980:Fig. 2).

and Buckingham 1978:267), and the axes typically consist of 10 holes plus 4 between the circles and another 4 beyond the outer one. The emphasis on counts of 4, 18, and 20 is significant in these designs, and these 260-hole devices can also accommodate calculations of periods in the 365-day solar calendar (Worthy and Dickens 1983).

It has not escaped attention that the pecked crosses resemble calendrical diagrams known in Maya books of the chilam b'alams, in Mexican and Maya Postclassic codices, and in common quadripartite glyphs for completion (Fig. 3.6b), and they demonstrate east-west connections between the axis of the cross and the summer solstice sunrise or sunset (Smith 1950:21–22; Aveni 2000:260–261; Aveni, Hartung, and Buckingham 1978; Coggins 1980). Further experimentation might reveal their use with other relevant periods of time, such as lunar, planetary, or eclipse cycles, or other phenomena. Dating these petroglyphs is difficult; although most seem to be Early Classic—the time of Teotihuacan expansion—some at Tlalancaleca, Puebla, may be considerably earlier, circa 500 to 100 B.C. (Aveni, Hartung, and Buckingham 1978:273).

Here it is also useful to remember the discussion of quadripartition in Chapter 1: quadripartition is a common feature of prehistoric cosmologies worldwide. The earthly domain or built world typically mimics that four-part structure, as regions, cities, and architectural groups are, like the universe, divided into four parts (Eliade 1979:335). Eliade suggests that founding rituals include erecting a "fence in the form of a circle or a square broken by four doors which correspond to the four cardinal directions" (p. 335). This ritual structure seems remarkably isomorphic with the image conveyed by the pecked circle devices.

The 260-day tzolk'in has deeply enduring and mythical roots in Mesoamerican ritual. To people of the modern heliocentric Western world, calendrical cycles of 365 days (based on the sun) and 29 to 30 days (based on the moon) are familiar, but a calendar based on 260 days demands explanation. The foundations of this 260-day sacred almanac could be as simple as a multiple of thirteen day gods times twenty fingers and toes (Thompson 1930a); however, since it is the twenty days that are named—for natural phenomena, in a sequence that is nearly universal throughout Mesoamerica—this begs the question of where the thirteen gods came from. Other suggestions for the origins of the 260-day calendar include the approximation of the human gestational cycle from last menstruation (Thompson 1960:98; Earle and Snow 1985; Brotherston 1983; Tedlock 1985:232); the time of solar zenith passage at 15° North latitude, the location of Izapa and Copán (Nuttall 1928; Malmström 1973); the duration of an "agrarian year," from February through late October (Tichy 1981:236–237; also Šprajc 2000; Milbrath 1999:13–14; Girard 1962:328–342; Thompson 1930b:41); cycles of visibility of the planet Venus (Aveni 1981; Flores 1989; Tedlock 1985:40, 233–34; cf. Justeson 1989:78); and average segments—7, 9, 13, and 20 days—of lunar cycles (Macri in press).

Mesoamerican calendars most likely had their origins in the beginnings of historical record keeping in Preclassic Mexico, to judge from carved dates and other writing in central and western Mexico (Cuicuilco, Chalcatzingo), Oaxaca (San José Mogote, Monte Albán), and the Gulf coastal lowlands (see Edmonson 1986b, 1988:20–21; Justeson 1986, 1989:79; Pohl, Pope, and von Nagy 2002). The earliest recorded calendrical dates in these areas refer to the years 679 and 667 B.C. The isthmian area of Mesoamerica in particular has long been seen as a zone of early calendrical elaboration and differentiation (Rice n.d.a), though researchers differ as to which side of the isthmus may claim precedence.

Edmonson (1986b:85) believes the Gulf Coast Olmec calendar is ancestral to all other Mesoamerican calendars. The Olmec calendar counts days of the month from 0 to 19 and names the year for the yearbearers of the last day (terminal naming). Edmonson (1988:117) thinks it is probable that Olmec calendric specialists had invented the 52-year Calendar Round by 739 B.C., and by 433 B.C. Mesoamerican astronomers "had attained the accuracy of modern astronomy in [their] estimate of the length of the tropical year: 365.2422 days." He also suggests that the Olmec began using the Long Count of 7,891 years in 355 B.C. He bases this on the coincidence of the completion of a Calendar Round with that of the last k'atun of a b'ak'tun, an event that only happens every 936 years. Its occurrence on 6.19.19.0.0 1 Ajaw 3 Kej (June 8, 355 B.C.) probably represents the initiation of the Long Count, as well as other important intervals such as the *may* (thirteen k'atuns) and the b'ak'tun (twenty k'atuns); a cycle of thirteen b'ak'tuns is equivalent to twenty *mays* (Edmonson 1988:101, 118–119, 124; see also Justeson and Campbell 1997:52). Similar coinciding cycles of b'ak'tun and Calendar Round occurred in A.D. 582 and, fatefully for the Aztecs, in 1519. Several early monuments were erected in the Gulf Coast region, including the La Mojarra stela, with Long Count dates ranging from A.D. 143 (8.5.3.3.5 13 Chikchan 3 K'ayab') to 157 (8.5.17.15.2 12 Ik' 5 Yaxk'in) (Kaufman and Justeson 2001:2.74), and the Tuxtla Statuette (A.D. 162).

Other arguments about the isthmian origins of Mesoamerican calendars focus on the Pacific coast. One suggestion (Malmström 1978) is that the 260-day almanac began in 1358 B.C. around the Mexico-Guatemala border (see also Tichy 1981:237) and that the 365-day vague year began a few decades thereafter. In this view, the initiation of the Long Count, by which time is accounted simultaneously in both calendars, would have occurred on September 12, 236 B.C. This date was the k'atun ending of 7.6.0.0.0 11 Ajaw 8 Kumk'u, when calendar priests may have attempted to standardize the calendars and extrapolate backward to an "origin" date, thereby establishing the "beginnings of time" in 3114 B.C. on another day 8 Kumk'u. K'atuns ending on 7.6.0.0.0 (236 B.C.) and 7.5.0.0.0 (256 B.C.) had been proposed many decades previously by John E. Teeple and Thompson, respectively, as starting dates for the Long Count (cited in Kubler 1977:16).

The earliest surviving Maya dates (depending on how "Maya" and "date" are defined) may lie in late b'ak'tun 7, and they correspond to 36 B.C. on a fragmentary Long Count date on Stela 2 at Chiapa de Corzo (in Chiapas, Mexico) and A.D. 36 on Stela 1 at El Baúl on the Pacific coast of Guatemala. Edmonson (1988:100–101, 121–122) sees the early inscriptions and dates from Chiapas and the Pacific coast as examples of the existence of a Preclassic "Kaminaljuyú calendar," which he named after the highland Maya site in the valley of Guatemala City, the present capital of Guatemala. Kaminaljuyú might have been a meeting ground for multiple cultural and linguistic groups, where they shared a common creation mythology but struggled among themselves for calendrical and ritual dominance (see Coggins 1996:33).

Edmonson believes the Kaminaljuyú calendar is the ancestor of two major versions of the solar calendar used in Classic period Mesoamerica. One is central Mexican—what he calls the "Teotihuacan calendar," named after that huge city northeast of Mexico City—the precursor of which he identifies on Kaminaljuyú Stela 10 dating to 147 B.C. The Teotihuacan calendar used initial (rather than terminal) dating, as did the other major Classic calendar (Tikal), but it diverged from the Olmec calendar before the incorporation of the Long Count dating system in the fourth century B.C. The Tikal calendar diverged from the Olmec a century or so later and was initiated in 236 B.C. (7.6.0.0.0 11 Ajaw 8 Kumk'u) (Edmonson 1986b:86, 1988:23). From Tikal Stela 29, dating to A.D. 292, he concludes that the Tikal calendar would have been inaugurated on July 13, A.D. 84.

All three post-Olmec calendars, Kaminaljuyú, Tikal, and Teotihuacan, shared a pattern of counting days of the month from 0 to 19 (like the Olmec calendar) and dated solar years from the beginning or initial day. The accurate estimation, by 433 B.C., of the length of the tropical year may be related to abandonment of terminal naming of the solar year (Edmonson 1988:117). The Long Count was shared by the Olmec and Tikal calendars but was not known at Kaminaljuyu or Teotihuacan. It "diffused to the Maya from the [Epi-]Olmec quite separately from the genetic derivation of the Tikal calendar round from Kaminaljuyu" (Edmonson 1988:120).

The "classical" or "Tikal" calendar of the Classic Maya, then, was in use from b'ak'tun 7 through 11.17.0.0.0 (A.D. 1539; see Edmonson

1986a). The 365-day calendar used initial naming and 0–19 numbering, which means that it began on day 0 of month Pop. Terminal naming was used for cycles in the 260-day almanac and Short Count, which means that k'atuns, b'ak'tuns, and *mays* were identified by their last day. The final k'atun of the 13-k'atun cycle or round ended on a day 8 Ajaw, so it was always known as a K'atun 8 Ajaw. Also, a K'atun 8 Ajaw always ended the 256-year *may* cycle and a K'atun 6 Ajaw always began it; that is, the final day 8 Ajaw of the thirteenth k'atun in the cycle was always followed by a day 1 Imix of a new k'atun, which ended on a day 6 Ajaw, hence a K'atun 6 Ajaw.

Calendrical Transformations

Maya calendars underwent numerous adjustments during the course of their history. For example, the Maya recognized that there was a gap of a quarter of a day between their 365-day calendar and the true solar or tropical year. This discrepancy would have meant a difference of one day every four years, or 100 days (more than three months) every 400 years, an unsettling state of affairs for farmers depending on calendrical auguries to plant and harvest their crops. Two of the month names in the ja'ab' apparently originally referred to agricultural seasons: the seventh month, *yaxk'in*, 'first, green day' (time of planting) and the fourteenth month, *k'ank'in*, 'yellow, ripening, maturity' (time of harvest).

During the Early Classic period at Tikal and surrounding sites, Maya astronomers inaugurated the new Uniform System of recording lunar eclipses and other lunar dates, perhaps as early as 8.16.0.0.0 (A.D. 357) and certainly by 9.4.13.0.0 (A.D. 527) (Justeson 1989:87–88). This system may go back to Late Preclassic efforts to track lunar eclipse cycles. Alternative systems were known at Altar de Sacrificios and Palenque to the west and also at Copán to the southeast.

In the seventh century A.D., new calendars—the Palenque and the Campeche—may have emerged in or been introduced to the lowlands (Edmonson 1988:36–37, 103, 126). Both calendars abandoned the 0–19 counting of days in favor of 1–20 and used terminal naming of the solar years. This latter practice is distinctively non-Maya: Edmonson (1988:103) calls it an "intrusive foreign idea," attributing it to Ch'olan speakers and calendars used in the Gulf Coast or Oaxaca region. The Palenque calendar, believed to have been inaugurated on the summer solstice, June 22, A.D. 177 (8.6.17.13.18 12 Etz'nab 1 Pop), was first documented at the k'atun ending in A.D. 692 (Edmonson 1979:13, 1988:126). This calendar, which was also used at Yaxchilán, Naranjo, and Piedras Negras but primarily as a "secondary calendar," retained the Tikal yearbearers Ik', Manik', Eb', and Kab'an (Edmonson 1988:103, 126).

The Campeche (or Uxmal, Puuc) calendar was inaugurated on the spring equinox, March 20, A.D. 568 (9.6.14.3.14 1 Ix 2 Pop) and first documented at Uxmal in A.D. 649 (Edmonson 1988:126–127; cf. Bricker 1989:235, who claims A.D. 672). Derived from the Palenque calendar and ancestral to that of Postclassic Mayapán, the Campeche calendar advanced the calendar by one day (essentially a leap year correction) in the ja'ab', resulting in new Late Classic yearbearers: B'en, Etz'nab', Ak'b'al, and Lamat (Bricker 1989:235; Edmonson 1988:103). This calendar was used in much of the western lowlands (e.g., Uxmal, Kabah, Edzná, Jaina, Toniná, Holactún, Yaxchilán, Bonampak), and it may represent Zapotec or Mixtec influence (Edmonson 1988:148).

The Late Postclassic Dresden Codex yearbearer pages depict yearbearers of the Late Classic Tikal calendar in the upper register and those of the Campeche calendar in the lower two registers (see Fig. 1.2, above), as if correlating the two calendars. The Madrid Codex uses yet another set of yearbearers (K'an, Muluk, Ix, Kawak), which represent a shift of one day from those of the Late Classic and may be traceable to western Yucatán.

At the beginning of the Colonial period, continuing conflicts over calendrical issues between the Xiw and the Itza/Kokom, the two principal lineages in Yucatán, led to a compromise known as the Mayapán calendar in 1539. Edmonson (1988:127) believes that the Mayapán calendar was actually invented sometime before December 21, A.D. 937 (10.5.9.6.4 7 K'an 2 Pop) but "not successfully promulgated" until 1539. There are "no native correlations" with the Mayapán calendar, and although it is the "direct successor to" the Tikal calendar, it seems to have been derived through the Campeche calendar (Edmonson 1988: 203). Two centuries later, in 1752, at the behest of the Itza, yet another calendar came into use at Valladolid, allowing Itza sun priests to rule twenty-four instead of twenty years; this calendar ceased to be used actively in 1848 (Edmonson 1982:11).

The Postclassic Maya *May*

During the early Colonial period in the northern lowlands, informants described the political organization at Mayapán to the Spaniards as having been centralized, hierarchical, and chartered by the endlessly repetitive cycles of cosmic time. Although there is some debate (see Chap. 2), remnants of this organization seem to have survived, as politico-ritual power continued to be concentrated in important cities that seated the *may* cycle; that is, they were "capitals" of a region for a period of 256 years. Within that territory and interval, the jalach winiks or ajaws of the most prominent towns took turns seating the thirteen constitu-

ent k'atuns, from which the jaguar priests, or b'alams, presided, for periods of twenty years (Edmonson 1979).

This geopolitical organization was described in the late seventeenth
century by the Franciscan father Andrés de Avendaño y Loyola, who,
like early Spaniards throughout the Yucatán, used the word *age* to refer
to k'atuns:

> These ages are thirteen in number; each age has its separate idol and
> its priest with a separate prophecy of its events.
>
> These thirteen ages are divided into thirteen parts, which divide
> this kingdom of Yucathán, and each age, with its idol, priest, and
> prophecy, rules in one of these thirteen parts of this land, according
> as they have divided it; I do not give the names of the idols, priests,
> or parts of the land, so as not to cause trouble, although I have made
> a treatise on these old accounts with all their differences and expla-
> nations, so they may be evident to all, and the curious may learn
> them, for, if we do not understand them, I affirm the Indians can be-
> tray us face to face. (1987:39)

This "treatise" that Avendaño purports to have written has never been
found (ibid.:n.121).

The May *and Its Seats*

The word *may* incorporates broad reference to the calendar, the number
20, and objects with four corners, the latter perhaps a symbolic reference
to completion or quadripartition. Etymologically, *may* can be traced to
highland Maya languages, including Colonial K'iche' and particularly
Kaqchikel, in which *may* refers to a cycle of twenty "years" of four hundred days (Recinos and Goetz 1953:31; Lounsbury 1978:762; Lowe
1982:281). *May* might also relate to Kaqchikel *meho* 'to go out and return', or to cycle (Brinton [1885] 1969:31). Other related terms include
amayte 'the first 20 years'; *ahau k'atun* and *amaytun* 'squared stone on
which the *ahau k'atun* was placed'; *lamay* 'four-cornered'; *lamay tun*
'squared stone; the course of the twenty years engraved on a stone'; and
kan amay 'thing of four corners' (Lowe 1982:321).

The most thorough linguistic discussion comes from John S. Justeson
and Lyle Campbell (1997:49–52), who note that the term is widely diffused in Mesoamerica and probably entered Greater Lowland Mayan
languages from Mixe-Zoquean in the Gulf Coast area. Because Cycle 7
and 8 monuments in this area used the Long Count, Justeson and Campbell presume that Mixe-Zoquean languages and script had a term for
k'atun. The earliest form of the lowland Maya hieroglyphic compound

for k'atun was *ma-tun* (T74:548) rather than *k'a-tun* (T28:548), and the prefix T28 *k'a* differed in early versus late forms, the early form being indistinguishable from T74 *ma* (which can also be read "great"). It was not until after 9.3.0.0.0 (e.g., Uaxactún Stela 3, at 9.3.13.0.0; A.D. 507) that the later form of T28 began to be used consistently. The authors deduce from this that *k'a* and *ma* both meant "twenty" and call on an analogy with the K'iche'an term *may* meaning "20 (of years)." They conclude that the lowland Maya term *may* referred to a twenty-year cycle—the k'atun itself—explicitly rejecting Edmonson's interpretation of *may* as a thirteen-k'atun cycle of 256 years.

The *Diccionario maya* translates *may* as *polvillo, espuma* (powder, dust, foam) as well as several terms relating to deer: *pata hendida, nombre ritual del venado, venadillo.* Indeed, the glyphic sign for *may* has been read as the cleft hoof of a deer (T294) (Montgomery 2001a: Fig. 9.3). Associations between deer (*Odocoileus virginianus yucatenensis;* white-tailed deer) and calendrical ceremonies are evident in the five sets of "deer almanacs" of the Madrid Codex. Lacadena's (n.d.) reading of *may* from Classic Maya glyph T174 (also read as *kuch* 'burden') recalls Mary D. Pohl's (1981) synthesis of ethnohistoric and archaeological data relating to the transfer of ritual cargos, or burdens (kuch), in ceremonies involving the hunting and sacrifice of a deer at a tree or newly erected pole in the month of Sip.

May can also be a verb meaning "to sacrifice," "to count," and—from proto-Mixe-Zoquean—"to count, divine, adore" (see also Campbell and Kaufman 1976:85). With reference to sacrifice, it is possible that deer bones—particularly foot bones?—were used in blood sacrifice. At the site of Blackman Eddy in Belize, for example, a polished deer metapodial bone bloodletter was found in an early Middle Formative ritual deposit (Brown 1999). In addition, *may* can be a noun or modifier conveying "a large or indefinite number," "a higher unit of measure for counting years," and "a unit of measure for scores of years" (Justeson and Campbell 1997:51). Coggins (1992:104–105) read the glyphs ending the text on the south side of Copán's Stela A as *ti ma lamay* 'at the completion of the great cycle.'

In light of these interpretations, the identifier "Maya" could be interpreted to mean "people of the four quarters" or "people of the cycle," and various Postclassic site names in the northern lowlands incorporate this reference. For example, Mayapán (a partly Nahuatl toponym: -*apan* 'cycle water place', referring to the site's water-filled sinkhole, or *cenote*) is similar to Yukatekan Maya *chi ch'en maya* 'mouth of the well of the people of the cycle' (Edmonson 1986a:5).

During the Postclassic and Colonial periods in Yucatán, as the k'atun cycle or *may* ended—"turned" or "folded" (*utz'*) is the Maya term in the books of the chilam b'alams—every 256 years, the Maya ritually "seated" the new cycle in a particular city. Edmonson (1979:11, 1982: xvi, 1986a:4–5) describes the seat of the *may* as it was recognized in early Colonial Yucatán: The cycle seat, or *may ku* (also *may ku(l)*, *ukul may*), was the primate city of a region. It was a capital of sorts (*tan kaj* 'front town'), but more important it was a sacred or holy city bearing the title Born of Heaven (*ich kan* or *siyaj kan*). It had a temple housing the cycle (*may ku,* the "cycle seat" proper) and its plaza (*sak lak tun*) was the crossroads (*jol kan be*) and religious center of the country and the navel of the world. The city also had a sacred ceiba tree (*yax che'* 'green' or 'first tree'), sacred grove (*tzukub te'*), and sacred well (*ch'en*). The seat of the *may* held "dynastic and religious primacy over the whole country" for 256 years, after which the city and its roads and idols were ritually destroyed and the city was "abandoned," although this might have been simply the departure of the ruling dynasty.

During the 256-year period of *may* rule in the Postclassic and Colonial periods, important towns in the region overseen by the *may ku* claimed the privilege of ritually seating each of its thirteen constituent k'atuns. Every twenty years as one k'atun folded, the new k'atun was ritually seated in a particular town, the *jetz'* (seat) k'atun. The jetz' k'atun was not only a ritual center, home of the b'alam and his chilam; each k'atun seat controlled tribute rights, land titles, and appointments to public office in the realm for the twenty-year duration (Edmonson 1979:11, 1982:xvii). Consequently, the thirteen-k'atun, 256-year *may* cycle held great political significance in the Postclassic period. Because of the extensive powers vested in the jetz' k'atun, conflicts frequently erupted among towns competing for the honor of seating the k'atun. After 1441–1461 and the collapse of Mayapán, sources generally agree on the k'atun seats of northern Yucatán (Edmonson 1986a:275–276, App. D). At that time, most k'atuns rotated among multiple towns, typically two or three, but sometimes as many as seven.

As the physical k'atun seat, or jetz' k'atun, changed, so did the layers of administrative lordship or priestly oversight of the period. The chief priest of each k'atun, who held office for the full twenty years, was referred to as b'alam (jaguar) or, less commonly, *ajaw kan may* 'lord [rattle]snake of the cycle'. Some priests were also given the title *aj k'in may*, which Edmonson (1986a:4) translates as "sun priest of the cycle," or *aj k'in;* I would also follow Barbara Tedlock's (1992:2) broad interpretation of the latter title as keeper of time, or "daykeeper." Each b'alam or k'atun priest had a spokesman or speaker (chilam), who was the official prophet of the k'atun. According to Edmonson (1982:31), the chilam was "always a trained sun priest (ah kin). He was not only a prophet (ah bobat) but *the* official Prophet for a particular katun. Finally . . . he was supposed to be a sage (ah miatz). When disagreement arose over the prophecies, it was up to the Spokesman to resolve it."

The Books of the Chilam B'alams and Rituals of the May

The momentous occasion of the ending of one *may* and the beginning of another—the "folding" and "seating" of these cosmic eras—was celebrated by the early Colonial period Maya with great ceremony. The *Book of Chilam Balam of Chumayel* describes these celebrations as ritually structured, historico-mythological "dramas" of multiple "acts" that included processions, feasting, speeches and recitations, sacrifice, recognition of ranks and titles, and other activities (Edmonson 1986a: 21–29, Chaps. 12 and 29). For example, the ending of the b'ak'tun (400 tuns, or 394 solar years) was celebrated in Mérida in 1618 and consisted of twenty acts (there are twenty k'atuns in a b'ak'tun); earlier turnings of the b'ak'tun had occurred in 435, 830, and 1224. The characters in these acts were costumed and masked, and the "whole ceremonial must have involved hundreds of participants and thousands of spectators" lasting twenty-four to forty-eight hours, with many activities taking place at night (Edmonson 1985:261).

The ceremony of the turning of the *may* in 1539 in Mérida paralleled that of the b'ak'tun, except that it took place in thirteen acts (thirteen k'atuns in a *may*). For this, the first seven acts of the b'ak'tun drama were assimilated into acts 8–14, for a total of thirteen acts. Although k'atun ritual is not explicitly described in the Chumayel, Edmonson (1986a:21–23, 82–99) deduced that it was patterned fairly closely on the thirteen-act *may* ceremony and described it as follows.

Act 8: Ceremonial Circuit. To judge from the b'ak'tun and *may* ceremonies, this was a counterclockwise procession, or perhaps merely a verbal tour, through the towns of the *may* realm or around the town itself. Edmonson says the circuit is "implied" in k'atun ritual and ended in a *b'alche'* drinking ceremony. (B'alche' is an alcoholic beverage made from the bark of the leguminous *jab'in* tree [*Lonchocarpus longistylus*] fermented in water and honey, with other added flavorings.)

An early Colonial example of this or a similar process (see Act 11, below) may have resulted in the so-called Land Treaty of Maní, dated August 15, 1557 (Roys [1943] 1972:175–194; Marcus 1993:126). In 1545 don Juan Kokom (Nachi Kokom), ruler of the Sotuta province, had surveyed the boundaries of his territory, but portions were contested by the Xiw to the west and by the Kupul to the east. The document records the meeting of governors (b'atab's) of all the towns in the Maní province headed by the Xiw jalach winik, plus neighboring territories, to work out the boundaries of their lands (marked with crosses). At the conclusion of the deliberations, the governors had a feast and consumed more than ten gallons of b'alche'. Significantly, this territorial problem arose shortly after the resettlement ordinances of 1552 and during the K'atun 11 Ajaw immediately following the 1539 calendrical compromise between the Xiw and the Itza. The Maní agreement of 1557 was achieved just a little less than two years before the end of that k'atun.

Similar processionals occurred during Wayeb' rites (Coe 1965) and also in modern times, for example, the *jetz' lu'um* 'seats of the land' (securing the land) ritual walk in Tekanto every nine years (Thompson 1999:238–239). Among the Tzotzil Maya of Zinacantán, Chiapas, counterclockwise processions are the direction of "historical process" (Gossen and Leventhal 1993:198–200). Syncretistic vestiges of a procession to symbolically order space continue today on Flores Island in Lake Petén Itzá: on All Saint's Day, the local priest leads a procession counterclockwise around the perimeter of the island, stopping for prayers in each of the four residential quarters of the island.

Act 9: Seating of the K'atun. The new b'alam, or jaguar priest, of the k'atun takes his place on the "mat of the k'atun" in the cycle seat. A mat (*pop*) is and was important to the Maya as a symbolic seat of authority, and woven or plaited matlike elements are frequently incorporated in royal costumes (Robicsek 1975). In addition, the first month of the secular year, or ja'ab', is named Pop, identified by a glyph showing a mat. The selection of the new jaguar priest had been made ten years earlier in mid-k'atun. This parallels the seating of the ruling "k'atun idols" (wooden or ceramic images of gods, probably figurine incense burners), which, according to Landa, were placed in the temple ten years before their actual rule (see also Morley and Brainerd 1956:212; D. Chase 1985).

Act 10: Seating of the Yearbearers. These are the four *b'akab's* 'Fathers of the Land', or calendar priests, who represented not only the years but also various quadripartite entities in nature such as the sky-bearers (*Pawajtuns*) and the gods of wind, sun, death, rain-lightning (*Chaks*), and fire (*Aj Tok*, also called "Burners"). Each Postclassic city had its own set of four yearbearers, identified with a direction and color.

Act 11: Pacing of the K'atun. This was a ceremonial procession of seven priests, the "Pacers," who measured the land and confirmed land titles. Payments of tribute were made. Restall (1997:189–205; see also Hanks 1989:99–100) describes a Colonial period Yucatán "walk of possession" that occurred when there were land tenure disputes and emphasized piles of stone and trees as boundary markers. The K'iche' *Popol Vuh* myth of creation also mentions "measuring, four-fold staking, halving the cord, stretching the cord" in taking land measurements (Tedlock 1985:72; see also Coggins 1996:20n11).

Act 12: Dawn. At this time the mats—symbolic seats of authority—of the lords were "counted" (i.e., ranked). In addition, there were declarations of candidacy for priesthoods, for governor (jalach winik), and for other officials such as b'atab's in the coming period. This is analogous to the procedure in highland Zinacantán, Guatemala, where candidates for priestly duties in the cargo system declared themselves as much as twenty years in advance (Vogt 1964:35).

Act 13: Sacrifice. Sacrifices were carried out in a variety of ways, including heart removal, hanging, burning, and drowning, all accompanied by music and dancing. At Chich'en Itza, the sacrifices took place by hurling the designated individual(s) into the cenote.

Act 14: Examination. This consisted of a ceremonial feast and ritual riddling, or "interrogation of the chiefs," on the last day of the k'atun, to "examine the knowledge of the chiefs of the towns, [to see] whether they know how the ruling men came, whether they have explained the coming of the chiefs, of the head-chiefs, whether they are of the lineage of rulers, whether they are of the lineage of chiefs, that they may prove it" (Roys [1933] 1967:88–89). As told in a section of the *Chumayel* (Roys [1933] 1967:88–98; Edmonson 1986a:168–204; cf. Burns 1983) dating to the seventeenth century, seven highly esoteric questions were asked or commands given: "Bring the sun . . . and so the sun they will be asked for is the lord's fried egg. . . . Go get the brains of heaven . . . that is incense . . . ," and so on.

Act 15: The Word. The new chilam, the speaker of the jaguar priest, proclaimed the prophecy, or "word" (*mut*), for the upcoming k'atun with richly poetic imagery. A highland parallel can be found in the "ancient word" of the *Popol Vuh,* an "extended discourse that carries the authority of tradition" as proclaimed by the "Mothers/Fathers of the Word," and also claimed by the writers of the *Popol Vuh* itself (Tedlock 1985: 325, 339, 351).

Act 16: Penance. This includes reference to containers, such as gourds, bowls, plates, and cups of the k'atun. Edmonson believes this act incorporated reference to autosacrifice (bloodletting) by the yearbearers, the priesthood, and the jaguar priest.

Act 17: Commemoration of the Ancestors (natab'al). In late Colonial times, a cross was erected, and Edmonson (see also Morley and Brainerd 1956:22) believed that in Classic times this was the moment when a carved stone stela was erected (*tz'ap*) or perhaps "unwrapped" (Stuart 1996:156–157). During the Late Postclassic period the Maya of Yucatán revived this Classic practice of erecting carved stone monuments at the turning of the k'atun. Bishop Landa (Tozzer 1941:38–39) noted that the

Table 3.4. K'atun seats of the Fifteenth through early Seventeenth centuries, from the Codex Perez

K'atun	Maya Date	Year	Town
1 Ajaw	11.9.0.0.0	1401	Izamal
12 Ajaw	11.10.0.0.0	1421	Zizal
10 Ajaw	11.11.0.0.0	1441	Kuldche
8 Ajaw	11.12.0.0.0	1461	Hunucmá
6 Ajaw	11.13.0.0.0	1480	Chacalaá
4 Ajaw	11.14.0.0.0	1500	Tixkulchá
2 Ajaw	11.15.0.0.0	1520	Ewan
13 Ajaw	11.16.0.0.0	1539	Colop Petén
11 Ajaw	11.17.0.0.0	1559	*llegaron los espanoles, no se labraron sus piedras**
9 Ajaw	11.18.0.0.0	1579	*llegaron los espanoles, no se labraron sus piedras*
7 Ajaw	11.19.0.0.0	1599	*no se labraron sus piedras*
5 Ajaw	12.0.0.0.0	1618	*no se labraron sus piedras*
3 Ajaw	12.1.0.0.0	1628	*no se labraron sus piedras*

*the Spaniards arrived, the stelae were not worked (carved)

Maya living near Mayapán, seat of the Postclassic multepal, "were accustomed to erect one of these stones every twenty years," and thirteen carved stelae have been found at that site (Morley 1920:574–576; Proskouriakoff 1962b:134–136).

More information comes from the "Codex" Perez (Solis Alcalá 1949b:187), which identies the k'atuns of the fifteenth through early seventeenth century and gives the names of the towns in northern Yucatán in which *se labraron sus piedras,* or carved the stelae commemorating the k'atun (Table 3.4). Note that after the arrival of the Spaniards, stelae were no longer carved, even for completion of the b'ak'tun in 1618.

Act 18: Counting of the K'atun. This was probably more an *account-*ing of the k'atuns, a recitation or verification of the calendrical basis of the current place in mythic time.

Act 19: Farce. In the Colonial period this provided comic relief in the form of a "morality play" about various sins.

Act 20: Sermon. The "sermon" was a review of past history and, like the "farce," incorporated references to wars as well as introduced elements of Christianity such as saints.

Overview

I propose that the political organization and political geography of the Maya lowlands during the Classic period was structured by the same principles as the Postclassic calendrical celebrations of the k'atun cycle or *may,* as Edmonson prophetically suggested in 1979. Modeling political rotations on cosmic cycles allowed power to be shared predictably, minimizing the potential chaos of political succession and disruption of the social order (Farriss 1987:577–578; Coe 1965; Thompson 1999).

The key to identifying Classic period *may* and k'atun cycles lies in dates inscribed on stone monuments. While the Maya memorialized many dynastic and other historical events on carved, dated stelae, period-ending monuments erected in commemoration of k'atun intervals carry striking politico-religious significance as seen with the hindsight afforded by Postclassic calendrical ritual. As noted in Chapter 1, there is an obvious danger in relying solely on dated, carved stelae to explore the *may* hypothesis because of missing and damaged monuments. However, as I (Rice 1997) have argued before and argue below, in the case of Tikal there are close correspondences between iconographic programs and other distinctive architectural and stylistic components, and many of these components are distributed more widely among other lowland sites.

At least five, possibly eight or more, acts of the period-ending ceremonies are of particular significance for retrodicting these rituals into the Classic period: Acts 8 and 11, the ceremonial circuit, or pacing of the k'atun; Acts 9 and 10, the seating of the k'atun and the yearbearers; Acts 13 and 16, sacrifice and penance; Act 14, examination and feast; Act 15, the chilam b'alam's prognostication (*mut* 'prophecy') for the incoming k'atun; and Act 17, the erection of a cross, pole, or, in Classic and Late Postclassic times, stela.

Apart from the ambiguous etymology and glyphic expression of the word *may* itself, other lines of evidence, including iconographic, calendrical, architectural, and archaeological data that I present in succeeding chapters, combine to form a persuasive argument for the recognition of 256-year cycles during the Preclassic and Classic periods in the lowlands. These 256-year cycles, consisting of 128 plus 128 years (or

260 tuns of 130 plus 130) can also be mapped onto other key astrocalendrical cycles of the Maya, including the 384-year cycle of Venus (128 plus 256 years) and the 394-year, 400-tun cycle of the b'ak'tun.

The most abundant and convincing evidence for this calendrically based political organization of the Classic lowland Maya comes from Tikal, in the Department of El Petén, Guatemala. This is the subject of the next two chapters.

CHAPTER 4

Tikal as Early Seat of the May

K'atun endings were celebrated throughout the Maya lowlands during the Classic period. As revealed in Morley's early twentieth-century monument surveys, the Maya regularly commemorated the completion of quarter, half, and full k'atuns by erecting sculptured, dated stelae. Several decades ago it became evident that at Late Classic Tikal, distinctive architectural complexes known as twin-pyramid groups were specially constructed for these k'atun-ending ceremonies (Jones 1969). Now, however, it is evident from review of inscriptions and iconography of period-ending monuments and related architectural complexes from Tikal and other sites that k'atun-and *may*-based politico-ritual organization existed in the Early Classic period, which I date to A.D. 179–435 (see Table 1.1), and very likely emerged considerably earlier.

The possibility that k'atun and *may* cycles and seats existed in the Preclassic period is difficult to evaluate directly owing to the lack of dated monuments and historical inscriptions. In addition, the earliest Preclassic occupations in most of the Maya lowlands hide beneath meters of construction fill, exposed only in small, discontinuous patches and dated by associated pottery fragments. However, at least five Early and Middle Preclassic ceramic spheres have been identified in the southern lowlands—Xe in the Río Pasión region, Mamom in central and northern Petén, Swasey in northern Belize, Cunil and Kanocha in west-central Belize, and Gordon at Copán. Middle Preclassic occupation also has been noted in the Puuc area (Carmean, Dunning, and Kowalski 2004) and elsewhere in the northern lowlands (Suhler et al. 2004; Bey et al. 1998). All of this indicates widespread, though not necessarily large populations at this time (see Andrews 1990). Other evidence for hypothesizing Preclassic political organization can be drawn from architecture and iconography uncovered in recent excavations at El Mirador and Nakbe in northern Petén, Calakmul in southeastern Campeche, and Cerros in Belize; another site with evident Preclassic importance is Copán, Honduras. If an early *may-* or calendar-based

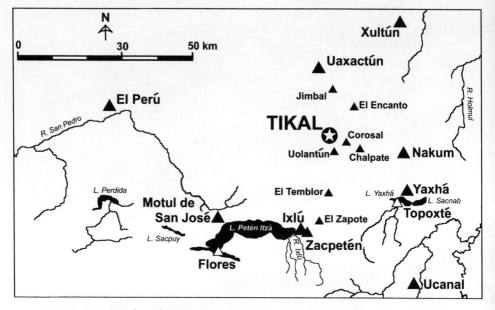

FIGURE 4.1 Map of northeastern Petén showing sites mentioned in text.

mode of politico-ritual organization, or a prototype, were in operation in the southern lowlands, current evidence suggests that its centers would be northern and central Petén, the Pasión, northern and west-central Belize, and the Copán region (see also Edmonson 1979:13–15).

Preclassic Ritual Architecture and K'atun Seats

Of particular interest in positing Preclassic origins of the *may* in the lowlands is the spatial disposition of distinctive structures and architectural complexes that could have been the *may ku* that embodied the cycle proper. In northern Petén, one of these is the "triadic structure" (Hansen 2000:59), a T-shaped platform with three structures located on the distal wings. In a common variant, the platform is not T-shaped but a pyramidal substructure with three small temples arranged at right angles to each other on the sides and back of the platform. These Late Preclassic triadic groups typically occur on the south side of a plaza or face south. The three structures have been interpreted as commemoration of the "original three lineages" or gods (the so-called Palenque Triad: GI, GII, and GIII) of the Maya or the "terrestrial counterpart of three cosmic hearthstones" (Taube 1998). One example can be seen in the main structures of the North Acropolis at Tikal.

Another architectural complex, which developed somewhat earlier and has more enduring importance, is variously known as the E-Group (from Uaxactún; Fig. 4.3), also sometimes referred to as a Commemorative Astronomical Complex (Complejo Conmemorativo Astronómico), or, the term most often used by Guatemalan archaeologists (Laporte 1996), Public Ritual Complex (Complejo de Ritual Público). These arrangements consist of a small platform on the west side of a plaza, fac-

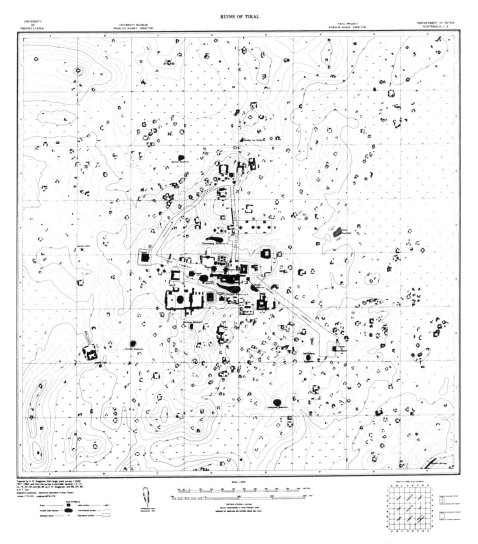

FIGURE 4.2 Map of Tikal (Carr and Hazard 1961; courtesy of University of Pennsylvania Museum, Philadelphia, neg. # Tikal 61-5-5).

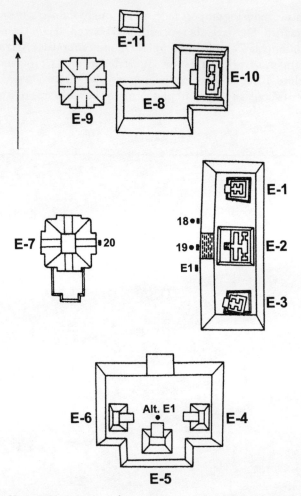

FIGURE 4.3 Uaxactún's E-Group "observatory" complex (after von Euw and Graham 1984).

ing the centerline of a single linear platform to the east that supports three temple structures in a north-south alignment. The western structure is usually "radial" (Cohodas 1980): a tiered platform, square in plan, with stairways on all four sides. It may or may not support a superstructure or temple, and it is often situated in the center of plazas. In its entirety, the E-Group configuration has been widely interpreted as a solar-seasonal observatory complex marking the dates of sunrise on solstices: from a viewing position on the western radial structure, sunrise at the summer solstice occurs over the northern temple, sunrise at the equinoxes occurs over the central temple, and sunrise at the winter solstice occurs over the southern structure (Blom 1924; Ricketson 1928; Ricketson and Ricketson 1937; Ruppert [1940] 1977; see also Aimers 1993; Aimers and Rice n.d.).

Middle Preclassic structures in the East Plaza of Tikal's Mundo Perdido, or Lost World, complex are the earliest known prototype of this presumed solar observatory configuration in the lowlands (Laporte and Fialko 1990, 1995). The arrangement consists of a radial platform, Structure 5C-54-1st, on the west side of a plaza facing an elongated platform with the three north-south temples of Structure 5D-84/88-1st to the east (Fig. 4.4). The first building episode (ca. 700–600 B.C.) of these structures was simple: a radial structure situated opposite but off-center of a long, narrow, north-south mound with stairs on the centerline of each side. These were later overbuilt with larger structures during the late Middle Preclassic period (Tzek ceramic complex and phase, 500–400 B.C.), followed by further remodelings in the early Late Preclassic (Chuen, 400–200 B.C.). These approximate construction dates fit well into 256-year *may* (or 128-year, half *may*) intervals retrodicted into Preclassic times from Postclassic and Classic K'atuns 8 Ajaw. In addition,

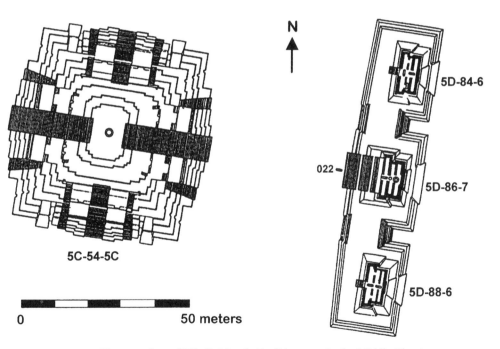

FIGURE 4.4 The east plaza of Tikal's Mundo Perdido group in the Middle Classic period (after Laporte and Fialko 1990: Fig. 3.9).

Late Preclassic expansion of these structures might have been occasioned by the hypothesized integration of the 365- and 260-day calendars into the Long Count in 354 B.C. and the count of cycles of thirteen k'atuns, that is, the *may* (Edmonson 1988:118–119). The year 354 B.C. marks the completion of B'ak'tun 7 as well as the beginning of a K'atun 8 Ajaw, which was completed—along with the completion of a *may*—twenty years later, in 334 B.C. (Table 4.1).

The facades of temples in early triadic groups and later E-Group assemblages were often embellished with enormous stuccoed and painted deity masks, most commonly depicting jaguars. Although numerous examples are found at Middle and Late Preclassic sites in Petén, the best known is at Late Preclassic Cerros, in northern Belize. There, stuccoed masks on the south-facing Structure 5C-2nd "feature blunt-snouted and long-snouted zoomorphs flanked by ear flanges" (Freidel and Schele 1988b:61). These have been interpreted in terms of cosmic cycling, with the rising and setting sun (the Jaguar Sun God) on the east and west sides, respectively, of the stairway on the lower tier and Venus as morning (east) and evening (west) stars on the upper tier of the substructure (Freidel and Schele 1988a, 1988b). At Tikal's Mundo Perdido, the three temples atop the eastern platform were built in the late Late Preclassic period, with the facade of the center structure featuring two jaguar masks. Numerous burials and caches were placed along the axes.

The significance of radial structures in the broader scheme of things might be understood in light of Lacadena's (n.d.) interpretation of *may* as related to something with four corners or four sides. At the same time, translations of *may* from highland Maya languages indicate meanings that include "to sacrifice, to count, to divine," all of which resonate with this interpretation of radial structures and solar observations. Radial structures also might be viewed as architectural embodiments of the circle-in-cross or quartered concentric circle petroglyphs widely distributed throughout Mesoamerica (see Chap. 3). It is not difficult to envision that through time, and perhaps as an outgrowth of literal or figurative site "founding" rituals, the four arms of the pecked cross and the quadripartite double circle-square were translated architectonically into four stairways arrayed around a tiered, square platform. Thus the radial structure—like the quincunx, k'in day glyph, kan cross, and *lamat*, or Venus glyph—is among the many Maya and Mesoamerican quadripartite figures signifying calendric and cosmic cycle completion (see Fig. 3.6b; Coggins 1980:Fig. 2). Importantly, because radial structures typically appear in the middle of open plazas, they also represent, in Maya cosmovision, the center of the universe, the joining of the four world quarters, and—in light of later sculptural and monumental programs associated with them (see Chaps. 5–7)—commemoration of

Table 4.1. Significant Preclassic and Early Classic dates for Tikal in the seating of the *may* and the turning of the b'ak'tun.

Era	Year Gregorian	Year Maya	K'atun	Phase	Archaeological Event
B.C.	590	6.8.0.0.0	8 Ajaw	Middle Preclassic	Tikal seats proto-*may*? Nakbe seats proto-*may*?
	354	7.0.0.0.0	10 Ajaw		B'ak'tun completion
	334	7.1.0.0.0	8 Ajaw	(early) Late Preclassic	Tikal seats *may* El Mirador seats *may*?
	77	7.14.0.0.0	8 Ajaw	(late) Late Preclassic	Tikal seats *may* Uaxactún seats *may*?
A.D.	41	8.0.0.0.0	9 Ajaw		B'ak'tun completion
	90?				Yax Moch Xok, Tikal dynastic Founder
	179	8.7.0.0.0	8 Ajaw	Early Classic	Tikal seats *may*
	292	8.12.14.8.15			First display of Tikal Emblem main sign
	317	8.14.0.0.0	7 Ajaw		Lady Une' B'alam celebrates period ending
	435	9.0.0.0.0	8 Ajaw	Middle Classic	Tikal seats *may*; b'ak'tun completion

Source: After Edmonson 1979:14–15; 1981:27.

agreements and compromises achieved through the ages by Maya calendar priests and sages in order to ensure and maintain cosmic order.

It seems likely that E-Group architectural complexes had their inception in rituals of annual solar and agricultural cycling. This cycling would explain why eastern orientations and observations—equinoxes, solstices, quarter years, and so forth, as observed by sunrise positions on the horizon—were important and commemorated architectonically. In the Early Preclassic these observation lines might have been established with perishable or temporary markers, such as poles or stones. From there, it is not difficult to conceptualize construction of permanent architectural markers for the sole purpose of carrying out such critical rituals.

These architectural complexes were also centers of early k'atun-ending celebrations, but it is not until carved and dated period-ending stelae began to be erected that this function can be recognized archaeologically. Several of the earliest k'atun-celebrating stela known in the Maya lowlands were found in E-Groups, particularly in front of or otherwise associated with the eastern structure. For example, carved Nakbe Stela 1, dating to the late Middle Preclassic, was found in an E-Group (Hansen 2000:56). And thirteen stelae, twelve plain and one carved, were found in the E-Group at El Mirador (Matheny 1987), raising the possibility that one was erected every twenty years during the roughly 250-year (100 B.C.–A.D. 150) florescence of the site. Uaxactún Stelae 18 and 19, celebrating the 8.16.0.0.0 K'atun 3 Ajaw ending in A.D. 357, were set in front of the east building of the E-Group at that site (Valdés and Fahsen 1995:204); Stela 19 shows a kneeling captive. The presence of kneeling or prone bound prisoners is a common theme on k'atun-ending monuments in both the Early and Late Classic periods (see Dillon 1982), recalling the meaning of k'atun as not only "twenty" but also "fight(er)," "combat," "battle," "war(rior)," "conquest" (Diccionario maya).

Early Classic Tikal and Its Rulers
The Institution of Kingship

Beginning perhaps as early as ca. 300 B.C., the growth in the importance of calendrical cycling was accompanied by transformations in the very fundament of leadership—a transition from emphasis on the personal and charismatic qualities of an individual to the more formal structure or institution of a "political office" that "represents a universal criterion of the state" (Kurtz 2001:176). Among the Maya, this new political office or role was that of ajaw (king, lord), a concept believed to have originated in the lowlands during the last century B.C. (Freidel and Schele 1988a, 1988b). Etymologically, the root of *ajaw* is *aw* 'shout', suggesting that the aj-aw is "the shouter" or perhaps "he who proclaims" (Stuart 1995:190–191), a reading that can be easily associated with the proclamation of the mut or prophecy of the k'atun. Embedded in such changes were new rules for power transfer, based on "firm genealogical principles of succession and firm ritual formulae, as carved on stone stelae[,] . . . [that ensured] the stable transmission of central leadership over generations" (Freidel and Schele 1988a:550).

Some two hundred years later, by A.D. 199, Freidel (1992:119) argues, the ajaw title began to be manifest as k'ul ajaw (divine or holy lord). Stuart (1995:197–198), however, notes that the k'ul ajaw title is rare until the Late Classic period and argues that this distinction of a divine or sacred king apart from other nobility may not have emerged until much later. Part of the evidence Freidel adduces for his earlier date is the conjuring of the Vision Serpent on the unprovenienced Hauberg Stela, dated 8.8.0.7.0 3 Ajaw 13 Xul (October 7, 199). The text on the back of the Hauberg Stela refers to the ruler letting blood fifty-two days before his accession. This monument shows B'ak Tul, k'ul ajaw of an unknown site, wearing a Jaguar Sun deity mask, with a down-gazing ancestor head in the Vision Serpent's gaping jaws and diminutive figures crawling about the serpent's body (Schele and Miller 1986:191; Freidel 1992:119; Stuart 1988:220). Down-gazing "ancestral" heads are known from iconographic programs elsewhere in the early Maya world, including El Baúl Stela 1 (at 7.19.15.7.12; A.D. 36), Kaminaljuyú Stela 11, and Abaj Takalik Stelae 2 and 3. As discussed in Chapter 5, these Late Preclassic and Early Classic elements—prone prisoners, small figures crawling in serpentine scrolls—prefigure the striking imagery of the Tikal region's Terminal Classic period-ending stelae associated with k'atun ritual.

The use of the "seating" glyph is also suggestive of early k'atun and *may* ritual. The Dumbarton Oaks "plaque," or pectoral ornament, a probable epi-Olmec quartzite tablet reportedly from the northern lowlands, shows a seated lord with a long-nosed head in his headdress, and the text refers to the "seating" of an ajaw (Freidel and Schele 1988a:555). The La Mojarra stela, dating to the mid-first century A.D. also uses the "seating" expression (Kaufman and Justeson 2001). The significance of a lord being "seated" (glyph T644; *chum*) rather than "acceding" (T684, the "toothache glyph") has been highlighted by Marcus (1992a:340): secondary-level sites used the accession glyph, whereas first-tier sites or regional capitals used the seating glyph. "Seating" is also the metaphor for beginning a month on a day 0 in the 365-day calendar.

I suggest that the seating event refers not only to the seating of the ruler in office but also to the seating of units of time, the *may* and k'atun, at these sites. It describes, in other words, not simply the installation of a human ruler or ajaw but also acknowledgment by a divine king, or k'ul ajaw, of acceptance of the burden, or sacred responsibilities, of office in ensuring uninterrupted calendrical cycling and cosmic continuity. During the Late Classic period, the main sign of the Tikal Emblem Glyph was sometimes combined with other glyphic prefixes to read *tan kun* (or ch'en) 'in the center of the seat (or cave) of' Tikal (see Fig. 2.4c).

Tikal's Dynastic Founding

Unfortunately, the record of Tikal's early dynasties, rulers, and monuments is quite fragmentary (Martin and Grube 2000:26–32; Martin 2003). Much of what we know comes from a historical text on the back of Stela 31 and from a painted vase listing royal successions. Other early dates come from the text on the roofcomb of the Late Classic Temple of the Inscriptions (Temple VI), where 5.0.0.0.0 (1143 B.C.) and 6.14.16.9.16 (456 B.C.) may refer to the actual or mythical founding of the site (Sharer 1994:271). Table 4.2 outlines the succession of Tikal's Early and Middle Classic rulers.

Tikal's principal dynasty is known as the Jaguar Paw dynasty, although there are no contemporaneous images linked with the founder or his name glyph to spell this out precisely. The dynasty was founded by Yax Moch Xok (variously read as Yax Eb' Xook 'First Step Shark', or Yax Ch'aktel Xok 'First Scaffold Shark'), who ruled in the late first century A.D. From the point of view of the *may* hypothesis, it is useful to note that *xok* also may be interpreted as "to count, to read"; recall, too, the interpretation of *may* as "to count, to divine." Tikal Burial 125, on the original central axis of the North Acropolis, may have been the Tikal founder's tomb, the grave goods of which were removed and reinterred to the east, thereby establishing a new centerline axis for that complex (Harrison 1999:68–69).

The next known ruler of Tikal is "Foliated Jaguar," whose nickname derives from a leafy element atop a jaguar head. Foliated Jaguar is probably the individual depicted on Tikal Stela 29 (A.D. 292) (Fig. 4.5), where he displays two images of the Jaguar God, one in his left hand and one on his chest; in his right arm he cradles the Maya double-headed serpent ceremonial bar. At the top of the scene is a down-gazing ancestor head, presumably his father, who might bear the name Chak Tok Ich'ak (Martin and Grube 2000:27). The ancestor wears a headdress consisting of a god image with a jaguar paw for a nose, providing evidence for descent in the Jaguar Paw dynasty. Recent interpretations suggest that Tikal Stela 29, discovered west of the North Acropolis, originally might have been erected in the Mundo Perdido E-Group. Directly in front of

Table 4.2. Tikal's Early and Middle Classic rulers.

Maya Name	Nickname	Date	Number in Succession
Yax Eb' Xok or Yax Moch Xok	First Step Shark	ca. 90?	Founder
(Chak Tok Ich'ak?)		ca. 250	
?	Foliated Jaguar	ca. 292	
?	Animal Headdress	?	
Siyaj Kan K'awil I		ca. 307	11
Ix Une' B'alam	Lady Une' B'alam	ca. 317	
?	Zero Moon Bird?	?	
K'inich Muwan Jol		ca. 359	13
Chak Tok Ich'ak I	Jaguar Paw	360–378	14
Yax Nun Ayin I	Curl Snout	379–404	
Siyaj Kan K'awil II	Stormy Sky	411–456	16
K'an Kitam	Kan Boar	458–486	
Chak Tok Ich'ak II	Jaguar Paw Skull	486–508	
?	Lady of Tikal	511–527	
Kalomte' B'alam	Curl Head	511–527	19
Ete I	Bird Claw	?	
Wak Kan K'awil	Double Bird	537–563	
?	Animal Skull	ca. 593–628	22
?		ca. 640	23, 24
Nun Ujol Chak	Shield Skull	ca. 657–679	

Source: After Martin and Grube 2000:26–43.

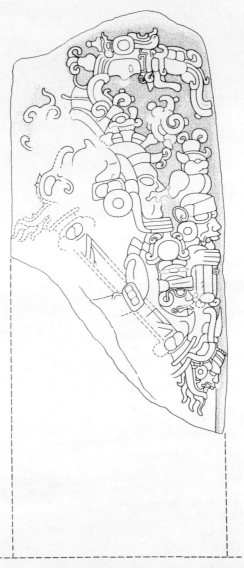

FIGURE 4.5 Tikal Stela 29. (a) The front may show the ruler Foliated Jaguar. (b) The back bears the earliest Long Count date in the lowlands (A.D. 292). (Jones and Satterthwaite 1982: Fig. 49; drawing by William R. Coe, courtesy of University of Pennsylvania Museum, Philadelphia, neg. #s Tikal 61-5-5, 61-5-2.)

A

Structure 5D-86, the central of three temples on the east side, is a small (3 m), low (30 cm) radial temple covering a mass grave; Stela 29 might have been set on top of this platform (Laporte and Fialko 1990:40–41; 1995:57).

Tikal's Name and Emblem Glyph

Tikal Stela 29 has the distinction of displaying the earliest known lowland Maya Long Count date, 8.12.14.8.15 13 Men 3 Sip (July 6, 292), inscribed on a monument (although Polol Altar 1 has been argued to have a Cycle 7 date; Pahl 1982). This first appearance of the Long Count system of dating on stelae customarily has been used by Mayanists to date the beginning of the Early Classic period in the lowlands. There is, however, considerable evidence for a Late Preclassic "stela cult" of plain monuments (Hammond 1982; Justeson and Mathews 1983), as at El Mirador, possibly erected to celebrate period endings, and the earliest record of a period-ending celebration might be that of 8.4.0.0.0 (A.D. 120) on an unprovenienced jade celt (Schele and Miller 1986:82–83).

Tikal Stela 29 also shows the site's Emblem Glyph main sign (see Fig. 2.4), appearing, significantly, in the headdress of a Jaguar God head held by the ruler, making Tikal the first site in the lowlands to display this political symbol. The appearance of names and titles in headdresses has long standing in Mesoamerica, as evident in the insignia of the "helmets" on the Olmec colossal heads. Viewed in cross-cultural perspective, headdresses are a common means of signaling cultural and "ethnic" identity (Wobst 1977).

The origin of Tikal's name and the interpretation of its Emblem Glyph—the main sign of which is glyph T569, a tied pouch (Thompson 1962:194–195) or knotted bundle—merit discussion, as meanings are disputed, but all support the *may* model. One point concerns whether the name "Tikal" is of modern or ancient origin. This toponym has long local usage in Petén and can be derived from two Yukatekan Maya words: *ti*, a locative identifier meaning "at, to" or "at the place of," plus *k'al*, which has many meanings, including "twenty" and "to fasten, bind, or enclose" (Stuart 1996:155–156). Teobert Maler (1911:3), who visited the site in the late nineteenth century, translated the name from Yukatekan Maya as *ti-kal* 'at the voice,' or "place where the spirit voices are heard" (provocative in light of the reading of *ti kal* as "to get drunk" [Harris and Stearns 1997:37; Montgomery 2001a:286]). A different derivation comes from Charles Andrew Hofling and Francisco Tesucún (1998), who derive the modern name from *ti ak'al* 'at the waterhole', referring to the site's large reservoirs (or perhaps its neighboring seasonal swamps, or *bajos*). This is the meaning given today by the local Itzaj Maya speakers of San José, on the north shore of Lake Petén Itzá.

Clemency C. Coggins (1987) accepts Tikal as the ancient name of the site and highlights Maya linguistic multivalency in suggesting multiple, complementary readings of the final syllable, glyph, and name. One meaning for *k'al* is "twenty," so that *ti-k'al* could mean "place of the count of twenty [years, i.e., k'atuns]." In addition, Coggins links the T60 *k'a* knot at the center of the tied bundle to *k'ax* 'tie' (also Stuart's "fasten"). Furthermore, the bundle itself is a powerful metaphor associated with k'atuns—as the burden (kuch) or prophecy of the k'atun, as tying up (i.e., completing) the burden of a k'atun, and as the folded paper or cloth on which the k'atun prophecies and other divinatory matters were written.

A different—but not necessarily contradictory—interpretation of the Tikal Emblem Glyph sees the main sign not as a tied-up bundle of things but rather as a hairstyle. It was early identified as *t'uch*, a bun or topknot of hair (Barthel 1968:171–172), and more recently as "the rear view of a human head with a knot tied across it" (Schele and Mathews 1998:63–64). Knots and knotted cloth or bundles symbolized "supreme authority" as early as the mid-first-century La Mojarra stela (Justeson and Kaufman 1993:1705, Figs. 7F, 7G). Related to this is the possibility that the main sign represents the rear view of the tied royal headband worn by rulers and by the Hero Twins in the *Popol Vuh* (see Coe 1973). This image of tied hair appears as such on Tikal Stelae 29 and 31, in the headdress of the "solar deity" head carried by the ruler (Coggins 1987) and in a death head in the basal panel of Stela 1.

Glyph T569 is now read *mut*, which in Yukatekan can mean "prophecy, news, tidings"; "bird" (Order Galliformes, which includes the noisy chachalacas as well as guans and curasows (Roys 1957:50); and (as *mutal* or *mutul*) "knot of hair" (Martin and Grube 2000:30; Schele and Mathews 1998:63–64). Macri (2000) derives *mut* from Mixe-Zoque *mu'ut* 'water pool'. Both translations indicate that today's Tikal was at the center of a kingdom called Mutal or Mutul by the Maya. Here we can also recall Act 15 of the Yucatán k'atun and *may* ceremonies: the mut or giving of the prophecy (as well as the "ancient word" of the K'iche' *Popol Vuh*). More significantly, the site of Tikal itself is proclaimed not only "the site of the prophecy" but also, in the Early Classic, as yax (first, new) mutul, "the site of the first prophecy."

In sum, T569 may be read *mut, kal, k'al, k'ax*, or "burden," or some combination of all of these, a classic example of the Maya love of polysemic and metaphorical language. All these meanings highlight reference to k'atuns and associated ritual. Furthermore, at Tikal as at other

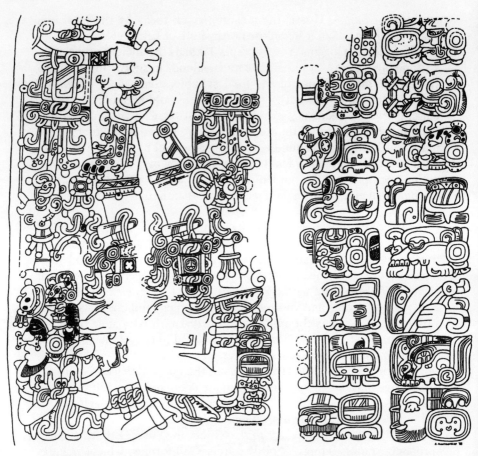

FIGURE 4.6 The basal portion of Tikal Stela 39. (a) The front of the stela portrays the ruler Chak Tok Ich'ak I standing on a captive; note the jaguar paw axe in his left hand and the Tikal Emblem main sign to the right of the captive's left ankle. (b) The text on the back of the stela celebrates completion of 8.17.0.0.0 K'atun 1 Ajaw (A.D. 376). (Drawing courtesy of John Montgomery.)

Classic sites, display of the main sign with the "water prefix" identifies the site as divine or holy, precisely the way Postclassic *may ku* or seats of the *may* were described.

The Dynasty Continues

The next reasonably well identified Tikal ruler is Siyaj Kan K'awil I, the first ruler definitely known as "Sky-born K'awil" and the eleventh in the dynasty established by Yax Eb' Xok. His name appears on Stela 1 at El Encanto, about 10 kilometers northeast of Tikal, dating to about 305 to 308. He is followed by a queen, Ix Une' B'alam, named after a "local goddess, in this case an infantile feline with Olmec antecedents" (Martin and Grube 2000:27). Mention of her on Stela 31 prompted Martin and Grube (2000:34) to suggest that she "seems to provide an important precedent for the transfer of the founder's bloodline through a woman." Ix Une' B'alam celebrated the 7 Ajaw k'atun ending (but not via a known monument) at Tikal in 8.14.0.0.0, A.D. 317.

There may then have been a ruler named Zero Moon Bird at Tikal, at least to judge from the Stela 31 text, although the evidence for this is disputed. A ruler by that name is identified on the Leiden Plate or Plaque, an incised jade celt originally discovered in Puerto Barrios, Guatemala, and deposited in a museum in Leiden, the Netherlands. The carving on this ornament is very similar to the style of early monuments at Tikal, and it has often been attributed to that site; the text on the back of it (8.14.3.1.12 1 Eb' 0 Yaxk'in; September 15, 320) refers to the seating of the ruler. The ruler faces the viewer's left and holds his hands in the distinctive position of later monuments: tight against his chest, back-to-back with fingers curled in. As on Stela 29, a Jaguar God head appears on the front of his belt. A key element of this carving is that the ruler is standing with a prone, naked individual, presumably a captive, behind his feet.

The thirteenth ruler in Tikal's dynastic line was K'inich Muwan Jol, whose death is recorded on a monument from the peripheral site of Corozal as 8.16.2.6.0 11 Ajaw 13 Pop (May 22, 359). Muwan Jol is perhaps best known as the father of Chak Tok Ich'ak I, otherwise known as Great Jaguar Paw (or Great Jaguar Claw). Chak Tok Ich'ak I came to rule on 8.16.3.10.2 11 Ik 10 Sek (August 6, 360) and died on 8.17.1.4.12 11 Eb' 15 Mak (January 14, 378).

Tikal Stela 39 (Fig. 4.6), only the basal portion of which is known, shows an Early Classic ruler believed to be Chak Tok Ich'ak I wearing an embellished loincloth and back ornament. In his left hand he grips an ax of some sort that terminates in a fearsomely clawed jaguar paw. Axes also are tucked into the tops of his elaborate anklets. He is standing on a bound, prone captive who has a beard and appears to be noble, given his attire—with knotted sandals, a mat-decorated loincloth, and complex headdress. Elsewhere he is identified as a *k'uhun,* or keeper of texts (Montgomery 2001b:49; Jackson and Stuart 2001). The monument displays the Tikal Emblem Glyph main sign in the text, though it lacks the "water-group" prefix meaning "holy, divine." The basal portion of this monument, which celebrates completion of 8.17.0.0.0 K'atun 1 Ajaw (376; Grube and Martin 1998:81), was found in Mundo Perdido, redeposited in the back room of Structure 5D-86-7, which is the central temple of the eastern three structures of the E-Group.

The Central Mexican Presence

It has long been known that central Mexico—most probably the enormous site of Teotihuacan—played an important but as yet undefined role in the Maya area during the Early Classic period (see Fash and Fash 2000; Braswell 2003a). Early attention focused on what was presumed to be a key interaction with Kaminaljuyú in the Maya highlands (Kidder, Jennings, and Shook 1946; Sanders and Price 1968; Coggins 1975, 1979), but more recent interest has been stimulated by epigraphic evidence of an "arrival event" of Teotihuacanos at Tikal on January 14, 378. On that day, according to David Stuart's (2000; see also Proskouriakoff 1993:4–10) reconstruction, a group of central Mexicans, including Siyaj K'ak' or K'ak' Sij (Fire Born; formerly known by the nickname "Smoking Frog"), Yax Nun Ayin I (First ? Crocodile, formerly Curl Snout), and Spearthrower Owl arrived at Tikal. On this same day the Tikal ruler Chak Tok Ich'ak I "entered the water," which is presumed to mean that he died. Stuart (2000:481, 487) sees Siyaj K'ak' as a military leader sent by Spearthrower Owl to overthrow Tikal's dynasty, consolidate power, and serve as regent for a new ruler, Spearthrower Owl's young son, Yax Nun Ayin I. Yax Nun Ayin I was installed on a day 5 Kab'an 10 Yaxk'in (September 11, 379), and on his accession monument, Stela 4, he wears a necklace of large shells and his face peers out from the maw of a huge feathered jaguar (?) head headdress. Above him a long-nosed deity head gazes downward.

Spearthrower Owl, Siyaj K'ak', and Yax Nun Ayin are identified in Tikal's texts as holding the important title kalomte', which conveyed, at least in later times, "a supreme status within a political hierarchy. It is the office for high kings of Late Classic Tikal and possibly Calakmul, and . . . it serves to mark overlords or 'emperors' of conquered territories" (Stuart 2000:486). The derivation of this title is unknown. Glyphically, it was originally identified as head variant T1030, with numerous variations (Fig. 2.3a–d), although a phonetic version is also identified as makuch or b'atab'. Later head variants can be distinguished by symbolic weaponry: in place of the back of the head and earplug is a left hand or arm grasping either a manopla ("brass knuckles") or an ax.

What has gone relatively unnoticed in this discussion of the 378 event is the substantial presence of central Mexicans in Tikal for more than a century before this "arrival" (cf. Laporte 2003) and the relative lack of evidence for dynastic disruption in the following century (cf. Borowicz 2003; Rice n.d.b). With respect to the former, a key variable in identifying central Mexican contact or influence outside the Mexican plateau is the presence of *talud-tablero* architectural facades. This term refers to the two-part construction of the tiers of a structural platform, in which a sloping batter (talud) is topped by a rectangular, bordered panel (tablero). At Tikal, talud-tablero architecture is first evident in Mundo Perdido around A.D. 250–300 (Laporte and Fialko 1990, 1995; Laporte 2003:200), about a century before the 378 "arrival" of central Mexicans in Tikal. Interestingly, it makes its earliest appearance in connection with modifications to the radial temple (Str. 5D-54) in the E-Group and shows up slightly later (ca. A.D. 350–378) on three platforms in residential Group 6C-XVI, a short distance to the south of Mundo Perdido (Laporte 1989).

Despite the evident importance of these central Mexican dignitaries in the lowlands, continuities with prearrival canons of dynastic legitimation were maintained. While subsequent Tikal rulers traced descent from Spearthrower Owl in the male line, they married Tikal women of presumably comparable high-status royal lines, perhaps from the Jaguar Paw dynasty. In addition, they appropriated the names of earlier, indigenous Maya rulers of the old Jaguar Paw dynasty, including Siyaj Kan K'awil I and Chak Tok Ich'ak (Table 4.2). This latter is of interest, because the father of the ruler on Stela 29 might have been named Chak Tok Ich'ak and would have ruled Tikal around A.D. 250. The next Tikal ruler named Chak Tok Ich'ak (I) died (or was killed) in 378, at the time of the Teotihuacan arrival. The third ruler named Chak Tok Ich'ak (but referred to as the second, or II) died in 508, as recorded on a monument from Toniná, Chiapas, Mexico (Martin and Grube 2000:37).

These dates and rulers' names bracket two roughly 128-year intervals in a 256-year interval of a *may* cycle. During the first 128-year period, 250–378, central Mexican "influence" in the form of talud-tablero architecture began to appear in Mundo Perdido; royal burials were in that complex rather than in the traditional domain of the ancestors, the North Acropolis on the north side of the Main Plaza. It was also during this period that Tikal first displayed its Emblem and adopted Long Count dating. During the next interval of 130 years, from 378 to 508, the North Acropolis resumed use as a royal burial ground with the interment of Tikal ruler Chak Tok Ich'ak I in 378, rulers appropriated the names of earlier kings in the Jaguar Paw line, and carved monuments display a wealth of evidence for continuity of tradition modes of dynastic legitimation.

For example, with certain outstanding exceptions, the imagery on stelae erected by Tikal's post-*entrada* rulers is purely Maya in concept, style, and execution. The famous Stela 31 (Fig. 4.7), for example, dates to 445 (a lajuntun) and shows Siyaj Kan K'awil II flanked by images of

FIGURE 4.7 The central figure of Tikal Stela 31, which dates to the lajuntun of A.D. 445, portrays Siyaj Kan K'awil II dressed in Maya garb, holding aloft his grandfather Spearthrower Owl's headdress and cradling a cruller-eyed GIII Jaguar Sun God head with the topknot of the Tikal Emblem Glyph. (Jones and Satterthwaite 1982:Figs. 51, 52; drawing by William R. Coe, courtesy of University of Pennsylvania Museum, Philadelphia, neg. # Tikal 69-5-175.)

his father in so-called Teotihuacan style. In the complex imagery on the face of this monument, Siyaj Kan K'awil II is dressed in Maya garb, holding aloft his grandfather Spearthrower Owl's headdress (Stuart 2000: 482) in his right hand. His left arm cradles a cruller-eyed GIII Jaguar Sun God head sporting the topknot of the Tikal Emblem Glyph, with more GIII heads adorning his belt (Freidel and Schele 1988b:71–72). This stela's long text, which resembles in content and style that of the later k'atun prophecies, mentions completion of the ninth b'ak'tun in 435 and the death of his grandfather, Spearthrower Owl. Stela 31, in other words, "proclaims the rebirth of orthodox kingship" by being

> consciously archaic in style and largely a copy of Stela 29 from 150 years earlier [A.D. 292]. [Siyaj K'an K'awil II's] complex head gear carries the crest of Yax Ehb' Xook, making his claims of dynastic revival explicit. . . . His father Yax Nuun Ayiin [the first] is shown three times on the monument. Above the king he floats as an ancestral sun god, a purely Maya form. (Martin and Grube 2000:34; see also Montgomery 2001b:80)

This monument was buried in the North Acropolis, the traditional burial ground of the Maya ruling dynasty. Stela 31 might originally have been paired with Altar 19, according to Coe (1990b:759–760), which shows a cross-legged seated figure on the front and an unusual, "seemingly quartered rope and knot design on the periphery."

Rather than being a formal military takeover of Tikal, this Teotihuacan arrival was clearly only one event in several centuries of interactions between central México and the lowland Maya (Cowgill 2003:328). As evidenced by architectural styles, these interactions took place in the ceremonial center of Tikal, included construction of a residential complex, and would have to have been facilitated by factions in Tikal (see Webster 2002:133). It is of interest that there is substantial evidence for internal dissention within Teotihuacan at this time, including termination of the Feathered Serpent Pyramid in the Ciudadela (Sugiyama 1998). In an argument detailed elsewhere (Rice n.d.b), I consider the central Mexican arrival that of a "stranger-king" and a prenegotiated merger of the dynasties of two great Mesoamerican cities. Tikal's young king Yax Nun Ayin I, perhaps the son of the mysterious Spearthrower Owl, would have been primarily a royal "placeholder" in this dynastic melding.

The text on the right side of Stela 31 refers to Yax Nun Ayin I as a "k'atun lord," which has been interpreted rather disparagingly: Stuart (2000:487) thinks it means he was less than twenty years old or ruled fewer than twenty years. Neither interpretation is entirely satisfactory, as he may have ruled from 379 until possibly 404, a span of twenty-five years. I interpret this term instead as referring to "lord of a k'atun," he being the lord of Tikal which took on the role of a regional k'atun seat during the antepenultimate k'atun of its *may* cycle. During his reign, he erected two monuments, Stelae 4 and 18, the latter commemorating the K'atun 12 Ajaw ending of 8.18.0.0.0 (396).

Yax Nun Ayin I's son, Siyaj Kan K'awil II, who may have been Spearthrower Owl's grandson, was the key outcome of the intermarriage between central Mexicans and Tikal's Jaguar Paw dynasty. Importantly, he adopted the K'awil title and patron, because his ancestor, Siyaj Kan K'awil I, seems to have been the last in the male line of the original dynasty founded by Yax Eb' Xok (Martin and Grube 2000:27). Siyaj Kan K'awil II's rule, or burden, occurred during a cosmically powerful transition for the Maya: a K'atun 8 Ajaw, which was not only the final k'atun of the thirteen-k'atun *may* cycle that had begun in 179 but also the final one of the b'ak'tun ending 9.0.0.0.0 (435). Tikal's newly fortified dynasty thus auspiciously came to rule over the new b'ak'tun while simultaneously seating the new *may*.

Tikal in the Middle Classic Period

Tikal's long political dominance in the Classic period lowlands began when the city seated the *may*, doubtless for a second time and quite probably a third, in the early fifth century A.D. This occurred during the rule of Siyaj Kan K'awil II, who was installed at Tikal on November 25, 411 (8.18.15.11.0 3 Ajaw 13 Sak), shortly after the completion of fifteen years (the jolajuntun) of a K'atun 10 Ajaw. Siyaj Kan K'awil II died in 456. His tomb lies on the central axis of the North Acropolis, beneath Structure 33; his magnificent Stela 31, dated 9.0.10.0.0 (445), was placed above his tomb at a later date.

Not long thereafter, the ruler K'an Kitam (Siyaj Kan K'awil II's son) mimicked Stela 31 on his own Stela 40, dated 468, holding aloft a Teotihuacan-style feathered and plated headdress and carrying a ceremonial bar. Another monument, Stela 2 (estimated to date ca. 455–475), shows Kan Kitam holding a ceremonial bar and wearing a jaguar mask–studded cape. Stela 2, like Kan Kitam's father's earlier monument, Stela 1, seems to celebrate descent through the matriline, that is, through indigenous Maya royalty (Martin and Grube 2000:34, 37) of the Jaguar Paw dynasty, as well as through the Mexican line.

Kan Kitam's Stelae 40, 2, 9, and 13 began a tradition of "staff stelae" at Tikal, which continued through the monuments of his son and successor, Chak Tok Ich'ak II. On two of these monuments, Stelae 40 (9.1.13.0.0) and 2, the ruler holds a double-headed serpent ceremonial

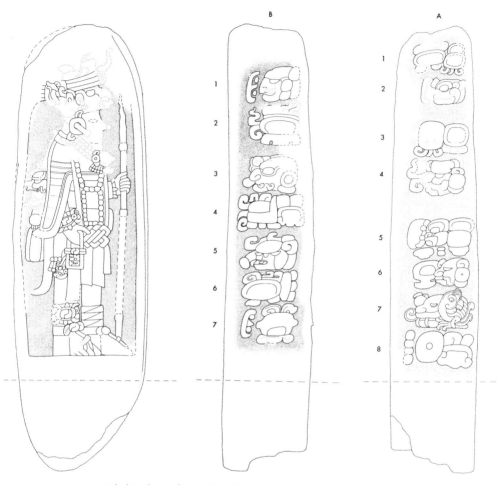

FIGURE 4.8 Tikal Stela 13 shows the ruler Kan Kitam holding a staff, possibly a fire drill (Jones and Satterthwaite 1982: Fig. 13; drawing by William R. Coe, courtesy of University of Pennsylvania Museum, Philadelphia, neg. # Tikal 69-5-11).

bar diagonally in his left arm, while on Stelae 9 (9.2.0.0.0) and 13 (style dated ca. 9.2.10.0.0; Fig 4.8) he holds a long staff in front of him. Martin and Grube (2000: 37) interpret the bar and staff as fire drills and suggest the ruler may be impersonating a fire deity. Although Stela 13 is dated only by style, it might have associations with fire drilling because the date would be a day 3 Ajaw, important in Burner rituals (see Chap. 8). Also, the staffs recall a Maya term for stela, *lakamtun,* in which *lakam* means "flag" or "banner"; thus *lakam-tun* is "banner stone," referring to "the conceptual origin of stelae as stone versions of the upright standards that once graced architectural plazas and terraces" (Stuart 1996: 154). Alternatively, the staff could be a digging stick, drawing attention to the ruler's responsibility for ensuring agricultural fertility (cf. Christie 1995: 142, who interprets the staff as a World Tree symbol).

Chak Tok Ich'ak II's five monuments, three of which commemorate the k'atun ending of 9.3.0.0.0 (2 Ajaw 18 Muwan; January 28, 495), show great elaboration of the staff. Instead of a single, presumably wooden pole, the staff now consists of three bent or curved poles, tied together by elaborate knots at both ends and in the middle (Fig. 4.9). (Here one might note the similarity to the staff carried by a god in the upper register of Dresden Codex page 25 [Fig. 1.2], one of the New Year's pages; he is also carrying a fan and a large backrack with a god figure in it. See Chapter 8 for discussion of New Year's ceremonies.) Other common features, variably present on these eight staff stelae, are the ruler carrying a small bag or pouch in one hand (4 examples), wearing nearly identical wrapped anklets (5) and a feathered headdress (6; Stela 9 may be the earliest depiction of this ornamentation), and bearing a supernatural head, often in a rack, on his back. Chak Tok Ich'ak II died in 508.

The succeeding years saw some dynastic disruption, with the six-year-old "Lady of Tikal" or Lady Kalomte' (Montgomery 2001b: 107), daughter of Chak Tok Ich'ak II, apparently coruling with Kalomte' B'alam from 511 to 527 (Martin and Grube 2000: 37–39). On Stela 10 (Fig. 4.10), Kalomte' B'alam is shown with a prone captive behind his feet; this monument was erected in what may be Tikal's first twin-pyramid group (5E-1sub), now destroyed, in the East Plaza. During the next decade or so (527–537), Tikal was led by the poorly known ruler Bird Claw (Martin and Grube 2000: 39). The final ruler in the first half of Tikal's *may* seating was Wak Kan K'awil (Double Bird), who returned to Tikal from exile (in Xultún?) and ruled from 537 to 562 (Martin and Grube 2000: 39; Montgomery 2001b: 116). He was a son of Chak Tok Ich'ak II and apparently the brother of Lady of Tikal, whom he may have murdered (Guenter 2000). In 562, Tikal was supposedly defeated in a star war attack by Calakmul.

K'atun endings were celebrated at Tikal throughout the first half of this Middle Classic *may* seating. For example, Stela 9 marked the end of a K'atun 4 Ajaw in 9.2.0.0.0, 475 (the monument was found in the Great Plaza); three monuments celebrated the 9.3.0.0.0 K'atun 2 Ajaw ending in 495; and Stela 6 commemorated the completion of the K'atun 13 Ajaw of 9.4.0.0.0, 514. Wak Kan K'awil's celebration of the ending of K'atun 9 Ajaw (9.6.0.0.0; 554) was noted not on a stela but in a text painted on a pottery dish that also depicted a Teotihuacan-like owl(?);

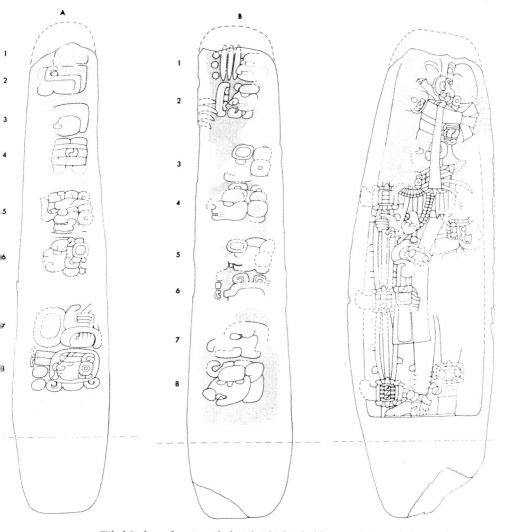

FIGURE 4.9 Tikal Stela 7, showing Chak Tok Ich'ak II holding an elaborately knotted staff (Jones and Satterthwaite 1982: Fig. 11; drawing by William R. Coe, courtesy of University of Pennsylvania Museum, Philadelphia, neg. # Tikal 69-5-6).

this vessel might be an example of the "plate of the k'atun" referred to in the Postclassic and Colonial books of the chilam b'alams (see Roys [1933] 1967:101, 150).

During Tikal's Early and Middle Classic terms as cycle seat, several sites in the surrounding region also commemorated k'atun endings:

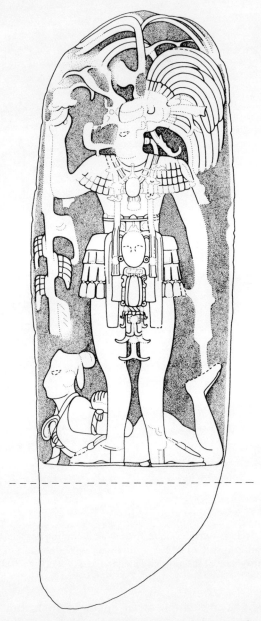

FIGURE 4.10 Tikal Stela 10, front, showing Kalomte' B'alam standing in front of a bound captive (Jones and Satterthwaite 1982: Fig. 14; drawing by William R. Coe, courtesy of University of Pennsylvania Museum, Philadelphia, neg. # Tikal 69-5-91). For text on right side, see Figure 3.4.

Uolantún (Stela 2), El Zapote (Stelae 1, 4, 7), Xultún (Stela 12), El Perú (Stela 15), and Yaxhá (Stelae 2 and 5, erected in front of the eastern structure of an E-Group). During this interval, El Perú and Yaxhá also displayed their own Emblem Glyphs, and a carved ceramic vessel from Ucanal, 51 kilometers southeast of Tikal, mentions the Tikal ruler Siyaj Kan K'awil II as overlord of Ucanal's king (Martin and Grube 2000:35). Similarly, the Tikal ruler Wak Kan K'awil "sponsored" the accession of the Caracol ruler Yajaw Te' K'inich in 553, then three years later led a *ch'ak*, or "ax," event against a Caracol lord.

Several peripheral sites around Tikal are of interest because their monuments mention Tikal's rulers: El Encanto Stela 1 mentions Siyaj Kan K'awil I and names his parents; Corozal Stela 1 notes the death of K'inich Muwan Jol in 359(?); and a stela at El Temblor may be the inaugural monument of Chak Tok Ich'ak I. It is likely that these early stelae were removed from Tikal and dispersed to these outlying areas (Martin and Grube 2000:27–30), perhaps by factions supporting Teotihuacan's dynastic interventions.

The Meaning of the Middle

The beginning of Tikal's Middle Classic role as *may* seat occurred in a K'atun 8 Ajaw, the last k'atun of the thirteen-k'atun cycle of the *may* seating. Siyaj Kan K'awil II's accession in 411 was in a jolajuntun year, five years before the ending of the K'atun 3 Ajaw. I believe the actual seating of the cycle at Tikal took place in 426 (8.19.10.0.0) (see also Edmonson 1979:13–15), the ten-year midpoint or lajuntun of a K'atun 8 Ajaw (416–435). It is probably also significant that Siyaj Kan K'awil II's monument, Stela 31, dates to 445, the lajuntun year of a K'atun 6 Ajaw, the first k'atun of the new 256-year cycle.

To explain the significance of intracycle intervals, it is necessary to return briefly to Maya calendrics and direct-historical analogy. It is well known that the Classic Maya commemorated certain intra-k'atun intervals by erecting stelae at the jotun (5 tuns), the half-k'atun lajuntun (lajun, "10" tuns), and the jolajuntun (5 tuns lacking to completion). The importance of the ten-year lajuntun interval in the Colonial period was noted by Bishop Landa and interpreted by Roys in terms of the successively overlapping decades of rule of the "idols" of the k'atun in their temples (Table 4.3):

Roys suggests that each katun idol remains in the temple thirty "years" of 360 days each. During the first ten, the idol (B) is a "guest" and acquires power from his predecessor (A) who still has a part to play, but retires at the end of these ten "years." During the second ten "years," B rules alone, receiving sacrifices. During the following third ten, B may be said "to share," still receiving reverence and offerings and his prognostics are still followed, and the new idol (C) also joins B as "guest," absorbing power from B during these ten "years" of B's reign. (Tozzer 1941:168n885)

With respect to the twenty-year rule of "idol B," Roys ([1943] 1972:81) also noted that "during the last ten years of this time it lost some of its power," presumably as it began accruing to its guest, "idol C."

A similar process occurred in human affairs during the Postclassic and early Colonial periods, as the half k'atun was the transitional moment when the kuch, or burden of office, was transferred from the present k'atun to the next one, and when the lord of the incoming k'atun, the Jaguar Priest (b'alam), was selected or confirmed. At this same mid-k'atun point, other individuals announced their candidacy or applied for the official positions they wished to occupy at the start of the new k'atun ten years hence (Edmonson 1982:86n2040).

The b'alam's preliminary initiation took place in a ceremony five years before the k'atun was to begin (i.e., the jolajuntun) (Edmonson 1982:70n1551). This ceremony is referred to as "taking the plate of the k'atun," the plate presumably being a shallow ceramic vessel. At this time the prophecy (mut) for the next k'atun was composed, to be read at the b'alam's installation in five years (Edmonson 1982:xii). Finally, it was the duty of the b'alam or his speaker (chilam) to write the history of

Table 4.3. Sequence of roles of Postclassic k'atun "idols."

	(A)	(B)	(C)	
Year	13 Ajaw	11 Ajaw	9 Ajaw	7 Ajaw
1521–1531	Rules			
1531–1541	Shares w/	Guest		
1541–1551		Rules		
1551–1561		Shares w/	Guest	
1561–1571			Rules	
1571–1581			Shares w/	Guest
1581–1591				Rules

Source: Tozzer 1941:168, note 885.

the k'atun five years after leaving office (i.e., within a jotun), since that provided the basis for future prophecy (Edmonson 1982:xii).

An excellent illustration of overlapping Late Classic–period k'atun seats—and also the role of warfare in their selection (see Chapter 8; also Rice n.d.)—comes from the Mopan region of southeastern Petén (Laporte 2004). The story begins with the inscription on Stela 2 at the large site of Ixkun, which mentions a "war" against neighboring Sacul, twelve kilometers to the east. This event occurred on 9.17.9.0.13 (December 19, 779), a date near the start of the last tun (or some 11.5 months) before the lajuntun ending of 9.17.10.0.0 (November 30, 780). Curiously, perhaps, this "war" was not recorded on the monuments at Sacul, which might be taken to indicate that site's "defeat." Ten years later, on 9.18.0.0.0, both Ixkun and Sacul celebrated the "turning" of the k'atun in the customary way, by erecting carved, dated period-ending monuments, Stela 1 at Ixkun and Stela 2 at Sacul (Laporte 2004). Significantly, both monuments record the same event: ruler Ch'iyel of the previously defeated site of Sacul visited Ixkun and its victorious lord Rabbit God K to celebrate the ending of this K'atun 11 Ajaw.

Ixkun enjoyed considerable Late Classic growth and construction activity, and this peaked around A.D. 790. But around A.D. 800 (or ca. 9.18.10.0.0, the midpoint of the new k'atun) the last carved monument was erected and piles of stones that Rabbit God K had amassed in the plazas for new construction were abandoned. Laporte (2004) interprets this as indicating that Ixkun's power waned and the site became dependent on the impressive site of Ixtonton, 7.5 km to the south. At this time, Ixtonton began to exhibit significant new Terminal Classic construction programs, including elements related to the northern Maya area such as mosaic masks with "flowery" noses and drum columns (Laporte 2004).

In terms of the model for sequential and overlapping k'atun seats, it can be suggested that during the ten-year period between 9.17.0.0.0 and 9.17.10.0.0, Sacul was a k'atun seat in this part of the Mopán region and Ixkun was its "guest" (having been previously selected for this honor). About a year before the lajuntun ending, Ixkun engaged in some sort of successful ritual jousting—perhaps a ballgame or the taking of captives—with Sacul, demonstrating that it indeed had cosmic sanction to be the next k'atun seat. Ten years later in 790, at the turning of the k'atun, Sacul's ruler came to Ixkun to meet with that site's king in a ceremony commemorating not only the calendrical interval but also the new seating of the k'atun in Ixkun. At that point, Sacul began "retiring," while Ixkun took on the role of fully empowered k'atun seat for the next ten years. In the meantime, Ixtonton had engaged in its own mid-k'atun acquisition of power, and was the incoming "guest" of Ixkun.

In 800, then, Ixtonton became the new k'atun seat and Ixkun began to retire, perhaps, given the unfinished construction, having desired but failed to continue for a second term as k'atun seat. Considering the new construction program at Ixtonton, plus the evidence for occupation continuing into the Postclassic period (Laporte 2004), Ixtonton might well have become a new *may* seat in the Mopán region. It is of interest, too, that the region's dated monuments span a narrow interval of A.D. 761–825 or only 64 years, which is a quarter of a *may*.

I propose that just as lajuntuns or half-k'atun intervals had significance in marking transfers of the burden of responsibility of office of the k'atun, so too did half-*may* cycles. By analogy to Postclassic k'atun politics, during the Classic period, new seats of the *may* were determined halfway through the 256-year cycle (i.e., 128 years after the original seating). If so, it is likely that a given *may* seat governed the cycle only during the first half; then, during the second half, it shared rule with whatever city was the incoming *may* seat.

This can be explained in terms of a *may* seat having three, rather than two, 128-year burdens, or periods of responsibility, in the same way k'atun deities had three ten-year terms of office. Say, for example, on Date X it is agreed that Tikal will next seat the *may*, a responsibility to be fully assumed 128 years, or half a *may*, later. For those next 128 years, Tikal "shared" the *may* with the existing seat, as its ascending "guest"; this was the first of Tikal's three burdens. This arrangement extended until Date Y (= Date X + 128) when the existing *may* seat retired; at this point, a K'atun 8 Ajaw, Tikal alone seated and ruled the *may*, with all the ritual rights and responsibilities thereto appertaining for its second and primary burden of 128 years. Then on Date Z (= Date Y + 128; i.e., 256 years after Date X), the new *may* seat was selected, and it was a "guest," sharing and absorbing power from Tikal for the last 128 years or third part of Tikal's term. The entire process covered 384 years, or 390 tuns, but the core of the *may* was the 13-k'atun, 260-tun interval beginning and ending with a K'atun 8 Ajaw.

With the mid-*may* selection of the new *may* seat, a portion of the burden of the current *may* cycle began to be transferred from its present seat to the new one, with the result that during the third part of the *may*, the ascending seat was expected to begin shouldering ritual responsibilities and activities befitting its new status. By analogy to k'atun idols, the current seat also began to descend, losing power as it accrued to the incoming one. Archaeological evidence suggests that this mid-*may* juncture was accompanied by radically differing roles, historical trajectories, or series of events at the *may* seat, when comparing the third part to the second.

Returning to Tikal and its Middle Classic *may* seating, then, the year

426 was significant to the Maya because it was a lajuntun, a ten-year k'atun midpoint, in a k'atun of great significance to the Maya: K'atun 8 Ajaw, the terminal k'atun of the 256-year cycle. But, as noted, this particular K'atun 8 Ajaw, spanning the years 416–435, was also the k'atun that ended B'ak'tun 8 and marked the beginning of Cycle 9. I believe that the primary burden of Tikal's Middle Classic *may* seating began in 426 and lasted 128 years, to circa 554, during which time the site alone seated the *may* and actively participated in regular k'atun celebrations marked by the erection of period-ending stelae, as discussed above.

The third part of Tikal's *may* seating, from circa 554 to 692, marks the infamous and enigmatic "hiatus," a 128-year period in which no monuments were erected at Tikal. However, instead of being a hallmark of Tikal's sudden decline, as it is traditionally viewed, this cessation in monument erection might have been an intentional change in practice and an anticipated decline in power of sorts, as another large lowland site or sites assumed the role of co-seat of the *may* and initiated its/their own mode of ritual celebration. One candidate for a late Middle Classic *may* seat was Caracol in Belize, which began celebrating its new status with distinctive Giant Ajaw altars that commemorated eighteen k'atun endings (nearly one and a half 256-year *may* cycles). Later, in the Late Classic period (see Chap. 5), a similar pattern can be seen: Tikal regularly erected stelae during the dominant portion of its term as Late Classic *may* seat, from 692 to 810, but not, with one exception, thereafter.

Overview

The existence of a formal, 256-year *may* politico-religious complex with its full architectural, astronomical, and territorial trappings might seem, on first glance, unlikely to have been functioning in the Preclassic period in the Maya lowlands, particularly in the Middle Preclassic. But several lines of evidence suggest that such a complex could have had its beginnings this early. As outlined in Chapter 3, Edmonson (1988) believes the Calendar Round was in existence by 739 B.C. and the Long Count was initiated in 354 B.C. At the same time, a radial pyramid and E-Group arrangement was being constructed and reconstructed at Tikal and also at Nakbe. Further corroboration comes from the Late Preclassic and Early Classic: the meaning of Tikal's Emblem Glyph, widespread early k'atun-ending stelae, and significant events occurring at 128- or 256-year intervals. Together, these data support the conjecture that the *may* in the Maya lowlands was initiated in this area of Petén during the latter part of the Middle Preclassic.

Edmonson (1979:14–15) derived hypothetical Preclassic and Classic *may* seatings by counting backward in time in units of ~256 years from known Postclassic *may* seating dates, all celebrating the ending of a K'atun 8 Ajaw. These dates correlate remarkably well with the Preclassic construction episodes at Tikal's Mundo Perdido as well as other events in the Early Classic period. But Tikal was not the only important Middle Preclassic site in the southern lowlands; other sizable sites—Nakbe is the closest example—are known. By the Late Preclassic, however, Nakbe had lost power and El Mirador had strengthened. Understanding the extent to which these sites shared calendrical ritual with Tikal, such as seating a *may* cycle, rests largely on evidence provided by shared architectural complexes and early k'atun-ending stelae (Table 4.4).

By the end of the Preclassic and beginning of the Early Classic, E-Groups had become the focus of ceremonial architecture at the major centers and were widespread throughout the southern lowlands (Aimers and Rice n.d.). These E-Groups played the same role in the Preclassic and Early Classic periods as did twin-pyramid groups in the Late Classic: they served as theaters in which calendrical ritual—k'atun celebrations—as well as dramatic displays of active engagement or agency within a divinely directed cosmos were enacted. Their presence at numerous sites in Petén and adjacent Belize, as well as in the valley of Guatemala (Valdés 1997) and the isthmian region (Clark and Hansen 2001), testifies to the power of the ideology shared by the participating communities. Sites constructing these complexes and erecting period-ending stelae had formal politico-ritual roles as seats of the k'atun for twenty-year periods, while another site or sites—for example, Tikal—embraced a more powerful role in controlling calendrics and time itself by seating the *may*. Construction of these complexes would have been part of the burden or kuch borne by those centers honored by the right to seat the k'atun.

In an idealized *may* model there would be thirteen k'atun seats in addition to (or perhaps including) the *may* seat. It is interesting, then, that shortly after the E-Group assemblages were first recognized, nineteen examples were identified in a relatively circumscribed area of northeastern Petén, southern Quintana Roo, and Belize, thirteen "in almost pure form" and six that were "less clear" (Ruppert [1940] 1977:222). Since then, these complexes have been identified, often in variant forms, at many other lowland sites (Aimers and Rice n.d.). Given the occurrence of early monuments, especially k'atun-ending stelae in central Petén, it is likely that El Zapote and Uolantún, plus El Encanto, Corozal, and El Temblor—all of which have stelae providing information on Early Classic Tikal rulers and to which early monuments from Tikal were removed (Martin and Grube 2000:27, 33)—also might have had these early "observatory" or commemorative assemblages; perhaps also El Perú and even Ixlú. Many of these complexes seem to have had

Table 4.4. Early dates and period-ending commemorations in the lowlands.

Site	Monument Number	Date	Year	Comment
Nakbe	S1		B.C. >200	(style date); in E-Group
Polol	A1	7.19.19.9.14?	A.D. 41?	
?	?	8.8.0.7.0	199	Hauberg Stela
Tikal	S29	8.12.14.8.15	292	Orig. in E-Group
Tikal		8.14.0.0.0	317	Period-ending celebration, no monument
Loltún		8.14.0.0.0 ?	317?	Cliff carving; (style date)
Tikal?	L.P.	8.14.3.1.12	320	Leiden Plaque
Uaxactún	S9	8.14.10.13.15	328	
Tikal	S33	8.15.0.0.0 ?	337?	(style date)
Uaxactún	S10	8.15.0.0.0 ?	337?	(style date)
Xultún	S12	8.15.0.0.0 ?	337?	(style date)
Uaxactún	S18	8.16.0.0.0	357	in E-Group
Uaxactún	S19	8.16.0.0.0	357	in E-Group
Yaxhá	S5	8.16.0.0.0 ?	357?	(style date)
Uaxactún	S5	8.16.10.0.0	366	lajuntun
Tikal	S39	8.17.0.0.0	376	Mundo Perdido
Bejucal	S2	8.17.17.0.0	393	year of a supernova?
Tikal	S18	8.18.0.0.0	396	
?El Zapote	S4	8.18.0.0.0	396	
Uaxactún	S4	8.18.0.0.0	396	
Uxbenka	S11	8.18.0.0.0 ?	396?	(style date)
Balakbal	S5	8.18.10.0.0	406	lajuntun
Uolantún	S1	8.18.13.5.11	409	
Tikal	S28	8.19.0.0.0 ?	416?	(style date)
Uaxactún	S17	8.19.0.0.0	416	
El Perú	S15	8.19.0.0.0	416	
Calakmul	S114	8.19.15.12.13	431	
Tikal	S1	9.0.0.0.0 ?	435?	b'ak'tun completion (style date)
El Zapote	S5	9.0.0.0.0	435	
Piedras Negras	A1	9.0.0.0.0	435	

primary use in the Late Classic, particularly in southeastern Petén. Given the widespread and extended duration of construction and use of these groups, it is not unlikely that their variability bespeaks participation in different *may* spheres.

It has been suggested that these assemblages are related to the earlier triadic structures, and the evolution of these architectural forms during the Preclassic accompanies a transfer in the "seat of power of the reigning lineage . . . from one architectural group to another over time" (Valdés and Fahsen 1995:199). I would link such a movement of the "seat of power" to changes in the seating of the *may* and k'atuns, as well as to transformations in the institution of kingship (ajawlil) itself, beginning around 100 B.C., although it is not unreasonable to suggest that there were accompanying shifts among powerful lineages. The likely dominant sites acting as *may* seats in the central lowlands for terms of 256 years in the Early and Middle Classic would have been Calakmul, El Mirador, Tikal, and Caracol.

From the symbol-laden year of 426, a forward movement of 128 years (or half a *may*) brings us to 554. This is the end of the last k'atun (a K'atun 9 Ajaw, 534–554) before the so-called Maya hiatus, a disjunction in the history of the southern lowlands marked most conspicuously by a gap in the tradition of erecting dated stelae, as well as by reduced ceremonialism and construction and perhaps also lower population densities (Culbert and Rice 1990). Usually dated from 534 (9.5.0.0.0) to 593 (9.8.0.0.0) in the lowlands, at Tikal the hiatus lasted much longer, from 562 to 692, a duration of 130 years or half a *may*. There, this interval has been interpreted as representing an internal power struggle accompanied by a "massive destructive campaign" (Jones 1991:117) in which monuments were defaced and moved. Other suggested causes are the waning of Teotihuacan's influence and the abandonment of Tikal by a defeated lineage, which decamped to Dos Pilas. Viewed from the perspective of Caracol and Calakmul, the hiatus and destruction at Tikal might be seen as the aftermath of its conquest by those apparently allied sites in 562. From the perspective of the Terminal Classic "collapse," the Middle Classic hiatus has been seen metaphorically as a "rehearsal" (Willey 1974).

In the context of *may* cycles and calendrics, however, if *may* seats had very different roles and responsibilities in the first and last halves of their 256-year cycles, the Middle Classic "hiatus" can be interpreted very differently. Given what is known about the seating of k'atuns and the *may* in the Postclassic and Colonial periods, this momentous event was often accompanied by significant conflict among sites, either over the right to seat the cycle or over the nature of the calendar itself. In addition, the previous seat was ritually terminated. Tikal's hiatus in monument erection and the attendant destruction and warfare is thus likely

Table 4.5. K'atun glyphs painted on three tripod plates from Tikal Burial 23.

Plate	Center	Wall Circumference
1	6 Ajaw 6	8 Ajaw 8, 8 Ajaw 8, 7 Ajaw 7, 8 Ajaw 8
2	8 Ajaw 8	7 Ajaw 8, 8 Ajaw 7, 8 Ajaw 8, 8 Ajaw 8
3	8 Ajaw 8	7 Ajaw 7, 7 Ajaw 7, 7 Ajaw 7, 7 Ajaw 7

to be the expression of multiple and intermediate contributory causes and events, but the ultimate cause would be the cycling of the *may*. In any case, the hiatus does not necessarily signal a terrible calamity befalling Tikal in Middle Classic.

For example, there continued to be rich burial furniture deposited during this period. While the rulers of Tikal during the hiatus are poorly known, owing to the absence of stelae texts, there is nonetheless a smattering of evidence about them and their rule, including k'atun-ending celebrations, and much of this evidence comes from tomb pottery of the Ik ceramic complex. Ruler Wak Kan K'awil (A.D. 537–562) celebrated the ending of K'atun 9 Ajaw (9.6.0.0.0; 554), as recorded on a polychrome plate (Martin and Grube 2000:39). The next known ruler of Tikal, nicknamed Animal Skull, ruled from about 593 to 628 and is believed to have been sumptuously entombed in Burial 195 (Coe 1990a:565–568) in Temple 32 in the North Acropolis, Tikal's traditional royal cemetery. A barrel-shaped vase dating from his rulership featured a glyph band listing early Tikal kings (Martin and Grube 2000:41). The massive Temple V, built in a single episode in the early seventh century, may date to his reign.

A later king, Nun Ujol Chak (formerly Shield Skull), ruled Tikal just before the end of the hiatus in monument erection. Possibly a usurper, as he refers only to his matriline, and father of the famous Jasaw Kan K'awil (see Chap. 5), he is thought to be the individual interred in Burial 23 (Coe 1990a:536–540) in the now-destroyed Temple 33 (Str. 5D-33), which originally stood front and center in the North Acropolis. Among the grave goods were three nearly identical Tepeu 1 (early Late Classic) red-slipped polychrome tripod, basal-ridge plates. The interior of each of these vessels was decorated with a quincunx arrangement of ajaw glyphs, one in the central base and four around the wall (Culbert 1993:Figs. 39–40). The bar-dot numbers (6, 7, 8) accompanying these ajaw glyphs appeared as both prefixes and postfixes and varied from plate to plate (Table 4.5).

The only K'atuns 8 and 6 Ajaw occurring around this time are those ending in 692 and 711, respectively, just after Nun Ujol Chak's reign. However, a K'atun 7 Ajaw ended in the Middle Classic period, 573, with the lajuntuns of 8 Ajaw and 6 Ajaw occurring ten years before and after this date, respectively (i.e., 564 and 583). Perhaps these plates were placed in the tomb as heirlooms, or perhaps Burial 23 held the remains not of Nun Ujol Chak but of an unknown Tikal king who ruled between Wak Kan K'awil (537–562) and Animal Skull (593?–628?). In any event, these dishes seem to be examples of the "plates of the k'atun" referred to in Postclassic texts (cf. Jones 2003).

A final point in connection with Early and Middle Classic *may* cycles at Tikal concerns the possibility of alternative calendrical cycles. The events highlighted here reflect the early significance of *may* cycles based on K'atuns 8 Ajaw. But as indicated in the discussion of the central Mexican presence at Tikal, another cycle of two roughly 128-year intervals, from circa 250 to 378 and from 378 to 508, can be identified. In terms of named k'atuns, 250 fell in the second half of the K'atun 13 Ajaw of 238–258; 378 just after the beginning of the K'atun 12 Ajaw of 376–396; and 508 near the end of another K'atun 13 Ajaw (495–514). This is of retrospective interest because by the Postclassic period in northern Yucatán, major disagreements had developed between two important lineages, the Xiw and the Kokom (Itza), about calendrical cycling. The Xiw, like the Classic period Maya of Tikal and elsewhere, counted and recorded k'atuns by their ending dates and completed their *may* cycles of 256 years on the last day of a K'atun 8 Ajaw. The Kokom (Itza), however, counted k'atuns from their initial dates, and their cycles began with a K'atun 13 Ajaw.

It appears, then, that different factions existed at Tikal in the Early Classic. One, the ruling Jaguar Paw dynasty, favored cycles ending with K'atuns 8 Ajaw. The dissident faction, apparently allied in some way with central Mexico and Teotihuacan, recognized cycles based on K'atuns 13 Ajaw, using that k'atun as the starting point or, perhaps, the following K'atun 2 Ajaw as the initiation of the *may* cycle. The broader significance of these differing conceptions of calendrical cycling becomes apparent in Chapter 6.

CHAPTER 5

Tikal's Late and Terminal
Classic Seating of the May

Tikal was renewed as a cycle seat, or *may ku*, in the Late Classic period during a K'atun 8 Ajaw (A.D. 672–692). In 682, the midpoint of this k'atun, Jasaw Kan K'awil I (the Tikal ruler formerly known as Ruler A or Ah Cacao) came to power on 9.12.9.17.16 5 Kib' 14 Sotz' (May 4), only four days before the lajuntun of 9.12.10.0.0. Thirteen years later, in 695, he claimed victory over his legendary competitor, Calakmul, a victory celebrated on September 14 of that year. Much has been made of the fact that this occurred 256 years (more precisely, one day short of 260 tuns)—a *may* completion—after the death of Spearthrower Owl in 439 (Martin and Grube 2000:45; Puleston 1979; Coggins 1980). These events were celebrated on the carved, wooden Lintel 3 of Temple I (see Fig. 5.9), which notes that Jasaw Kan K'awil I conjured and let blood as part of dedicating (a building?) "in the center of the seat (or cave) of Tikal" (*tan kun/ch'en Mutul*).

Jasaw Kan K'awil I, supposedly son of Nun Ujol Chak but also referred to as possibly "non-Tikaleño by birth" (Coe 1990a:608), inaugurated a return to the traditions of his forebears but with some innovations. The two distinctive elements of his reign and those of his successors (Table 5.1) were a combination of old and new imagery on period-ending stelae and elaboration of a distinctive architectural setting for k'atun celebrations, the twin-pyramid complex. The latter provide the most robust evidence for politico-religious continuities from the Classic to the Postclassic period, as the k'atun-ending dates, ritual bloodletting, and stela erection conform to numerous "acts" of Colonial period-ending ceremonies.

Tikal as Late Classic *May Ku*
Twin-Pyramid Groups

In the Late Classic period, Jasaw Kan K'awil I inaugurated Tikal's seating of the *may* by launching an expanded architectural program, twin-

Table 5.1. Tikal's Late and Terminal Classic rulers.

Maya Name	Nickname	Date	Number in Succession
Jasaw Kan K'awil I	Ruler A	682–734	
Yik'in Kan K'awil	Ruler B	734–746	27
???		746–768?	28
Yax Nun Ayin II	Ruler C	768–794?	29
Nun Ujol K'inich		c. 800?	
	Dark Sun	c. 810?	
	Jewel K'awil	c. 849	
Jasaw Kan K'awil II		c. 869	

Source: Martin and Grube 2000:44–53.

pyramid groups (see Jones 1969), for commemorating k'atun endings. These complexes consist of a large raised platform on which four cardinally oriented structures are arranged around a plaza (Fig. 5.1). The eponymous twin pyramids are five-tiered, radially symmetrical structures with a stairway on all four sides, opposing each other on the east and west sides of the plaza; no temple structure stood atop them. A north-south line of paired, uncarved stelae and altars stood in front of the eastern pyramid, facing west into the plaza. To the south was a low, rectangular "range structure," approximately 25 meters long, with nine doorways. On the north side was a small, square or rectangular stone enclosure, with walls roughly 3 meters high, in which a carved stela-altar pair were set (Fig. 5.2). This northern structure was unroofed and "open to the zenith, whence [the ruler] derives his power" (Aveni 2003:161).

The twin-pyramid group is a cosmogram, a physical representation of the trilevel and quadripartite Maya cosmos (Guillemin 1968; see also Coggins 1979, 1980). Together the east-west structures of twin-pyramid groups marked the journey of the sun and the moon as they rise in the east and set in the west. The nine-doorway structure in the south represents the Underworld, where these celestial bodies dwell after their disappearance in the west (nine is the number of levels and Lords of the Underworld). North represents the celestial level of the cosmos and the home of the divine ancestors. This is where the k'atun-ending commemorative stelae and altars were erected, the divine ruler on the monument symbolically looking "down" (south) on the earthly realm. Given the number of construction tiers (five) of the east-west pyramids of Twin-Pyramid Group Q, George F. Guillemin (1968:28–29) thought that a count of these tiers plus the plaza levels could be combined to represent the thirteen levels of the heavens and the nine levels of the Underworld (see Edmonson's [1986a:120–126] discussion of the "birth of the winal" in the *Chumayel*). Thus the twin-pyramid complexes symbolize the trajectories of celestial bodies both in the sky and in the Underworld.

According to Guillemin (1968:9), Tikal's "twin pyramid arrangements are mainly an imitation of the Great Plaza which, in turn, would represent an enlarged version of the North Acropolis." He emphasized what is now called the "triadic group" arrangement that can be seen in the Early Classic North Acropolis: three structures arranged to the north, east, and west sides of a patio (Strs. 5D-22, -23, and -24). In the Late Classic Great Plaza this arrangement was enlarged, with the entire North Acropolis—resting place of the Tikal dynasty's ancestors—serving as the northern point of the triad, flanked by Temples 1 and 2 facing each other across the open plaza. South of the plaza sits the Central Acropolis, a dense residential arrangement of palacelike rooms and

FIGURE 5.1 Restoration drawing of Tikal Twin-Pyramid Group Q (also known as 4E-4) (courtesy of University of Pennsylvania Museum, Philadelphia, neg. # Tikal 66-5-49).

FIGURE 5.2 The stela enclosure of Tikal's Twin-Pyramid Group Q, with Stela 22 and Altar 10 visible through the corbel-vaulted doorway (photograph courtesy of Don S. Rice).

courtyards. The entire Great Plaza itself thus represents a macro-scale twin-pyramid group.

I do not disagree with this interpretation, but I would add that the east-west radial platforms of twin-pyramid groups represent a direct link to the E-Group arrangements of the Preclassic and Early and Middle Classic periods. In these earlier complexes, a western radial pyramid stood across a plaza from a tripartite temple structure that marked solar positions, where lines of stelae, usually commemorating k'atun endings, were erected. In the case of twin-pyramid groups, the eastern structure was an identical radial pyramid, and the variable numbers of stelae in front of it were plain rather than carved. Thus the Late Classic twin-pyramid groups maintained east as the primary ritual direction, though slightly diminished through lack of architectural differentiation. Furthermore, if Macri's (in press) explanation is correct about the very ancient role of lunar cycles in the importance of numbers 13, 9, and 7, then the nine doorways of the southern structure suggest not simply the solar but also the lunar significance of these architectural complexes.

Nine twin-pyramid groups are known at Tikal, of which five are complete and dated by their carved stelae; the others have style dates based on attributes of the masonry and uncarved stelae (Jones 1969). The first twin-pyramid "group" at Tikal, Group 5E-1sub, was simply a pair of radial temples and lacked the distinctive stela enclosure and nine-doorway palace of the Late Classic complexes (Jones 1985:51; 1991: 114). The temples may date to the reign of Jasaw Kan K'awil's father (Valdés and Fahsen 2004), although they might have been built as early as 475 (Schele and Mathews 1998:67). In any case, their stairways were "refurbished at least twice" (Jones 1985:51) before they were destroyed by Late Classic construction of an overlying ballcourt and radial temple with Veracruz-style talud-tablero and flaring cornice in the East Plaza. It is not known if the other undated twin-pyramid assemblages, 4D-2 and 5B-1, also date to the Middle Classic, although this is certainly possible given their incomplete or damaged status.

In the Late Classic, beginning in 692, five twin-pyramid complexes were built at twenty-tun intervals, the carved monuments in the stela enclosure dating to successive k'atun endings. In other words, Jasaw Kan K'awil I and his successors commemorated k'atun endings from 9.13.0.0.0 (692) through 9.18.0.0.0 (790) in these complexes. The only exception to this pattern is the period ending at 9.15.0.0.0 (731); this event might have been celebrated in the small Twin-Pyramid Group O, lying across the Maler Causeway directly west of Groups R and Q. The stela-altar pair in the northern enclosure of Group O is plain rather than sculptured, and thus undated, and might reflect Jasaw Kan K'awil's absence from the site while visiting Copán on that occasion (see below). The Late Classic span of celebrating k'atun endings, from Jasaw Kan K'awil I's accession in 682 to the last sequential k'atun-ending monument in 810, lasted 128 years, half a *may* cycle.

The idealized *may* model postulates thirteen k'atun seats within Tikal's sphere, which would have erected twin-pyramid groups to commemorate k'atun endings. However, during Tikal's Late and Terminal Classic period *may* seating, only five proposed k'atun seats in Tikal's realm—Yaxhá, Ixlú, Zacpetén, Chalpate, and Uolantún—appear to have constructed twin-pyramid complexes, and none of these has been securely dated.

Yet there is epigraphic evidence that Tikal did indeed have thirteen provinces or k'atun seats in its Late Classic realm. Jasaw Kan K'awil I's accession came immediately following a war in 679 in which Tikal was supposedly conquered by the site of Dos Pilas to the southwest through alliance with Calakmul (see Houston 1993; Boot 2002; Fahsen 2002). The rulers of Dos Pilas commemorated their victory on Hieroglyphic Stairways (H.S.) 2 and 4. On H.S. 2, Steps III and IV display the Emblem Glyph of Tikal plus the glyphs for thirteen tzuk (parts, provinces) and u kab'iy (Schele and Mathews 1998:70). This last is read as representing agency—"by," "under the auspices of"—or as indicating subordinate relations to a political overlord. On H.S. 4, Step III refers to the Tikal lord as "he of thirteen provinces" (Boot 2002). These texts, then, refer to "thirteen provinces of Tikal," which could be simply a Maya metaphor for "many dead in Tikal's realm," or it could mean that Tikal literally had thirteen provinces or dependencies—thirteen k'atun seats—within its domain. Among these proposed k'atun seats are Uaxactún, Yaxhá, Nakum, Xultún, Motul de San José, Ixlú, Zacpetén, Chalpate, and Uolantún.

Jasaw Kan K'awil died in 734 and was buried in a splendid chamber (Burial 116; Coe 1990a:604–609) under Tikal's Temple 1. Shortly before he died, he (or a representative) traveled to Copán to participate in the meeting of lords of four major sites (Copán, Tikal, Palenque, and Calakmul), as commemorated on Copán Stela A. That he was truly a statesman of some "international" renown is suggested by the discovery of thirty-seven delicately incised bone fragments in his tomb, the fine lines accentuated by cinnabar. One of these bones bears a date corresponding to October 26, 726, and refers to the death of Ruler 2 at Dos Pilas; another refers to the death of a woman possibly from Cancuen on January 24, 727 (Harrison 1999:140). Painted pottery cylinders in the tomb might represent gifts from other lowland kings (Coggins 1975:515).

Tikal's Late Classic Monuments

Insights into the Late Classic seating of the *may* at Tikal also can be gleaned from the iconography and themes of k'atun-ending stelae at Tikal, in twin-pyramid complexes and elsewhere at the site, and monuments at other sites in the central Petén lakes region (see Christie 1995; Graham 1973; Stuart 1988; Chase 1985; Morley 1937–1938:415–448; also Marcus 1976; Proskouriakoff 1993). These valedictory monuments display a shared program of shapes, styles, and themes, including the presence of the Tikal Emblem Glyph and commemoration of k'atun- and lajuntun-ending intervals (Rice 1997) and the following:

- Calendrics: These monuments rarely use Initial Series dates; instead they record dates by the Calendar Round. They typically commemorate period endings, especially k'atuns (20 tuns or

7,200 days; approximately 20 years) and also lajuntun intervals (half-k'atuns of 10 tuns, or 3,600 days). Jotuns (5 tuns, 1,800 days) and jolajuntuns (15 tuns) are recorded only rarely, and are known primarily from "peripheral sites" (Proskouriakoff 1993:184).

- Primary theme: The central personage is extravagantly attired in an elaborate feathered headdress and often a jaguar-pelt kilt, bearing a backrack, carrying in one arm a ceremonial staff or bar, and performing the "scattering" rite with the other hand. Many of these details echo the costuming of the ruler on the Middle Classic period-ending and "staff" stelae. In particular, the ceremonial bar appears to be a smaller version of the tripartite, knotted staffs of the Early Classic, with diamond-shaped rather than curved bars and cradled in the arm rather than held vertically in front of the ruler.
- Secondary theme: The ruler is often shown standing atop or in front of bound, prone captives; sometimes the captive is depicted alone on an altar. The prone position is unusual, compared to the more typical kneeling posture. Seated captives are also shown on three "column altars" (possible ballcourt markers), two of which have rope borders, but only one is dated (Column Altar 1, at 9.15.17.10.4 10 K'an 12 Pax; December 12, 748) (Jones and Satterthwaite 1982:Fig. 62). The depiction of prone prisoners on k'atun-ending stelae was also seen in the Early and Middle Classic periods (Chap. 4) beginning with Tikal Stela 29 at 292. Their appearance recalls the alternative meanings of *k'atun,* "combat," "battle," or "warrior."
- Mat and rope motifs often appear as borders on the edges of altars and stelae or as separators creating quadripartite divisions of the decorative space.

The "scattering" gesture and glyph (T710; Stuart 1984) are significant new elements of Tikal's Late Classic k'atun celebrations and the iconographic program of these monuments, which otherwise are very similar to the site's Early Classic stelae. This glyph and gesture, an open hand with dots falling from it, is read *u chok'-wa ch'aj* 'he scatters drops,' but gives no clue as to what those "drops" might be. In the *Diccionario Maya-Español, chok'* is translated as "to pour water, salt, or other things by handfuls"; other definitions suggest that it refers to pouring dry goods rather than liquids, although *ch'aj* means "drops."

Thus the images of scattering have been interpreted as the ruler dispersing seeds or grains (e.g., maize, beans), crystals, or incense, perhaps in divination. More recently, it has been viewed as the ruler's blood sacrifice on period-ending dates (Stuart 1988:187, 188). Given Landa's accounts (e.g., Tozzer 1941:140–144), the scattered substance in the Late Classic might have been mixtures of specific counts of grains of maize mixed with copal incense (*pom*) or incense mixed with rubber tree sap (the latter called *k'ik'* 'blood').

Scattering rituals seem to be important and widespread in Mesoamerica, not just in the Maya area and not just in the Classic period. The mid-second-century A.D. stela from La Mojarra, Veracruz, has numerous textual references to scattering or sprinkling, using an open hand glyph, although there are no period-ending dates (Kaufman and Justeson 2001). The much earlier Humboldt Celt, possibly dating to as early as 900 B.C., may show an "iconic" reference to the scattering rite (Justeson 1986:Fig. 3e). In the Middle Classic, the scattering gesture and/or glyph may be earliest associated with k'atun endings on Yaxchilán Stela 27 at 9.4.0.0.0 13 Ajaw (514; Coggins 1983:53n22) and Caracol Stela 1, dated 9.8.0.0.0 (593).

Tikal's eight Late Classic stelae and their paired altars, dating between 9.13.0.0.0 (692) and 9.19.0.0.0 (810), constitute the largest and best-preserved corpus of such sculpture from central Petén. The monument sequence is summarized below.

Tikal Stela 30 (Fig. 5.3) and Altar 14 (Fig. 5.4), dated to the k'atun ending (9.13.0.0.0) 8 Ajaw 8 Wo (March 16, 692), were set in the intentionally destroyed (Jones and Satterthwaite 1982:62) Twin-Pyramid Complex M (3D-1 in Group H), adjacent to the northern end of the later Maudslay Causeway. Three plain altars stood before the eastern pyramid of the group. On Stela 30, Jasaw Kan K'awil I, who claimed descent from the early Middle Classic king Siyaj Kan K'awil II (Stormy Sky), is shown scattering. He carries a tripartite staff and wears a back ornament bearing a mask of the Maize God, which Bricker (1984:229, 1989:239) suggests may be a reference to the burden of the Ix Yearbearer. Ix, however, is not a Classic yearbearer but rather a Postclassic one. The stela text includes the *k'al tun* (stone binding) glyph, which Stuart (1996:156) suggests may refer to the walled enclosure within which the monument was set. Altar 14 is all-glyphic and displays an 8 Ajaw in the "Giant Ajaw" Caracol style. Jasaw Kan K'awil I is noted for his revitalization of Tikal's power and hegemony, evidenced by a major building program in the North Acropolis and the elaboration of public k'atun-ending rituals, commemorated by carved stelae and altars in a new ritual circuit of twin-pyramid complexes.

Tikal Stela 16 (Fig. 5.5) and Altar 5, dated (9.14.0.0.0) 6 Ajaw 13 Muwan (December 3, 711), are found in Twin-Pyramid Complex N (5C-1, west of the Great Plaza and adjacent to the Tozzer Causeway, just southeast of Temple IV). A human skull and bones were cached under

FIGURE 5.3 Tikal Stela 30 ([9.13.0.0.0] 8 Ajaw 8 Wo; March 16, 692), from Twin-Pyramid Complex M, shows the ruler Jasaw Kan K'awil I (Jones and Satterthwaite 1982: Fig. 50; drawing by William R. Coe, courtesy of University of Pennsylvania Museum, Philadelphia, neg. # Tikal 69-5-65).

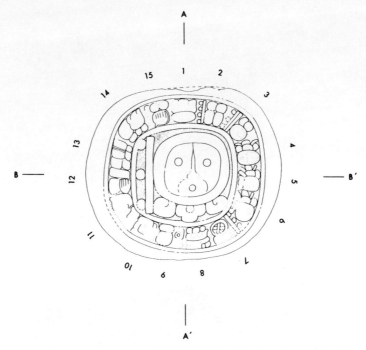

FIGURE 5.4 Altar 14, paired with Stela 30, displays a Giant 8 Ajaw in the "Caracol style" (Jones and Satterthwaite 1982:Fig. 50; drawing by William R. Coe, courtesy of University of Pennsylvania Museum, Philadelphia, neg. # Tikal 69-5-87).

the stela (Jones and Satterthwaite 1982:37). On the monument, Jasaw Kan K'awil I, who is not scattering, wears an elaborate feathered backrack and necklace and pectoral of large round beads; he carries a two-part ceremonial bar horizontally in front of him and a bag looped over his right wrist. His headdress incorporates a Venus sign, perhaps in acknowledgment of this date as the first appearance of Venus as Evening Star (Montgomery 2001b:158), and combines Ak'b'al (night) with Sun God imagery, symbols of the Paddler Gods (ancestor figures), although they are not depicted. Like Stela 20 and other monuments in twin-pyramid groups, the text of Stela 16 incorporates the k'al tun glyph. Loosely read, the text announces, "On 8 Ajaw 13 Muwan, the fourteenth k'atun was completed, the tun was ended [k'al tun] at the ? First Entrance [T769 'Maw'] to the Underworld by [Jasaw Kan K'awil], the Divine Tikal Ruler, Sun-eyed Man, the three k'atun [Kalomte']" (Harris and Stearns 1997:166–168). This appears to suggest that twin-pyramid groups were considered openings to the Underworld.

Altar 5 (Fig. 5.6) shows two lords, nearly identically dressed, each carrying a staff and a weapon (the left figure a manopla and the right a

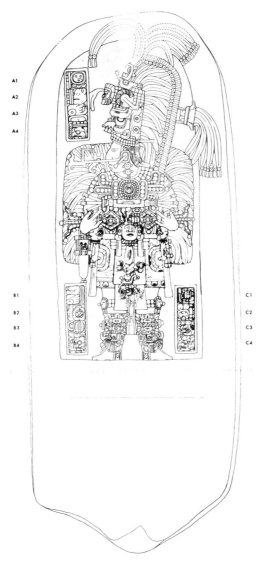

FIGURE 5.5 Tikal Stela 16 ([9.14.0.0.0] 6 Ajaw 13 Muwan; December 3, 711), from Twin-Pyramid Complex N, shows the ruler Jasaw Kan K'awil I (Jones and Satterthwaite 1982:Fig. 22; drawing by William R. Coe, courtesy of University of Pennsylvania Museum, Philadelphia, neg. # Tikal 69-5-55).

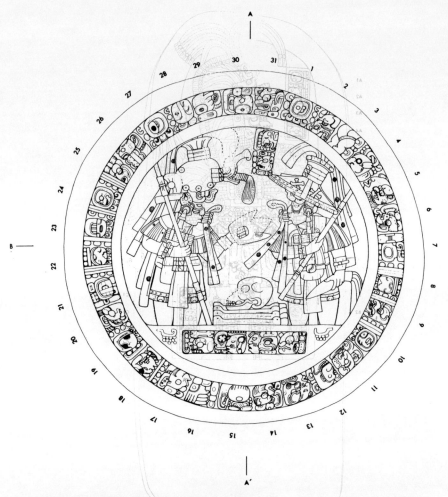

FIGURE 5.6 Tikal Altar 5, paired with Stela 16, shows Jasaw with another lord, ex-
huming the bones of a noble lady from Topoxté (Jones and Satterthwaite 1982:
Fig. 23; drawing by William R. Coe, courtesy University of Pennsylvania Museum,
Philadelphia, neg. # Tikal 69-5-75).

probable flint knife), with what looks like a folded and knotted cloth in
front of the face. Differences in costuming are evident in their unusual
and very elaborate headdresses and their belts. The scene and text have
been interpreted as describing the Tikal ruler with a lord of an unknown
place called Maasal or Masul (perhaps the site of Naachtun?), affiliated
with Calakmul, exhuming the bones of a noble lady (Martin and Grube
2000:46). Another reading of the text (Grube 2000b:260) is that it de-

scribes the death of a royal lady from Topoxté named Wayas Ch'ok Na Tetun Kaywak and her burial in the "house of the nine lords" on (9.13.1.6.7) 1 Manik 10 Mol (July 6, 693). It is tempting to speculate that this "house" could be the nine-doorway structure of a twin-pyramid group, or perhaps a metaphor for the Underworld. Montgomery (2001b: 155) interprets the scene as Jasaw Kan K'awil exhuming the bones and skull of his wife or consort, Lady Tun Kaywak of Yaxhá, at Calakmul in the company of Kan Sak Wayas of Masul. "Sak Wayas" is a noble title at Calakmul. It is of interest that a skull and bones were found under the accompanying Stela 16, although there is no way to prove they are those of Lady Tun Kaywak.

Tikal Stela 21 (Fig. 5.7) and Altar 9 were found near the Temple of the Inscriptions (Temple VI), not in a twin-pyramid group. On this monument, a barefoot Yik'in Kan K'awil (formerly known as Ruler B) scatters, carries a staff with three sets of knots in his left arm, and wears an elaborate backrack. Bricker (1989:234, 246) notes that in the Dresden Codex and in twentieth-century Chamula (Chiapas), a fire-walking rite accompanied the start of Kawak years, in which the priest sprinkled "wine" (b'alche'; or perhaps fermented cacao) on the coals. She also notes that the ruler's back ornament or burden displays a mask with a defleshed jaw, suggesting it represents a victim of human sacrifice or, as in the Postclassic and Colonial periods, the death god burden of Kawak years (Bricker 1984:229; 1989:237, 246). Again, however, Kawak (like Ix) is not a Classic yearbearer but a Postclassic one.

The face of Stela 21 has two glyphic panels, the uppermost of which is eroded and unreadable. Thus a missing dedication date had to be reconstructed on the basis of a Calendar Round distance number date in the lower panel and yielded 9.15.5.0.0 10 Ajaw 8 Ch'en (July 24, 736) (Jones and Satterthwaite 1982:47–48). I am rather suspicious of this non-k'atun-ending date on the monument, because iconographically it is almost exactly a copy of the later Stela 22 (see below), dating to 9.17.0.0.0, and scattering is normally a k'atun-ending ritual. In addition, the text uses almost verbatim the couplet structure (Harris and Stearns 1997:102–105) on the lower panel of the ruler's son's monument, Stela 22. However, as noted, the ruler Jasaw Kan K'awil was reportedly in Copán on the occasion of the k'atun ending in 731 and there is no known monument to that date. Yik'in Kan K'awil, who is named on Stela 21, did not accede until 734, and perhaps he celebrated this jotun completion in lieu of the earlier missed k'atun ending.

The surviving text on the lower panel of Stela 21, paraphrased in the style of that of Stela 22, reads: "Holy Tikal ruler, 4 k'atun kalomte' [Distance Number 12 k'ins, 11 winals, 1 tun] on 3 Lamat 6 Pax he was seated

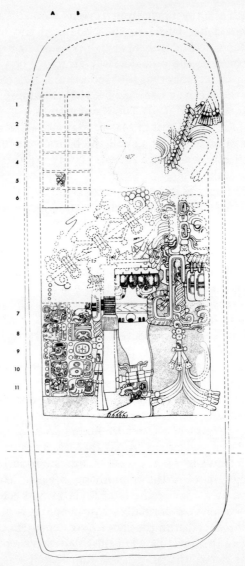

FIGURE 5.7 Tikal Stela 21 ([9.15.5?.0.0] 10 Ajaw 8 Ch'en; July 24, 736?), found near the Temple of the Inscriptions (Temple VI), shows the ruler Yik'in Kan K'awil (Jones and Satterthwaite 1982:Fig. 31; drawing by William R. Coe, courtesy of University of Pennsylvania Museum, Philadelphia, neg. # Tikal 69-5-58).

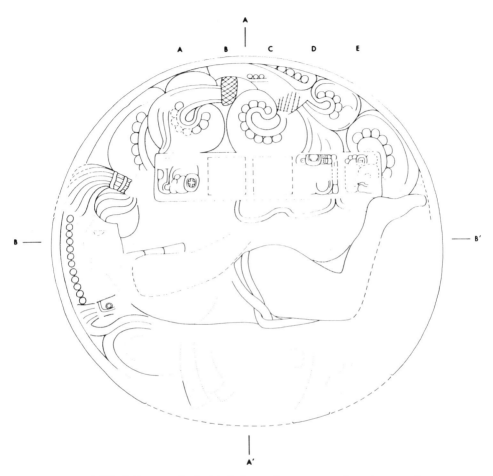

FIGURE 5.8 Tikal Altar 9, paired with Stela 21, shows a prone, bound captive from Calakmul (Jones and Satterthwaite 1982:Fig. 32; drawing by William R. Coe, courtesy of University of Pennsylvania Museum, Philadelphia, neg. # Tikal 69-5-81).

as kalomte' and then he scattered drops." The accompanying Altar 9 (Fig. 5.8), one of the largest of the Tikal altars (Jones and Satterthwaite 1982:47), shows a prone, bound captive from Calakmul (Martin and Grube 2000:48). I wonder if Stela 21 and Altar 9 originally could have been erected in the stela enclosure of Twin-Pyramid Group O (Group 4D-1) and later moved to the Temple of the Inscriptions and replaced by a plain stela and altar.

Tikal Stela 5 and Altar 2, dated (9.15.13.0.0) 4 Ajaw 8 Yaxk'in (June 12, 744), were placed in the North Acropolis, in front of Structure

5D-33-1st. Yik'in Kan K'awil stands facing the viewer's left, wearing a jaguar-skin kilt and a backrack holding a deity head with a defleshed jaw. He carries a manikin scepter in his right hand and in his left clutches the handle of a long conical bag. The kalomte' glyph appears twice in the text, along with a variant form of the Tikal Emblem Glyph. A prone prisoner, Naranjo king Yax May Kan Chak (Schele and Grube 1995:43), lies behind the ruler's feet. Altar 2 is heavily eroded but has a quadripartite division and upper rope border. Yik'in's victory over Naranjo, including the capture of its king and his palanquin, was celebrated on Lintel 3 of Temple IV. This lintel is remarkably similar, in both text and iconography, to Lintel 3 of Temple I (Fig. 5.9), which celebrates his father Jasaw Kan K'awil's victory over Calakmul, including the same reference to events taking place "in the seat of Tikal."

Tikal Stela 20 (Fig. 5.10) and Altar 8, dated (9.16.0.0.0) 2 Ajaw 13 Sek (May 7, 751), were set in Twin-Pyramid Complex P (3D-2, next to Complex M at the joining of the Maler and Maudslay Causeways). The stela celebrates the end of the first k'atun of Yik'in Kan K'awil's (Ruler B) reign. He wears a God K headdress and is neither scattering nor carrying a ceremonial bar. Instead, he stands in front of a jaguar throne, holding a halberd or long staff with three embedded blades (reminiscent of the club on earlier Uaxactún Stela 5) in front of him and a bag in his left hand, and wearing a backrack holding a large supernatural head. Altar 8 (Fig. 5.11) shows a prone, bound noble captive named Wilan Tok Wayib', who has a *wuk tzuk* title linking him to the Naranjo-Yaxhá region and who was sacrificed on December 10, 748 (Martin and Grube 2000:50). It was earlier suggested that this captive might have died in a ballgame (Schele and Miller 1986:249).

Tikal Stela 22 and Altar 10, dated (9.17.0.0.0) 13 Ajaw 18 Kumk'u (January 22, 771), were placed in the stela enclosure of Twin-Pyramid Complex Q (4E-4; Fig. 5.2), east of the Maler Causeway. Nine plain stelae-altar pairs sit in front of the eastern radial structure. Stela 22 (Fig. 5.12) is very slightly wedge-shaped and asymmetrical, a trait that becomes much more prominent in the Terminal Classic. It depicts the Tikal ruler Yax Nun Ayin II (formerly known as Ruler C or Kitam), second son of Yik'in Kan K'awil and probable grandson of Jasaw Kan K'awil I (Martin and Grube 2000:51). He is the twenty-ninth and last in the long Jaguar Paw dynasty of Tikal and the builder of two twin-pyramid complexes. Yax Nun Ayin II is shown barefoot, performing a scattering rite, carrying a tripartite bar and a long conical bag, and wearing a jaguar-pelt kilt, with the same death god mask in his back ornament as is shown on Stela 21. In dress and posture he appears to be copying the images of his father as seen on Stelae 21 and 5 (Miller 1993:362). The reference to ancestors is accentuated by the small figure in the

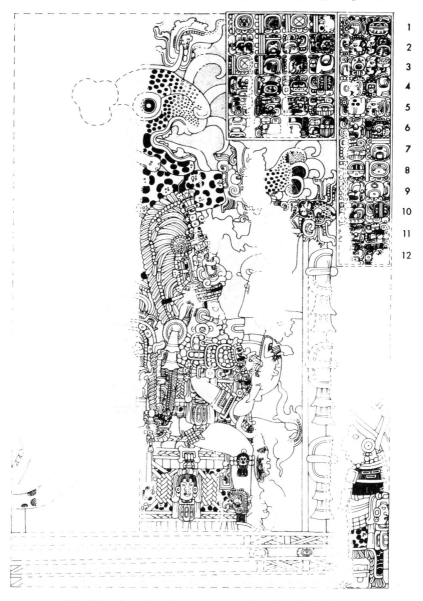

FIGURE 5.9 Tikal Temple 1, Lintel 3, shows Jasaw Kan K'awil after defeating Calakmul in A.D. 695 and records the thirteenth k'atun anniversary of Spearthrower Owl's
death (Stuart 2000:490). Note the enormous Jaguar patron of his dynasty looming
over him; also the mat and mask motif on his throne, similar to that on the sides
of Tikal altars, and *tan kun Mutul* 'in the seat of Mutul' at D6 (Jones and Satterthwaite 1982:Fig. 70; drawing by William R. Coe, courtesy of University of Pennsylvania Museum, Philadelphia, neg. # Tikal 69-5-96).

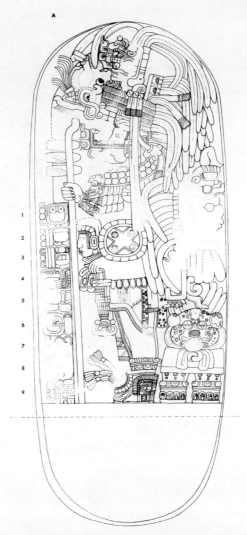

FIGURE 5.10 Tikal Stela 20 ([9.16.0.0.0] 2 Ajaw 13 Sek; May 7, 751), found in Twin-Pyramid Complex P (Jones and Satterthwaite 1982: Fig. 30; drawing by William R. Coe, courtesy of University of Pennsylvania Museum, Philadelphia, neg. # Tikal 69-5-57).

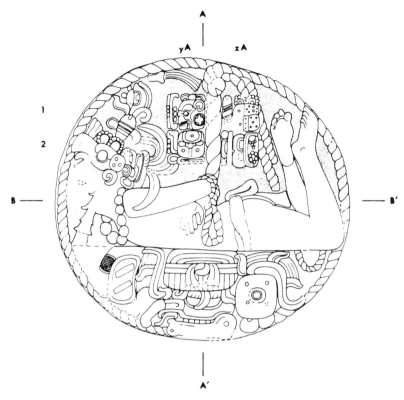

FIGURE 5.11 Tikal Altar 8, paired with Stela 20 (Jones and Satterthwaite 1982: Fig. 30; drawing by William R. Coe, courtesy of University of Pennsylvania Museum, Philadelphia, neg. # 69–5–80).

upper left corner of the stela, surrounded by dotted scrolls, another trait that becomes common in the Terminal Classic (see below).

As on Stela 21, the text consists of a couplet structure carved in two panels and reads: "On 13 Ajaw 18 Kumk'u the seventeenth k'atun, the tun was completed by Flower Mountain [Yax Nun Ayin II], the Divine Tikal Ruler, twenty-ninth successor of Yax Moch Xok. . . . He is the son [flower] of ? Kan K'awil, the Sun-eyed Man, the Divine Tikal Ruler, the 4 K'atun [kalomte']"; on 11 K'an 12 K'ayab [9.16.17.16.4] he was seated as [kalomte'] and then he scattered drops (Harris and Stearns 1997:102). The accompanying Altar 10 (Fig. 5.13) shows a prone, bound captive lying on a square framework set in a quatrefoil, rimmed by petaloid elements. Around the side are four captives separated by mat symbols, and a rope rings the altar's edge.

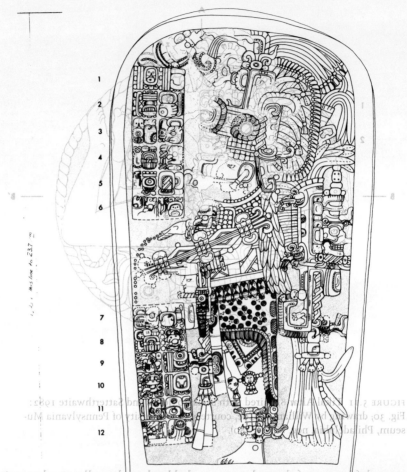

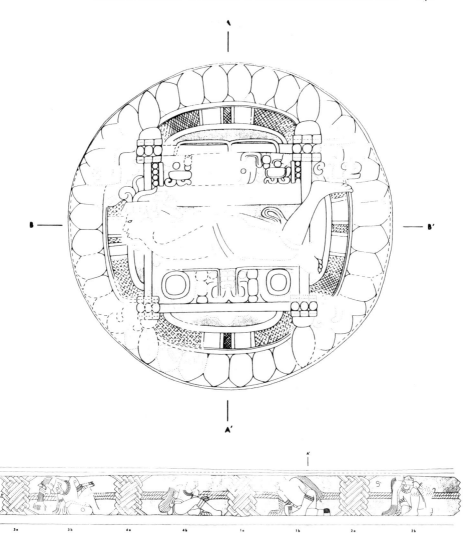

FIGURE 5.13 Tikal Altar 10, paired with Stela 22; (a) top, (b) sides (Jones and Satterthwaite 1982:Fig. 34; drawing by William R. Coe, courtesy of University of Pennsylvania Museum, Philadelphia, neg. #s Tikal 69-5-82a, 69-5-82b).

Tikal Stela 19 and Altar 6, dated (9.18.0.0.0) 11 Ajaw 18 Mak (October 9, 790), are found in Twin-Pyramid Complex R (4E-3), located between the Maler Causeway and Complex Q. At least five stelae-altar
pairs sat in front of the eastern radial structure. Stela 19 is virtually a
copy of Stelae 5 and 22, with Yax Nun Ayin II standing barefoot, scattering, carrying a ceremonial bar, and wearing a jaguar kilt and a back

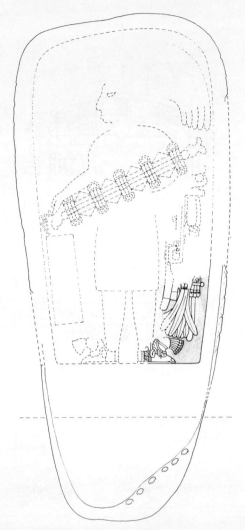

FIGURE 5.14 Tikal Stela 24 ([9.19.0.0.0] 9 Ajaw 18 Mol; June 26, 810?), in front of Temple III, may show ruler "Dark Sun" (Jones and Satterthwaite 1982:Fig. 40; drawing by William R. Coe, courtesy of University of Pennsylvania Museum, Philadelphia, neg. # Tikal 69-5-61a).

ornament with a death god mask. The top is eroded but probably had ancestor figures. Altar 6 shows a prone, bound prisoner and has a decorated border. The side shows four sumptuously dressed seated figures separated by thronelike elements bearing glyphs.

Tikal Stela 24 (Fig. 5.14) and Altar 7 (Fig. 5.15) are believed to have

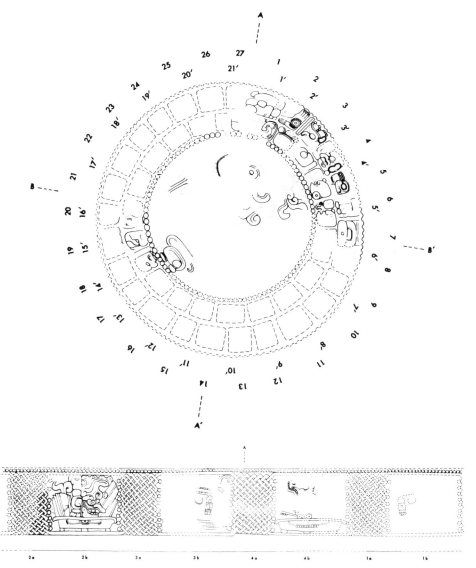

FIGURE 5.15 Tikal Altar 7, paired with Stela 24: (a) top, (b) sides (Jones and Satterthwaite 1982: Fig. 40; drawing by William R. Coe, courtesy of University of Pennsylvania Museum, Philadelphia, neg. #s Tikal 69-5-78, 69-5-79).

been carved by Yax Nun Ayin II's successor, nicknamed Dark Sun, and were set facing east in front of Temple III, which may have been Dark Sun's mortuary monument (Martin and Grube 2000:52–53; Montgomery 2001b:208). Like Stela 22, Stela 24 is slightly wedge-shaped. The face is extremely eroded, as are the extensive texts on the sides, but the date and motif have been tentatively reconstructed: the stela is believed to date to (9.19.0.0.0) 9 Ajaw 18 Mol (June 26, 810). It shows a ruler (Dark Sun?) performing a scattering rite and holding an elaborately knotted ceremonial bar. The text references the Paddlers, although the scene is too eroded to determine their presence. Schele and Grube (1995:99), noting the presence of a title, "Ab'ta," common in the Pasión region, suggest that "enemies" or captives taken in battle may have come to Tikal to participate in these period-ending ceremonies. Altar 7 shows a deity head in a footed dish (the "plate of the k'atun"?) and uses mat separators. Dark Sun is also believed to be the corpulent figure dressed in an elaborate jaguar suit and headdress, carrying a plain staff, and bearing a backrack with the head of a fleshless-jawed deity, that appears on Lintel 2, Temple III (Martin and Grube 2000:52).

Late Classic Period–ending Monuments in Tikal's Realm

Late Classic monuments displaying similar themes are found throughout central Petén, at sites in Tikal's immediate proximity and a short distance to the south around Lake Petén Itzá. Farther to the east and southeast, sites in the vicinity of Lake Yaxhá show iconographic ties, although this region of eastern Petén was in territory contested by Tikal, Calakmul, Caracol, and Naranjo (see Chap. 6).

In 1921, on the Tayasal peninsula, Morley found three stelae and a lintel around Structure T123 in Structure Group 25 (formerly Plaza A). This is probably a radial structure, described as a platform approximately 5.8 x 5.8 meters in the center of the plaza, topped with a small, square structure with a doorway on each side (Chase 1983:468, 976). Fragmentary Stela 1, tentatively dated to (9.17.0.0.0) 13 Ajaw 18 Kumk'u (January 22, 771), shows "a human figure seated cross-legged on a mask panel . . . [holding] a Ceremonial Bar in his left arm, the right hand grasping some other object" (Morley 1937–1938:427). "Stela" 2, possibly a lintel and in fragmentary condition, was discovered 11 meters north of Structure T123 and provisionally dated (9.19.0.0.0) 9 Ajaw 18 Mol (June 26, 810). Lintel 1, also broken, was tentatively dated (9.18.0.0.0) 11 Ajaw 18 Mak (October 9, 790).

Located approximately 3 kilometers from the northwest shore of Lake Petén Itzá, the site of Motul de San José is believed to be that identified by the "Ik'" sign in its Emblem Glyph. Alternatively, this Emblem might refer to several sites in this area, including Bejucal. Still a third possibility is that the Emblem might refer to the recently discovered large site known as Nixtun-Ch'ich' on the Candelaria peninsula on the western shore of Lake Petén Itzá. Regardless, these sites or the region are the only one(s) in the immediate Lake Petén Itzá region to have their own Emblem Glyphs (Stuart and Houston 1994:28, Fig. 28; see also Proskouriakoff 1993:150–151). The site referenced by the "Ik' Emblem" was one of four Terminal Classic capitals named on Stela 10 at Seibal (Marcus 1973, 1976). Motul Stela 1, broken and badly eroded, was provisionally dated to (9.19.0.0.0) 9 Ajaw 18 Mol (June 26, 810), whereas Stela 2 was thought to date a k'atun later, (10.0.0.0.0) 7 Ajaw 18 Sip (March 13, 830) (Morley 1937–1938:417). However, the scene of two dancers on Stela 2 suggests it dates no later than 9.19.0.0.0 (Proskouriakoff 1993:150–151).

Lakes Yaxhá and Sacnab are the easternmost lakes in the Petén chain. The toponyms of the sites of Yaxhá, Topoxté (both of which had Emblem Glyphs but Topoxte's lacked the *k'ul* prefix), and Sacnab are known from glyphic texts on Classic period monuments (Stuart and Houston 1994:5–7, 29), and these may be among the few place-names of the Petén lakes region to survive from Classic glyphic texts into twentieth-century use. Toponyms for both sites appear on monuments at Naranjo, Tikal, and La Naya.

Yaxhá, on the north shore of Lake Yaxhá, shows strong affiliations in material culture with Tikal, including an apparently unfinished twin-pyramid complex, but its inscriptions record repeated conquests by Naranjo, 12 kilometers to the northeast. Yaxhá's monuments are primarily Early Classic in date, and the bases of several, including Stelae 4, 6, and 10, have evidence of an earlier style of carving. This is also known on Actun Can Stela 1 and Nakbe Stela 1 (see also Justeson and Mathews 1983; Hammond 1982). Only two Late Classic stelae are known from Yaxhá.

Stela 13 was found recumbent in front of the westernmost pyramid in the site's twin-pyramid complex rather than in the stela enclosure. It shows a ruler depicted in frontal view, scattering, with a small ancestor figure peering down from the sky. The stela has a full basal panel under the standing figure. Proskouriakoff (1993:150) believed the monument commemorated the lajuntun of 9.17.10.0.0 12 Ajaw 8 Pax (November 30, 780), while suggesting that the twin-pyramid complex (in which Stela 13 was found) dates to 9.18.0.0.0 or later. Schele and Grube (1995:80; Grube 2000b:262) interpret the three dates on the monument as a series at peculiar four-year intervals: a possible date on the right might be 9.17.19.0.0 3 Ajaw 13 Pax (December 6, 789), the date on the front of the monument is 9.18.3.0.0 12 Ajaw 3 Mak (September 23, 793), and the one on the left side of the text records 9.18.7.0.0 9 Ajaw 3 Kej (September 2, 797).

Yaxhá's last dated monument is Stela 31, at 9.18.5.16.4 3 K'an 12 Yax (August 2, 796) (Grube 2000b:262–263; cf. Schele and Grube 1995:80, 82), and records a capture. The main figure is dancing with a small bound prisoner seated in front of him; a full basal panel is under his feet.

The Topoxté Islands lie off the southwestern shore of Lake Yaxhá near the mouth of the Río Ixtinto. Four sculptured stelae (Lundell 1934; Grube 2000b:267–268), as well as other small plain stelae in the main plaza, are known from the islands. Stelae 1 and 2 were found on the main island, Topoxté, west of the small, low platform opposite Structure D, the central structure of the island's Postclassic temple assemblage. Stela 3 was found in the center of Paxte Island at the southeast corner of a low platform, and Stela 4 was similarly positioned on Cante Island. Stelae 2 and 3 mention the Yaxhá Emblem Glyph and also the toponym for Topoxté itself, although the latter lacks the affixes for k'ul 'divine' and ajaw 'lord'. Stela 2 shows a figure depicted frontally, holding a staff; Stela 3 is a distinctly asymmetrical monument showing a seated figure. The Topoxté toponym also is known from Altar 5 at Tikal and a polychrome cylinder vase of unknown provenience (Grube 2000b:252).

Interpretations: Tikal's Late Classic May Seating

During the Late Classic period, the sites and populations around Lake Petén Itzá were subordinate to the site of Tikal to the north. Specifically, they were rotating k'atun seats (jetz' k'atun) within the realm Tikal ruled as seat of the 256-year may cycle of thirteen k'atuns.

The late monuments of the Tikal realm have been described as stylistically conservative because they primarily depict standard royal portraiture scenes (Mathews 1985:52; Jones 1991:120; Miller 1993:362). The mythical or historical ancestors floating in scrolls of clouds, blood, or smoke from burning incense above the principal figure are considered archaisms, because they harken back to Early Classic Tikal Stela 31 and other monuments. However, as I have argued earlier (Rice 1997), I believe this "conservatism" is not a mere stylistic rerun but rather a major politico-religious revitalization asserting dynastic revival and power (see also Martin and Grube 2000:44–53).

Significantly, these Late Classic stelae at and around Tikal display a number of themes, images, and elements that have precedents in the site's Early and Middle Classic monuments celebrating k'atun endings. The ruler's regalia is of special importance, typically a jaguar-skin kilt and a feathered backrack holding a deity image; in the Middle Classic, rulers wore nearly identical sandals, whereas in the Late Classic they were sometimes depicted barefoot. Throughout the Classic period, rulers held knotted staffs or bars; in the Middle Classic, they were tripartite and held vertically in front; and in the Late Classic, they were more elaborate and cradled in one or both arms. Rulers stood on or in front of prone, bound captives, or captives appeared on paired altars. The sides or peripheries of the altars were often encircled by ropes, sometimes joining four mat motifs that established quadripartite space; similar altars are also seen on carved lintels (see Fig. 5.9) depicting rulers seated on thrones. And divine ancestors floated above the ruler in clouds of incense smoke in the Late and especially the Terminal Classic.

How does the imagery on these Classic monuments conform to the imagery and ritual of the k'atun and *may* ceremonies as known or reconstructed from the early Colonial period lowlands? We have seen that these ceremonies were celebrated in "dramas" of thirteen "acts." Eight (perhaps ten) of these can be posited to have direct material connections to the Late Classic period-ending celebrations taking place in Tikal's twin-pyramid groups.

Act 8: Ceremonial Circuit (and/or Act 11: Pacing of the K'atun). This was a counterclockwise procession around the town or the realm, presumably led by priests or the ruler and involving measurement of the land and confirmation of land titles. Similar processionals occurred as part of annual Wayeb' rites (Coe 1965) and in modern times. At various points in the b'ak'tun ceremony held in 1618 (Edmonson 1986:25–27), god-impersonators, priests, or yearbearers conducted fire ritual and carried World Tree symbols and surveying sticks (*p'iz te*). These might be analogs of the staffs and bars carried by rulers depicted on Classic stelae.

It is likely that ritual circuits originated in the Preclassic or earlier: at the Late Preclassic site of Izapa on the Pacific coast, the placement of some two hundred fifty stone monuments in various plazas may have been in accordance with a ceremonial procession (Lowe, Lee, and Martínez 1982:31; Kappelman 2001; Rice n.d.a). With reference to the Classic period, Baudez (1991) discussed such perambulations commemorating Late Classic period endings, especially k'atun endings, at Copán. He viewed the sites as cosmograms and argued that such ritual processions would have been associated with radial temples and other cruciform structures, including orthogonal causeways, or sakb'es. He also noted relationships between these kinds of structures and the representation of the Maya tzolk'in calendar in the Madrid Codex, with its four arms to the cardinal directions and footprints marking symbolic ritual paths. A virtually identical representation is seen in the Mexican Codex Fejérváry-Mayer.

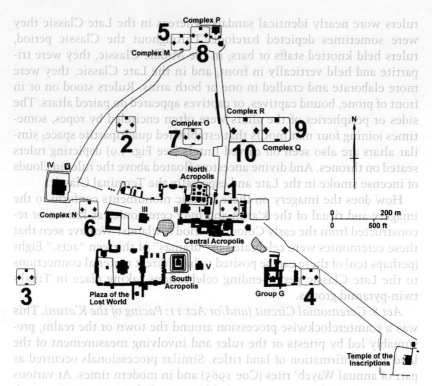

FIGURE 5.16 Diagram of hypothesized counterclockwise ritual circuits at Tikal based on locations of twin-pyramid groups. The groups are numbered here in order of hypothesized (Early Classic) and known (Late Classic) dates of construction, beginning with number 1, now destroyed, under the East Plaza, just to the east of the Great Plaza. Number 4 is conjectural. Twin-pyramid icons not to scale.

At Tikal, it is likely that such processionals were an important part of k'atun-ending ritual, as all the twin-pyramid groups known at the site are located adjacent to one or more of the site's three causeways. Indeed, the locations of several sequentially built twin-pyramid groups suggest that they themselves may have marked counterclockwise circuits around the site by the late Late Classic (Fig. 5.16): beginning with Complex M (constructed in 692) in the north, a procession would move southwest along the Maudslay Causeway to Complex N (711) lying at the west end of the Tozzer Causeway, then northeastward (without benefit of an extant causeway) to Complex O (731?), and from there along the northern half of the Maler Causeway to Complex P (751), just to the east of Complex M.

Such processions could have been initiated in earlier examples of these assemblages, but these are not well dated because carved stelae were not found in the northern enclosures. The earliest twin-pyramid complex known thus far, Jones's (1969) 5E-1sub, is located east of the Great Plaza at the southern end of the Maler Causeway and may date to the late fifth or early sixth century. Presumably next in the sequence, to judge from a counterclockwise perambulation, would be Group 4D-2 to the northwest, south of the Maudslay Causeway. The third in this hypothetical sequence would be Group 5B-1, farther to the southwest, well away from causeways. If the procession model holds, I would not be surprised if a fourth twin-pyramid group, not yet identified archaeologically, might lie somewhere to the south or southeast of the Great Plaza to complete the ritual circuit. It would probably lie under Group G, the Temple of the Inscriptions, or the Late Classic Méndez Causeway, which joins these complexes to the Great Plaza. In any case, these complexes could have celebrated k'atun endings beginning perhaps as early as 9.2.0.0.0.

The next twin-pyramid complex, Group M, well dated at 692, represents a reinvigorated Late Classic tradition and a new circuit, described above, inaugurated by the new ruler, Jasaw Kan K'awil I, who may have begun erecting carved stelae in the northern enclosures. It is of interest that these hypothesized processions begin near, and may have continued to pass through, the Great Plaza.

Act 9: Seating of the K'atun (and/or Act 12: Counting of the Mats). In the Colonial period, the new b'alam, or jaguar priest, of the k'atun took his place on the "mat of the k'atun" in the cycle seat after having been selected ten years earlier in mid-k'atun. No evidence of this part of the ceremonies is clearly seen on the period-ending stelae, although Stela 20 and other representations (e.g., lintels) show rulers sitting on jaguar skin–covered seats or stools marked on the sides with mat motifs. In this light, the altars with mat motifs in Late Classic twin-pyramid groups could be symbolic thrones.

Act 10: Seating of the Yearbearers. This probably represents the seating of the yearbearer for the incoming year. As discussed above, some of the rulers shown on the stelae are carrying a burden, or kuch, represented by an elaborate backrack holding a deity head, which may be the yearbearer or other quadripartite god such as skybearers or the gods of wind, sun, death, rain and lightning, and fire.

Act 11: Pacing of the K'atun. This may have been similar to or a component of the procession in Act 8.

Act 12: Dawn. At this time the mats of the lords were "counted" (i.e., ranked) and candidates for various civic and ritual duties in the coming period declared their intentions. Again, as in Act 9, this may be alluded to by the presence of quadripartite mat motifs on the sides of altars, signifying the establishment of ritual order in the four corners of the world.

Act 13: Sacrifice (see also Act 16: Penance). In the Colonial period, sacrifices were carried out in a variety of ways—heart removal, hanging, burning, drowning—all accompanied by music. At Tikal, the sacrificial victim is clearly the prone, bound prisoner lying under or behind the ruler's feet or on the accompanying altar. This distinctive imagery was also present on Early Classic period-ending monuments. In the Late and Terminal Classic, if not earlier, sacrifice was carried out in the context of ballgame ritual (see Chap. 8).

Act 14: Examination. This consisted of a ceremonial feast and ritual riddling, an interrogation intended to demonstrate the rulers' knowledge and therefore their right to rule. At Late Classic Tikal, this activity might have taken place in the nine-doorway palace on the southern side of the plaza complex, or elsewhere at the site, perhaps in a popol naj (council house).

Act 15: The Word. In the Postclassic and Colonial periods, the new chilam, the "speaker" of the jaguar priest, announced the prophecy, or "word" (*mut*), for the upcoming k'atun with grandly poetic imagery. This probably has no surviving material counterparts, as the prophecy and history of the k'atuns were doubtless scribed in bark-paper books.

Act 16: Penance. This is likely a reference to bloodletting by the year-bearers, the priesthood, and the jaguar priest. It is probably represented on Classic stelae by references to bloodletting and "scattering." In the books of the chilam b'alams, there is also frequent mention of objects and containers, such as rattles, gourds, bowls, plates, and cups of the k'atun, which might be identifiable in Classic period material culture. For example, Late Classic plates of the k'atun—slipped ceramic vessels with painted central Ajaw glyphs—were found in burials: a plate in Tikal Burial 77 was painted with 13 Ajaw 12 (A.D. 771, 780), and an eroded but similarly painted vessel came from Burial 191. (Elsewhere, at Topoxté, Burial 49 included an orange-polychrome tripod plate with Ajaw 13 painted in the center [Hermes 2000:Fig. 142.1], and in Burial 128 at Altar de Sacrificios, two tripod plates—painted red over an orange background, with a green stuccoed rim—bore a 12 Ajaw in the center [Adams 1971:66, 76–78, Fig. 89]. These plates, which Richard E. W. Adams describes as possible imports from the Usumacinta area, accompanied a high-status individual who is believed to have died between 9.16.2.0.0 and 9.16.3.0.0. A 12 Ajaw day falls on November 12, 753 [9.16.2.10.0 12 Ajaw 3 Muwan].)

Act 17: Commemoration of the Ancestors. Given Colonial period references to the erection of stelae (at Mayapán), wooden poles, and then crosses every twenty years in Yucatán, it requires no stretch of the imagination to envision that this was when a stone stela was erected or unwrapped (Stuart 1996) during the Classic period and even earlier in the

Preclassic. That in the Late Classic these stelae were erected in the northern portion of a plaza, symbolic home of the ancestors, and that both early and late monuments in the Tikal region depicted symbolic ancestors (Paddlers) in the "sky" above the ruler, establishes a clear precursor of this Colonial period practice.

The last three acts of the Late Postclassic and early Colonial period celebrations (Act 18: Counting of the K'atun; Act 19: Farce; and Act 20: Sermon) have no immediately recognizable material correlates in the Classic record at Tikal. They likely were public dramas, dances, and other rituals enacted on the summits of the twin pyramids to entertain and inspire awe in a populace gathered in the plaza below.

Tikal and Its *May* Realm in the Terminal Classic Period

In the past twenty years or so, there have been major shifts in thinking about the Terminal Classic and Postclassic periods in both the northern and southern lowlands (Chase and Rice 1985; Sabloff and Andrews 1986; Webster 2002; Demarest, Rice, and Rice 2004). In both areas, Postclassic lowland Maya civilization is recognized as something distinctly different from that of the Classic period, but the strong continuities that exist are rarely highlighted (cf. Marcus 1993). The Terminal Classic is the period during which these continuities and changes sorted themselves out.

In the southern lowlands, the Terminal Classic is traditionally identified with the so-called collapse of Classic Maya civilization, characterized by the cessation of erection of carved, dated stelae; a decline in architectural construction, mortuary ritual, and polychrome pottery production; and the abandonment of large Classic period centers. The Terminal Classic demise has been interpreted as reflecting widespread social, political, economic, dynastic, and demographic upheaval. Given this catastrophist scenario, it is not surprising that when addressing the Terminal Classic in the southern lowlands, archaeologists have tended to focus rather single-mindedly on determining the cause(s) for the collapse (see Culbert 1973), including war, invasion, epidemic disease, and natural disasters. Subsequent investigations, however, have acknowledged that the crisis was first apparent in the arena of elite power (e.g., the fall of some dynasties) and the region was not totally depopulated.

The *may* hypothesis posits a different scenario. In this model, the Terminal Classic period is the second half of Tikal's "official" tenure as full Late Classic *may* seat beginning in the K'atun 8 Ajaw of 672 to 692 (its earlier role as incoming "guest" would have coincided with the 128-year hiatus, during which it was also the outgoing seat; see Chap. 4). During the first half of its full tenure, 692–820, Tikal ruled alone as *may ku*; then during the second half, 820–948, the next K'atun 8 Ajaw, Tikal would have shared rule with the incoming cycle seat. During this latter interval, as during the last half of its Middle Classic *may* cycle, Tikal would have experienced an expected and preordained reduction of activity in its architectural and iconographic programs. Through this line of reasoning, I consider the Terminal Classic period, traditionally dated circa 790/800–950/1000 in the southern lowlands, to encompass the 128-year interval from 820 to 948; in the Maya calendar, this is from 9.19.10.0.0 8 Ajaw 8 Xul to 10.6.0.0.0 8 Ajaw 8 Yax.

Monuments and Themes

Only one period-ending stela is known to have been erected at Tikal itself during the Terminal Classic period, but sites of probable k'atun seats within its realm regularly celebrated k'atun and lajuntun endings by erecting carved, dated monuments. Similar shapes and a shared iconographic program plus display of the Tikal Emblem Glyph on these stelae and altars bespeak continued recognition of Tikal as a politico-religious power in northeastern Petén (Rice 1997). Terminal Classic monuments in the realm maintained many of the characteristics of the Late Classic styles, as described above, and added others:

- Shape: Instead of being parallel-sided, Terminal Classic stelae often exhibit marked asymmetry and are "wedge-shaped," broader at the top and narrower at the base.
- Calendrics: These monuments celebrate period-ending dates, especially k'atuns and lajuntuns, and there is relatively scant reference to completion of b'ak'tun 9, on 10.0.0.0.0, in 830. As on the Late Classic monuments, dates on these late stelae are shown as Calendar Round rather than Long Count dates and as such are primarily reconstructions.
- Primary theme: As on Late Classic stelae, Terminal Classic monuments in the Tikal region show a central dignitary who wears a feathered headdress and jaguar-pelt kilt, carries a ceremonial staff or bar, and scatters. He is often standing atop or in front of bound, prone captives, which may also appear on an accompanying altar.
- Secondary theme: Many Terminal Classic stelae highlight the Paddler Gods (or sky figures, cloud riders; Marcus 1992a:297; Proskouriakoff 1993:185), one to four humanlike figures entwined in large scrolls or S-shapes with dotted borders floating above the central personage.
- Additional iconographic elements and themes are quadripartite designs, mat and rope motifs, and all-glyphic monuments.

- Location: Some Terminal Classic or Cycle 10 stelae in Petén are found at sites with significant Postclassic occupation, many suggesting repositioning or reuse.

The theme of "cloud riders" in dotted scrolls on these stelae merits further discussion. For a time the S-shapes or scrolls were believed to represent blood, a sacred substance that serves as "a physical background for supernatural beings" (Stuart 1988:184), and the logograph for cloud (*muyal*, T632; Stuart and Houston 1994:44–45, Fig. 51). They can also be identified as the undulating, serpentlike Milky Way, path to the Maya Underworld of Xibalba, and Hofling (pers. comm., September 19, 1996) connects them to serpents, the Vision Serpent, in particular. The Vision Serpent is also seen on the Hauberg Stela, dated A.D. 197, which shows the ruler letting blood, with four small human or god figures—forerunners of the Late Classic Paddlers—clambering around the serpent's body; an ancestor head looks down from the Vision Serpent's mouth.

I believe, however, that these "cloud scrolls" or representations of "blood" are instead representations of clouds of smoke of burning incense, the congealed sap of the copal tree (*Protium copal*) or other resinous trees or shrubs. The key here is the dots that line the scrolls: these are the same dots that are part of the glyph for incense, or pom (T647, 687), and the dots that are shown in the scattering glyph and gesture. They are also the dots that surround the "k'ul" element of Emblem Glyphs identifying *may* and k'atun seats and ajaws as divine. Similarly, these dots occur in a number of other glyphs where, I believe, they function to indicate a sacred, ritual, or divine element or essence. Incense or pom is the substance used by the Maya to cleanse, purify, and sanctify sacred space and also to call forth the ancestors; incense may be burned in pottery incensarios or molded into balls and studded with beads as offerings. Related to this, a verb (*ati*) associated with these scenes of human figures riding on clouds has recently been deciphered as "to bathe," with the interpretation "'bathing the ritual' . . . [as] an act of consecration [through] ritual purification" (Stuart, Houston, and Robertson 1999:169). The "bathing" here is clearly immersion in the perfumed smoke of burning incense.

The humanlike figures in the incense clouds are ancestors, a depiction that goes back to Preclassic Olmec, Izapan, and Pacific coast art. Late La Venta Stela 3, with six human figures floating above the central personage, is a particularly close comparison to the Terminal Classic scenes in the Tikal area. More specifically, these figures are identical to the aged Paddler Gods identified on a carved bone from Tikal Burial 116

FIGURE 5.17 A carved bone from Tikal Burial 116, showing the Paddler Gods in a canoe (courtesy of University of Pennsylvania Museum, Philadelphia, neg. # Tikal 63-5-87).

(Fig. 5.17): deceased ancestors paddling the canoe that carries kings and gods to the Underworld. According to Quiriguá Stela C, the Paddlers oversaw creation and "planted" three hearthstones in the sky; these are the three stars in the belt in the Orion constellation (Montgomery 2001a:302).

David Stuart (1988:189; see also Miller and Taube 1993:128) notes that two of the four figures in the upper register of Ixlú Stela 2 (below, Fig. 5.23) appear to be human warriors and two are Roman-nosed deity figures. Of the latter he writes, "[T]he left figure is marked by a large, round eye, a jaguar-head cap, and feline paws and tail. These identify him as the Jaguar God of the Underworld. The right figure also has a round eye, but his distinctive traits include a fish-head (?) cap and a bone or stingray spine placed through his septum" (Stuart 1988:189). The two Paddlers are often distinguished by ak'b'al (night) and k'in (sun, day) glyphs, respectively, distinctions that can be traced to the Late Preclassic period, with the identification of ak'b'al and k'in glyphs on the incised jade Pomona Flare (Freidel and Schele 1988a:558; see also Justeson, Norman, and Hammond 1988).

Tikal Stela 11 and Altar 11 were found in a line of (primarily Early Classic) stelae and altars on the northern edge of the Main Plaza, in front of the North Acropolis. They are the latest and only Terminal Classic monuments at Tikal, dating to 10.2.0.0.0 3 Ajaw 3 Kej (August 15, 869). Although Stela 11 (Fig. 5.18) is unusual for the Terminal Classic in that it uses an IS Introducing Glyph and is not wedge-shaped, it portrays two Paddler sky figures and a segmented, decorated border. The central scene shows a ruler holding a large quadripartite ceremonial bar and performing a scattering rite; he is wearing a feathered backrack holding a deity head with fleshless jaw. A bound captive is evident behind his feet. The monument's text refers to the "lineage house," to Tikal's founder, to the thirtieth successor, and gives the name Jasaw Kan K'awil II (Schele and

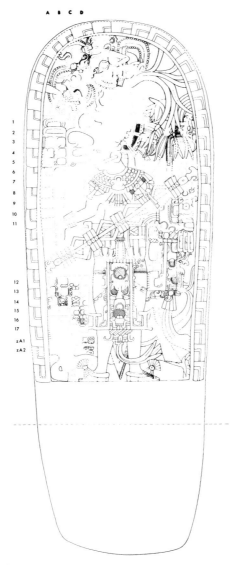

FIGURE 5.18 Tikal Stela 11, dated 10.2.0.0.0 3 Ajaw 3 Kej (August 15, 869), set at the base of the North Acropolis (Jones and Satterthwaite 1982:Fig. 16; drawing by William R. Coe, courtesy of University of Pennsylvania Museum, Philadelphia, neg. # Tikal 69-5-54).

Grube 1995:127; Martin and Grube 2000:53), who may be the ruler depicted. The placement of Jasaw Kan K'awil II's monument in front of the North Acropolis may be homage to his eponymous ancestor, his dramatic building program, and the hallowed burial ground of his dynastic predecessors.

Other Sites in Tikal's Terminal Classic May Realm
UAXACTÚN AND JIMBAL

Uaxactún, 20 kilometers north of Tikal, has four late stelae commemorating k'atun endings in the Group A main plaza. Two of these have reconstructed dates of 9.19.0.0.0 (Stelae 7 and 14) and another, Stela 13, commemorates the end of the b'ak'tun with a Long Count date of 10.0.0.0.0 7 Ajaw 18 Sip (830). The ruler's name on the monument is Olom Chik'in Chakte (Valdés and Fahsen 2004). Stela 12, which is not wedge-shaped, dates to (10.3.0.0.0) 1 Ajaw 3 Yaxk'in (May 2, 889) and shows the Tikal ruler with the "west kalomte'" title, and Uaxactún king K'al Chik'in Chakte, celebrating the period ending by scattering. The text ends by recording the arrival of a third unidentified individual (ibid.).

The site of Jimbal, 12.5 kilometers north of central Tikal, has been regarded as a "tertiary center" in Classic lowland Maya site hierarchy schemes (e.g., Marcus 1976: Table 13), as it lacks its own Emblem Glyph and has a small number of plazas. Six Terminal Classic stelae and four altars were reported from the site (Jones and Satterthwaite 1982:110–12). Jimbal Stela 1 (Fig. 5.19), dated to (10.2.10.0.0) 2 Ajaw 13 Ch'en (June 24, 879), was found with Altar 1 on the east side of the main plaza. The stela text announces that the ruler, identified as an "ochk'in kalomte'," scattered on the half period and played the ballgame, and refers to the Paddlers as itzat, or artists and sages (Pugh 1999). It also incorporates three square glyph cartouches that give the sequential day names 12 Chikchan, 13 Kimi, and 1 Manik' (12 Snake, 13 Death, and 1 Deer). These days, the significance of which is unclear, would have occurred either seven weeks earlier (April 30–May 2, 879) or nearly seven months after (January 15–17, 880) the dedication date in June. Stela 1 has a decorated border and shows a ruler standing with his head in profile, holding a round shield and a God K or manikin scepter, with two Paddler Gods in dotted S-shaped motifs above him. The one on the left, the jaguar Paddler, has animal feet and is scattering.

Jimbal Stela 2 (Fig. 5.20), with its companion Altar 2, was found in the center of the plaza. The stela, with an IS date of 10.3.0.0.0 1 Ajaw 3 Yaxk'in (May 2, 889), is a small, wedge-shaped monument with a deco-

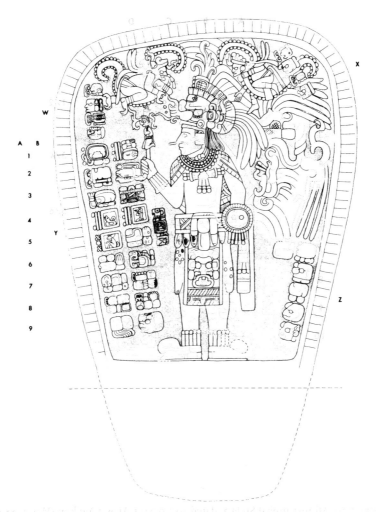

FIGURE 5.19 Jimbal Stela 1, dated (10.2.10.0.0) 2 Ajaw 13 Ch'en (June 24, 879); note Paddler Gods in the "sky" above the ruler and squared glyph cartouches at A-B4 and A5 (Jones and Satterthwaite 1982:Fig. 78; drawing by William R. Coe, courtesy of University of Pennsylvania Museum, Philadelphia, neg. # Tikal 69-5-133).

rated border. Lacking a figural scene, it consists entirely of glyphs: one indicates scattering, and another is the Tikal Emblem Glyph. The text may indicate that Jimbal's ruler was the son of Olom Chik'in Chakte of Uaxactún (Valdés and Fahsen 2004). It also incorporates the same three day names in square glyph cartouches as on Stela 1. Altar 2 is unusually small and has a decorated border.

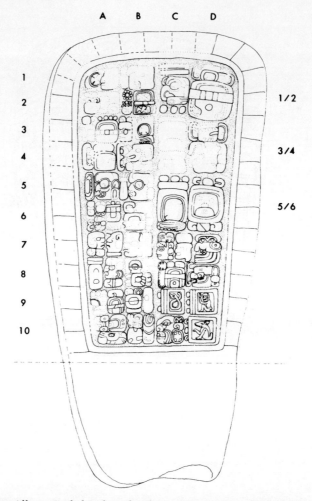

FIGURE 5.20 All-text Jimbal Stela 2, dated 10.3.0.0.0 1 Ajaw 3 Yaxk'in (May 2, 889), is read in unusual order: D–C, then A–B; note squared glyph cartouches (Jones and Satterthwaite 1982:Fig. 79; drawing by William R. Coe, courtesy of University of Pennsylvania Museum, Philadelphia, neg. # Tikal 69-5-134).

LAKES MACANCHÉ AND SALPETÉN

The basins of Lakes Macanché and Salpetén, just to the east of the main arm of Lake Petén Itzá, witnessed transitional settlement from Classic through Terminal Classic into Postclassic times. Stelae dating to the Late and Terminal Classic periods adhere closely to the canons of traditional Tikal and Tikal-related iconography and themes.

At Yalain, a small site on the western edge of the Lake Macanché basin, a plain stela and altar were found in the large Main Plaza; Stela 1 had the asymmetrical shape characteristic of Terminal Classic monuments in this region but is otherwise undatable.

Zacpetén, the peninsular site on the north shore of Lake Salpetén (Pugh 2001a), saw occupation beginning in the Middle Preclassic period, but its major constructions and occupation date to the Terminal Classic and Postclassic. In 1980 two stelae were discovered in Plaza B, a probable twin-pyramid complex. While Stela 2 was plain, the slightly wedge-shaped Stela 1 (Fig. 5.21) lay in two pieces, with its carved but heavily eroded face up. It showed a principal figure standing in profile, facing the viewer's left, performing the scattering rite, holding a ceremonial bar diagonally in his left arm, and wearing an ornate plumed headdress.

During 1996 excavations around Structure 601 on the south side of

FIGURE 5.21 Zacpetén Stela 1 was found in Plaza B, a probable twin-pyramid complex (photograph by Don S. Rice).

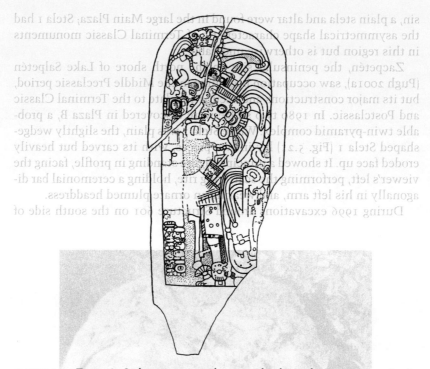

FIGURE 5.22 Zacpetén Stela 4, reset into the east side of Postclassic Structure 601 in Group A (field drawing by Paulino Morales).

Zacpetén's Group A, a Postclassic temple assemblage, two stelae—one plain (Stela 3) and one carved—were discovered. Carved Stela 4 (Fig. 5.22), mortared into the eastern side of the substructure, showed a single figure in profile, facing the viewer's left, possibly scattering, and wearing a large headdress and a feathered back ornament. Above the figure was a dotted scroll holding a human figure. Stela 4 is parallel-sided rather than wedge-shaped, but stylistically it appears to date to the very Late Classic or Terminal Classic period. Preliminary readings (David Stuart, pers. comm., 1994; Rockmore 1998) suggest a Calendar Round date beginning with 7 or 8 Ajaw (possibly 9.19.10.0.0 or 10.0.0.0.0). There also may be a *sak-pet* logograph and reference to Paddlers.

Elsewhere in Group A at Zacpetén, a plain stela (Stela 5) and a broken carved altar (Altar 1) were incorporated into the construction of the platform of Structure 606a/b, facing south into the plaza. Altar 1 (Fig. 5.23) was broken into two halves, each half placed to the side of the plain stela. The unusual design consists of a large central element (a serpent deity? mask) surrounded by a narrow ring of glyphs. The broad outside design is quadripartite, with four blocks of four glyphs separated by four large mat elements. According to Houston (pers. comm., August 28, 1997), the thirty-six glyphs in the ring and blocks are read in a continuous text. The text begins with a Distance Number Introductory Glyph referring to 10.0.0.0.0, suggesting that the altar was originally placed with a stela and the text is continuous from that monument. He suggests the text records a birth on the winter solstice of A.D. 809, with the father having Tikal connections. The central emblem is a toponymic "icon" bearing the signs ik', k'an, and nal (Stuart, pers. comm., September 14, 1998). Nikolai Grube (pers. comm., June 18, 1998), however, believes the text refers to the accession on 9.16.0.16.8 5 Lamat 16 Sip (March 30, 752; soon after the beginning of a K'atun 13 Ajaw) of Zacpetén's ruler, K'inich Pa-?. This individual claimed to be the son of the Tikal ruler Yik'in Kan K'awil (Ruler B) and held the titles Aj Chak Kalomte' and Aj K'al B'ak (He of 20 Captives).

Ixlú, a heretofore poorly known site on the isthmus between the eastern end of Lake Petén Itzá and the western edge of Lake Salpetén, has been regarded as a "tertiary"-level site in hierarchical approaches to

FIGURE 5.23 Zacpetén Altar 1, broken in two and set into the facade of Structure 606 in Group A, dates ca. 10.0.0.0.0? (A.D. 830) (drawing by David Stuart).

Late Classic political geography (Marcus 1976). Like Zacpetén, this site was occupied beginning in the Middle Preclassic, but its significant occupation dates to the Terminal Classic and Postclassic. The site did not have its own Emblem Glyph, but the presence of the Tikal Emblem on Altar 1 suggests Ixlú had close relations with that *may* seat. In addition, Ixlú has an undated twin-pyramid complex and fragments of a carved stela were noted in its stela enclosure.

Ixlú Stela 1 (Fig. 5.24), dated (10.1.10.0.0) 4 Ajaw 13 Kank'in (October 7, 859), depicts a lord almost identical to the ruler on Tikal Stelae 5, 20, and 11: wearing a jaguar kilt, bearing an enormous back ornament with a deity head, holding a quadripartite staff with four sets of knots, and scattering. Behind the principal individual is a seated, bearded subsidiary figure. Above is a complex scene of the Paddlers—four human figures, warriors above and Roman-nosed below—in S-shapes and dotted scrollwork.

Ixlú Stela 2 (Fig. 5.25) was originally dated by Morley (1937–1938: 441–443) as a lajuntun ending (10.2.10.0.0) 2 Ajaw 13 Ch'en (June 24, 879), the same date as Jimbal Stela 1. On the basis of the iconography, however, I disagree with the recent revision of this date (Schele and Grube 1995:118) to 10.0.19.4.11 9 Chuwen 14 Sip (March 2, 849), marking an accession. The monument shows a profiled central figure scattering, wearing a jaguar-skin kilt and an ornate feathered headdress, and holding a God K or manikin scepter (Stuart 1988:184; Schele and Miller 1986:Fig. IV.2). He also appears to be carrying a backrack. Four sky figures in dotted cloud scrolls float above the central individual. The iconography strongly suggests a period-ending date for the monument.

Ixlú Altar 1 (Fig. 5.26), now set into a cement wall on the main plaza of Flores Island, has a date of (10.2.10.0.0) 2 Ajaw 13 Ch'en (June 24, 879), a lajuntun ending. The altar's face consists only of heavily eroded glyphs. Houston (pers. comm., 1994) reads the text as, "'in the middle of his 10th tun' 'he seated/offered the stone' (referring to the dedication of the altar) and 'he scattered the drops' . . . 'he of the 20 captives.'" This is the same epithet used on Altar 1 at Zacpetén, and both monuments may refer to the same individual. The individual referred to here is apparently the ruler of Ixlú named Aj K'al Bak Tok'ak'il, who celebrated the occasion in the company of an unknown person who was a [kalomte'] (Schele and Grube 1995:136), probably from Tikal.

I see this text as confirming the mid-k'atun ritual of seating the cycle, reading it as "he seated the tun or k'atun" in the initial ten-year role as "guest host," in preparation for full responsibility ten years hence, in a K'atun 1 Ajaw. Schele and Freidel (1990:389) suggest the Ixlú ruler may be claiming status as k'ul ajaw (divine lord) over Tikal. According to the *may* model, however, he would be claiming the right to rule over the

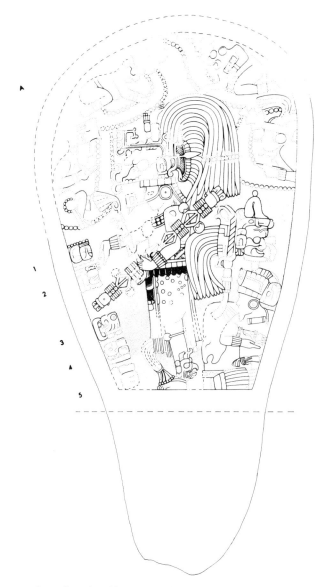

FIGURE 5.24 Ixlú Stela 1, dated (10.1.10.0.0) 4 Ajaw 13 Kank'in (October 5, 859) (Jones and Satterthwaite 1982: Fig. 80; drawing by William R. Coe, courtesy of University of Pennsylvania Museum, Philadelphia, neg. # Tikal 70-5-124).

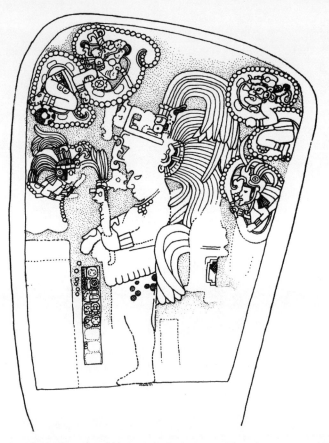

FIGURE 5.25 Ixlú Stela 2, dated (10.2.10.0.0) 2 Ajaw 13 Ch'en (June 22, 879) (drawing by Linda Schele, © David Schele, courtesy Foundation for the Advancement of Mesoamerican Studies, Inc.).

next k'atun as conferred by Tikal as cycle seat. The Paddler Gods are mentioned, but the remainder of the text on Altar 1 is not clearly understood. One interpretation (Schele, Grube, and Boot 1995 : 12; Schele and Grube 1995 : 136) suggests a reference to a "regional lord" holding the title chakte' (now read kalomte'), a title associated with the Late Classic "Tlaloc-Venus war complex," who came to Ixlú and participated in the ceremonies. Another interpretation (Houston, pers. comm., 1994), however, sees the text as referring to "a version of Chak, 'K'an tun Chak.' The 'K'an tun' or 'yellow stone' occasionally refers to objects like this altar."

I believe there might be some relationship between this stone and Landa's description of Colonial period rites during Wayeb' days when Kan was yearbearer and the incoming yearbearer was Muluk. Keeping in mind that Colonial period yearbearers (K'an, Muluk, Ix, Kawak) are one day later than those of the Campeche calendar (Ak'b'al, Lamat, Ben, Etz'nab'), the yearbearer on 10.2.10.0.0 was Lamat, corresponding to Muluk. The ritual for Muluk (and so Lamat?) days involved bloodletting using a stone called the Chak Akantun (Thompson 1999:235), perhaps the "k'an tun Chak" identified by Houston.

Ixlú Altar 2 was discovered in December 1993, just before the initiation of the 1994 field season of Proyecto Maya-Colonial. The poorly preserved sculptured scene (Fig. 5.27) has two registers, each with two seated, facing figures. The figures in the upper register are probably nobles, but neither is elaborately attired: both wear pectorals, and the figure on the right sports a feathered headdress. The individual in the lower right is obviously a captive, with bowed head and arms tied behind his back. According to Houston (pers. comm., 1994), this altar portrays the presentation of a captive to a principal lord in a palace; alternatively, the figure opposite the captive could be a woman offering a drink. Houston suggests the altar dates sometime after 800, roughly 9.18.0.0.0 or 9.19.0.0.0. Héctor Escobedo (pers. comm., 1994) estimates a later date of 10.1.0.0.0 (849) on stylistic grounds and suggests that the figure in the upper right may have an Emblem Glyph, possibly Tikal's. I am inclined toward this latter and later date.

FIGURE 5.26 Ixlú Altar 1 (drawing by Linda Schele, © David Schele, courtesy Foundation for the Advancement of Mesoamerican Studies, Inc.).

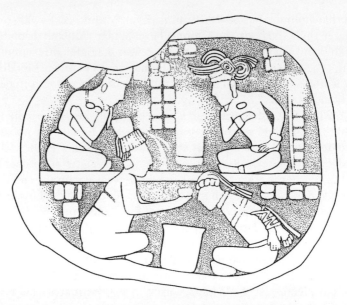

FIGURE 5.27 Ixlú Altar 2, discovered in 1994 (field drawing by Paulino Morales).

Overview

On the basis of architectural, iconographic, and epigraphic data, the following sites were suggested as possible k'atun seats in Tikal's Preclassic *may* (or proto-*may*) seating: Uaxactún, El Perú, Bejucal, Nakbe, and, to judge from close similarities of Preclassic ceramic complexes, probably several sites in the Petén lakes region.

During the Early and Middle Classic period, Tikal's *may* realm included at least six k'atun seats, as determined by the presence of E-Groups (E) and period-ending monuments (M): Uaxactún (EM), Yaxhá (EM), Xultún (EM), El Zapote (M), Uolantún (M), and El Perú (M). Additional sites constructed E-Groups or variants (E), but dated period-ending monuments are thus far lacking: Ucanal, Nakum, Ixtinto, Chalpate, Holtún, La Tractorada, Cenote, Paxcamán, and Tayasal. In addition, El Encanto, Corozal, and El Temblor had monuments mentioning Tikal's Early Classic rulers, but these stelae are thought to have been moved from Tikal to the small peripheral sites at some later time, perhaps during the period immediately after central Mexican contact. In addition, Río Azul was very likely a Tikal satellite, although it lacks both period-ending stelae and, apparently, the E-Group assemblage. Ucanal seems to have been part of this system, if only briefly, as its ruler in the early fifth century was a yajaw of Tikal's king.

During Tikal's Late Classic *may* seating, some of the earlier k'atun seats continued and new ones were added, judging from the presence of twin-pyramid groups (T) and erection of period-ending monuments (M): Uaxactún (M), Motul de San José (M), Ixlú (TM), Zacpetén (TM), Chalpate (T), Uolantún (T), and Tayasal (M). The positions of Yaxhá (T), Nakum (M), and Ucanal (M) are difficult to assess, because these sites seem to have been in a region contested by Calakmul, Caracol, and Naranjo. It is interesting, however, that the Late Classic ceramic complexes of Yaxhá and Calakmul are very closely tied to (i.e., full sphere participants in) the better-known ones of central Petén, that is, Tikal and Uaxactún (Rice and Forsyth 2004).

In the Terminal Classic, Tikal's *may* seating would have involved Uaxactún, Jimbal, Ixlú, Zacpetén, El Perú, Motul de San José?, and perhaps also Yaxhá/Topoxté and Nakum. It is useful in this regard to recall Marcus's (1976) model of political geography, which proposed nine centers within the Tikal regional state: Naranjo, Aguateca, and Machaquilá as secondary sites; Jimbal, Ixlú, and Uaxactún as tertiary; and El Encanto, Xultún, and Nakum as quaternary. New evidence accumulated since she proposed this model requires that El Perú, Motul de San José?, and probably Yaxhá be added to the list and that Naranjo be eliminated because of its affiliation with Calakmul. In addition, it is now known that several of these sites—Yaxhá, Topoxté, Xultún, and Motul de San José?—have their own Late Classic Emblem Glyphs, often assumed to be an indicator of some degree of political independence. In particular, since Xultún's stelae do not share features of monuments in the Tikal realm, it is more likely that it was a satellite of Calakmul.

It is difficult to identify Tikal's successor, the midcycle incoming *may* seat to rule during the Early Postclassic period (948–1204) in central Petén. On the basis of epigraphic, iconographic, architectural, ceramic, and settlement continuities from the Late Classic through the Terminal Classic and into the Postclassic periods, Ixlú and Zacpetén might have been likely candidates. Another possibility is the newly discovered site of Nixtun-Ch'ich', on the Candelaria peninsula on the western end of Lake Petén Itzá. However, the east-west socioethnic divisions characteristic of Postclassic Yucatán also seem to be present in Terminal Classic central Petén (Rice and Rice 2004), and the western Lake Petén Itzá basin is unlikely to be Tikal's direct heir. As I discuss in succeeding chapters, evidence from other sites in Petén suggests that the political situation in the Terminal Classic period in Petén was decidedly complex and that both Seibal and Ucanal played significant roles.

CHAPTER 6

Other Classic Period
May-based Realms

There is persuasive evidence that, as Edmonson earlier conjectured, the Classic Maya observed *may* cycles and that the *may* was seated at Tikal. Edmonson (1979:15) also suggested that, besides Tikal, other southern lowland seats of the *may* might have included Copán, Palenque, Altar de Sacrificios, and Seibal. His suggestions can be compared to the regional "capitals" proposed in other centralized models of Classic Maya statehood: Tikal, Copán, Palenque, and Toniná, in Morley's (1946) model; Tikal, Copán, Calakmul, Palenque, and Seibal, in the Barthel-Marcus scheme; and Tikal, Copán, Calakmul, Palenque, and Yaxchilán, in Adams's Late Classic vision.

Here I discuss two sites, Copán and Calakmul, long associated with regional state models; I also offer a brief overview of Palenque, Caracol, and the Petexbatún region in the context of the *may*. These sketches support the hypothesis that the lowland Classic Maya shared a politico-religious structuring based on 256-year calendar cycles, but it is evident that the means of participation varied and each cycle seat and region maintained distinctive ritual identities. Except where other citations are given, the data on dynasties and related matters discussed in this chapter have been drawn from the site summaries in Martin and Grube's *Chronicle of the Maya Kings and Queens* (2000), and this source is not specifically cited further except in the case of direct quotations.

Copán, Honduras, and Quiriguá, Guatemala

Copán is a reasonably convincing site to advance as a Classic cycle seat, or *may ku*, with Quiriguá some 70 kilometers to the north-northwest as one of its constituent k'atun seats (see Fig. 1.1). Copán is a relatively small center on the left bank of the Copán River in northwestern Honduras. The Maya name for the site or territory is Xukpi: *xuk* 'corner'; *xukpi* 'corner bundle'; *xukup*, the motmot bird (genus *Momotus* or *Aspatha*) (Schele and Mathews 1998:133). Its Emblem Glyph (see Fig. 2.5), with a leaf-nosed bat (T756) as its main sign, was first displayed on Stela 9 on 9.6.10.0.0 8 Ajaw 13 Pax (January 27, A.D. 564). Copán has long been postulated as a regional "capital" based on its Stela A, which refers to three other such "capitals" (Marcus 1976; Adams 1986). More recently, the site has been characterized as governed by "multiple, effective political interest groups in the polity" or "maximal lineages" (Webster 1992:153; see also Viel 1999).

Archaeological excavations at Copán have yielded evidence of occupation dating back to the Early and Middle Preclassic periods, circa 1100–400 B.C., with ceramics similar to those of the Pacific piedmont and coast (Fash 1991:64–70). However, Copán's inscriptions on Stelae 4 and 17 indicate that the "kingdom" of Copán was established on the period-ending 8.6.0.0.0 10 Ajaw 13 Ch'en (December 16, 159). The 159 date is commemorated also on Copán Stela I, with reference to completion of the sixth k'atun. A later k'atun-ending Copán inscription dated 8.17.0.0.0 1 Ajaw 8 Ch'en (October 19, 376) is mentioned on a carved peccary skull recovered in a tomb. In this inscription, an otherwise unknown "Foliated Ajaw" is one of two seated individuals facing a stela and altar; the text includes reference to "wrapping" a stela (Fash 1991:87).

Copán's dynastic history (Martin and Grube 2000:190–213) is known primarily from two sculptured monuments, Altar Q in the plaza of the Acropolis and a bench in Structure 11, to the north of that plaza (see Viel 1999). The Copán and Quiriguá dynasties were, more explicitly than that of Tikal, "founded" in the mid-k'atun or lajuntun of 426, in a K'atun 8 Ajaw, ten years before the k'atun and b'ak'tun endings of 9.0.0.0.0 (December 9, 435) were commemorated. This dynastic founding is also likely to represent the seating of a *may* cycle at Copán. More specifically, Copán's dynasty was founded on 8.19.10.11.0 8 Ajaw 18 Yank'in (September 7, 426) by K'inich Yax K'uk' Mo' (Great-Sun First Quetzal Macaw).

K'inich Yax K'uk' Mo''s origins are not certain, but there is increasing evidence that he was from central Petén and perhaps Tikal. A text dating to 8.18.10.8.12 (1 Eb' 10 Yax; November 3, 406) on the back of a statue of a seated human, known as the Hombre de Tikal, mentions an individual named K'inich Yax K'uk Mo', and the same or an earlier individual named K'inich Yax K'uk' Mo' might be represented opposite Foliated Ajaw on the carved peccary skull (Sharer 2003:325–327). In addition, strontium-isotope analysis of human bone believed to be the remains of K'inich Yax K'uk Mo', found in the Hunal Tomb, indicates that he was not a Copán native but rather from central Petén (Sharer 2003:340).

Sharer (2003:322–323, 350) proposes that Tikal orchestrated a military conquest of Copán under the leadership of K'uk' Mo', an elite warrior, in 426 or 427. Simultaneously, Tikal seems to have aided in the founding of the ruling dynasty of Quiriguá under the authority of Copán, presumably in the person of Yax K'uk' Mo'. Yax K'uk' Mo, in other words, overthrew the established ruling dynasty of Copán and married a woman from that lineage in a sequence of events very like those transpiring at Tikal half a century earlier. K'inich Yax K'uk' Mo is thus a "stranger-king," like Tikal's Siyaj K'ak' (Rice n.d.b), who is referred to on the Xukpi Stone buried under Copán Structure 26.

Early stelae at Copán and Quiriguá share distinctive iconographic traits with Tikal's early monuments, including frontal portraiture with upturned, back-to-back hands with curled fingers in front of the chest, plus a distinctive semi-in-the-round or "wraparound" style. At the same time, Yax K'uk' Mo''s personal artifacts (Stuart 1997) and the general architecture at the time show strong Mexican influences and one early building, Structure 16, had central Mexican talud-tablero architecture and brightly painted murals. The Classic foundations of Copán, Quiriguá, and other sites (such as Palenque) may be linked to complex Tikal–central Mexican dynastic interactions throughout the region.

Yax K'uk' Mo' (426–437?) was succeeded by his son, K'inich Popol Hol (Mat Head), who erected two monuments: Stela 18, which uses the rare "ladder" or "scaffold" glyph Eb' of the Tikal's founder's name, and Stela 63. Stela 63, the earliest dated carved monument at Copán, celebrates the 9.0.0.0.0 k'atun/b'ak'tun ending in 435, as does, retrospectively, Waterlily Jaguar's all-glyphic Stela 15 (dedication date, 524), after which little is known of succeeding rulers.

The next period endings that were celebrated at Copán were on Stela 17 at 554 (9.6.0.0.0) and on Stela 9 at 9.6.10.0.0 (564), a lajuntun ending on a day 8 Ajaw, with the first known display of Copán's Emblem Glyph. The 119-year hiatus in erecting k'atun-ending monuments, from 435 to 554, is roughly one-half k'atun less than the 128-year half-*may* cycle. This suggests a situation like that described for Tikal in Chapters 4 and 5, in which different kinds and levels of ritual activity were carried out in one half of a *may* versus the other. Yax K'uk' Mo's dynasty lasted 396 years, until 9.19.11.14.5 3 Chikchan 3 Wo (February 8, 822).

Copán's Great Plaza, which lies at the northern extreme of the site center, is a dramatic architectural celebration of dynastic power (Fig. 6.1). The stelae in this plaza were erected by the city's Late Classic kings, Smoke Imix (K'ak' Nab' K'awil?) and Waxaklajun Ub'aj K'awil. Smoke Imix ruled from 628 to 695 and was buried in Temple 26. Quiriguá Altar L, a variant of the Giant Ajaw altar format common at Caracol, names him "as the subject of a *tzak jul* event—perhaps meaning his 'conjured arrival here'" as part of celebration of the k'atun ending

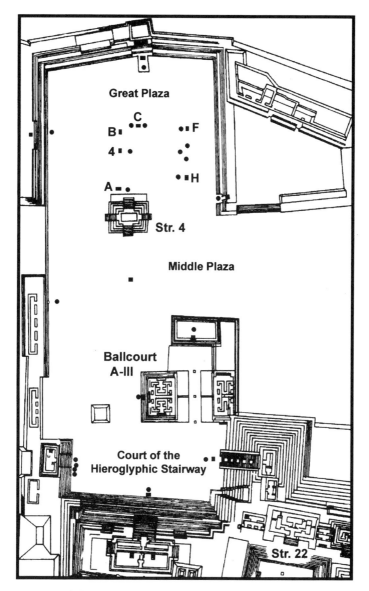

FIGURE 6.1 Map of the northern portion of the Copán ceremonial center, showing the Ballcourt, Structure 10L-22, and the Great Plaza with Waxaklajun Ub'aj K'awil's stelae (after Fash 1991:Fig. 8).

9.11.0.0.0 (652) (Martin and Grube 2000:201, 217). Waxaklajun Ub'aj K'awil (also known as 18 Rabbit or 18 Jog), possibly Smoke Imix's son, ruled from 695 to 738 and presided over the greatest florescence of Copán.

Waxaklajun Ub'aj K'awil celebrated the k'atun 9.14.0.0.0 to 9.15.0.0.0 by erecting six stelae in the Great Plaza in the northern part of the site, placed in two north-south rows on the eastern side and in the center of the plaza. Interpretations, below, of the iconography on these monuments are taken from Schele and Mathews (1998:141–161).

Stela C, near the center of the plaza, shows the ruler on recto and verso, looking both east and west, and commemorates the period ending 9.14.0.0.0 (December 5, 711). Ropes mark the edges of both faces, and small spirit companions—nawals or *way* figures—are visible in the upper corners. Stela F, the northernmost of the east-side monuments, commemorates the lajuntun of 9.14.10.0.0. Waxaklajun Ub'aj K'awil is shown in the role of the Bearded Jaguar God, wearing a long feathered back ornament with ropes around his knees; a series of *way* figures clamber on ropes edging the face of the monument. The back of the stela has four blocks of four glyphs, each wrapped by a twisted cord or rope. Stela 4, in the center of the plaza west of Stela C, commemorates the jolajuntun of 9.14.15.0.0. The ruler is dressed as Bolon K'awil, one of Copán's patrons, and wears an enormous backrack; the text references reenactment of an event (the founding of the first dynasty?) in 8.6.0.0.0 (159). It is accompanied by a carved stone ball tied with rope and a rectangular altar wrapped like a gift box, with four *way* figures guarding the knots.

During the final year before the end of this k'atun, Waxaklajun embarked on an ambitious program involving structural modification and erection of three more monuments in this plaza. The construction project was the remodeling of Structure 10L-4 (Str. 4), which separates the Great Plaza to the north from the Middle Plaza to the south and also faces into the Great Plaza, closing it off on its southern end. An earlier version of Str. 4, believed to have been commissioned by the dynastic founder, Yax K'uk' Mo', or his son, incorporated Stela 35 in its fill. Style dated to circa A.D. 400, this monument may show Yax K'uk' Mo' carrying a serpent-bodied ceremonial bar (Fash 1991:88). In his later remodeling of this platform, Waxaklajun added east and west stairways, turning it into a radial structure (Baudez 1991:85).

Copán's famous Stela A was erected on the north side of this radial platform, facing east across the plaza toward Stela H, which in turn stood south of earlier Stela F. Together, Stelae A and H celebrate the period ending of 9.15.0.0.0 4 Ajaw 13 Yax (August 20, 731). Both monuments were erected over cruciform cache chambers, with the one under Stela H containing the earliest artifacts of gold in the Maya area (Schele and Mathews 1998:158). On Stela H, dedicated 9.14.19.5.0 4 Ajaw 18 Muwan (December 3, 730), or 260 days before the k'atun ending, Waxaklajun is attired as the Maize God, wearing a netted skirt of jade, a Maize God headdress, and a large Maize God backrack. As on his other stelae, twisted cords provide an edging, with a *way* or miniature Maize Gods (one holding a perforator) clinging to the rope.

Stela A may show Waxaklajun in the costume of Kan Te Ajaw, another of Copán's patrons, wearing an ornate matlike headdress (Schele and Mathews 1998:159). The lengthy text of Stela A (Fig. 6.2), dedicated only sixty days after Stela H on 9.14.19.8.0 12 Ajaw 18 Kumk'u (February 1, 731), continues that of its partner. This text, appearing on three of the four sides of the monument, has defied clear decipherment as it appears to describe some esoteric ritual and cosmological activity that has little parallel in monuments elsewhere. The best known part of the inscription is found near the end, on the south panel, where the Emblem Glyph of Copán appears with those of Tikal, Palenque, and Calakmul. This occurrence, accompanied by reference to "four skies" and the four cardinal directions (or the four positions of the sun's journey), contributed to inferences of a quadripartite cosmological and geopolitical model of Classic Maya political organization, with four regional-directional capitals (Barthel 1968; Marcus 1973, 1976). What the text actually seems to record, however, is that the lords of these sites gathered together as part of the ceremony involving deposition of objects in the caches (D. Stuart, pers. comm., June 23, 2002; Schele and Mathews 1998:160–161; see also Coggins 1992).

The reference to "four skies" is of interest because these collocations can be read syllabically: *kan te kan (na), kan [Zip?] na kan (na), kan ni kan na, kan may kan na.* The variable second element in each of these compounds might be a numerical classifier; in the second of the four, this classifier is a bird head variant with a possible "Zip Monster" prefix, while the fourth is distinguished by a *may* glyph or deer hoof. It is possible that these four glyphs could be matched with the four individual sites, just as the directional glyphs were interpreted to indicate symbolic regions of political control. It is equally likely, however, that they are general descriptors and metaphors for "the whole world": earth and sky; sunrise, zenith, sunset, Underworld; the four quarters; and the four sacred seats of the *may* that provide the geopolitico-ritual structure that links the earthly domain with the cosmos.

The final monument in Waxaklajun Ub'aj K'awil's sequence was Stela B, which commemorated the 9.15.0.0.0 period ending in 731. This monument was the northernmost of the line of three stelae in the center of the Great Plaza, with Stelae 4 and A standing to its south.

Copán's Late Classic stelae, despite their distinctive sculpture-in-the-

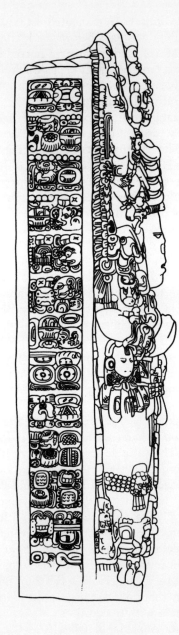

FIGURE 6.2 The south side of Copán Stela A, dated 9.15.0.0.0 (A.D. 731), mentions Tikal, Calakmul, and Palenque, and was used by Barthel and Marcus in postulating four capitals in the Late Classic lowlands (drawing by Linda Schele, © David Schele, courtesy Foundation for the Advancement of Mesoamerican Studies, Inc.).

round style and frontal portraiture, display some traits reminiscent of Tikal's period-ending monuments. These include the ruler holding a serpent-headed ceremonial bar, wearing a backrack and/or impersonating the Maize God; also, ropes or twisted cords form borders. The "spirit companions" or *way*-nawal figures clinging to the ropes—and to the Vision Serpents on the later jotun marker, Stela D (9.15.5.0.0)—are analogous to the ancestral Paddler figures riding cloud scrolls on Tikal's late monuments, as well as the figures on the Preclassic Hauberg Stela. In addition, the Copán program of erecting five monuments in the vicinity of a radial structure is similar to that at Terminal Classic Seibal (see Chap. 7). Scattering is not shown on Waxaklajun's stelae: Stela B celebrates the k'atun ending 9.15.0.0.0 4 Ajaw 13 Yax (August 20, 731), with the ruler in his usual stance, but the text includes the phrase "he scattered drops" (Schele and Mathews 1998:164).

Waxaklajun Ub'aj K'awil also created the final version of Ballcourt A, which was finished in early January 738. This large and elegant ballcourt, first constructed during the fourth century, sits on the north side of the Hieroglyphic Court, open to the south, with the adjacent west-facing Temple 26 and its hieroglyphic stairway to the southeast. Shortly after finishing the ballcourt, in what appears to have been a major reversal of Copán's fortunes, Waxaklajun Ub'aj K'awil was captured on May 1, 738 (9.15.6.14.6 6 Kimi 4 Sek) by the ruler of Quiriguá, K'ak' Tiliw Kan Yoat (formerly Kawak Sky). Waxaklajun's fate was reported as beheading, according to Quiriguá's texts, but Copán claims merely that he died in "battle." Stuart (1995:300) provides a variant interpretation of the Quiriguá text, reading the ax verb as *ch'akba*, a reflexive form—that is, self-decapitation—as known from mythological scenes on Classic vases.

Not long after Copán's "defeat," its ruler, K'ak' Yoplaj Kan K'awil (Smoke Monkey) built Structure 10L-22A. This structure was identified as a popol naj (Mat House; a community or council house; see Fash 1992; Fash et al. 1992; Fash 1991:130–134; Schele and Mathews 1998:492–493n73) on the basis of the mat motifs on its façade. It is thought to have been dedicated on a day 9 Ajaw on the basis of large 9 Ajaw medallions "repeated in pairs numerous times on all four facades of the structure" (Fash, Andrews, and Manahan 2004), suggesting its dedication on a jolajuntun ending 9.15.15.0.0 9 Ajaw 18 Xul (June 2, 746). K'ak' Yoplaj was successor to the unfortunate Waxaklajun Ub'aj K'awil, and his small new structure abutted Waxaklajun's much more imposing Structure 22 to the west. The front and back facades of Structure 10L-22A were decorated with six mat symbols alternating with eight carved human figures, each wearing individualized headdresses and neck ornaments and seated cross-legged over large glyphs believed to be toponyms (Fig. 6.3). The nine toponymic glyphs on the structure appear to name sites in and

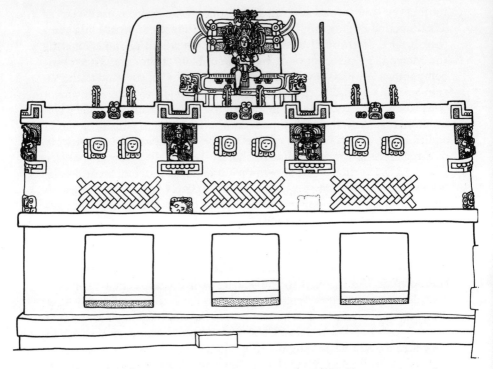

FIGURE 6.3 Plan of Copán Structure 10L-22A, a popol naj (Mat House; a community or council house), decorated with mat symbols, human figures seated on place-name glyphs, and glyphs reading *ajawlil* 'ajawship', 'governance' (drawing courtesy of Barbara Fash and William Fash).

around the Copán area, perhaps including Río Amarillo, El Paraíso, El Puente, and Los Higos (Fash 1991:134). Above the mats were glyphs reading *ajawlil* 'ajawship; governance'. Roof ornaments labeled the building as a *nik te'il na* 'flower house', a Colonial period gloss for council house (Fash, Andrews, and Manahan 2004).

Using an analogy with Ralph Roys's study of sixteenth-century Yucatán, Barbara W. and William L. Fash and others (Fash et al. 1992; see also Cheek 2003) suggest that Structure 10L-22A may have been an administrative structure for meetings of the Copán ruler and jolpops (council members, or those at the head of the mat). The insights into Classic Maya political organization afforded by Structure 10L-22A and its sculptures highlight two points:

First, they suggest that governors and subsidiary lords were of sufficient importance to wield strong authority in the fate of large

Classic Maya city-states, particularly in political crisis. Second, if one of the fundamental characteristics of statehood is the separation of political institutions from kinship lines, then from A.D. 746, if not before, Copán was at that stage of development. The statesmen are identified not by their personal names, but rather by the name of the subdivision of the kingdom which they represent. (Fash 1991:135)

I believe the implications of Structure 10L-22A extend further. First, as Fash notes, one definition of jolpop is "head of the banquet." This suggests to me that the feasts (Act 14) were part of k'atun-ending celebrations in the Postclassic and Colonial periods (see Chap. 3). In addition, I suspect the nine toponyms or subdivisions of the kingdom refer to nine tzuk, or k'atun-seating provinces and allies, within the Copán polity. Finally, Baudez (1991) has suggested that ritual processions (i.e., Act 8: Ceremonial Circuit, or Act 11: Pacing of the K'atun) also might have been part of k'atun-ending ceremonies at Copán. He (1991:85) believes radial platform Structure 10L-4 sat in the center "of a huge cross that divides the Main Group into four quadrants" and the east-west arms of the cross are now-destroyed causeways that extended from Structure 10M-1 on the east to Structure 10K-29 or 10K-16 to the west.

South of Copán's Great Plaza is the Middle Plaza, with the small Court of the Hieroglyphic Stairway immediately to the south. The hieroglyphic stairway ascends the west side of Temple 26 (Str. 10L-26) and faces west into the courtyard. Its 2,200 glyphs incorporate those of the earlier stairs set by Waxaklajun Ub'aj K'awil in his remodeling of the temple over Smoke Imix's tomb in A.D. 710. This earlier hieroglyphic stairway, which recorded the city's dynastic sequence up to Waxaklajun Ub'aj K'awil's rule, was demolished and the carved blocks reset into a new stairway with an extended text. The rebuilding of Temple 26 and dedication of the hieroglyphic text in 755 were part of a revitalization of Copán carried out by K'ak' Yipyaj Kan K'awil, who ruled from 749 to 761(?). It has been suggested that Temple 26 was dedicated to the site's dual Maya and Mexican heritage, with sculptures of Copán kings dressed in Teotihuacan warrior style standing on the stairway, and a quasi-"bilingual" text in Maya and "Mexicanized" or non-Maya glyphs inside the temple (Stuart 2000:496–497).

The hieroglyphic stairway was excavated and closely studied by epigraphers to test two hypotheses, that it was either (1) a conquest monument imposed by Quiriguá to celebrate the capture and beheading of Waxaklajun Ub'aj K'awil or (2) a Copán-inspired monument created to rebuild the prestige and legitimacy of Copán's ruling dynasty (Fash 1991:143). Evidence supports the second hypothesis, indicating that the inscription summarizes events from 553 to 756 and emphasizes the role of the twelfth Copán ruler Smoke Imix God K, 628–695 (Fash 1991: 144–145). "Thus, it appears all but certain that the Hieroglyphic Stairway was an indigenous Copán dynasty monument, built to relegitimize their ruling order in the face of the humiliating loss of 18 Rabbit," that is, Waxaklajun Ub'aj K'awil (p. 146).

The Copán ruler K'ak' Yipyaj Kan K'awil was succeeded in 763 by Yax Pasaj Kan Yoat/Yopat (nicknamed Yax Pak or Madrugada), whose father is unknown but whose mother was from Palenque. Yax Pasaj is known for many constructions, including the final version of Temple 16 and, at its base, Altar Q, a square altar with portraits of Copán's first sixteen kings. Yax Pasaj's depictions of himself are unusual in that he is shown with

> a group of named "companions" that partner him on many monuments. These characters behave very much like kings themselves, they have "seating" events, perform the "scattering" rite and bear either full or modified emblem glyphs. Initially it was thought that these were siblings of the king and a sign that he was obliged to share power with an extended family, though more recent evidence suggests that they were companions of a more supernatural kind. (Martin and Grube 2000:210)

These could be *way*-nawal figures like those accompanying Waxaklajun Ub'aj K'awil, or ancestor figures analogous to the Paddlers of the Tikal realm. Alternatively, given that Copán and Quiriguá commonly personify or anthropomorphize day and number glyphs, one wonders if these could be personified k'atuns or k'atun seats, or rulers of k'atun seats.

The last period-ending stela at Copán was Stela 11, dated to the lajuntun 9.19.10.0.0 (May 4, 820), which "explicitly proclaimed the 'toppling of the founder's House' or lineage of Yax K'uk' Mo'" (Montgomery 2001b:210). Copán's end was violent, as indicated by the burning of structures and collapse of vaults in Courtyards A and B (Fash, Andrews, and Manahan 2004). It is not known who was responsible. The final Copán ruler, Ukit Tok', was inaugurated in February 822. On his only monument, Altar L, he tried to mimic his predecessor Yax Pasaj's monument, Altar Q, but it was never completed.

The Copán dynasty begun by K'inich Yax K'uk' Mo' lasted from 426 to 822, or 396 years. This exceeds the duration of 1.5 *may* cycles, or the three phases "guest," full seat, and retiring seat (i.e., 128 + 256 years = 384 years), by 12 years. This total of 396 years is, however, close to the duration of a bak'tun, 394.5 years, raising the possibility that one and a half *may* cycles might have been designed to correspond to b'ak'tuns. If, however, *may* cycling at Copán is considered to begin with the first period-ending stela, which was on the momentous b'ak'tun ending of 9.0.0.0.0 (435), this brings us to 386 years, almost exactly one and a half *may* cycles. Although not commemorated by carved stelae, the earlier k'atun ending of 8.6.0.0.0 (159) and the rule of Foliated Ajaw are mentioned several times in the site's texts and might also play a part in these cycles.

The site of Quiriguá plays an intriguing role vis-à-vis Copán. Lying 70 kilometers north-northwest of Copán on the left bank of the Motagua River in Guatemala, Quiriguá has long been considered a colony of that site (Morley 1935), and recent work confirms Copán's role in its dynastic founding (Sharer 2003). Quiriguá's Emblem Glyph (T559/560) is read *k'ank'in* (fourteenth month in the solar calendar), as a "cacao tree with pod" (Sharer 1994:Fig. 13.6), and as tzuk (partition) (Schele and Mathews 1998:346n6). Quiriguá's dynasty (Martin and Grube 2000:214–225) was founded very shortly after Copán's, and its first ruler, nicknamed Tok' Casper, took office u kab'iy—under the supervision of—Yax K'uk' Mo'. The two sites show great similarities in layout, architecture, and monumental sculpture. Fash (1991:150) suggests that Quiriguá's imitation of the Copán layout was "a deliberate ploy by Quiriguá's ruler . . . to outdo his former masters from Copán." I suggest that in the very Late Classic Quiriguá itself might have become a *may* seat.

Quiriguá celebrated early period endings, including that at 9.1.0.0.0 (455) and perhaps also the jotun of 9.2.5.0.0 (480). This date occurs along with mention of a later ritual that took place "'under the supervision' of an ochk'in kalomte'" (Martin and Grube 2000:217) or "kalomte' of the west." This title has often been interpreted as having some reference to Teotihuacan, located in central Mexico to the west of the Maya lowlands. However, because the kalomte' title is particularly associated with Tikal and Copán's Late Classic Stela A's mention of Tikal seems to associate that site with the west, this may mean that the Tikal ruler K'an Kitam had some hand in the event.

Quiriguá experienced a similar Middle Classic hiatus in monument erection as that at Tikal and other lowland sites, with no dated stelae or altars for some one hundred eighty years between 493 and 672. It is possible that the site might have experienced disastrous floods during this interval and been abandoned for a time (Sharer 1990). In any case, Altar L (Monument 12), featuring a variant Giant Ajaw layout, was dedicated in about 9.12.0.0.0 (672), celebrating the completion of K'atun 10 Ajaw. It is of interest that one k'atun later, Tikal ended its own hiatus in the same manner, with a Giant Ajaw on Altar 14.

During the last decade or so of the Copán ruler Waxaklajun's reign, Quiriguá seems to have grown increasingly assertive. According to

Quiriguá Stela E, K'ak' Tiliw came to rule Quiriguá in 724 "under the supervision of" (u kab'iy) the very man he is said to have subsequently killed, Copán's ruler Waxaklajun Ub'aj K'awil. Some years later, in 734 (9.15.3.2.0.), Quiriguá displayed its Emblem Glyph, and in 736, K'ak' Tiliw claimed to have erected a stela (not known) in a ceremony that has a reference to Chik Nab', perhaps a district within the Calakmul polity. Two years later, in 738, Quiriguá defeated Copán, although none of the Quiriguá accounts of this event refer to it using a term for war (Martin and Grube 2000:205). Viel (1999:393) interprets the rivalry between the two cities as one between the two major lineage groups in the region as identified by insignia on their pectorals on Copán's carved monuments.

After that event, as Copán's fortunes declined, Quiriguá enjoyed a period of expansive construction and power. K'ak' Tiliw rebuilt and enlarged the site's acropolis, plaza, and ballcourt, and at the jolajuntun of 9.15.15.0.0 (746) he began the practice of erecting a monument every five years. Quiriguá's Late Classic carved monuments (Sharer 1990) were either very tall obelisk-like stelae with deep relief—K'ak' Tiliw's Stela E (Monument 5), erected in 771, is a stone column more than 7 meters aboveground—or, as at Copán, zoomorphic altars—large boulders carved to resemble turtles or jaguars. Quiriguá's last dated text, on a building facade rather than a stela, refers to the rulers of both Copán and Quiriguá scattering in commemoration of the k'atun ending of 9.19.0.0.0 (810) (Martin and Grube 2000:225).

The pattern of stelae dates at Quiriguá supports the model of 128- or 256-year intervals indicating the site's participation in a *may ku* system. The interval from the founding of the site in 426/427 to the last dated text in 810 is 384 years (= 256 + 128), suggesting that Quiriguá might have experienced the three roles of guest seat, full seat, and retiring seat in much the same way that Copán did. Also of interest is the interval between the Giant Ajaw Altar L, carved at the end of Quiriguá's hiatus in about 672, and the last dated text (810). This interval spans 138 years, ten years longer than a half *may*. However, it seems clear that throughout the Classic period Copán was the leading site in the southeast region and Quiriguá was largely subsidiary. The very late display of an Emblem Glyph, plus Quiriguá's raid on Copán and the subsequent capture and death of Waxaklajun Ub'aj K'awil, accompanied by decline at that site, probably signaled the shift in power as Copán moved into the role of retiring *may* seat and Quiriguá was ascendant as "guest."

One controversial topic in interpreting the southeast region's history concerns the length of occupation of the Copán valley after the collapse of dynastic rule. After 737 Copán was effectively no longer the seat of the *may* in this region (despite the continuation of its dynasty until 820 or 822), having been usurped by Quiriguá. Ceramic evidence—the scarcity of Postclassic pottery—traditionally suggested an ending of occupation at Copán around 850–900. However, debris around Terminal Classic Ballcourt B, south of the site center, included at least six Early Postclassic Tohil Plumbate jars (Fox 1996:492). Moreover, suites of radiocarbon dates from occupation just south of this ballcourt (Manahan 2002), plus obsidian hydration dates from sites in the rural valley (Freter 1992; Webster, Freter, and Storey 2004), provide strong evidence of occupation in the area for another one hundred fifty to perhaps as much as four hundred years, until around 1200–1250 (cf. Fash, Andrews, and Manahan 2004). In other words, while the attempt by Copán's last ruler, Ukit Tok', to establish himself (and also a new *may* seat?) at Copán in 822 apparently failed, the effort might have rallied the remaining elites sufficiently to account for the continued occupation of the Copán pocket and other rural settlements. This could represent another 1.5 *may* cycles of continuing settlement in the Copán valley.

Several sites in and around the Copán valley could have served as k'atun seats in the Copán or Quiriguá realm. These are Santa Rita, 12 kilometers up the Copán River from Copán, with its Stela 23 celebrating the 9.11.0.0.0 (652) k'atun ending, and Los Higos, 70 kilometers northeast of Copán. That satellite's Late Classic Stela 1 (781?) mentions Butz' Chan with one of his titles and an "aj-po" (ajaw) superfix but lacks the "water group" prefix of an Emblem Glyph (Fash 1991:97).

A number of sites in southern Belize appear to have been k'atun seats in the southeastern Copán-Quiriguá domain in the Late Classic. One of these is Uxbenká, with twenty-two stelae, eighteen of them arranged in a stela plaza (Leventhal 1990:134–137; 1992:145–150). Unfortunately, only four can be dated: two are style dated to approximately 8.18.0.0.0 (396), and two celebrate the lajuntun of 9.17.10.0.0 (780). Another k'atun seat is Pusilhá, farther to the south, with more than three dozen carved monuments (Wanyerka 2002). Rulers at the site celebrated the k'atun ending of 9.7.0.0.0 (573) and the jolajuntun ending of 9.10.15.0.0 (647); Stela D (dated 9.8.0.0.0) gives a retrospective date of 9.3.0.0.0 (493) (Braswell 2002). Nim Li Punit in southern Belize is still another possible k'atun seat in the Copán realm, as texts on the site's many monuments mention the Xukpi (Copán) ajaw five times (Wanyerka 2002).

Wanyerka (2002) suggests, on the basis of epigraphy and iconography, that these southern Belize sites demonstrate a pattern of shifting alliances. In the Early Classic these sites seem to have relations with central Petén, and Uxbenká Stela 11 mentions Tikal ruler Chak Tok Ich'ak (Wanyerka 1996a). But Uxbenká and the southern Belize region experienced a hiatus in monument erection that lasted for one hundred thirty years (Wanyerka 2002)—in other words, half a *may*—and then when monuments again were erected in the Late Classic they demonstrated affiliations with Copán-Quiriguá. Pusilhá, for example, shares the main sign (tzuk or yaxk'in) of Quiriguá's Emblem Glyph, and Pusilhá rulers adopted the names of the Late Classic Copán kings Butz' Chan (578–628) and Smoke Imix (628–695). At Pusilhá, Stela K gives a retrospective reference commemorating the 8.6.0.0.0 period ending (corresponding to Copán's founding date of 159) and the mysterious Foliated Ajaw (Wanyerka 2002), and Stela 1 mentions Smoke Imix as "Holy Tzuk Lord" in an u kab'iy expression (Schele and Mathews 1998:346n6). Nim Li Punit celebrated the lajuntun of 9.14.10.0.0 (721), and its rulers displayed the distinctive turban headdress characteristic of Copán rulers. The Nim Li Punit ruler attended an event in Copán in 771 (Braswell 2002).

It is difficult to fit Lubaantun into this scheme, as it was founded late (in the early eighth century) and has no carved, dated stelae (Hammond 1975). The latest dated monument in the Copán-Quiriguá *may* region is on Stela 1 from Tzimin Che in southern Belize, which celebrated the 10.4.0.0.0 k'atun ending on January 15, 909 (Wanyerka, pers. comm., June 25, 2002).

Calakmul, Campeche, Mexico

Calakmul, 100 kilometers north of Tikal in southeastern Campeche, is considered to have been Tikal's principal rival during the Classic period (Martin and Grube 1995:101–115). The site was little known when Edmonson suggested the existence of Classic period *may* cycling, and thus he did not include it in his scheme. Subsequent archaeological work at Calakmul since the 1980s indicates that the city is unusually large whether measured in terms of its numerous urban and extraurban causeways, site area (70 km^2), population (approximately 50,000), or number of monuments (119) (Folan et al. 1995, 2001); the size of the Calakmul state is estimated at more than 13,000 km^2 (Folan, Gunn, and Domínguez Carrasco 2001:227; Braswell et al. 2004). Calakmul has the characteristics of "overkingship," or political primacy over a number of sites within a large realm, and it is one of the postulated capitals of regional states in several models of lowland political organization (Marcus 1976; Adams 1986). With its political and military apogee between A.D. 652 and 752 (Braswell et al. 2004), Calakmul clearly would have been a Late Classic *may ku.*

Calakmul's Emblem Glyph (T764; Chikchan snake) suggests that the site was originally named Kan 'snake' or Kanal, although it was also known as Ox Te' Tun 'three stones', and the larger realm it oversaw was named Chik Nab' or Nab Tunich 'waterlily place' (Marcus 2001:40). The latter could refer to the water lilies growing in Calakmul's thirteen large reservoirs, which had a capacity totaling some 200 million liters

(Braswell et al. 2004). Calakmul came to prominence during the Late Preclassic period (350 B.C.–A.D. 250; Folan et al. 1995:316; Pincemin et al. 1998:312), and its Classic rise, like Tikal's, coincided with the decline of Late Preclassic El Mirador.

As with many large Late Classic sites, comparatively little of Calakmul's early occupation is known as it was buried under heavy later construction. In addition, few Early Classic stelae have been found, and thus it is difficult to know when the site first displayed its Emblem Glyph, for example. Unlike most Classic cities, Calakmul's early dynastic history is primarily detailed on Late Classic texts painted on pottery vases rather than on sculptured monuments (Martin and Grube 2000:102). Most of these vessels painted in the so-called codex style were produced by later occupation at the primarily Middle Preclassic site of Nakbe (Hansen 1992), lying to the south near El Mirador. The founder of Calakmul's dynasty is nicknamed "Skyraiser," but the date of his founding is unclear.

Despite the paucity of information on Calakmul's early occupation and dynasties, available evidence suggests the city participated in the same general kinds of *may* ritual known from Preclassic and Classic Tikal and elsewhere. While Calakmul's earliest known monument dates to A.D. 431 (see below), nearby Balakbal has an earlier stela dated 8.18.9.17.18 (406), two days before the lajuntun, and the Calakmul Emblem Glyph appears on a hieroglyphic stairway at Dzibanché dating to 495 (Braswell et al. 2004).

A large E-Group complex sits at the very center of Calakmul, with a triadic structure at the north end of this plaza. Stelae 8 and 9 were set in front of the east building of the complex (Folan et al. 1995:314–315), as were monuments at Tikal and Uaxactún, but at Calakmul these stelae date to the Late Classic rather than to the period of the structural assemblage itself. This suggests that this complex (Fig. 6.4) may have continued in use into the Late Classic period, as complexes were in southeastern Petén and the Río Mopán area. The entire complex seems to have considerable late modifications, as an unusually large square platform, rather than a radial structure, sits on the central axis of the west side. Some forty Late Classic stelae have been found in this plaza, eighteen of them in front (west) of the eastern structure (Folan et al. 2001).

Calakmul's largest temple is Late Preclassic Structure IIA, comparable in size to El Mirador's El Tigre pyramid, which overlooks the southern end of the site's E-Group plaza. In the Early Classic period, Structure II was enlarged and six masks were placed on the north (front) facade, flanking its central staircase. This structure continued to be used and modified into the Late and Terminal Classic period, with thirteen stelae erected on and around it.

The evidence for Calakmul's participation in a *may*-type organiza-

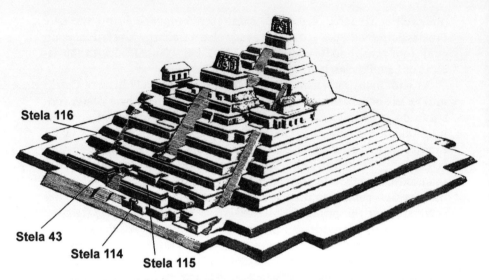

FIGURE 6.4 Front of Calakmul Structure II (Pincemin et al. 1998:Fig. 3; redrawn by Kay Klahassey from drawing by E. Tamay Segovia and photograph by E. Leiter; courtesy of Joyce Marcus and William J. Folan).

tion in the Late Preclassic and Early Classic is equivocal, owing to the lack of early stelae and reference to allied sites. The presence of the widespread E-Group suggests that Calakmul might initially have been a jetz k'atun, or k'atun seat, within Tikal's *may* realm. The Early Classic king Tun K'ab' Hix (?) was buried in Structure IV, the central building on the east side of the complex (Braswell et al. 2004). If, instead, Calakmul itself seated the *may* during the Early Classic, it is likely k'atun seats include Balakbal, with its eighth-cycle Stela 5. In addition, Calakmul's many causeways link it to satellite centers (Folan et al. 1995:313) that flourished earlier in the Preclassic, including El Mirador 38 kilometers to the southwest, El Tintal another 30 kilometers beyond, and Nakbe.

It is easier to propose a Middle Classic seating for Calakmul. The site's earliest known monument, Stela 114, is relatively late, having an IS date of 8.19.15.12.13 8 Ben 6 Mol (September 16, 431) (Pincemin et al. 1998). This historical monument (Fig. 6.5) deals with the twenty-year anniversary of an event that occurred in 411, probably an accession, and perhaps that of Skyraiser. The principal figure is shown cradling a ceremonial bar in his left arm and holding in his right hand the same distinctive knotted staff, consisting of three bent poles, seen on Tikal monuments dating several decades later. Another early monument at Calakmul, Stela 43 (Fig. 6.6), dating to the termination of a K'atun 13 Ajaw in 514, bears a scene very like that on the Leiden Plaque from the

Tikal area, with a prone captive behind the ruler's feet, except the ruler is carrying a ceremonial bar (Pincemin et al. 1998:Fig. 9). Both of these stelae were reset, probably in Terminal Classic times, into niches constructed at the base of the huge Preclassic Structure II platform (Pincemin et al. 1998). Their careful curation indicates that these rulers and dates were of supreme significance in Calakmul's history. Given the date of 431, very close to the beginning of Tikal's Middle Classic *may*

FIGURE 6.5 Calakmul Stela 114, erected in A.D. 435, shows the ruler (Skyraiser?) holding a staff like that on later Tikal "staff stelae" (Pincemin et al. 1998:Fig. 6, redrawn by Kay Clahassey; courtesy of Joyce Marcus and William J. Folan).

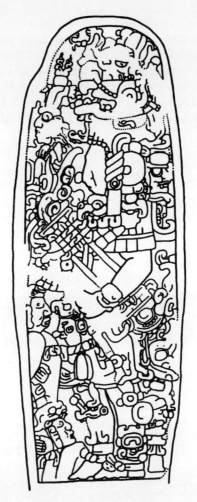

FIGURE 6.6 Calakmul Stela 43, erected in A.D. 514 (Folan et al. 1995:Fig. 15, redrawn by Kay Clahassey; courtesy of Joyce Marcus and William J. Folan).

seating, it is not unlikely that this monument commemorates the be-ginning of a Middle Classic *may* at Calakmul.

Two likely candidates for k'atun seats within a hypothetical Calak-mul *may* realm in the Middle Classic are Dzibanché and El Resbalón to the northeast, in what is now Quintana Roo. Both sites have hiero-glyphic stairways. At El Resbalón, the stairway has a date of 529 and in-dicates that the local rulers were subject to Calakmul (Carrasco and Boucher 1987). Excavations at Dzibanché revealed a stairway in which the blocks primarily depict prone, bound captives. The date is uncertain, and although the name of an early Calakmul ruler, Yuknom Ch'en I, appears, this ruler is otherwise unknown. Tikal's ally El Perú was apparently involved with Calakmul at this time, because a monument at El Perú records a woman named Lady Star (Na Ek') celebrating an event in A.D. 520; she was the wife of the Calakmul ruler (Montgomery 2001b:107).

A later Calakmul king nicknamed "First Axewielder" celebrated the k'atun ending of 9.7.0.0.0 (573) at Dzibanché. He may have ruled for only a few years, perhaps 572 to 579, but his name glyph appears to be an early variant of the later glyph known as kalomte' (T1030i-k), as it shows a head with the left arm grasping the "brass knuckles" weapon.

Although these data provide some support for Calakmul as a Middle Classic *may* seat, the relatively few early stelae mean that the evidence is not nearly as substantial as that for Early and Middle Classic Tikal. Two of Calakmul's early monuments, Stelae 43 and 114, show ties to the Tikal or central Petén Early–Middle Classic iconographic program and the city was clearly a large, powerful center of calendrical ritual, on its way to becoming an independent Late Classic *may* seat if it was not yet one already. Following the dedication of Stela 43 at Calakmul in 514, there ensued a 109-year gap in monument erection (one k'atun less than half a *may*). This hiatus, from 514 to 623, partially overlaps Tikal's half-*may* hiatus in monument erection, which dates from 562 to 692; Tikal's hiatus, of course, has been thought to be at least partly caused by Calakmul's machinations.

During its hiatus, Calakmul or its rulers are mentioned at a number of sites, some of them separated by substantial distances. This pattern is not unlike that of Tikal during its hiatus. Calakmul seems to have been both creating alliances and competing with sites in the Usumacinta region as well as to the southeast (Marcus 1987, 1995). In the former region, for example, a Calakmul lord was captured by Yaxchilán in 537, while to the southeast, in 546 Calakmul's ruler Tun K'ab' Hix facilitated the installation of Naranjo's ruler Aj Wosal. An alliance between Calakmul and Caracol resulted in Tikal's "defeat" in 562. It is known from later stelae that the Calakmul ruler Scroll Serpent (579–611) celebrated the 9.8.0.0.0 k'atun ending of 593, but if a monument was erected then it no longer survives. Later, Calakmul returned to action in the Usumacinta region, "attacking" Palenque in 599 and again in 611.

In 619 the Calakmul ruler Yuknom Chan supervised the Caracol ruler K'an II in some activity, and four years later Calakmul ended its hiatus in monument erection. Beginning with Stelae 28 and 29 dated to the lajuntun ending of 9.9.10.0.0 2 Ajaw 13 Pop in 623, Calakmul began commemorating k'atun and lajuntun endings emphatically with multiple—often paired—monuments (Marcus 1987). For example, the lajuntun ending of 9.13.10.0.0, on a day 7 Ajaw (702), was celebrated by seven stelae; another seven monuments were dedicated in 731 to the K'atun 4 Ajaw ending in 9.15.0.0.0 (the same period ending celebrated by Copán Stela A); and in 741, five stelae were erected at the lajuntun ending of 9.15.10.0.0 on a day 3 Ajaw. The interval of intense period-ending monument display ended around 751, 128 years after it had begun.

It would seem, therefore, that in 623, on a lajuntun 2 Ajaw, Calakmul ended its hiatus and emerged as a Late Classic *may* center, demonstrated by its commitment to commemorating period endings with carved monuments. There does not seem to have been any distinctive architectural program associated with this seating, comparable to the twin-pyramid groups or radial temples constructed for k'atun endings at Tikal, or a consistent ritual or motif such as scattering. Instead, the key element at Calakmul seems to be the erection of multiple monuments, often in pairs and often showing both king and queen.

At the beginning of its *may* seating, Calakmul was still involved with Naranjo, which, under Aj Wosal's successor, had apparently disengaged itself from Calakmul sponsorship. In a star-war event on December 24, 631, five years after Caracol's defeat of Naranjo, Calakmul delivered the final blow: it "seized" Naranjo, whose king was "k'uxaj' 'tortured' or 'eaten', perhaps a special punishment for his secession. We are told that this took place at Calakmul . . . on the very day of the battle and seemingly he was already a captive in their hands" (Martin and Grube 2000:106). This story is related on the Naranjo hieroglyphic stairway, built in 642. Fifty years later, in 680, Naranjo defeated Caracol, after which the Naranjo dynasty abruptly ceased.

Calakmul's alliances with Dos Pilas, Naranjo, and Yaxhá suggest that these sites were incorporated into Calakmul's orbit at various times in the late seventh and early eighth century, but they seemed to function at a different level of interaction than as k'atun seats. El Perú seems to be another ally, as suggested by mention of Na Kan Ajaw (Divine Woman of the Snake Polity) on that site's Stela 34 dating A.D. 692 (Wanyerka 1996b). The inscription on this monument includes the title South Divine Jaguar, which might refer to her husband or, more likely, her father at Calakmul, since Calakmul is identified with the south direction on Copán Stela A. Other likely k'atun seats in Calakmul's Late Classic period *may* realm (see Fig. 2.2a) are Oxpemul, La Muñeca, Altamira, Naachtún, Uxul, and Sasilhá (Marcus 1976:Fig. 1.15, 1983; Folan et al. 1995:330), which were equidistantly spaced in a hexagonal lattice around Calakmul, as well as Los Alacranes (B'uuk'), La Corona, and other sites that enjoyed continuing relationships from the Early Classic. Braswell et al. (2004) mention some twenty secondary-level sites in the Calakmul region. It is not difficult, in other words, to postulate the idealized thirteen jetz' k'atuns within Calakmul's Late Classic sphere of politico-ritual control.

Relations between Calakmul and sites to the northeast, such as Río Bec and Becan, are not easily understood. Around 771—in the latter half of Calakmul's *may* seating—Calakmul's influence in the area seemed to wane as a new architectural style, known as Río Bec-Chenes, developed. This style, characterized by elaborate "false pyramid" facades, flourished at Río Bec itself, Hormiguero, Chicanna, Xpujil, and Becan. Some elements were also present at Calakmul (Braswell et al. 2004). It has been suggested (Jones 1969:7, 128) that the twin towers of this new architectural style might be related to the twin-pyramid groups at Tikal. It might also be proposed that the elaborate mosaic "zoomorphic portals" at numerous sites in this area (Gendrop 1980) represent the regional architectural signature of a *may* seating similar to those of the E-Group assemblages, twin pyramids, and later ballcourts (at Chich'en Itza; see Chap. 7).

Throughout the Late Classic period, the most prominent political relationships in the lowlands seem to have been those between Calakmul and Tikal, but these are difficult to comprehend. Recent interpretations have been couched primarily in warfare terminology, with defeats, conquests, and alliances as the operative interactions between these two superpowers. In particular, interpretive scenarios have hinged on the existence of factions in Late Classic Tikal, with Calakmul supporting the Tikal-ruler-in-exile at Dos Pilas. In January 657, near the end of Tikal's hiatus, Calakmul supposedly "attacked" Tikal in a "star war" and Tikal's ruler "fled." But subsequent events are murky and suggest that relations were very complex. A scene on a painted vase dated 691 shows a Calakmul lord delivering tribute to a Tikal lord (Martin and Grube 2000:110, citing Houston and Mathews 1985). Significantly, perhaps, this is the year before the postulated 692 reinauguration of Tikal as a Late Classic *may* seat. Tikal thereupon defeated Calakmul on August 5, 695, and captured at least two important lords; the king, Yuknom Ich'ak K'ak', may have died in battle and was buried in Structure II (Braswell et al. 2004). Forty years later, in 736, Tikal's Altar 9 (see Fig. 5.8; erected along with Stela 21), celebrating the Tikal ruler Yik'in Kan K'awil's inauguration, suggests a defeat of Calakmul as it portrays a bound Calakmul lord. Yet five years later, in 741, Calakmul erected five stelae at the lajuntun ending of 9.15.10.0.0. Shortly thereafter, Tikal defeated two of Calakmul's allies, El Perú in 743 and Naranjo in 744.

As discussed in Chapters 4 and 5, Tikal's Classic period *may* cycles can be divided into four sets of intervals of ~128 years: A.D. 435 to 562, 562–692, 692–820, 820–948. Can a similar series of intervals be identified for Calakmul? The best starting point seems to be the site's Late

Classic pattern of erecting multiple monuments, particularly on period endings, between 623 and 751. This, of course, is an interval of 128 years or half a *may*, from a lajuntun date of 9.9.10.0.0 2 Ajaw 13 Pop to the ending of a K'atun 2 Ajaw in 9.16.0.0.0. This interval of intense monument dedication was preceded by a 109-year "hiatus" from 514 to 623, an interval nineteen years (approximately one k'atun) less than the 128-year pattern evident at Tikal. Moving backward in time another 128 years from 514 (the beginning of the Calakmul hiatus), we reach 386, a lajuntun of 8.17.10.0.0, on a day 13 Ajaw 18 Xul. Nothing suggests this date is particularly significant at Calakmul; the only seemingly relevant date is ten years later, in 396, when a stela at the satellite of Balakbal commemorated the k'atun ending of 8.18.0.0.0. However, given the paucity of surviving early stelae at Calakmul, it is not unlikely that one or more "missing monuments" originally existed or could eventually be found at the site dating to 386.

If, instead of moving back into the past from 623 (the start of intense monument erection), we move ahead 128 years to 751 and then another 128 years (total 256 years), we come to the lajuntun year of 879. During this Late and Terminal Classic interval, Calakmul continued to erect stelae, including celebrations of period endings in 790, 800 (two monuments), and 810 (three). In addition, it was during the Terminal Classic that earlier stelae, apparently curated for centuries, were set into the base of Structure II. A recent discussion has suggested that the latter was a triadic structure and proposed that Calakmul's sociopolitical organization was tripartite, a material manifestation of the site's place-name, Ox Te' Tun, or place of three stones (Folan, Gunn, and Domínguez Carrasco 2001). The three components of that organization were sacred, secular, and military, and centered on Structure II since Late Preclassic times (ibid.:253). Regionally, Calakmul also continued to play a significant role, as indicated on Seibal Stela 10 by the mention of its ruler, Kan Pet, participating in a k'atun-ending event with other rulers of *may* seats at 10.1.0.0.0 (849).

The small and stylistically late Calakmul Stela 61 mentions the last named ruler, Aj Tok', and scattering, a ritual suggesting a period-ending date of 10.3.0.0.0 (899) or 10.4.0.0.0 (909) (Martin and Grube 2000: 115). My preference—following from the 128-year intervals described above—would be a lajuntun-ending date of 10.2.10.0.0 2 Ajaw 13 Ch'en, 879, as it could have marked the end of Calakmul's Late Classic seating of the *may*, which began in 623. On stylistic grounds, at least four other monuments may date to Cycle 10 or even later (Proskouriakoff 1950: 152). Several of Calakmul's satellites also erected Cycle 10 monuments (Marcus 1987), including Oxpemul and Nadzcaan in 10.0.0.0.0 (830) and La Muñeca and Xamantún in 10.3.0.0.0 (889).

Another Calakmul satellite might be Xultún, lying northeast of Uaxactún near the headwaters of the Río Azul. Xultún displayed its own Emblem Glyph perhaps as early as 396 (Mathews 1985:Fig. 10) and was probably in Tikal's Early Classic *may* realm. Circumstances seem to have changed later, however, as Xultún's monuments dated to Terminal Classic k'atun endings—Stela 9 at 9.19.0.0.0?; Stela 8 at 10.0.0.0.0; Stela 1 at 10.1.0.0.0; Stela 3 at the lajuntun of 10.1.10.0.0; and Stela 10 at 10.3.0.0.0—lack the characteristic features of late monuments in the Tikal region. Xultún might have been incorporated into Calakmul's Late–Terminal Classic *may* realm.

The absence of Early Classic stelae at Calakmul is unusual. The site's later residents might have moved, buried, or destroyed most monuments dating to that interval. The stelae positioned in front of Calakmul's E-Group seem to be Late Classic replacements. The site's earliest known monument thus far, dated 431, was guarded for several centuries, but it is unclear why this monument was saved when so much of the rest of Calakmul's Preclassic and Early Classic history was obliterated. Perhaps this relates to another peculiar feature of the site's early history: the seeming absence of evidence for central Mexican contact or influence, so prominent at other major sites in the lowlands. Such references might have existed but were later seen as representing ties to unpopular dynasties, ideologies, or rituals and thus destroyed. The absence of early texts at Calakmul reduces us to extremely speculative scenarios, but what little evidence exists raises tantalizing questions about the early role of this large and important city.

Other Sites and Regions

Several other southern lowland sites deserve brief consideration in terms of the *may* model, although supporting evidence is often difficult to marshal. In some cases this is because of the unique way the site recorded its history (Palenque erected only one stela, for example), or because the site has not been amply excavated or published. Again, considerable dynastic history presented here is drawn from Martin and Grube (2000).

Caracol, Belize

Caracol, lying about 75 kilometers southeast of Tikal in western Belize, was established in the Middle Preclassic period. It is an enormous city, covering an area of 177 km^2 with an estimated population of more than 115,000 (Chase and Chase 2001:107). Nine major causeways (of a total of some twenty-seven) radiate out from the site to nearby satellites, including Cahal Pichik, La Rejolla, Retiro, and others. Caracol's dynasty was apparently founded in A.D. 331 (Chase and Chase 2001:125; see also Martin and Grube 2000:85–99); its founder is Te' K'ab' Chak, associated with the dates 331 and 349. Caracol's Emblem Glyph does not incorporate the k'ul ajaw or divine lord phrase (Martin and Grube 2000:87). The ancient name of the site is believed to be Oxwitza' 'Three Hills Water' (ibid.), but this may be a specific place within Caracol.

Caracol's Late Preclassic and Early Classic architecture displays characteristics of the Tikal *may* realm in northeastern Petén. Its largest edifice, nicknamed Caana 'Sky Place', is a triadic structure in its latest form—a huge pyramidal platform with three Late Classic structures arranged at right angles on top—like those from El Mirador and elsewhere. Similarly, an E-Group was constructed at Caracol beginning circa 300 B.C. In this group, Structure A-2 sits on the west side of a plaza facing a line of three structures on the Structure A-5/6/7 platform. Two monuments, Stelae 12 and 20, stood in front of central Structure A-6; Stela 20 shows the ruler Yajaw Te' K'inich I seated in a throne or cave and dates to 487. A cache of Early Classic monuments (Stelae 13, 14, 15, 16, and Altar 7) was found in association with Structure A-5. These monuments celebrate a sequence of k'atun endings, including 9.4.0.0.0 (514) and 9.6.0.0.0 (554). Stela 16, which celebrates the k'atun ending of 9.5.0.0.0 (534), mentions the Copán ruler Waterlily Jaguar, a reference that "demonstrates that Copán was a politically dominant center in the Middle Classic and that it was somehow prestigious for the Caracol lord to mention his interactions with Waterlily-Jaguar of Copán" (Fash 1991:96, citing Grube).

Caracol celebrated Classic k'atun endings with Giant Ajaw altars, eighteen of them, the first dating to 9.3.0.0.0 2 Ajaw (495) and the last dating to 9.12.0.0.0 or 9.13.0.0.0. (672, 692). These can be considered the site's unique *may* celebratory program. Otherwise, Caracol stelae are "deeply conservative in their sculptural style, retaining anachronistic details of costuming and pose" (Martin and Grube 2000:90). The ruler is shown frontally, with his head in profile, cradling a ceremonial bar in upraised arms in front of his chest, a posture typical of Tikal's Early Classic monuments as well as those from Copán and Quiriguá. Small figures—dwarfs?—appear on either side of his feet, and he is surrounded by "the open maws of serpents . . . each of which disgorges an ancestor" (ibid.:91).

A key event occurred on 9.5.19.1.2 9 Ik' 5 Wo (April 16, 553, near the end of a K'atun 11 Ajaw), when Yajaw Te' K'inich II came to rule at Caracol "by action of the king of Tikal" (Houston 1991). In the following year Caracol displayed its Emblem Glyph. In April 556 an "ax event" occurred, interpreted as Tikal's attack on and defeat of Caracol, and not long thereafter, in April 562, Calakmul and Caracol "defeated" Tikal in a star war. The story of Tikal's "conquest" in 562 is told on Caracol Altar 21, set into the alley of the A-Group ballcourt, which celebrates the 9.10.0.0.0 k'atun ending in 633. This supposed defeat marked the beginning of Tikal's 130-year hiatus, during which Caracol flourished. However when Tikal staged a resurgence in the late seventh century, Caracol then experienced its own corresponding hiatus in monument erection. This interval lasted 128 years, from 9.12.0.0.0 (672) to 9.18.10.0.0 (800). (An exception in this disruption is an unusual slate stela commemorating the lajuntun of 9.13.10.0.0 [702]).

Caracol's "defeat" of Tikal in 562 marks the beginning of a long period of apparent conflict among Tikal, Caracol, Calakmul, Naranjo, and Dos Pilas. It is tempting to speculate from Maya calendrics that these interactions involved Caracol's status as an existing or emerging cycle seat. Caracol defeated Naranjo twice, in 9.9.18.6.3 (631) and again in 9.10.3.2.12 (636).

During the Terminal Classic, Caracol enjoyed a renaissance and seems to have had close relations with Ucanal, perhaps beginning as early as 793 (Chase, Grube, and Chase 1991; Chase and Chase 2004). Caracol Altar 23 (800) celebrates the capture of two kings, one from Ucanal, who are shown with arms bound behind their backs. Caracol Altars 12 and 13, dated to 820, show the Caracol ruler, K'inich Tob'il Yoat, conversing with the Ucanal king, Papamalil; one shows a captive named Makal Te'. K'inich Tob'il Yoat may have set the last Giant Ajaw altar of the site marking the K'atun 7 Ajaw ending and b'ak'tun ending of 10.0.0.0.0 in March 830. The final monuments of Caracol, the small and asymmetrical Stela 17 and its accompanying Altar 10, date to 849, while all-glyphic Stela 10 commemorates the lajuntun of 10.1.10.0.0 (859).

With respect to Caracol's *may* seating, then, the interval from 859, the date of the last stela, to 495, the date of the first Giant Ajaw altar, is 364 years, 20 years or one k'atun short of the 128 + 256 year full *may* cycle. Significantly, the site's Giant Ajaw altar series began in commemoration of the completion of a K'atun 2 Ajaw.

Satellite sites within Caracol's seating of the *may* might include La Rejolla, Mountain Cow, Hatzcab Ceel, Sacul, Naj Tunich, Ixtutz, Ixkun, and B'ital, among others. Other possibilities are Ucanal and Nakum, both of which seem to have been pawns in the competition among Caracol, Calakmul, Naranjo, and Tikal at various points in their history. To judge from epigraphic and ceramic evidence, or more specifically, lack thereof, Caracol's influence does not seem to have extended into or south of the Maya mountains and southern Belize (Wanyerka, pers. comm., June 14, 2002; Prufer, pers. comm., June 18, 2002), territory apparently dominated by Copán and Quiriguá.

Palenque and Toniná, Chiapas, Mexico

The site of Palenque lies 160 kilometers west of Tikal on the boundary between the Gulf Coast plain and the Chiapas hills. The site's ancient name was Lakam Ja 'Big Water' and the kingdom was called Bak or B'aakal 'Bone'. Palenque used several main signs in its Emblem Glyph, the most common being T570 (*bak* 'wavy bone,' 'captive') but also T590 (a mandible).

Palenque's early dynastic history (Martin and Grube 2000:155–175) is known only from a series of Late Classic retrospective texts rather than from successive historical monuments erected by its rulers. Indeed, no Early Classic inscriptions are known for Palenque except for a statement of ownership on an unprovenienced travertine bowl. The site's mythic history, however, as related by texts in the Cross Group, goes back to the late fourth millennium B.C. and refers to the birth of several deities, including the well-known "Palenque Triad" of gods GI (Hunapu of the Hero Twins [Lounsbury 1985]; also Chak Xib Chak); GII (an infantile k'awil); and GIII, the Jaguar Sun God. The final ruler in this series, presumably also mythical, was Bloodletter of the Snake in the late Early Preclassic period, who was born in 993 B.C. and acceded in 967 B.C. (ca. 5.9.2.0.0). The structure of Palenque's recorded mythic history closely parallels that of the *Popol Vuh* (Tedlock 1985:62–63).

One of Palenque's Late Classic texts mentions Siyaj K'ak', leader of the Mexican "arrival" at Tikal in A.D. 378. It is possible, then, that Palenque's dynastic founding—like those of Tikal and Copán—was related to that event. However, the dynasty is said to have been founded on 8.19.15.3.4 1 K'an 2 K'ayab (March 9, 431) with the accession of ruler K'uk' B'alam I. K'uk' B'alam holds the title Toktan Lord, referring to an unknown site that might be his original home. Edmonson (1979) suggested that Palenque seated the cycle shortly thereafter in 435 on the b'ak'tun completion of 9.0.0.0.0. A series of poorly known rulers follow, one of whom was K'an Joy Kitam I, who ascended in 529. It is recorded that in 496 he had taken on "a junior title and presumed heir-apparency at the age of six" and that the "ceremony took place at Toktan" (Martin and Grube 2000:158).

During the Early Classic, Palenque's rulers may or may not have celebrated k'atun endings; if they did, their rituals did not entail the erection of commemorative stelae. We are informed of early k'atun observances only from one of the inscribed panels in the Late Classic Temple of the Inscriptions, which gives a history of rulers linked to nine k'atun endings (Schele and Mathews 1998:105–106). The record of several accessions on thirteen-tun completions is an unusual pattern and may be an idealized, reconstructed history.

The best-known portion of Palenque's history begins with the ruler K'inich Janab' Pakal I. Pakal was born on 9.8.9.13.0 8 Ajaw 13 Pop (March 24, 603), son of Lady Sak K'uk', and acceded to the throne at the age of twelve on July 27, 615 (9.9.2.4.8 5 Lamat 1 Mol). He married a woman from Toktan, had at least two sons with her who succeeded him, and died at the age of eighty in 683 (9.12.11.5.18). Pakal celebrated the k'atun endings of 9.11.0.0.0 K'atun 12 Ajaw (652) and 9.12.0.0.0 K'atun 10 Ajaw (672). His Late Classic palace complex is assumed to be a popol naj, or council house (Schele and Mathews 1998:368n31).

In the k'atun preceding Pakal's reign, Palenque was "attacked" twice by Calakmul some 250 kilometers to the northeast and once by Bonampak, about half that distance to the southeast. The first attack by Calakmul, probably in April 599, involved an "axing" and "throwing down," interpreted as the sacking of the city and the overthrow of its rulers and patron deities (Martin and Grube 2000:160). The second attack came twelve years later, in April 611. The palace structure at Palenque commemorates these and other events with carvings of prisoners. Apparently the site was in disarray for a k'atun or so, and the fact that major rituals were not performed at the turning of the ninth k'atun in 613 was sufficiently worrisome to be noted in the site's later inscriptions. Two years later, in 615, K'inich Janab' Pakal I assumed rulership.

A significant event occurred in 659, when Pakal was visited by someone named Nun Ujol Chak, once thought to be the exiled ruler of Tikal but who is now believed to have been a native of a site in Tabasco (Martin 2003:28). This event was recorded on buildings Pakal constructed (Schele and Mathews 1998:97) and apparently also resulted in the importation of Petén-style polychrome pottery into Palenque's Murcielagos ceramic complex (see Rands 1973:58). It also marks the beginning of the effigy censer stand "cult" or set of mortuary rituals that celebrated the Jaguar Sun God of the Underworld (JGU) (Rice 1999).

Edmonson (1979:15) suggested that Palenque again seated the cycle in A.D. 692 (9.13.0.0.0). One of the most splendid architectural complexes in the Maya lowlands, Palenque's "Cross Group"—consisting of the Temple of the Cross, the Temple of the Foliated Cross, and the Temple of the Sun—were dedicated in 692, perhaps as part of this renewal. Also, Palenque's only carved stela was erected to commemorate this period ending (Martin and Grube 2000:169). Satellites within Palenque's realm would have included Tortuguero, 61 kilometers west of Palenque, whose ruler "conquered" Comalcalco in 649 and also "attacked" a Palenque ally in 644 and 655. Another is Toniná, 64 kilometers to the south, which attacked Palenque in 711 and seized its ruler, K'an Joy Kitam. Piedras Negras might also lie within Palenque's realm, as a sajal of that site's ruler was taken captive in 725.

I agree with Edmonson in proposing dates for Palenque's *may* seating that parallel those of Tikal. In other words, the seating began in 435, shortly after the founding of the site's dynastic line in 431 and the year of the inauguration of the long-ruling king nicknamed "Casper." The second seating of the *may* at Palenque would have been in 692. The last of Palenque's rulers was Wak Kimi Janab' Pakal III, who acceded in 799. Residential occupation of the site ended shortly thereafter, to judge from the ceramic remains, and the last known reference to Pakal III is around 814 at Comalcalco (Martin and Grube 2002:175). Palenque's last *may* seating, then, would have lasted barely 128 years or a half cycle (692 + 128 = 820).

One candidate for Palenque's successor as *may* seat is Toniná, perhaps known in ancient times as Po or Popo, which first displayed its Emblem Glyph on or around 9.8.0.0.0 (593) (Mathews 1985). The site is poorly known in the Early and Middle Classic periods (Martin and Grube 2000:177–189), and there are numerous gaps in dates on the city's more than two hundred monuments (Mathews 2001). Retrospective reference is made to a king in A.D. 217, and various monuments date to the sixth century but give few rulers' names. The site's Late Classic history is better understood. Sculpture from the reign of Ruler 2 (668–687) shows emphasis on Giant Ajaw altars, otherwise known primarily from Caracol, and depictions of bound captives, also prominent on Tikal's monuments. A stucco mural at the eastern end of the fifth terrace of the Toniná acropolis shares the theme and layout of the Atetelco compound murals at Teotihuacan, displaying a gridded, feathered frame with medallions incorporating inverted figures. It also shows spirit companions, or *way*.

Ruler 2's lordship came to an end when Toniná was raided by Palenque in September 687, just before that site's reseating of the *may*. The next ruler, K'inich B'aknal Chak (688–715), is described as a powerful regional lord, or overking (Martin and Grube 2000:184). He constructed the sunken Ballcourt 1, probably dedicated in 699, which depicted six prisoners, all said to be vassals of the Palenque ruler K'an B'alam. The name glyphs of these prisoners give insights into other sites in the Palenque-Toniná orbit, including Amayte, La Mar, and Yaxchilán.

Toniná's monuments register 39 period-ending dates, a relatively small proportion of the total of 131 dates at the site (Mathews 2001), and only 18 of them were k'atun-ending dates (the remaining 22 commemorate jotuns, etc.). Toniná has an unusual pattern of performing some activity on Ajaw days of dates ending in 9.0 (i.e., nine tuns or "years," zero k'ins) (Table 6.1). Stuart (n.d.) has also called attention to dates nine years apart. Perhaps both refer to the jetz' lu'um (securing the land)

Table 6.1. An unusual pattern of dates at Toniná.

Maya Date	Day Names	Gregorian Year	Ruler	Monument Number
9.12.7.9.0	6 Ajaw 13 K'ank'in	679	Ruler 2	85
9.12.17.9.0	5 Ajaw 3 Kej	689	B'aknal Chak	F88
9.13.7.9.0	4 Ajaw 13 Ch'en	699	B'aknal Chak	141, p47
9.13.17.9.0	3 Ajaw 3 Yaxk'in	709	Ruler 4	p18
9.14.2.9.0	7 Ajaw 18 Sek	714	Ruler 4	p38
9.14.12.9.0	8 Ajaw 8 Sip	724	Ich'ak Chapat	p25
9.14.17.9.0	1 Ajaw 3 Wo	729	Ich'ak Chapat	7
9.18.7.9.0	7 Ajaw 18 Wo	798	Ruler 8	1
10.0.7.9.0	3 Ajaw 3 Sak	837	Uj Chapat	104
10.3.17.9.0	9 Ajaw 18 Sak	906	Ruler 10	p1

Source: Mathews n.d.:Table 2.

ceremony, which in modern Tekanto, Yucatán, must be performed every nine years (Thompson 1999:239).

If we take the display of the Emblem Glyph in 593 as Toniná's possible seating of the *may*, moving forward 128 years puts us at the lajuntun of 9.14.10.0.0 (A.D. 721), slightly less than two years before the accession of Ich'ak Chapat, who ruled more than fifty years. Another 128 years, the slowdown period of the last half of the *may* seating, takes us through the long rule of Ruler 8 to A.D. 849; only two dated monuments were carved after 800, however. The last date at Toniná, on Monument 101, is 10.4.0.0.0, a k'atun ending on January 15, 909, one of the latest Long Count dates in the lowlands.

Dos Pilas, Petén, Guatemala

Dos Pilas, situated 115 kilometers southwest of Tikal in the Petexbatún region between the Pasión and Salinas Rivers, is another site that was part of the complex web of Late Classic period politico-religious machinations. Two sites in the Petexbatún were dominant in the Early Classic, Tamarindito and Arroyo de Piedra, but the region's history changed profoundly in the early seventh century when Dos Pilas was established (Houston 1987, 1993; Martin and Grube 2000:55–67; Fahsen 2002; Demarest 2004). While it is unlikely that Dos Pilas itself seated the *may*, the site appears to have played a critical role in the balance of power between the two major political rivals of the Late Classic period, Tikal and Calakmul.

Newly discovered sections of a hieroglyphic stairway at Dos Pilas indicate that the site was founded by Tikal in A.D. 632 when Tikal's ruler dispatched his four-year-old son, B'alaj Kan K'awil, to the Petexbatún (Fahsen 2002). This founding was motivated in part by Tikal's desire to control trade from the highlands along the Río Pasión (Demarest, pers. comm., July 1, 2002). Those and subsequent events are extremely confusing as to motivations and internal and external relations of the principals. In addition, it is difficult to distinguish places because, as the son of the Tikal ruler, B'alaj Kan K'awil seems to have felt entitled to display the Tikal Emblem Glyph. There was apparently some intradynastic conflict between B'alaj Kan K'awil at Dos Pilas and Nun Ujol Chak, a younger (?) brother currently ruling Tikal, and Calakmul was brought into the fray. By 648 B'alaj Kan K'awil described himself as yajaw, or vassal, of Calakmul, and in 652 Calakmul defeated Dos Pilas. Then, in 657, in a star-war event, Calakmul "defeated" Tikal, forcing Nun Ujol Chak into exile at Palenque.

In 672 Nun Ujol Chak of Tikal struck back: he returned from exile, overthrew Dos Pilas, and forced its ruler, B'alaj Kan K'awil, into five-year exile. B'alaj Kan K'awil then returned to Dos Pilas on the same day in 677 when Calakmul "defeated" Tikal and two years after that led his own "battle" that resulted in the "defeat" of Tikal. It was after that defeat that Dos Pilas, under the guidance of B'alaj Kan K'awil's son and successor, built the commemorative Hieroglyphic Stairway 2, which referred to the thirteen tzuk or divisions (k'atun seats) in Tikal's realm.

Perhaps because of these conflicts and exile, it was not until around 682 that Dos Pilas and its rulers were able to begin a major program of monument erection and construction. During that year, B'alaj Kan K'awil visited Calakmul to celebrate the lajuntun of 9.12.10.0.0 9 Ajaw 18 Zotz (he also erected Dos Pilas Stela 9 to commemorate that event) and then returned four years later for the accession of Calakmul's ruler Yich'ak K'ak'. Also in 682 his daughter, Lady Six Sky, was sent to establish a new dynasty at Naranjo. Her son, K'ak' Tiliw Kan Chak, came to rule Naranjo in 693 at the young age of five years; he was probably merely a figurehead under her leadership until her death in 741. His father is not named but was likely a lord of Calakmul, as her son proclaims himself a vassal of that site.

B'alaj Kan K'awil's son, Itzamnaj K'awil, came to rule Dos Pilas in 698 and erected numerous stelae commemorating the events and period end-ings of his reign (Stuart and Houston 1994:84–92). Dos Pilas Stela 1, for example, commemorated the jolajuntun at 9.13.15.0.0; on Stela 14, dated 9.14.0.0.0 6 Ajaw 13 Muwan, Itzamnaj K'awil is shown standing atop an "earthband," with a crouching bound captive below. Stela 15, dated 9.14.10.0.0 5 Ajaw 3 Mak (October 11, 721), was erected in the El Duende complex on the east side of the site. This stela is of particular interest because the text in the upper register of the monument includes "five distinct place names, each in association with a different event" (Stuart and Houston 1994:91). According to this text, Itzamnaj K'awil scattered at El Duende, was adorned at Seibal, and then, apparently on the same day, erected a stela at Aguateca; eighty days later, he erected a stone—probably Stela 15 itself—at El Duende and then danced at Dos Pilas (Stuart and Houston 1994:92).

An apparent regent, known as Ruler 3, whose wife was from Can-cuen, led Dos Pilas following the death of Itzamnaj K'awil in 726. Ruler 3 "conquered" Seibal in 735 in a conquest and "axing" event that was commemorated on stelae at Dos Pilas and Aguateca; both show the ruler standing on top of the captive Seibal king (Stuart and Houston 1994:61). Following this event, he initiated the use of what is often re-ferred to as the barrel-like variant of the Tikal Emblem Glyph but is also T716, the twice-bound snouted head of an animal. In addition, Ruler 3 erected the beautifully carved Stela 8, touting the achievements of his predecessor; the monument's text mentions the Paddler Gods (Stuart, Houston, and Robertson 1999:166).

A text from Seibal on Hieroglyphic Stairway 1 refers to a later Dos Pi-las ruler, K'awil Kan K'inich (741–761), who in 746 scattered at Seibal and then again at Tamarindito two days later (Stuart and Houston 1994:92). These events recorded on Seibal H.S. 1 and Dos Pilas Stela 15 provide some evidence that Late Classic kings, in the Petexbatún-Pasión area at least, participated in ceremonial visits to sites in their realms and carried out important rituals, such as scattering. Whether such ritual circuits were generally part of their duties as kings or specifically part of their obligations through the burden of the k'atun or *may* is impossible to determine, although it could of course be both.

After 761, Dos Pilas's fortunes were dramatically reversed: there are no further references to Itzamnaj K'awil, the site seems to have been vir-tually abandoned, and a series of petty-king pretenders ruled from sev-eral sites. The upstart Dos Pilas kingdom, which was established around A.D. 632 and began using a distinctive Emblem in 735, collapsed around 761, to judge from the last mention of the site or its ruler at Tamarindito. Dos Pilas thus endured some 129 years, approximately half a *may* of 128 years, its downfall (or last reference) occurring in the lajuntun of a

K'atun 13 Ajaw. The final appearance of the Mutul main sign of an Emblem Glyph in the Petexbatún area occurred in 807, by which time the region was essentially abandoned.

Meanwhile, as the Petexbatún sites were collapsing in the late eighth century (Demarest 2004; O'Mansky and Dunning 2004), other sites at some remove were briefly flourishing. One of these was Machaquilá, on a tributary of the Río Pasión southwest of Dos Pilas, which was conquered by that site in 652 (Demarest, pers. comm., July 1, 2002). In 664, Taj Mo', ruler of Machaquilá, was captured by the Dos Pilas ruler B'alaj Kan K'awil (Fahsen 2002). Machaquilá erected stelae over a half-*may* period of 128 years, beginning on 9.14.0.0.0 6 Ajaw 13 Muwan (December 3, 711) and ending on 10.0.10.0.0 6 Ajaw 8 Pop (January 20, 840) (Graham 1967; Fahsen 1984). The sites of Machaquilá, Cancuén to the south, and Dos Pilas had fairly close relations, perhaps through marital and other alliances, as the wife of Dos Pilas Ruler 3 was from Cancuén. Farther to the north, however, Seibal was poised to take over as Terminal Classic *may* seat in the Pasión region (see Chap. 7).

Overview

Although the sites and events described here fit into the overall *may*-based model of lowland politico-ritual centers, they do so in ways that differ considerably from Tikal and from each other. This does not weaken the *may* hypothesis; rather, it illustrates the flexible and independent agency of individual rulers and cities as actors within this cosmic structure. It is not at all unreasonable to suggest that each individual Classic period cycle seat would develop its own program of architecture, iconography, and ritual asserting the unique historical, genealogical, and divine claims to power of its ruling dynasty. At the same time, however, key elements of the highly ritualized celebrations of cyclical calendrical intervals, k'atuns and *mays*, were broadly shared and very publicly proclaimed the participation of cycle seats and their satellites in rituals designed to ensure cosmic continuity throughout the lowland Maya world.

It is interesting that two of these probable *may* seats, Copán and Palenque, in addition to Tikal, were apparently visited by (or otherwise involved in) the central Mexican arrival of Siyaj K'ak' in the late fourth century. Moreover, texts carved on bones from Tikal Burial 116, presumably the tomb of Jasaw Kan K'awil, include "a long list of death-dates for foreign nobility, while others supply intriguing, but still largely opaque, references to the kingdoms of Copan and Palenque" (Martin and Grube 2000:47) and to a captive from Calakmul. All this supports the concept that some broad-scale underlying themes or plans united these sites.

With respect to Copán's seating of the *may*, the site exhibits patterns that are considerably different from those of Tikal, although these cities had very close early relationships in the founding of their dynasties and styles of their monuments. Copán did not appear to adhere as strongly as did Tikal to K'atuns 8 Ajaw as significant ritual nodes, although the series of significant dates seems to conform to units of 128 and 256 years. Architectural programs also differed: although Copán has one radial structure, it does not have Tikal's E-Group assemblages or twin-pyramid complexes, and Tikal lacks the hieroglyphic stairway program found at Copán and many other sites.

Calakmul and its seemingly continuous hostilities with Tikal warrant some discussion, because the complexity of these interactions suggests something far more intricate and deep-seated—a political pas de deux—than simple territorial aggression. To recapitulate, in A.D. 623, a lajuntun dated 2 Ajaw, Calakmul ended its hiatus in monument erection. A vase probably dated 691 shows a Calakmul lord delivering tribute to Tikal, but four years later in 695 Calakmul was "defeated" by Tikal. In 736 Tikal's Altar 9 celebrating the Tikal ruler Yik'in Kan K'awil's inauguration suggests another "defeat" of Calakmul, as it portrays a bound Calakmul lord. Five years later, in 741, five stelae were erected at Calakmul commemorating the lajuntun ending of 9.15.10.0.0, the midpoint of a K'atun 2 Ajaw. Shortly thereafter, Tikal "defeated" two of Calakmul's allies, El Perú in 743 and Naranjo in 744.

While in some cases the textual evidence for conflict between the two sites is fairly clear, other data raise questions. In particular, ceramics recovered from excavations of tombs and other contexts indicate that Calakmul residents used types and groups of the Tikal-related ceramic spheres in the Early and Late Classic (Tepeu, Eznab) (Folan et al. 1995). As Braswell et al. (2004) note with respect to artifacts in general, Late Classic Calakmul participated in an "essentially Petén-focused interaction sphere."

In the *may* model, the obvious competition between Calakmul and Tikal would revolve around the seating of the *may* at 256-year intervals, and perhaps other calendrical issues as well. One point that emerges from examination of significant dates at Calakmul is that while a few of them adhere to the K'atun 8 Ajaw dates so important at Tikal, the major transitions seem to coincide with K'atuns 2 Ajaw or lajuntuns on a day 2 Ajaw in the Maya tzolk'in, or 260-day sacred calendar. K'atuns 2 Ajaw occur at asymmetric intervals of 60 tuns after a K'atun 8 Ajaw or, differently stated, 196 tuns before a K'atun 8 Ajaw. If this observation is not an artifact of stela preservation at Calakmul but truly represents a different calendrical emphasis, it might indicate that the conflict between Tikal and Calakmul and their allied sites centered on calendrics and associated ritual. In addition, the two sites might have had ethnolinguistic differences (Stuart 1995:271–272) that could have exacerbated conflict. Whatever led to this different calendrico-ritual emphasis, if real, must have occurred or been initiated during the Calakmul hiatus, which began in 514 and ended 109 years later with a renewed emphasis on commemorating period endings. As noted, two stelae were erected in 623, the lajuntun ending of 9.9.10.0.0 on a day 2 Ajaw 13 Pop.

Caracol's relations with Calakmul are of interest in this context, because its pattern of celebrating k'atun endings with Giant Ajaw altars inaugurated its seating of the *may* at the end of a K'atun 2 Ajaw in 495. In addition, Caracol was often allied with Calakmul against Tikal, and Caracol's star-war defeat of Tikal in 562 is sometimes considered to have brought about Tikal's hiatus. The pattern of creating Giant Ajaw altars at Tikal and Quiriguá, after a "hiatus" and apparently at the start of k'atun or *may* seatings, warrants further investigation.

As a last note on Late Classic calendrics, it bears mention that Edmonson (1988:148–149, 233) identified two closely related "new" calendars that appeared in the western Maya lowlands during this period, the so-called Campeche and Palenque calendars. These differ from the Tikal calendar in seemingly minor ways, primarily in the count beginning with 1 instead of 0 and the use of terminal dating. At the time of Edmonson's writing he noted only eighteen examples of the use of these calendars, which appeared in a 277-year interval between 665 and 942. They are found at only eleven sites: Uxmal (earliest and latest examples), Edzná (three times, including two period-ending stelae), Jaina, Holactún, and Kabah in the Puuc area of Campeche, and in the Usumacinta area at Toniná, Palenque, Yaxchilán (3), Piedras Negras (2), and Bonampak. In addition, Dos Pilas Stela 8 records dates in both the Tikal and the Campeche calendars (Bricker 1997a:2). Only one nonwestern site, Naranjo (2), used these calendars.

One peculiar feature of the dates recorded by these calendars is that they refer to the month Yaxk'in ($n = 7$) in the Maya 365-day calendar, then equivalent to the month of June ($n = 8$) in the Gregorian calendar (Table 6.2).

Edmonson (1982:179n4981) notes that Yaxk'in is the only month that is distinctively referred to as being "born." The clustering of these dates in mid- to late June suggests an association with the summer solstice, although many dates do not specifically correspond and others occur in other months with no solsticial or equinoxial associations. Of

Table 6.2. An unusual pattern of Late Classic dates recorded in the Campeche and Palenque calendars.

10 Ajaw 7 Yaxk'in	June 26, 672 (Edzná)
6 Etz'nab' 19 Yaxk'in	June 24, 733 (Toniná)
13 Manik 20 Yaxk'in	June 15, 767 (Palenque)
1 Eb' 20 Yaxk'in	June 14, 768 (Yaxchilán; "flapstaff dance")
2 Eb' 20 Yaxk'in	June 12, 776 (Naranjo)
1 Kab'an 20 Yaxk'in	June 11, 781 (Piedras Negras)
3 Eb' 14 Mol	June 26, 781 (Yaxchilán)
9 Ajaw 17 Mol	June 22, 810 (Edzná; Period Ending)

Source: Edmonson 1988:148–149, 233.

particular interest is the appearance of this calendar at Naranjo, well outside the Usumacinta and lower Campeche areas.

Finally, it should be reiterated that my discussion here is an overview intended to demonstrate the possibility that the *may* structured "politics" over a wide area and that Tikal was not the only *may* seat or "capital" in the lowlands. Adequate testing of the validity and appropriateness of the *may* model for explaining inter- and intrasite political structure and affairs at these sites, as well as other patterns of commemorative dating, demands study by specialists in each site's political history and excavations.

CHAPTER 7

New Terminal Classic May Realms

Archaeologists' attention to the lowland Maya Terminal Classic period, typically dated from circa 790–800 to 950–1000, has long been focused on two topics: "collapse" in the south and "Toltec" influence and chronology in the north. These concerns were identified by archaeologists early in the twentieth century and have molded research and historical reconstructions since. There have been few discussions of events and processes common to both regions (but see Demarest, Rice, and Rice 2004).

The *may* model proposes a different interpretation of Terminal Classic circumstances in the lowlands. This period—which I date to the 128-year interval from 820 to 948, or 9.19.10.0.0 8 Ajaw 8 Xul to 10.6.0.0.0 8 Ajaw 8 Yax in the Maya calendar—was the last half of the Late Classic *may* seating at Tikal and other sites in the southern lowlands. Those sites that were *may* seats during the Late Classic continued to play a role—albeit a diminished one—during the Terminal Classic. Other sites, at the same time, in both southern and northern lowlands, seem to have risen to greater prominence and adopted new responsibilities as Terminal Classic and Early Postclassic *may ku*. Among them are Seibal and likely Ucanal in the south and Chich'en Itza, Dzibilchaltún, Uxmal and its Puuc satellites, and Cobá in the north.

The Southern Lowlands

Some central Petén sites in Tikal's *may* realm, such as Ixlú and Zacpetén around Lake Salpetén, continued to celebrate Terminal Classic period endings with monument styles and shapes shared with Tikal. Others, however, did not participate in this Tikal-centered period-ending program and instead displayed equally distinctive, Terminal Classic iconographic styles and programs of their own. One such center is Seibal in the Pasión region of southwestern Petén, along with sites in the southwestern portion of Lake Petén Itzá, closer to Tikal. Terminal Classic monuments in these areas differ significantly from those of the Tikal realm, displaying a suite of characteristics that suggest a major infusion of "foreign," that is, non-Classic and nonsouthern Maya, influences:

- Shape: Terminal Classic stelae are often small and occasionally asymmetrical. In contrast to the monuments of the Tikal realm, with their markedly broadened upper portions to better display the important Paddler ancestor figures, these stelae often have narrow tops.
- Calendrics: As in the Late Classic, these Terminal Classic monuments celebrate period-ending dates, especially k'atuns and lajuntuns. Dates are commonly given by the Calendar Round rather than Long Count and thus are primarily reconstructions.
- Primary themes: While some stelae continue to show a central dignitary scattering, a new theme appears: two (or more) unadorned seated figures conversing and gesturing.
- Secondary themes: Captives continue to appear on these monuments; Paddlers do not.
- Additional iconographic elements: These include rope motifs, often as decorated borders; scenes in two or more registers; and so-called foreign or non-Classic Maya elements such as facial features (nose, beard), dress, accoutrements (atlatls), and squared glyph cartouches.
- Nonfigural monuments: A number of Terminal Classic stelae and altars, a few in the Tikal realm but distributed over a much wider area, lack figural scenes and instead consist entirely of texts. These include Nakum Stela C (9.19.10.0.0); Flores Stela 2 (10.1.0.0.0); Ixlú Altar 1 (10.2.10.0.0); Jimbal Stela 2 (10.3.0.0.0); Uaxactún Stelae 13 (10.0.0.0.0) and 12 (10.3.0.0.0); Caracol Stela 10 (10.3.0.0.0); Uxmal Stela 17 (10.4.0.0.0) (Schele and Mathews 1998:288). This trait may have started in the Late Classic in some areas: La Naya Stela 1 (9.14.3.0.0); Uxbenká Stela 15 and 19 (9.17.10.0.0; Leventhal 1992:148); Naranjo Stelae 10 (9.19.0.0.0) and 32 (9.19.0.0.0).
- Location: Marcus (1976:193; also Houston 1993) noted that 65 percent of all Cycle 10 monuments were erected at relatively small sites that were in second- or third-order ranks in the Late Classic rather than at the large, primary centers. In addition, 40 percent of Cycle 10 Maya centers erected monuments for the first time.

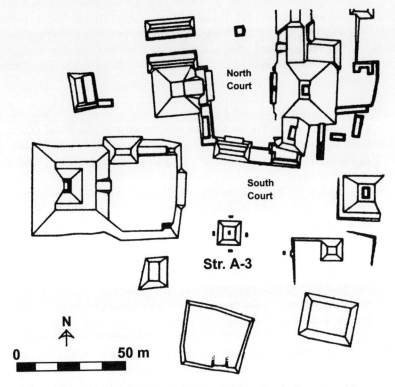

FIGURE 7.1 The southern part of Seibal Group A, showing the location of Structure A-3 (after Willey 1990:Fig. 4).

Seibal as May Ku: *Structure A-3 Monuments*

The long-occupied site of Seibal (Fig. 7.1) on the Río Pasión has three major structural groups, A, C, and D, laid out in a T-shaped arrangement and joined by causeways. Two of these groups, A and C, have ballcourts (Willey et al. 1975; Mathews and Willey 1991). The site appears to have been a major center in the Preclassic period and is of particular interest here because it has a large number of Cycle 10 stelae. The Emblem Glyph of Seibal consists of triple kawak signs and Coggins (1990:93) suggested that it "signifies the role of the site as a cyclic completion center" for the death and rebirth of b'ak'tuns. More recent readings of the Emblem suggest that it represents a "hearth" (Taube 1998), that is, the three hearthstones of creation. These readings are not incompatible.

During the Late Classic period, Seibal seems to have been under the overlordship of Dos Pilas to the south, but with the decline of that site in 761 Seibal achieved a greater degree of independence. Ten years earlier, Seibal displayed its Emblem Glyph on the hieroglyphic stairway on Structure A-14, constructed in 751 (9.16.0.0.0). A k'atun later, a new Seibal ruler, perhaps temporarily under the patronage of the king of Aguateca, was inaugurated on the k'atun ending 9.17.0.0.0 13 Ajaw 18 Kumk'u (January 22, 771). With the final collapse of the petty kingdoms of the Petexbatún region, Seibal assumed primacy as a cycle seat in the Pasión area during the Terminal Classic.

Seibal has fifty-six stelae, of which twenty-two are carved, and twenty-two mostly plain altars (Willey et al. 1975:42–43). The lack of carved stelae may be explained by the statement on Dos Pilas Stela 2 that others "chopped the writing" at Seibal (Schele and Mathews 1998:177). For the present purposes, the most interesting of Seibal's late stelae are from Group A on the western part of the site, an area of primarily Terminal Classic occupation. Also in Group A are Structure A-10, the eastern structure of an E-Group, and Structure A-14, whose hieroglyphic stairway records much of the earlier history of the site (Mathews and Willey 1991:50).

Seibal's sculpted monuments are frequently divided into Maya and non-Maya styles. In an early study of the so-called non-Classic-Maya Seibal monuments, Graham (1973) grouped them into facies A and B. Facies A stelae, dating from 10.1.0.0.0 through 10.3.0.0.0 (849–889), portrayed figures dressed in more or less Classic style but with distinctive non-Classic facial features. This grouping includes Stelae 8, 10, 11, 20, and 21, which closely resemble Stelae 1 and 2 from Ixlú and Stela 4 of Ucanal (Graham 1973:213). Facies B monuments, showing individuals with extremely long hair and lacking typical Classic attire, are Stelae 2, 3, 13, 14, 15, and 17. Tying these stylistic elements to both Puuc and Gulf Coast origins, Graham (1973:217; cf. Tourtellot and González 2004) dated them to the K'atun 1 Ajaw falling between 10.2.0.0.0 and 10.3.0.0.0 (869–889).

In a later discussion, Graham (1990) reordered Seibal's monuments into five groups: Group I consists of the Late Classic (late Cycle 9) "Palace Tablets," plus Stelae 5, 6/22, and 7. The Palace Tablets appear to have been reset into the lowest terraces of Structure A-14 in the Central Plaza of Group A, which dates to the Terminal Classic, suggesting continued veneration of ancestors. "Stelae" 5 and 7 are paired relief panels dated 9.18.10.0.0 (800) flanking the hieroglyphic stairway of Structure A-10 in the E-Group; the panels display ballgame imagery. Group II includes the "temple stelae," that is, those monuments on and around Structure A-3, along with Stela 12. Group III monuments, Stelae 1 and 20, also in Group A, commemorate the k'atun ending of 10.3.0.0.0. Stelae in Group IV include monuments numbered 2, 3, 13, 14, 17, 18, and 19; four of these were erected in Group A. Stelae 4 and 15 constitute Group V.

Stela 10

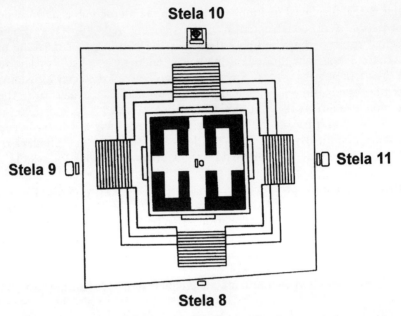

Stela 9

Stela 11

Stela 8

FIGURE 7.2 Plan of Seibal Structure A-3, a radial temple, showing placement of Stelae 8–11 around the exterior; Stela 21 is in the interior (after Schele and Mathews 1998:Fig. 5.7).

The five monuments of Structure A-3, situated in the center of the South Plaza of Group A, are particularly significant. Structure A-3 (Fig. 7.2) is a radial temple—a square platform with stairways on four sides and a small three-roomed vaulted structure on top with doorways opening to the four directions. The red-painted superstructure incorporated Puuc-style masonry and vault construction (Andrews and Robles 1985:65), and the multicolored frieze around the top bears the date 7 Ajaw 18 Sip, probably 10.0.0.0.0. This frieze contained sculptured images of twelve individuals, in all likelihood the lords of the twelve polities, or tzuk—the k'atun seats—within Seibal's Terminal Classic *may* realm. As such, it calls to mind the depictions of eight lords in the frieze around Copán's earlier Structure 10L-22, the popol naj. In the context of Maya architectural symbolism, Structure A-3 itself is highly symbolic, as symmetrical, four-stairway, radial buildings and other quadripartite figures had been associated with calendrical cycle completion since Middle Preclassic times and continued through the Postclassic.

Structure A-3 and its stelae were built and/or dedicated at the k'atun ending of (10.1.0.0.0) 5 Ajaw 3 K'ayab' (November 28, 849) by a new ruler at Seibal, Wat'ul Chatel, formerly known as Ruler E. The text on one of the monuments, Stela 11, refers to a day 6 Kawak 17 Sip reconstructed as 9.19.19.17.19 (March 12, 830), exactly one day before the ending of the tenth b'ak'tun (Grube and Martin 1998:109). This suggests that events commemorated by these stelae and the structure itself are those of the b'ak'tun ending in 830.

Wat'ul might be yet another foreigner—a "stranger-king" (as earlier at Tikal and Copán)—at Seibal, because he gives no parentage statements and there is little information available about his accession other than that he "arrived" at Seibal (see below). He held numerous titles, including Aj Jun K'in 'He of one Day' and Aj B'olon Tun (see Schele and Freidel 1990:387–389; Schele and Grube 1995:113, 119–121; Schele and Mathews 1998:175–196; Stuart 1988:206, 208). The latter seems to be a regional title, used earlier in the Petexbatún and by a previous Seibal ruler, and has been translated as "He of Nine Tasks" (Schele and Mathews 1998:351n5), but it also has been read as Aj B'olon Jaab'tal (Martin and Grube 2000:227). This suggests a reading "He of Nine Jaab's" or years, though not necessarily nine years of age. It might refer to some kingly ritual occurring at nine-year intervals, such as the jetz' lu'um walk of securing the land in modern Tekanto (Thompson 1999:238–239). A pattern of dates on Ajaw days ending with 9.0, or 9 tuns completed within a k'atun, suggests a similar pattern (see also dates at Toniná, Chap. 6).

Five stelae were placed with Structure A-3, one at the foot of each of the four platform stairways and one in the center of the temple superstructure. Although each of these stelae depicts a different scene, all have been said to represent ways in which period endings were commemorated (Stuart 1988:206; Schele and Grube 1995:119–121) as well as the varied responsibilities of Maya sovereigns in the cosmos.

Stela 11 (Fig. 7.3) has a somewhat unusual layout in three registers, with a horizontal text across the top of the monument and a short panel opposite the ruler's face. The text records that Aj B'olon Tun arrived in the center of Seibal under the sponsorship of an individual named Kan Ek' Jo Pet from a place named K'anwitz 'Yellow Mountain', tentatively identified as the site of Ucanal (Stuart and Houston 1994:20–21).

In addition to the arrival date of 6 K'awak 17 Sip, the day before the 10.0.0.0 b'ak'tun completion, this monument records a day 5 Ajaw 3 K'ayab', also noted on the other Structure A-3 monuments, which is the day of completion of the first k'atun of Cycle 10. The sculptured scene shows a mustachioed Wat'ul Chatel in his role as guarantor of earthly abundance, wearing a jaguar pelt skirt, a headdress with a sky-band, and a World Tree apron, carrying a long stick or baton, and scattering; a prone captive figure lies in the lower register. Wat'ul Chatel's portrait may also have appeared in the frieze above the south doorway

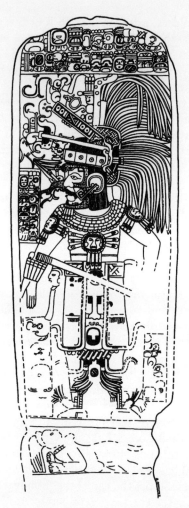

FIGURE 7.3 Seibal Stela 11, on the east side of Structure A-3, records the arrival of
Aj B'olon Tun Wa'tul Chatel at Seibal and shows him scattering (drawing courtesy
of John Montgomery).

on Structure A-3 (Willey 1990:199). Stela 11 stands on the east side of
the structure; east in Maya cosmology is associated with sunrise, rain,
fertility, and birth and is also the starting point of ceremonial circuits.

Stela 10 (Fig. 7.4) is slightly asymmetrical but with a narrow rather
than wider top; in its text layout it recalls Late Classic Tikal Stelae 19,
21, and 22, with two panels of glyphs on the left side of the face of the
monument. The text begins with a date of 5 Ajaw 3 K'ayab' (10.1.0.0.0;
849) and records that "his first k'atun he scattered incense, he of one day,

K'ak' Aj B'olon Tun, Wat'ul, holy Seibal." This event happened "in the center of" (*tan*) Seibal and was "watched" (*ila*) by three visiting ajaws: Jewel[?] K'awil from Tikal, Kan Pet [Lo?] from Calakmul, and Kan Ek' from Nal or the Ik' site, possibly Motul de San José (Grube and Martin 1998:128–129; Martin and Grube 2000:53; Montgomery 2001b:213). Wat'ul Chatel, bedecked with mat symbols in his collar and headdress, is depicted frontally, holding a cosmic monster or serpent ceremonial bar across his chest, a symbol of blood and royal genealogy. He wears a

FIGURE 7.4 Seibal Stela 10, on the north side of Structure A-3, shows Wat'ul Chatel and mentions a ritual watched by visitors from three other sites identified by Emblem Glyphs in A9–B11 (drawing courtesy of John Montgomery).

FIGURE 7.5 Seibal Stela 9, on the west side of Structure A-3, shows Wat'ul Chatel as the Maize God (drawing courtesy of John Montgomery).

jaguar skirt and belt that repeats some of the same sky-band glyphs of his bar. This stela stands on the north, home of the ancestors and the sun at zenith.

Stela 9 (Fig. 7.5), on the west side of the structure, shows Wat'ul as the Maize God. His head, face, and costuming are "classically" Maya, particularly evidenced by his flattened forehead. His headdress is nearly identical to that worn by the principal figure on Ucanal Stela 4. The inscription mentions that he witnessed the appearance of a Vision Serpent, and he holds the same ceremonial bar with astronomical symbols seen on Stela 10, depicting the cosmic or celestial serpent. It again states the titles "Ah B'olon Tun" and "Aj Jun K'in." West is associated with sunset, death, and the entrance to the Underworld.

Stela 8 (Fig. 7.6) is slightly wedge-shaped and asymmetrical. In iconographic detail, this monument is the most "classic"of these monuments in style. Wat'ul is shown in the costume of the Bearded

FIGURE 7.6 Seibal Stela 8, on the south side of Structure A-3, portrays Wat'ul Chatel as the Jaguar God of the Underworld (drawing courtesy of John Montgomery).

Jaguar God or Jaguar Sun God of the Underworld (JGU or GIII) with cruller eyes and jaguar gloves and booties and holding a God K head. His headdress, similar to that on Stela 11 in having a sky-band bar, displays a diving bird that also appears on warriors' headdresses at Chich'en Itza. The inscription mentions that Wat'ul celebrated the end of the k'atun in the plaza of Seibal with a witness named Hakawitzil, possibly from Chich'en Itza. The JGU/GIII imagery worn by the ruler is appropriate for the placement of this monument on the south side of Structure A-3, as south is linked symbolically to death and the Underworld in Maya cosmology.

Stela 21, inside the temple and facing east, has a very eroded text. The scene shows Wat'ul again wearing the eye cruller and beard but little else of the Bearded Jaguar Sun God costuming. He holds a K'awil or manikin scepter in his right hand and in his left a shield depicting the Sun God.

Several other stelae in Seibal's Group A, especially from its South Plaza, are of interest. These monuments generally do not display standard Classic lowland styles of portraiture and some have atypical placements. Two are k'atun-ending markers: Stela 1, on the north end of the South Plaza, celebrates 10.2.0.0.0; Stela 20 dates to 10.3.0.0.0. Both show similar figures carrying a similar staff. Stela 20 is one of three stelae (Stelae 13 and 17 are the others) that formed an east-west alignment of monuments on Structure A-24 and its large frontal terrace on the west side of the South Plaza.

Another monument in Group A, Stela 19, is unusual not only in its asymmetrical shape but also in the figure's beaked mask and ornamented speech scroll. Dating of the monument is uncertain, but its 1 B'en 1 Pop reading suggests either a "ritualistic calculation" or a date of 10.1.18.6.13 (Graham 1990:60). I am inclined instead to believe the date is a jotun, lajuntun, or jolajuntun ending, as the figure is performing the scattering rite.

Stela 3 (Fig. 7.7), found in front (west) of Structure A6 and now in the Museo Nacional in Guatemala City, has three registers (Graham 1990: 61–64), reminiscent of monuments in Yucatán. The upper and lower registers show pairs of seated individuals conversing. Those in the upper register are long-haired and barefoot, wearing loincloths, necklaces of large round beads, and masks. The figures in the lower register are also barefoot and long-haired, but they have different ornaments and are holding objects that suggested to Graham (1990:62) "the rattle and drum of the katun." The middle register shows an individual standing in a "plumed and conventionalized serpent mouth." The text has squared glyph cartouches, and Graham dates Stela 3 to (10.2.5.3.10) 1 Ok 8 Kank'in (September 28, 874).

FIGURE 7.7 Seibal Stela 3 (drawing courtesy of John Montgomery).

Lake Petén Itzá

In central Petén, the political situation is far more complex than indicated by the content and distribution of monuments of the Tikal realm (see Chap. 5). Several stelae found around the southwestern part of Lake Petén Itzá—including those on Flores Island in the smaller, southern arm of the lake, and in the modern community of Santa Elena on the mainland across from Flores—display non-Classic Maya characteristics similar to those seen on the Seibal monuments. In addition, Terminal Classic ceramic complexes recovered from sites in the lakes region, in-

FIGURE 7.8 Flores Stela 1 (after Morley 1937–38:Plate 45a).

cluding Tayasal (Chase 1983) but also Tikal-related Ixlú, Zacpetén (Rice 1996), and Macanché (Rice 1987), incorporate elements from the Pasión area, such as large incurved-rim basins and rare (and mostly imitation) Fine Orange.

In 1915 Morley (1937–1938:432–436) encountered three carved monuments or fragments on Flores Island, all of them reset near the church. It is not clear, therefore, whether these stelae were originally part of the occupation of Flores or if they had been moved there from some location elsewhere around the lake. All appear to represent period-ending markers. Flores Stela 1 (Fig. 7.8), dated (10.2.0.0.0) 3 Ajaw 3 Kej (August 15, 869), has a seated figure in the jaws of an upturned serpent and another seated figure above; the back bears a text. Flores Stela 2, "the top portion of a small all-glyphic stela," is dated (10.1.0.0.0) 5 Ajaw 3 K'ayab' (November 28, 849); its glyphs are large and crudely carved. Flores Stela 3, the upper portion of a monument, has a carved date of (10.0.0.0.0) 7 Ajaw 18 Sip (March 13, 830). Flores Stela 4, discovered in 1975, was carved in a stiff, blocky style. It depicts the lower torso and legs of a poorly proportioned profiled striding figure who carries a bag in his right hand and is wearing taloned sandals (Navarrete 1988:9; Hellmuth 1976:66); it is probably Postclassic in date.

Flores Stela 5 (Fig. 7.9) has a text of squared glyphs and shows a winged, barefoot diving figure in profile, flanked by diving birds interpreted variously as quetzals (Taube 1992:72, 73), guacamayos or macaws (Navarrete 1988:9–10), and turkeys (Chase 1983:1075). In Postclassic Yucatán, descending images were usually considered to represent "God E," the Maize God (Taube 1992:41–50). The figure on the Flores stela displays many of this deity's associated traits: foliage appearing out of the head (often out of a k'an sign), featherlike elements projecting from the arms, and holding something (maize? tamales? a mirror?) in outstretched hands. God E is associated not only with maize, life, fertility, and agricultural cycles but also with death and sacrifice, and may also represent "the idealized ancestor" (ibid.). The figure on Flores Stela 5, however, has been identified as wearing a God K headdress and might be God K (ibid.:73).

Stela 5 is not satisfactorily dated. Its 2 Ajaw 13 Yaxk'in date might be a misreading for the number or month of the ja'ab' (or perhaps it was a date recorded in the Campeche/Palenque calendar?). A day 2 Ajaw coincides with a day 13 Ch'en in 10.2.10.0.0 (879), 13 Mak in 10.9.0.0.0

FIGURE 7.9 Flores Stela 5 (after Navarrete 1988:Fig. 5, who refers to it as Monument 2).

(1007), 13 K'ayab' in 10.15.10.0.0 (1135), 8 Sip in 11.2.0.0.0 (1263), and 8 Yaxk'in in 11.8.10.0.0 (1392). I feel it is more likely that number 8 could be misread for 13 than that the month sign of Yaxk'in could be mistaken for any of the above alternatives, and I am inclined toward the latest date of 1392.

In the modern community of Santa Elena, on the south shore of Lake Petén Itzá and joined to Flores Island by a causeway constructed in the mid-twentieth century, several monument fragments can be seen cemented into the courtyard of the Escuela Normal Rural "Julio E. Rosado Pinelo." It was reported to me that a Classic period site was destroyed in order to construct the school at this location.

Santa Elena Stela 1 is the upper portion of a stela with carving on both faces. It has a distinctive non-Petén-style pointed shape, with both "corners" removed, a form similar to monuments in the Puuc area (see below). One side of the monument shows a single figure facing left, wearing a beaded collar with a round pectoral and holding a ceremonial bar over his chest. A glyphic text appears to the right of the figure. The reverse side shows a figure also facing left, holding a ceremonial bar at the waist, suggesting a Late Classic date.

Ucanal

Ucanal lies in eastern Petén, Guatemala, on the west bank of the Mopán River. It is located some 51 kilometers southeast of Tikal, closer to and southeast of Naranjo, and directly west of but at a slightly greater distance from Caracol. In this location Ucanal's political history seems to have been dominated by those two large sites.

As noted above, it has been suggested that the Maya name for Ucanal might have been K'anwitz 'Yellow Mountain' (see also Grube and Martin 1998:109–113). Early maps suggested Ucanal was a quaternary-level site in the Classic lowland Maya settlement hierarchy (Marcus 1976:Table 13). However, recent mapping and excavations at the site reveal that it was substantially larger than originally supposed, with 114 structure groups, an E-Group, two ballcourts, two causeways, and two canals that descended to the river (Laporte and Mejía 2002; see also Corzo, Alvarado, and Laporte 1998). The site had 26 stelae, 18 altars, 7 monuments, and a hieroglyphic stairway in Ballcourt 1.

During the reign of Siyaj Kan K'awil at Tikal, A.D. 411–456, Ucanal's ruler was yahaw, or subordinate, to him (Martin and Grube 2000:35). But the site later displayed its own (?) Emblem Glyph, suggesting that by 9.8.0.0.0 (593) Ucanal occupied a relatively high rank and had its own territorial polity. Recent surveys in southeastern Petén reveal numerous sites in the Mopán area that were within Ucanal's dominion, including

Calzada Mopán, El Calabazal, El Camalote, La Amapola, La Blanca, Sacul, Ixkun, and El Chal (Corzo, Alvarado, and Laporte 1998:192). The text on Stela 1 at Sacul states that in February 760 its ruler received the manikin scepter in the presence of someone from Ucanal (ibid.:193), suggesting that Sacul was under that site's hegemony. Ixkun Stela 2 refers to a war with Ucanal in May 780.

Although occupied since the Middle Preclassic, Ucanal seems to have reached its peak in the Terminal Classic and Early Postclassic, experiencing three waves of external contacts. The first brought mosaic sculpture facades, the second brought new monuments and grandiose remodeling of structures, and the third saw construction of round structures (Laporte and Mejía 2002:43–44). Laporte and Mejía suggest that the site flourished some two hundred fifty years beyond the end of the Late Classic and into the eleventh century; I would see this as a *may* cycle running from 820–830 to 1076 or so.

Of the ten sculptured stelae at Ucanal, one probably dates to the lajuntun of 9.12.10.0.0 9 Ajaw 18 Sotz' (682; Laporte and Mejía 2002:30), five commemorate Late Classic k'atun or lajuntun endings beginning in 9.19.0.0.0, and three date to the Terminal Classic period. Iconographically, they share much with monuments in the Tikal *may* realm, suggesting that by the Terminal Classic, Ucanal's ties to Naranjo, Caracol, and Calakmul had been ruptured. In addition, ceramics from the site's Late and Terminal Classic complexes are members of the Tepeu (Tikal-Uaxactún) sphere.

It will be recalled that the monuments around Seibal Structure A-3 (particularly Stela 11) celebrated the arrival of a new king, Wat'ul Chatel, in 830, who was apparently sponsored by king Kan Ek' Jo Pet from a place named K'anwitz, possibly Ucanal (Grube and Martin 1998:109). The occurrence of the name or title Kan Ek' in the Terminal Classic period is important in connection with the later series of Itza rulers of Tayasal in Lake Petén Itzá, all of whom held that title in the early Colonial period.

Ucanal Stela 3 is the northernmost of three monuments erected in a small stela plaza, Plaza H, on the west side of Structure A-26, a large platform at the south end of the central or main plaza of the site. Its carved face has deteriorated badly, but Morley (1937–1938:195) tentatively dated it to (10.0.10.0.0) 6 Ajaw 8 Pop (January 20, 840). Altar 3, found 2 meters in front of this stela, shows five seated or kneeling figures, four of which are bound captives. Translations of the nineteen glyphs that accompany this scene have not yet been published. Graham's newly discovered Altar 1 at Ucanal also shows a frontal seated prisoner with his arms bound behind his back.

Ucanal Stela 4 (Fig. 7.10) was found to the north (front) of Structure

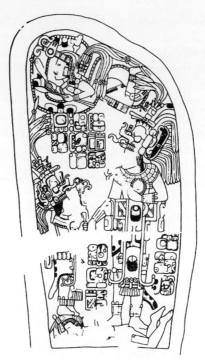

FIGURE 7.10 Ucanal Stela 4, dated (10.1.0.0.0) 5 Ajaw 3 K'ayab' (November 28, 849). Note the warrior figure in the "sky" above the ruler, the scattering glyph at B2, and the squared glyph cartouches at C2 and C6a; the Ucanal Emblem appears at C3 and D1 (after drawing by Ian Graham, from Stuart 1988:Fig. 5.12).

A-26, accompanied by a plain altar and a plain stela (Morley 1937–1938:196–198). Dated (10.1.0.0.0) 5 Ajaw 3 K'ayab' (November 28, 849), this asymmetrical monument celebrates a scattering event overseen by a Paddler God clad in warrior garb (including atlatl and darts) in a dotted scroll, at the "setting of a stone" (Schele and Grube 1995:122). Two barefoot figures, the one on the right considerably larger than the one on the left (a son?) but each in identical costume of jaguar-skin kilt and holding a God K scepter, stand upon a captive. As on the later Stela 1 from Jimbal, squared day name glyphs occur, but these are different, nonsequential days: 10 Kawak and 13 Ajaw. At C3 is a glyph reading "divine K'anwitz kalomte'."

The Northern Lowlands

Although the iconographic elements on the Seibal and Lake Petén Itzá stelae in the southern lowlands have been identified as non-Maya—that is, "Mexican," "Putun," Chontal, and so on—their source and the mechanisms of their arrival in Petén are not yet clearly understood. Indeed, some archaeologists continue to oppose the notion of foreigners in the area at all. On closer analysis, some of these elements appear to be most closely related to monuments in the northern lowlands, especially those of the Puuc region, where the new Campeche and Palenque calendars came into use in the Late and Terminal Classic.

The Puuc Region
UXMAL

The Puuc region of Campeche and Yucatán, in the northwestern corner of the peninsula, is characterized by fertile soils and low hills (*puuk*) rising about 175 meters above the flat limestone plain. Uxmal and other centers in the eastern Puuc region, such as Sayil, Kabah, and Labná, reached their florescence primarily in the Terminal Classic period, 750/ 800–1000 (Carmean, Dunning, and Kowalski 2004). Neighboring "western Puuc" sites such as Edzná, Xcalumkin, and Oxkintok peaked slightly earlier, have fewer carved monuments, and lack the elaborate mosaic facades of sites to the east (Andrews and Andrews 1980:300). Terminal Classic stelae in this northern area are distinctive because of their proportions (relatively tall compared to width), use of multiple registers (reminiscent of the layout of codices), decorated borders, and pointed tops and truncated corners. In addition, stelae in the northern lowlands are frequently found at the termini of, or otherwise associated with, causeways. Like these other prominent Terminal Classic northern lowland cities, Uxmal lacks a true Emblem Glyph (Stuart and Houston 1994:5).

According to the books of the chilam b'alams, Uxmal was established in a K'atun 2 Ajaw (A.D. 731–751) by a Mexican group known as the Xiw or Tutul Xiw, part of migrations of Mexicans into the Maya lowlands beginning in a K'atun 8 Ajaw (672–692). The leader was Aj Kuy Tok' Tutul Xiw, who supposedly reigned from K'atun 2 Ajaw (9.16.0.0.0, 751) through K'atun 10 Ajaw (10.5.0.0.0, 928). Aj Kuy Tok' means "Lord of the Owl-Flint," which is interpreted as referring to Teotihuacan connections (Schele and Mathews 1998:259). Uxmal appears to have been the "primate religious and political capital" in the Puuc area around A.D. 1000 (Kowalski 1994:95; Carmean, Dunning, and Kowalski 2004). A causeway links the site to two subsidiary sites, Nohpat and Kabah, and possibly also to Hunto Chac (Kowalski 1994:113; Carmean, Dunning, and Kowalski 2004).

Uxmal and its satellites exhibit typical Puuc-style architecture characterized by multiroom palaces with elaborate stone mosaic facades and vault stones. As at many Terminal Classic and Postclassic sites in the northern lowlands, the ceremonial precinct is surrounded by a wall. One unusual structure at Uxmal, the Adivino or Temple of the Magician, has a substructure with an apsidal plan and two temple superstructures; it was built in four stages. Most of the constructions with carved dates were built at the beginning of the tenth century. For example, the ballcourt has sequential days of 2 Ix 17 Pop (10.3.15.16.14; January 13, 905) and 3 Men 18 Pop (10.3.15.16.15; January 14, 905) carved on two stone rings.

Structures in the Nunnery Quadrangle are dated to sequential years: (10.3.17.12.1) 2 Imix 19 Kank'in (October 2, 906) and (10.3.18.9.12) 4 Eb' 5 Kej (August 9, 907). The Nunnery Quadrangle can be recognized as a cosmogram and a variant of Tikal's twin-pyramid groups (Kowalski 1994). The North Building, which sits on the highest elevation, represents ancestors and "the sky": the structure has thirteen doorways (recalling the thirteen levels of heaven) and is decorated with muyal, or cloud symbols, and bicephalic serpents resembling the ceremonial bars carried by Classic rulers. It also has four elaborate mosaic masks of stacked long-nosed deity heads and symbols recalling Mexican Tlaloc-year sign glyphs. The South Building has nine doorways, like the nine-doorway palaces of the twin-pyramid complexes (nine levels of the Underworld and lords of the night), and thus has Underworld associations. It sits at the lowest level of the Nunnery complex, and its central doorway and southern stair access are aligned with the ballcourt to the south. The flanking East and West Buildings sit on the same, intermediate level between those to the north and south. Each has a broad stairway running across its entire front, perhaps recalling the important frontal stairways of the radial structures in twin-pyramid complexes. The western structure has seven doorways and is decorated with God N/turtle figures; the eastern structure has five doorways and is decorated with owls.

The only identified Uxmal ruler is "Lord Chak," believed to be the figure on Uxmal Stela 14 (Fig. 7.11), one of sixteen monuments on a stela platform west of the Monjas structure. He is shown standing inside a structure (or palanquin?) on top of a double-headed jaguar throne, wearing jaguar booties and carrying a bag in his right hand and holding aloft an ax and shell trumpet in his left. Two small figures are on the right side of the central figure; the larger of the two, in Chich'en Itza–style dress, is standing atop a fallen captive. The basal panel shows two naked, dead captives sprawled in what is apparently a cave or cenote, judging from its border. Above the scene are two Paddler-like figures, the one on the left with the clawlike foot of Jimbal Stela 1, plus complex quasi-floral imagery vaguely similar to Yaxhá Stela 31. The unusual "seat-shaped" Stela 17 has a lengthy but largely undecipherable text and

FIGURE 7.11 Uxmal Stela 14; the name Lord Chak appears at A3 (after drawing by Taube 1992:Fig. 4e).

records the period ending of 10.4.0.0.0 in 909 (Schele and Mathews 1998:288).

In addition to its (relatively few) stelae, Uxmal and some of the other Puuc sites (e.g., Sayil) display numerous phallic sculptures, perhaps material manifestations of the varied penis titles (e.g., *at, ach, yoat*) used in the Classic (Montgomery 2001a:206) and Postclassic periods (e.g., thirteen Itza k'atun priests known as Ach Kat in Petén; Jones 1998:61). The word *Uxmal* has been read as "Thrice Built" (Schele and Mathews 1998:257), perhaps referring to the city's having been a *may* seat for three terms beginning in the Terminal Classic.

OTHER PUUC SITES AND MONUMENTS

The large site of Sayil dates primarily to the early Terminal Classic (Tourtellot and Sabloff 1994; Carmean, Dunning, and Kowalski 2004).

FIGURE 7.12 Sayil Stela 5; note the pointed top and braided border (after Proskouri-akoff 1950, from Pollock 1980:Fig. 276c).

The southern B Group, one of three major architectural assemblages, is of particular interest. Lying at the end of a causeway, the group consists of a ballcourt, a huge terrace, several courts, and a large palace (Pollock 1980:124). In addition, a low "monument platform" (Str. 4B4) sits on the causeway a short distance north of the ballcourt. This platform supported eight stelae and seven or more altars, which stood in an east-west row and faced south toward the ballcourt (Pollock 1980:131, 133). Four of these stelae (nos. 3, 5, 6, 8) are characterized by being very narrow in comparison to their height and having pointed or triangular tops. On Stela 3 the principal figure may be scattering, and the 5 Ajaw day suggests a 10.1.0.0.0 k'atun-ending date. Stela 5 (Fig. 7.12) shows a figure, possibly dancing, who holds a serpent-footed scepter, and the border has braid motif. It too appears to be early Cycle 10 in date (Pollock 1980:135, citing Proskouriakoff 1950:162). Stela 6 shows a small figure standing on a pedestal or throne and is thought to date to the period ending 9.19.0.0.0 (Pollock 1980:135, citing Proskouriakoff 1950:162).

Oxkintok is located far in the northwest corner of the Yucatán peninsula, on the edge of the Puuc zone. This site flourished in the Middle Classic (A.D. 400–500) and has the distinction of having the earliest known Long Count date in the northern lowlands—Lintel 1 at 9.6.0.0.0 (475); plus Stela 4, with a figure standing in a position similar to those on Early Classic Petén stelae—and also Manik III blackware pottery

(Coggins 1983:39). This evidence led Coggins (1983:39) to suggest that "an important person may have moved directly to Oxkintok from the southern lowlands" in the late fifth century. Twenty-five stelae have been identified at the site, nineteen of them sculptured. Virtually all the Late and Terminal Classic monuments are carved with scenes in multiple registers separated by a band of glyphs (Pollock 1980:316–322), which might be interpreted as some form of political power sharing (Carmean, Dunning, and Kowalski 2004).

Thirteen of Oxkintok's sculptured stelae were erected during the Terminal Classic period, A.D. 850–1000 (Carmeann, Dunning, and Kowalski 2004). Stela 3, currently in the Museum of Archaeology in Mérida, has a dentil-decorated border. Its carved scene is set in two major registers separated by a glyph band, with a third partial register at the top; it has a tentative date of 10.1.0.0.0 (849) (Pollock 1980:317–318, citing Proskouriakoff 1950:151). Stela 9 (Fig. 7.13) stood on the west side of Structure 2B7, facing west, on an axis with the portal vault of Structure 2B8 and the east-running causeway on the east side of Structure 2B7 (Pollock 1980:318). It has a braided border and two registers separated by a glyph band. The upper figure might be ballplayer; his headdress is similar to that of the right-hand figure on Tikal Stela 5 (Fig. 5.6). Stela 21 has a rectangular shape and a twisted rope border, with the design scene shown in three registers (Pollock 1980:Fig. 547). It dates to the lajuntun

FIGURE 7.13 Oxkintok Stela 9; note the scene in two registers and the braided border (after Proskouriakoff 1950, from Pollock 1980:Fig. 545a).

10.1.10.0.0 4 Ajaw 13 Kank'in (Grube 1994:344). Thirty-one altars are also known from Oxkintok, of which eight were carved. Four "column altars" were carved with a twisted-rope-and-pleat design around the upper exterior (Pollock 1980:322), similar to that seen on later Mayapán stelae.

Chich'en Itza, Yucatán

Archaeologists' interest in the Terminal Classic period in the northern lowlands has focused on chronological relations among and between distinctive architectural styles (indigenous Puuc Maya vs. "Toltec" Mexican) and ceramic styles, subsumed by two ceramic spheres (Cehpech and Sotuta). Questions have revolved around the sequencing versus contemporaneity of these architectural and ceramic styles and the kind and degree of "Mexican" influence versus autochthonous development in the region, particularly in terms of sociopolitical relations.

Early archaeological work, especially the investigations at Chich'en Itza by the Carnegie Institution of Washington under the direction of Sylvanus Morley, led to the interpretation that around 450–600, during the late Early Classic (Early Period I or Regional period, as it was variously called in the northern lowlands), a distinctive culture developed in the Puuc, Río Bec, and Chenes areas of Campeche and spread northward (Morley and Brainerd 1956:42–43). This culture flourished particularly in the Puuc region of the northwestern peninsula and east to Chich'en Itza during the Late and Terminal Classic periods (also known as Early Period II, Florescent, or Pure Florescent), and was identified by the spread of the Cehpech ceramic complex (Smith 1971). This culture came to an end with the postulated Toltec conquest of the northern lowlands and establishment of a capital of sorts at Chich'en Itza. This Early Postclassic period, from about 1000 to 1200 (known as the Early Mexican or Modified Florescent period), saw the spread of Toltec influence throughout the peninsula and is recognized by pottery of the Sotuta ceramic complex.

Since the late 1970s, however, this unilinear scenario has been questioned by Joseph W. Ball (1977, 1979a, 1979b), and he and other archaeologists began to debate models postulating various degrees of overlap of the Cehpech and Sotuta ceramic spheres, since their constituent ceramics had not been found in clear stratigraphic relationship. Today, most archaeologists working in the northern lowlands have come to recognize a complex situation that includes earlier development of the characteristic slatewares of the Puuc Cehpech sphere, an eastern subsphere of Cehpech centered around the site of Cobá, possible early and late faceting of the Sotuta complex (Cobos 2004), and considerable temporal overlap of the Cehpech and Sotuta spheres (Ringle et al. 2004).

Chich'en Itza, in the north-central Yucatán peninsula, is well known from Maya histories, legends, and early explorers' reports. Despite Morley's excavations in the 1940s, this primarily Terminal Classic site remains poorly understood. Chich'en Itza did not deploy a traditional Emblem Glyph with a place-identifying main sign; instead, the site used only the k'ul ajaw label for its principal lords (Stuart and Houston 1994:5).

The founding of Chich'en Itza—*chi ch'en its a* 'mouth of the well of the itsa [water witches]' (Edmonson 1982:5)—is reported in numerous sources, and the various books of the chilam b'alams suggest that the city seated the *may* at least twice. According to *The Chilam Balam of Tizimin,* the city was founded in a K'atun 8 Ajaw (692, 948) and was siyaj kan 'born of heaven', that is, a seat of the *may* cycle (Edmonson 1982:5–6). *The Chilam Balam of Chumayel* states that Chich'en Itza was "discovered" in a K'atun 4 Ajaw (731, 987) by the calling together of "the four divisions of the nation," and the site's occupants—the Itza—ruled for thirteen k'atuns (Roys [1933] 1967:139–140), again indicating its role as *may* cycle seat. According to Landa (Tozzer 1941:177; Schele and Mathews 1998:197), Chich'en Itza was founded by three brothers, K'ak'upacal (Kelley 1968a), Aj Joltun B'alam, and Jun Pik Tok'. The ballcourt disk from Chich'en Itza refers to an "Aj Joltun Balam, Peten, Itzamal Ajaw" (Krochock 1997), reinforcing suggestions of relations between the Itza and the Petén area.

Despite the multiple sources of information on Chich'en Itza, the site and its history have remained enigmatic to generations of archaeologists. A considerable part of the problem was what seemed to be two sequential and spatially distinct architectural components of the site, Maya and "Toltec," which were originally interpreted as evidence of conquest of the Maya by central Mexicans. Normal kinds of clarifying evidence for such an interpretation were lacking, however. Ceramic complexes associated with these architectural styles, at Chich'en Itza itself and at contemporaneous sites elsewhere in the northern lowlands, have rarely been found in clear stratigraphic association. Dated inscriptions are rare, difficult to read, and fall into a very narrow time range. In the past ten years or so there has been considerable progress in untangling these complexities: it is agreed that the ceramic and architectural components overlap in time, but the exact *degree* of overlap is still debated.

The central ceremonial precinct of Chich'en Itza (Fig. 7.14) is divided into two walled portions, northeastern and southwestern, each with a

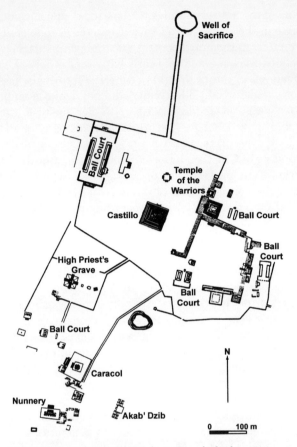

FIGURE 7.14 Map of the central ceremonial portion of Chich'en Itza.

mix of shared and unique structural forms. The southwestern sector has numerous structures with indigenous Maya characteristics, particularly mosaic facades like those of the Puuc area to the west. These include Las Monjas and the Casa Colorada, both with associated ballcourts, and the Ak'ab Tz'ib. The Caracol is the earliest of numerous radial structures at the site and topped by a circular "observatory" building, entered from the west. The High Priest's Grave, another radial structure, is set on a platform at the junction of three causeways.

The northeastern portion of the site has structures that are in some ways similar to (but larger than) those to the southwest, including radial temples (the Castillo and the Venus platform) and ballcourts. Other structures and layouts in this precinct bear a striking resemblance to those of the highland Mexican site of Tula, capital of the Toltecs. These include the colonnaded Temple of the Tables, the Temple of the Warriors (which combines Puuc vault stones with talud-tablero platform facings), and the Group of the Thousand Columns, as well as abundant feathered serpent iconography.

The most studied portion of Chich'en Itza is the Great Ballcourt Complex on the western side of the northern precinct. This ballcourt is the largest known in the Maya lowlands, and the complex has four temple structures. Two lie on the north and south end zones, facing down center court; the North Temple has three doorways, the South Temple seven. According to Schele and Mathews (1998:207), "[T]hese two buildings carry relief murals that apply Creation imagery to the two critical domains of statecraft—the sacred art of warfare and sacrifice, and the role of the ballgame in the passage of authority from generation to generation through rites of accession."

The Upper and Lower Temples of the Jaguar, situated on the eastern wall of the ballcourt, are extravagantly embellished with relief carvings. The Lower Temple of the Jaguar is entered at ground level, from the east, and its reliefs, in five registers, show a procession of warriors approaching a figure dressed in ballgame garb (Wren 1991:53). The Upper Temple of the Jaguar, facing west and accessed from atop the eastern wall of the court, also appears to be dominated by warrior imagery. One mural scene illustrates the "conquest" of a village that Miller (1977) believes may be in Petén.

Of particular interest is the "Atlantean Altar" in the front (west) room of the Upper Temple of the Jaguar. This is a flat, carved tabletop held up by fifteen "Atlantean" figures—actually carved stone pairs of human legs disjoined from the torso at the hips and buttocks—decorated so that the loincloths appear to represent sumptuously costumed individuals (Fig. 7.15). The distinctive costuming of each of these figures is reminiscent of Structure 10L-22A at Copán, the popol naj with portrayals of its local rulers, and perhaps also the frieze of Seibal's Structure A-3, with twelve individuals. Schele and Mathews (1998:243) interpret these fifteen figures as b'akab's who "represent a set of specific offices and ritual functions in the Itza state" and as "office-holders who were part of the council that ruled their kingdom." More precisely, these figures are k'atun lords, the heads of lineages or rulers of individual k'atun seats within Chich'en Itza's *may* cycle seating. The presence of fifteen of these figures approximates the sixteen lineages and regions that formed the later multepal (rule by council, or confederacy) government of Late Postclassic Mayapán. It may be that such a political structure had its origins at Chich'en Itza during the Terminal Classic (see also Kowalski 1994:117).

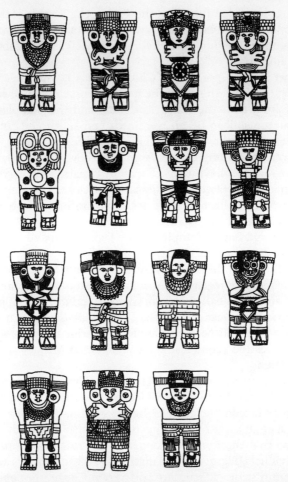

FIGURE 7.15 The "Atlantean" figures supporting the altar top in the west room of the Upper Temple of the Jaguar in the Great Ballcourt Complex at Chich'en Itza (after Schele and Mathews 1998:Fig. 6.39).

Chich'en Itza's Great Ballcourt Complex dates to the early Terminal Classic period (Wren and Schmidt 1991). This determination is based in part on the Great Ballcourt Stone, which has a Calendar Round date of 11 Kimi 14 Pax, probably indicating 10.1.15.3.6 (November 15, 864) (Wren 1991:53, 56). The text on the stone also has a ballgame glyph and perhaps the name of K'ak'upacal, and Wren (1991) believes the monument was probably used as an altar on which to spread victims for heart sacrifices.

I suspect that the building of thirteen ballcourts at Chich'en Itza was a consequence of that site seating the *may* in the Terminal Classic. One ballcourt would have been built at the site to commemorate every k'atun in the thirteen-k'atun cycle of the *may*. The wide occurrence of ballcourts in the western peninsula (but comparative rarity in the eastern part; see Kurjack, Maldonado, and Robertson 1991) might then mark the site of k'atun seats within Chich'en Itza's Terminal Classic *may* polity. This practice would represent continuities with the Preclassic importance of the ballgame (some twenty-five Middle and Late Preclassic ballcourts are known in the northwestern corner of the peninsula; A. Andrews, pers. comm., August 14, 2002), as well as with central Petén. In central Petén during the Preclassic and Classic periods, distinctive structural complexes—E-Groups and twin-pyramid groups—were built at *may* seats and their subordinate centers for the purpose of commemorating k'atun terminations every twenty years. These complexes often have ballcourts adjacent or nearby (Aimers 1993).

It is now widely agreed that Chich'en Itza had strong ties to central Petén and the Itza homeland (Wren and Schmidt 1991; Krochok and Freidel 1994:359; Boot 1995; Schele and Mathews 1998). The practice of celebrating k'atuns with commemorative architecture, and also the role of the ceremonial ballgame, would have moved northward along with the Petén migrants. (In this regard, it is interesting to contemplate the suggestion [Laporte and Fialko 1990:57] that in Early Classic Tikal the ballgame was associated with a specific lineage or part of a lineage with central Mexican affiliations occupying Group 6C-XVI.) It is important to note, however, that few dates at Chich'en Itza record period endings.

Indeed, inscriptions and dates have posed problems for interpreting the history of Chich'en Itza and resolving long-standing questions about Maya-"Toltec" overlap. The earliest inscribed date at the city is 9.2.10.0.0 3 Ajaw 8 K'umk'u; this date, found in the Temple of the Initial Series, registers the midpoint or lajuntun ending of 485 within a K'atun 2 Ajaw. It would seem to correspond to some other early dates in the western peninsula and the Puuc area (e.g., Oxkintok's Lintel 1 dating ten years earlier). The means of six calibrated radiocarbon dates from the site fall between 663 and 891 (Krochok 1998:5), again supporting an occupation dating from the beginning of the Late Classic period.

But structures of the Terminal Classic period, which saw Chich'en Itza's major expansion of construction and occupation, do not display period-ending dates. The site's dated inscriptions do not occur on stelae, commemorate k'atun intervals, or celebrate dynastic rule or individual rulers with dates of their birth, accession, and death (Wren and Schmidt 1991:212), as in central Petén. Instead, the most commonly celebrated event at Chich'en Itzá is the "lintel dedication ceremony" (Kelley 1982; Wren and Schmidt 1991:213). The texts of Chich'en Itza, unlike those of the southern lowlands, appear principally to record ceremonies dedicating structures and the lintels seem to be "owned" by individuals (Kelley 1982; Krochock 1991:49). K'ak'upakal, the most frequently named person on the lintels, is "never named in direct association with the transcribing or carving of the lintels or the dedication of the temples. He does seem to be mentioned in association with the playing of the ball game," however, and his parents are identified as "Lady K'uk' and Jawbone-Longbone" on the Las Monjas lintels (Wren and Schmidt 1991: 213; Kelley 1962, 1968a, 1982).

Inscribed dates at Chich'en Itza are found within a relatively narrow interval. Wren (1991:56) writes that "virtually all the dated inscriptions at Chichén Itzá fall within a forty-year period" between 866 and 906 (10.1.17.5.13 and 10.3.8.14.4). Others have noted that carved inscriptions occur primarily and earliest in buildings with Puuc-style architecture, dating from 800 to 948. More specifically, however, inscribed glyphic dates span a period from 832 (Temple of the Hieroglyphic Jambs) to 998 (the High Priest's Grave, a radial structure in the southern ceremonial precinct). This latter date is one year after the lajuntun ending of 997, at 10.8.10.0.0 3 Ajaw 3 Pax. Despite this relatively brief series of Terminal Classic dates, it is clear that the site was occupied far longer than they would allow, and the Chich'en-related Sotuta ceramic sphere lasts two and a half centuries (Cobos 2004).

Archaeologists, art historians, and epigraphers working with the Chich'en Itza materials have concluded that the site sat at the head of a multiethnic, multepal–like polity with elements drawn from many areas of Mesoamerica, Maya and non-Maya. The lords of Chich'en Itza were known and identified themselves as Itza, an ethnic group or lineage traceable to Classic period central Petén. The lack of stelae, period-ending inscriptions, and genealogical information, however, suggests that these Itza—in Petén and in the north—were a faction opposed to the k'atun-based political traditions and practices of the ruling dynasty of Tikal and allied sites. Instead, the emphasis on mural art and carved lintels suggests a cultural heritage in the Late Classic traditions of the Usumacinta area in the southwestern lowlands, for example, at Palenque, Bonampak, and Yaxchilán, where lintels were extremely important vehicles for royal inscriptions. Yaxchilán, possibly a Classic *may* seat in the middle Usumacinta region, had fifty-eight carved stone lintels and, on Structure 33, thirteen ballgame-scene panels. The presence of mosaic facades is clearly a component of the local tradition of the neighboring Puuc area to the west, which in turn has a history of relations with central Petén.

The real innovation at Chich'en Itza is the emphasis on ballcourts, possibly as k'atun-commemorating complexes, which have a long history extending throughout the western part of the peninsula. While many if not most large sites in the southern lowlands had at least one ballcourt, I know of none with as many as Chich'en Itza. The only sites that approach this number of ballcourts are Kaminaljuyú in the Guatemala highlands, with twelve (Middle and Late Classic, ca. 400–700), and El Tajín in north-central Veracruz, with eleven. Of the latter, four date to the Early Classic (beginning ca. 300–400), five to the Late Classic, and two to the Epiclassic (ca. 900–1000) (Wilkerson 1991:50). Like most Classic period Mexican sites, El Tajín did not celebrate k'atun endings but rather 52-year Calendar Rounds, and the beginning of new Rounds conceivably could have been celebrated by construction of ballcourts and play of the game. A Totonac calendar initiated in 456 (Edmonson 1988:130) might have marked the commencement of such a practice; if so, eleven ballcourts constructed every fifty-two years beginning in A.D. 456 would take us close to the year 1000. In any event, the shared emphasis on the ballgame between El Tajín and the western peninsula is significant in light of the widely acknowledged similarities of ballgame paraphernalia at Chich'en Itza and the Gulf Coast, plus Tajín-style architecture elsewhere in the lowlands (e.g., Tikal), and the legendary arrival of the "Mexican" Tutul Xiw peoples in the Maya area in the Terminal Classic.

Another innovation—or perhaps better said, a renewed emphasis—at Chich'en Itza is fire ritual. Recent studies of that site's inscriptions and iconography have revealed that a common royal title at Chich'en Itza was *yajaw k'ak* 'lord of the fire' (Grube 1994:9). Texts on several buildings, for example, the Casa Colorada, describe the drilling of sacred fires (Grube 1994:9). Fire drilling was also a popular theme in the iconography of Naranjo (Martin and Grube 2000:70). The significance of fire ritual among the Maya, particularly its association with calendrical ritual, is explored further in Chapter 8.

To summarize Chich'en Itza's seating of the *may*, Edmonson earlier (1979:15–16) postulated that Chich'en Itza seated the cycle in 692 (9.13.0.0.0) and again in 948 (10.6.0.0.0), the former date according well with the span of radiocarbon dates for the site. A.D. 692 is also the date of inauguration of Dzibilchaltún as a *may* seat (see below). Dzibilchaltún seems to have been the formal seat during the first half of this period, erecting numerous period-ending monuments, whereas Chich'en Itza appears to have been the incoming seat or "guest." Chich'en Itza would have celebrated its role in k'atun celebrations in the latter half of the Terminal Classic cycle seating, beginning in about 820, with a flurry of construction of ballcourts and temples with inscribed, dated lintels. By 948, the occasion for a new *may* seating, however, there is little to suggest that Chich'en Itza held much prominence except for the 998 date on a column of the Temple of the High Priest's Grave. While the chronicles suggest the site was renewed as cycle seat for another 256 years, until the next K'atun 8 Ajaw in 1204 and the primacy of Mayapán, there is little confirmatory evidence from archaeology, epigraphy, or ceramics. However, Chich'en Itza was a pilgrimage site through the Late Postclassic period, suggesting an important continuing ritual role.

Dzibilchaltún and Cobá

Dzibilchaltún is a large city in the far north-northwestern part of the Yucatán peninsula, north of Mérida and only 20 kilometers from the coast (Andrews 1981). Its program of public architecture, like that of nearby Komchen, began in the Middle Preclassic, circa 800 B.C. and continued through the Late Preclassic, until circa A.D. 250. During this time, both sites could have been *may* seats in the region, with Dzibilchaltún seemingly more important in the late Middle Preclassic and Komchen flourishing in the early Late Preclassic, from circa 400–300 B.C. to A.D. 150 (Andrews 1981:320–321). Both sites share some Preclassic ceramic ties to the southern lowlands, but they lack triadic groups and Komchen is not known to have an E-Group. Dzibilchaltún was nearly abandoned in the Early Classic but then heavily reoccupied in the Late Classic and Terminal Classic, from around 700 to 1000. At that time, its population is estimated to have been as large as twenty thousand. Dzibilchaltún has some 7,500 structures, including 4 major radial structures and 25 monuments. Stela 9 is the only k'atun-ending monument, with a date of 10.1.0.0.0 (849).

One of the important architectural complexes of Dzibilchaltún's Late Classic resurgence is the "Seven Dolls" Group (Fig. 7.16). This complex is identified by its principal building, radial Structure 1-sub and its four-doorway superstructure, known as the House (or Temple) of the Seven Dolls after the seven Postclassic figurines found in a cache in the structure. This temple sits just east of a distinctive arrangement consisting of three range-type structures on separate platforms in a north-south line, with a low radial "stela platform" west of them in the center of the plaza. This entire complex lies at the eastern end of a 2-kilometer-long causeway, with a similar group at the western terminus. Andrews (1981) comments that both groupings are similar to the E-Groups of the Late Preclassic and Early Classic in the southern lowlands.

Coggins (1983) discussed the significance of the Seven Dolls Group and the group of structures at the western end of the causeway that joins them. Rather than emphasize their resemblance to E-Groups, however, she posits that they represent "a widely separated twin-pyramid com-

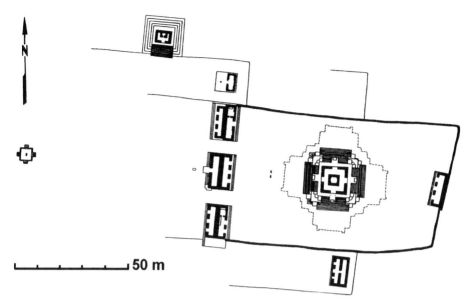

FIGURE 7.16 Dzibilchaltun's Temple of the Seven Dolls Group (after Andrews and Andrews 1980: Fig. 83).

plex that spans the center of Dzibilchaltún and that dictated its plan at about A.D. 700" (Coggins 1983:1, 54). The base of Structure 1-sub was decorated with a stucco water frieze, Underworld associations that Coggins (1983:61–63) links to a cenote cult of divination and prophesy. Coggins (1983:57, 60) concluded that the city was "capital of an interrelated Mexicanized Maya people" who shared rituals and iconography with Petén and, following Edmonson (1979), Dzibilchaltún was the "northern seat of the katun during the katun cycle that began at 9.13.0.0.0 8 Ahau (A.D. 692)."

I would argue, however, that Dzibilchaltún became a Late Classic seat of the *may* and, under influence from Petén migrants, adopted and modified some of the distinctive architectural forms of the southern lowlands. Substantial architectural similarities between Dzibilchaltún and various sites in Petén supplement the iconographic evidence from stelae, lintels, and other sculptured and painted surfaces in the northern lowlands. For example, there are general architectural ties to contemporaneous Palenque, including standardized spaces, masonry style, and other features (Andrews 1981:330), as well as basal water friezes (Coggins 1983:50–52). Other ties can be seen in E-Group complexes. One such complex (or variant) sits on the east side of the Central Plaza, opposite Cenote Xlacah. Those at the ends of Causeway 2 date to the Late rather than Early Classic period, and, according to Andrews (1981:330; emphasis added), "it appears that their builders were *consciously reviving* an ancient southern architectural form." Here it bears recalling that in southeastern Petén and at Calakmul these E-Group assemblages apparently continued to be actively used for k'atun ceremonies into the Late and Terminal Classic periods.

The presence of numerous radial temples at Dzibilchaltún is also of interest. The largest of these, Structure 89, is the latest at the site and sits at the western end of Sacbe 6. The two at either end of the long causeway, particularly the Temple of the Dolls itself, recall Structure A-3 at Seibal and its five carved stelae apparently celebrating a gathering of lords from four sites. Monuments in the Temple of the Dolls complex at Dzibilchaltún are arranged differently from those at Seibal, however: four stelae and one altar were placed along the centerline of the Temple of the Dolls complex. These include Stelae 1 and 2 in front (west) of the temple, Altar 1 in front of the central of three structures to its west, and Stela 3 atop the small radial platform comprising the western structure of the E-Group.

If Dzibilchaltún flourished as a Late and Terminal Classic center in the northern lowlands between 700 and 1000, this would appear to accompany a seating of the *may* in the K'atun 8 Ajaw of 692 and lasting until 948. It is more likely, however, that Dzibilchaltún served its first term as a formal *may* seat from 692 to 830, during which time Chich'en Itza was ascendant as the "guest," or incoming, seat and succeeded as *may ku* from 830 to 948. According to the model advanced here (see Table 4.3), the geopolitical sequence of *may* seatings involves 128-year intervals of incoming and outgoing centers. This means that if Dzibilchaltún were the principal seat of the *may* for 128 years beginning in 692, its role would actually have begun 128 years earlier, in 564. At that time the site would have been the guest of some other, then-current *may ku*. It is difficult to identify such a potential senior site outside of the southern lowlands at this time, although possibilities are Oxkintok (with heavy Petén influence beginning in the fifth century; see Coggins 1983:39) and Uxmal or Cobá.

Cobá sits among five small lakes some 100 kilometers east-southeast of Chich'en Itza in Quintana Roo (see Folan, Kintz, and Fletcher 1983; Andrews and Robles 1985; Robles and Andrews 1986) and covers more than 70 km^2. It had sixteen causeways, or sacbes, connecting to its satellites (probable k'atun seats), the longest of which extends from the Terminal Classic Nohoch Mul architectural complex more than 100 kilometers west to Yaxuná. It also appears to have had a Caribbean port at Xelha.

Cobá has a long occupational history, as evidenced by a continuous ceramic sequence from the Late Preclassic to the Late Postclassic period. During the Early and Late Classic, the site and the eastern peninsula in general had close affinities with central Petén, as evidenced by Petén-style architecture, ceramics, and sculpture (Robles and Andrews 1986:77). It has been suggested (Schele and Mathews 1998:202) that Cobá might have been part of the Calakmul hegemony. However, around A.D. 750 Cobá's ceramic assemblage changed with the introduction of a slateware tradition similar to that of the Puuc area to the west, although Puuc-style architectural elements were not in evidence. Cobá is thought to have been the capital of a sphere or realm in the eastern peninsula from about 700 to 1200, perhaps in competition with that of Chich'en Itza (Andrews and Robles 1985). Around 1100, however, public works construction ceased and satellite sites at the sacbe termini were abandoned (Andrews and Robles 1985:71).

Cobá has thirty-two known stelae, twenty-three of them sculptured. Nearly all datable monuments were erected in the seventh century (Folan 1983:81), with the earliest stela dedicated in 623 (9.9.10.0.0 2 Ajaw 13 Pop) and the latest around 780. Apparently, "many" of them show a single individual "standing on the back of one or two men," presumably captives. Stylistically, they "bear a close resemblance" to Petén monuments, particular those of Naranjo (Folan 1983:81).

Overview

What can these data from inscriptions, iconography, and architecture contribute to a new understanding of the Terminal Classic period in the southern lowlands, and what do they mean in terms of the *may* model of political organization? In central Petén, long dominated by Tikal and its realm, the Terminal Classic period (820–948) represented the last or outgoing half of Tikal's *may* seating that had begun in 692. It was essentially a dormant period when ritual responsibilities were shared with the incoming seat of the cycle. Who was Tikal's successor? It is not clear; Ixlú, Zacpetén, Tayasal, Flores, or Nixtun-Ch'ich' all seem to be likely sites.

In southwestern Petén, in the Pasión region, Seibal became a new *may* seat in 761, with a new king inaugurated in 771. As indicated by radial Structure A-3, a major program of building and monument erection was initiated in the early ninth century, probably in commemoration of a meeting of kings, calendar priests, or sages to discuss calendrical matters and especially the turning of the b'ak'tun in 10.0.0.0.0 (830).

The latest stelae at Seibal (and also Flores) are circa 10.3.0.0.0 (889). If we go back in time half a *may* or 128 years from 889, we come to 761, and then another 128 years from 761 brings us to 633, the end of a K'atun 1 Ajaw and the founding (in 623) of Dos Pilas to the south in the Petexbatún. Dos Pilas might have been a *may* seat—or perhaps merely a pretender—unifying a number of sites in the Pasión-Petexbatún region until 761, at which time the site slipped from power. In any case, there seems to have been a Late and Terminal Classic *may* seating in southwestern Petén that lasted at least 241 years and probably closer to 256, with Dos Pilas seating the cycle from 623/633 to 761 and Seibal from 761 to 889.

Seibal is one of numerous sites in the southern lowlands where Terminal Classic stelae and altars seem to celebrate the arrival of strangers, persons bringing with them distinct cultural elements that differed from those of the Classic period southern lowland Maya. These elements, including dress, weaponry, and glyph styles, become evident in the iconography and monuments beginning around 810–820 (9.19.0.0.0 or 9.19.10.0.0) and continue through about 889 (10.3.0.0.0). The new "Mexican" (probably originating in the Gulf Coast) calendars are evident a bit earlier in the late sixteenth k'atun (767) in the Usumacinta region, and still before (ca. 665) to the north in the Puuc area. In other words, whoever these interlopers were, they initiated entry into the southern lowlands from the west (and/or north: Puuc) just a few k'atuns before the turning of the b'ak'tun at 10.0.0.0.0 (830). Note the similarity to events some four hundred years earlier, when an arrival of Mexicans in the southern lowlands occurred just before the turning of the b'ak'tun at 9.0.0.0.0 (435).

The seated figures shown conversing on the many southern lowland Terminal Classic monuments are simply dressed, conspicuously devoid of kingly regalia and accoutrements of office, which suggests that the individuals were not flaunting symbols of status and power. Conversation scenes also appear on Terminal Classic Fine Orange (Pabellon Molded-Carved type) pottery bowls and vases, perhaps vessels used for serving food and beverages at such meetings. While captives continue to be depicted on the monuments, they are seated rather than hog-tied and trampled under the king's feet. The innovation of all-glyphic monuments appears to accentuate the paramount interest at this time—the fact that these discussions were taking place, rather than the power and charisma of the individual speakers. The texts could very likely record decisive outcomes of these summit meetings. More significantly, this new iconographic program and accommodation of other socioethnic groups might reveal the earliest stages in the lowland Maya political transition from Classic period divine kingship to Postclassic multepal, or rule by council, but still within the *may* framework (as suggested to me by A. Hofling, pers. comm., August 29, 2002). Similar movements toward shared government—variously referred to as "concilar," "collective," or "shared power"—can be found in the Terminal Classic northern lowlands (Carmean, Dunning, and Kowalski 2004; Ringle et al. 2004; Suhler et al. 2004).

The occurrence of squared day glyph cartouches in the Petén area is another indication of foreign (or at least nonsouthern lowland Maya) influences. These glyphs occur on Seibal Stela 13 on a day 7 Muluk, on Calakmul Stela 86 (Graham 1990:63), and on Flores Stela 5. They also are found at three sites in the Tikal realm (Edmonson 1988:40): Jimbal Stelae 1 and 2, giving dates of 12 Chikchan, 13 Cimi, and 1 Manik, and El Zapote Stela 5. In addition, Ucanal Stela 4 shows a scattering glyph on a period ending of 10.1.0.0.0 5 Ajaw 3 Kayab (September 5, 848), with squared glyph cartouches reading 10 Imix 13 Eagle(?). This latter, "obviously in a foreign writing system," refers to the date of the Olmec year beginning forty days before the Tikal date and is "the closest thing we have to a direct correlation of the Mayan calendar with any other native system" (Edmonson 1988:40). Edmonson (1988:229–230) believes that these "aberrant day glyphs" in square cartouches "are certainly not Mayan" but Gulf Coast, most likely "Late Classic (and provincial) Olmec," and accompanied the introduction of the so-called Campeche and Palenque calendars.

The suggestion that foreigners coming into the Terminal Classic lowlands were from the Gulf Coast region has been argued as far back as Thompson's (1970) identification of them as "Putun." Possibly Chontal speakers, possibly with ties farther west into Mexico and particularly to El Tajin, possibly the producers and traders of Fine Orange pottery, possibly using the script and calendrics of the Late Classic Olmec region, possibly related to the introduction of the so-called Campeche calendar—these "possibles" are increasingly becoming "probables" as more and more research is done.

Seibal's Structure A-3 and Stelae 8–11 and 21 appear to record a regional assembly of lords similar to that reported in the prophetic histories as having taken place earlier at Dzibilchaltún. Distinctive radial platforms or temples, sometimes accompanied by equally distinctive stelae, are also seen at Dzibilchaltún (Temple of the Dolls), Copán (Str. 10L-4 and Stela A), and Tayasal (Str. 123; Chase 1983). According to the *Book of Chilam Balam of Chumayel*, during the last tun of a K'atun 13 Ajaw in 771, a high-level assembly took place at Ichkansiho (Dzibilchaltún), which included the lords of Mutul, Chich'en Itza, Dzibilchaltún, Itzamal, Chable, and other towns (Schele and Mathews 1998: 259). Schele's interpretation of this meeting was that it resulted in the formation of an Itza confederacy in the northern lowlands (Schele and Mathews 1998:218). It also could have resulted in a decision about where to seat the *may* at the close of the b'ak'tun.

Copán Stela A and Seibal Stela 10 are often discussed together because their texts mention the Emblem Glyphs of three other powerful sites. These two monuments are also usefully considered in the context of iconographic programs on other stelae erected in their vicinity. In Copán's Great Plaza, for example, a stela series was erected by Waxaklajun Ub'aj K'awil north of a radial structure. These begin with Stela F, showing the ruler in Bearded Jaguar costume and dated A.D. 721, while three companion monuments mark the ending of K'atun 4 Ajaw ten years later, in 731, or 9.15.0.0.0, the three-quarter-b'ak'tun mark. Copán Stela H shows the ruler dressed as the Maize God, on Stela A he wears a mat headdress and displays *kan te,* or World Tree symbolism, and Stela B shows earth monster symbolism. Similarly at Seibal, Stela 10 is one of four stelae dedicated in 849 commemorating the ending of the b'ak'tun in 830 and erected around a radial structure. On Stela 8 Wat'ul Chatel is dressed in Bearded Jaguar costuming, on Stela 9 he is dressed as the Maize God, on Stela 10 he wears a mat headdress identical to that on Copán Stela A, and on Stela 11 he wears a World Tree apron that suggests the kan te symbolism on Copán Stela A. The interval between Copán's Stela F and Seibal Stelae 8–11 is 128 years.

Copán Stela A identifies three other sites (Tikal, Calakmul, and Palenque) and associates them with cardinal directions (or points of the solar cycle) but gives no personal names; Seibal Stela 10 gives Emblem Glyphs of Tikal, Calakmul, and the Ik' site (presumed to be Motul de San José) and the personal names of individuals associated with those sites but gives no directional or solar associations (other than the positions of all four stelae around Str. A-3). The production of these monuments is also of interest, because it has been suggested that the Copán stelae might represent the work of two sculptors or workshops (Schele and Mathews 1998:139). Similarly, the Seibal monuments might have been carved by different "master sculptors" (Graham 1990:25); Proskouriakoff (1993:181) suggests a stylistic relationship to the stelae of Machaquilá, upriver. All in all, the stylistic sharing evident among these monuments at Copán and Seibal invokes key cosmic referents rather than mere artistic license, and the events they commemorate were sufficiently significant that the participants might have brought their own master sculptors on the journeys with them.

The gatherings at or commemorated by these buildings might have an analogy in Postclassic and Colonial period practice. In Colonial Yucatán, for example, high-level meetings held among regional lords "reaffirmed the political legitimacy of the rulers . . . [and] served to ratify territorial boundaries" (Restall 2001:347). Similarly, Edmonson notes that the b'alam and his chilam were priests and sages with responsibility for resolving any disagreements about calendrical matters. If these conflicts could not be settled,

> a convocation of sages could be called. The authority of such a meeting appears to have exceeded that of the lord of the katun himself, and, though it was largely confined to the religious sphere, its ability to concert calendrical changes had a sweeping impact on political and economic affairs. (1982:31n483)

It is likely that such meetings would have been called to deliberate the turning of the b'ak'tun, the selection of new *may* seats, and similar momentous events.

Finally, accelerating conflict is apparent in the southern lowlands during the Late Classic period, and at least one—perhaps more—disaffected lineage or faction of elites existed within Tikal. One such group in the Petexbatún, originally displaying the Tikal Emblem Glyph, changed its allegiance to Calakmul. Possibly other factions—leaving voluntarily or being ousted; perhaps joined by like-minded groups from other Petén sites—moved northward and were responsible for the introduction of Peténlike architectural and iconographic traits to the northern lowlands. Some of these are closely associated with *may-* and k'atun-based geopolitical organization in the lowlands, indicating that such calendrical rituals and beliefs ostensibly traveled as well, either being introduced or strengthened by a Petén-based population presence beginning perhaps in the sixth century or so. At the same time, it is equally obvious that other groups of people were moving in the opposite direction, from the northern lowlands as well as the Gulf Coast into Petén. Beginning later, perhaps around the completion of the b'ak'tun in 830, such movements introduced new ideas, styles, and material goods into Petén, particularly in the western part of the region. These kinds of "foreign" intrusions and population movements might have been implicated in the wars and abandonments prompting construction of defensive barricades around some sites in the northern plains of Yucatán (Dahlin 2000).

It is of no little interest to compare one obvious trait of Terminal Classic monuments—shape—in Tikal and the Puuc region. The monuments in the Puuc area, and the stelae in west-central Petén that share some Puuc traits, have narrow tops; the corners are often removed, creating points. It could be that the sculptured monuments are modeled after the painted end walls of corbel-vaulted structures, where the inslanting walls of the vault cut off the upper corners of the scene. Or it could be a specific repudiation of the Tikal program and its glorification of divine ancestors. Terminal Classic stelae at Tikal and other sites in its realm emphasized their upper portions, making them asymmetrical and wedge-shaped. The expanded upper area heralded deference to royal ancestors, the Paddler Gods floating among serpentine clouds of copal smoke and nearly dwarfing the ruler below. The new iconographic program of the Terminal Classic explicitly rejects such displays of kingly power and dynastic glorification. Instead, the monuments seem to herald multepal by commemorating significant conversations and diplomacy. Their presence in the Lake Petén Itzá region also bespeaks longstanding ties between this area and the Puuc–Chich'en Itza region to the north.

CHAPTER 8

Implications of the May *Model*

The Maya geopolitical organizational structure based on the *may* would have had broad ramifications and implications for other major cultural institutions, including political economy, intra- and intersite relations, and various aspects of ritual. Here I consider the implications of *may*-based political organization for such institutions as ritual celebrations, the ballgame, warfare, and the nature of rulership itself.

Identifying the *May*

According to the evidence, the 260- and 130-tun cycles of the *may*, folded into 400-tun b'ak'tuns, operated for nearly two and a half millennia, from the Middle or Late Preclassic through the Classic and Postclassic periods into Colonial times. If this is true, why is there no direct mention of it in the inscriptions? Indeed, references to the *may* in the surviving texts of the late prophetic histories themselves are rather oblique but were teased out by Edmonson (1979). Did the Colonial period Maya intentionally conceal this armature of their politico-ritual organization from the Spaniards? Have we not yet deciphered the glyphs for such organization in Classic period texts? Could it have been discussed in the codices but, for whatever reason, not referenced in stone sculptures?

The problem may lie in part in the unclear etymology of the word *may*, and it might have come to mean different things—or the cycle might have been known by different terms—at different points during the two millennia that it was in operation. Textual references to *may* are rare and shed little light on this institution as a mechanism of geopolitical structuring.

Because one of the meanings of the word *may* relates to deer hooves (Fig. 8.1), it is useful to investigate references to or depictions of deer and their hooves in the inscriptions. One use of a deer hoof glyph is in the

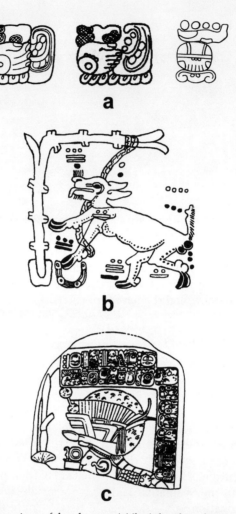

FIGURE 8.1 Representations of deer hooves: (a) (l–r) the "heir designation" glyph; 'since he ended the *may*'? (Palenque Palace House A–D Palace Tablet; after Macri n.d.); deer hoof as numerical classifier? (Copán Stela A); (b) a portion of Madrid Codex, page 49b, showing a deer caught in a tree-snare, with the glyph for "cenote" below a forehoof; note the exaggerated toes (after Vail 1997: Fig. 3–15); (c) deer haunch headdress on Aguateca Stela 2 (after drawing by Ian Graham).

so-called heir designation event (Montgomery 2001a: Fig. 9-3); it may refer more broadly to initiation into adulthood for young boys of the nobility, perhaps through deer hunting (Joyce 2000: 124–128). The deer hoof also appears on Copán Stela A, where it has been interpreted as a numerical classifier in the sequence of "four sky" glyphs (Schele and

Mathews 1998:161) (see Fig. 6.2). A more suggestive occurrence is on the Palenque Palace Tablet dated to the lajuntun 9.14.10.0.0 (A.D. 721), which appears to read "since he ended the *may*."

The deer hoof also appears in identical balloon-like headdresses worn by rulers on Aguateca Stela 2 (735) and Dos Pilas Stela 2 (736), both of which appear to show the entire haunch of a deer with the hoof projecting forward over the ruler's face. The front of the headdress is decorated with the distinctive trapezoidal framework of the central Mexican year sign. Both stelae commemorate a Venus event, presumably the successful war against Seibal. A deer hoof in a headdress also can be seen on a relief panel from Jonuta (Joyce 2000:126).

As discussed below, deer hunting appears prominently in certain almanacs of the Madrid Codex and is linked to tzolk'in-based Burner rituals (see von Nagy 1997; Vail 1997; Bricker 1997b). In the codex depictions of deer, the hooves are exaggeratedly large, but the significance of this is not clear other than the meaning of *may* as "deer hoof."

Occurrences of deer hooves or foot and toe bones (metapodials and phalanges) in archaeological contexts are rarely noted. A comparison of deer parts represented at deposits at four sites in the northern lowlands (Carr 1996:255) indicated that 30 to 40 percent of the fragments represent metapodials and phalanges. Deer toe bones were used by shamans in divining rituals and a cache of nineteen of them, "some worked," was found in a burial at the Classic site of Holmul (Hamblin 1984:142). In addition, a deer metapodial bloodletter was found in a Middle Preclassic cache (Brown 1999). The hooves themselves are cartilage and not likely to survive deposition; they are known to have been strung together as rattles among native North American groups. Perhaps the "rattle of the k'atun" mentioned in some prophetic histories could have been made from deer hooves.

Calendrical Rituals Involving Fire

Classic inscriptions and Postclassic and Colonial period chronicles reveal an impressive array of calendrical ceremonies carried out across Mesoamerica, in addition to those associated with Maya period endings, and these could have played a role in political organization and the structuring of geopolitical authority. Many of these involved the ritual starting and quenching of fires in temples and other public structures. The ceremonial drilling of fire and iconographic portrayals of possible fire drills as part of royal paraphernalia is known from Early Classic monuments, as the knotted staffs held by rulers (see Figs. 4.8, 4.9) might be ornately embellished ceremonial fire drills.

Burner Rituals

Some of the scenes and inscriptions on Classic period stelae could correspond to Late Postclassic and Colonial Burner rituals known from the codices, books of the chilam b'alams, and Landa's writings. The Maya divided their sacred 260-day calendar into four "burner periods," with a Burner (Aj Tok) presiding over each. The Burners were like other quadripartite gods in presiding over each of the cardinal directions. Each burner period consisted of 65 days, subdivided into intervals of 20 days, 20 days, 20 days, and 5 days (see Long 1923:174; Thompson 1960:99–101; Bricker 1997a:2–3; Edmonson 1982:180, 1986a:125). The sequence of ceremonies was centered on a day with the numerical prefix 4, and occurred with only four day names: Chikchan, Ok, Men, and Ajaw. In this complicated ritual cycle, an "announcement" of the cycle was made, for example, on a day 3 Chikchan, when the Burner "gets the fire" (u ch'a k'ak'). Twenty days later, on a day 10 Chikchan, the Burner begins the fire (u hopol u k'ak'); another twenty days after that is the day 4 Chikchan, the key day of the ceremony, when the fire "runs" (y alcaba). After another twenty days, on a day 11 Chikchan, the fire is extinguished (u tup k'ak'). Five days later is a day 3 Ok, when the cycle begins again for the series of Ok days and focused on 4 Ok, followed by Men days, and then Ajaw days.

The Madrid Codex contains several almanacs (43b–c; 90a–92a) with dates and iconography relating Burner ceremonies to deer-trapping and deer-sacrificing activities, especially during the dry season (equivalent to February through May) (Vail 1997). In particular, an image of a deer standing in a cenote with a 9 Men date may be associated with the tup k'ak, or fire quenching, ritual. According to Landa (Tozzer 1941:163), the rituals associated with Burner periods were carried out to ensure good rains for their crops; in this context, the final ceremony of extinguishing the fire is of interest. For this event, in the Maya month of Mak there was a festival celebrated by old men for the Chaks or rain gods:

> They hunted for all the animals and creatures of the field[,] . . . and they came together with them in the court of the temple in which the Chacs and the priest took their places . . . each having a pitcher of water. . . . They placed in the middle a great faggot of dry sticks tied together and set upright, and first burning some of their incense in the brazier they set fire to the sticks, and while they were burning, they took out a great many of the hearts of the animals and birds and threw them into the fire to burn. . . . When all the hearts were consumed, the Chacs extinguished the fire with the pitchers of water. (Tozzer 1941:163)

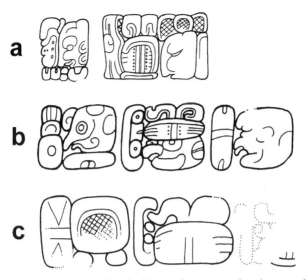

FIGURE 8.2 The Fire Sequence identified by Grube (2000c, after drawings by Ian Graham): (a) "drill fire" on Yaxchilán Lintel 29; (b) "light fire" on Motul de San José Stela 3; (c) "quench fire" on Ixkun Stela 2.

As Long (1923) points out, the symbolism here is that of the rain gods extinguishing the fires in the burning milpas so that planting can begin. Tup k'ak' agricultural ceremonies are still carried out in twentieth-century Maya villages in Yucatán (Villa Rojas 1969:270).

Recently, Grube (2000c) identified what he calls the "fire sequence" in Late Classic Initial Series inscriptions from various sites, which clearly reflects the Burner activities. This sequence, three glyphs between Glyph A and the ja'ab' day, consists of the possessive *u k'ak' il* 'his fire' (T122:563a, *k'ak* 'fire'), preceded by the verb "to light," "to burn," or "to extinguish," and followed by a god head (Fig. 8.2). On nine of the dated monuments and two of the undated ones the verb is a "hand scattering fire" logograph that may be read as *pu-ki* or *puuk*. "Scattering" the fire might be a better interpretation of the third and most central of the Burner rituals, which has been translated variously as "runs" the fire or "gives the fire scope" (Thompson 1960:100). Clearly this latter refers to steps of the Burner rituals known from Postclassic and Colonial sources. None of the recorded dates coincide with significant astronomical events.

Grube (2000c:Table 1) identified thirty-five dated occurrences of this fire sequence expression, ranging from A.D. 573 through 849, but most (*n* = 29) occur between 9.13.10.0.0 (A.D. 702) and 9.19.0.0.0 (A.D. 810).

Twenty-four occur on period endings: thirteen on k'atun endings, nine on lajuntuns, and two on jolajuntuns. On period endings the fire glyph variant is T44:563b with T153 (crossed bands) infixed into 563 (Thompson 1962:186; Kelley 1968b:143). The remainder occur on miscellaneous dates, while another six examples are undated. In terms of specific days, the majority ($n = 24$) of these rituals are associated with days Ajaw, which is one of the "official" Burner days.

The spatial occurrence of these fire sequence, or Burner, expressions is also of interest. With three exceptions, they do not occur at Classic regional capitals or *may* seats such as Tikal or Copán; the exceptions are Motul de San José, Calakmul, and Palenque, with one occurrence each. Otherwise they are found in east-southeastern Petén and Belize, including Naranjo (with 6 examples), Pusilhá (5), Sacul (3), Ixkun (2), Nim Li Punit (2), Polol, La Milpa, Uxbenká, Itzan, Naachtun, and Xnaheb.

Burners and fire-related ceremonies may have origins deep in Mesoamerican prehistory. The Burner days (Chikchan, Ok, Men, Ajaw; or Snake, Dog, Eagle, Lord or Flower) are known as Type V yearbearers and were used only in the Olmec calendar (Edmonson 1988:21, 231). Although yearbearers changed several times during the course of Maya calendrical history, this particular set seems to have been retained and venerated via Burner ceremonies for more than two thousand years. That rituals involving fire and burning incense were important to Preclassic societies such as the Olmec and Izapa can be seen in their iconography, which shows people holding torches, sitting facing each other over a fire or incense burner, and so on.

Possibly related to these ceremonies is the emphasis on fire ritual at Terminal Classic Chich'en Itza, where a royal title was *yajaw k'ak* 'lord of the fire' (Grube 1994:9). While the same title is known from a text at Palenque (Martin and Grube 2000:173), at Chich'en it was among the "principal titles of the local nobility." Texts on several buildings, for example the Casa Colorada, describe the drilling of sacred fires (ibid.). In addition, it has also been suggested that the structure known as the Venus Platform "commemorates a specific calendar ceremony aligning the Maya and central Mexican calendars, referring to both the New Fire Ceremony and the end of the ninth bak'tun on the day 7 Ajaw" (Milbrath 1999:187, citing Coggins and Drucker 1988:23).

New Year's Ceremonies

Throughout Mesoamerica, the five days ending the solar year cycle—known as Wayeb' among the Maya and as Nemontemi in central Mexico—were unlucky days in which there was uncertainty as to whether the sun would emerge from its Underworld journey to begin a new annual cycle. Best known from Aztec-Mexica ritual, the observances associated with the ending of the old year and beginning of the new included the quenching of all fires and ceremonial renewal of fire with first sighting of the rising sun: these are known as New Fire ceremonies. These ceremonies enjoyed added significance every fifty-two years with the start of a new Calendar Round, that is, the coincidence of days and numbers of the 365-day ja'ab' and the 260-day tzolk'in. At this juncture, it would have been of paramount importance for priests to ensure the sun's appearance after the five unlucky days. Thus New Year's and other kinds of fire-related ceremonies were occasions of crucial kingly and priestly celebrations and quite worthy of note on Classic monuments.

In the Maya area, it has long been known that significant portions of the extant codices—Dresden pages 25–28 (see Fig. 1.2), Madrid pages 34–37, and Paris pages 19–20—treat ceremonies carried out at the start of a new year (Thomas 1882; Seler 1904:26–35; Thompson 1934, 1972:89;). Bricker (1984, 1989) has woven evidence from ethnographic, ethnohistoric, codical, and Classic iconographic sources to postulate continuities of calendrical ritual celebrating New Year's ceremonies between the codex pages and certain of Tikal's Late Classic monuments. In addition, half-year stations of the ja'ab' have been recognized in the codices, though not in the ethnohistoric literature, but it is not known if these might have been commemorated in the Classic period (Vail 1996:50).

As discussed previously, the ruler portrayed on Late Classic k'atun-ending stelae in the Tikal area typically carries a ceremonial bar and wears a jaguar costume, suggesting a role similar to that of the Postclassic b'alam, or jaguar priest. Bricker focused on similarities between the striking imagery on Tikal Stelae 30, 21, 22, and 19 and the Dresden Codex New Year's pages, but similar parallels can be drawn to the Madrid. Page 34a of the Madrid (Fig. 8.3), for example, depicts a scene with the principal individual (the Kawak yearbearer or Pawajtun) clad in a jaguar pelt and headdress, carrying a staff, and performing the scattering rite, with an ancestor in the upper left corner.

It will be recalled that Tikal Stela 30 (see Fig. 5.4), at A.D. 692 the earliest of these possible New Year celebratory monuments, shows the ruler scattering, with a tripartite staff and a back ornament bearing a Maize deity mask, perhaps a reference to the burden of the Ix yearbearer (Bricker 1984:229, 1989:239). Tikal Stela 21 (see Fig. 5.7), dated 736, shows the ruler barefoot, scattering, carrying a ceremonial bar, and wearing an enormous back ornament displaying a head with a defleshed jaw. Tikal Stelae 22 (see Fig. 5.12) and 19, dated 771 and 790, respectively, are virtual copies of each other and show the ruler barefoot, scattering, carrying a tripartite bar, wearing a jaguar pelt kilt and a Venus

FIGURE 8.3 Main scene of the upper portion of Madrid Codex page 34a (after Villacorta and Villacorta 1976:292) includes the almanac for the Kawak yearbearer. In one interpretation (Vail 1996:176–177) this is seen as a black-painted Pawajtun, holding a digging stick and planting seeds of corn. I would see it in terms of Late Classic Tikal k'atun-ending stelae, showing the ruler or jaguar priest (note jaguar tail) scattering, with an "ancestor" figure (?) seated in the "sky" above. This figure may be a Postclassic conflation of the Paddlers, as the figure has a jaguar ear and what might be a stingray spine (?) in the forehead and is depicted in a blue-painted cartouche surrounded by dots of "divinity."

mask, and with the same death god(?) mask in his back ornament as shown on Stela 21.

The principal argument against seeing these Late Classic monuments as depicting annual yearbearer rituals is that the yearbearers of the Classic period were different from those in the Postclassic and Colonial periods. Ix, Kawak, and Muluk are yearbearers in the Madrid Codex and in the Late Postclassic and Colonial periods, but the yearbearers of Late Classic Tikal were Ik', Manik', Eb', and Kab'an. The Tikal monuments clearly commemorate k'atun endings every twenty years, rather than New Year's commemorations (there are no fifty-two-year intervals that correspond).

Fire Walking

A related event is the fire-walking ritual of purification that, according to the *Relación de Valladolid* (Yucatán), took place at the end of Wayeb' days during New Year's ceremonies (or possibly, according to Landa, specifically for Kawak years). An enormous pile of wood, about 25 feet square and 6 feet high, was burned and then the coals were spread. Just before dawn the chief priest and his assistant sprinkled balche' around the edges of the embers, then the priest removed his sandals and walked across the hot coals, still sprinkling balche', followed by the other participants (see Tozzer 1941:148–149; Thompson 1960:100–101). Landa noted that "some passed over [the coals] without harm, but others got burned and still others were half burned up. And they believed that in this was the remedy for their calamities and bad omens" (Tozzer 1941:149). Thompson (1960:101) suggested fire walking as "the chief ceremony" of the Burners when "the fire spreads" on 4 Ajaw, 4 Chikchan, 4 Ok, and 4 Men.

The rulers on the three Tikal monuments described above are shown barefoot, and Bricker (1984, 1989) posited a relationship to these fire-walking rites. The heads on the back ornaments worn by the rulers represented gods associated with each of the four yearbearers, and the individuals who walked the fire were the priests of those gods. Bricker suggested that the death mask in the ruler's backrack represents a victim of human sacrifice or, in the Postclassic and Colonial periods, the death god burden of Kawak years (1984:229; 1989:234, 237, 246). In twentieth-century Chamula (Chiapas), a fire-walking rite continued to accompany the start of Kawak years, with the priest sprinkling balche' on the coals. There are also resemblances to the Chamula "jaguar skin dance" (Tzotzil *ak'ot chilon*), which is part of New Year's rituals for Muluk (yearbearer) years, and also a military victory dance. In the jaguar skin dance, an official of the community dons a jaguar pelt and carries a beribboned staff or spear while he dances to the accompaniment of drums (Bricker 1979).

It is entirely possible that through time certain rituals associated with New Year's and k'atun-ending calendrical celebrations became modified, conflated, separated, or otherwise transformed from their Classic origins to the Colonial period program. As Baudez (1991:87) remarked, "even if [Tikal's] twin-pyramid complexes were built for celebrating katun endings, it is very possible that they were also used for

New Year ceremonies during the whole length of a particular katun." Although there seems to be some discrepancy in the yearbearers depicted on the Tikal monuments, the fact that the ruler is barefoot and scattering—perhaps balche' or coals rather than blood—is suggestive of fire-related rituals.

Ballcourts and the Ballgame

One of the most enduring icons, temporally and geographically, of the Mesoamerican cosmovision is the ballgame. Known from the Early Preclassic period through the twentieth century, and occurring outside the Mesoamerican culture area proper from the southwestern United States into the Caribbean (see Scarborough and Wilcox 1991), the ballgame and its courts of play served as ritual touchstones. Indeed, the ballgame has been posited as the basis for the earliest manifestations of "government" in Mesoamerica (Hill and Clark 2001). Although Mesoamericanists speak of "the ballgame" as if it were everywhere identical, different rules and styles of courts existed in various times and places. There were also several game variants, including hip-ball, hand-ball, and stick ball, each with its own paraphernalia, equipment, and setting (Cohodas 1991).

In the Maya area, the ballgame (*pitz*) and the ballcourt (*hom;* also *b'ate'*) were long-sanctified elements of cosmic creation as revealed in the *Popol Vuh:* the Hero Twins played in the aboveground ballcourt described as the "great abyss" to the northeast, as well as in the ballcourt of the Underworld with its associated "Place of Ballgame Sacrifice." The significance of the ballgame throughout Maya history is recognized archaeologically through the construction of stone and plastered ballcourts with temples and sculptures, as well as depictions of the ballgame and its ceremonially attired players on stelae, wall panels, and ceramics. Discussion of the role of the ballgame in the Maya area has tended to focus on the iconography as it relates to myth and astronomical correlations. But the ballgame also had an association with calendrical ritual and political organization.

A ballcourt dating to the Early Preclassic period has been identified at Paso de la Amada, Chiapas (Hill, Blake, and Clark 1998; Hill and Clark 2001). Early Olmec chiefs were depicted as ballplayers or warriors with insignia-bearing helmets on the colossal head sculptures (Clark 1997:223; also Coe 1968; Taube 1992), and clay figurines of ballplayers were abundant in the Olmec heartland in the Middle Preclassic (Coe and Diehl 1980) as well as in central Mexico (Tolstoy 1989). A tall stela from the site of Alvarado on the Gulf Coast shows an Olmec captive seated before a ruler-ballplayer (Covarrubias 1966:Fig. 29, cited in Coggins

1996:27n30). It is not unlikely, then, that the Olmecs might have had a creation myth similar to, or the prototype of, the Maya creation epic *Popul Vuh*. Rulers-as-ballplayers were powerfully linked to cosmic creation. In the Maya lowlands, perhaps the earliest known ballcourt was identified at Nakbe and dated circa 500–400 B.C. (Hansen 2000:5).

Interpretations of the Maya-Mesoamerican ballgame (see Scarborough and Wilcox 1991) focus on a wide range of possible ritual associations: life, death, and rebirth; trials of the Hero Twins in the Underworld (see also Coe 1989); cyclical movements of celestial bodies; and symbol of, or portal to, the Underworld. Also, the ballcourt was seen as the setting of the "Third Creation." Ashmore (1991, 1992) interprets the placement of ballcourts in a site's overall layout in cosmological terms, as a liminal or transitional zone between north and south, between up and down, and between celestial world and Underworld. Aimers (1993:179–185, Table 3) noted that ballcourts are often located near E-Groups. Fox (1996) emphasizes the role of the ballgame as part of more complex "extended ritual cycles."

The ballgame typically ended with the sacrifice (see, e.g., Wilkerson 1991) by decapitation of one or more players, their death (and symbolic rebirth) standing as a metaphor for celestial and agricultural cycles. The presence of skull racks near ballcourts, for example, at Chich'en Itza and Aztec Tenochtitlan, underscores the role of decapitation in these events. Similar fates seem to have befallen players—often kings—in the Classic period. For example, in 738 Copán's king Waxaklajun Ub'aj K'awil completed construction of a ballcourt near his hieroglyphic stairway, then shortly thereafter he was "captured" by the ruler of Quiriguá. Quiriguá claims to have decapitated Waxaklajun, whereas Copán says he died in "battle" (Martin and Grube 2000:205). The likely subtext here is that the rulers of the two cities engaged in a ballgame contest, which Waxaklajun lost in his home court, whereupon he was beheaded.

Classic Maya ballgame iconography contributes numerous insights into the political significance of the ballgame in the lowlands. For example, there are two logographs for ballcourt, one showing a U-shaped cross section of a court and the other showing a staircase (Fig. 8.4a). This plus architectural evidence suggests that the game was played in two distinct settings: one took place in a formal ballcourt (although there are virtually no images of this game), and the other—abundantly illustrated in carved and painted media—was played on or near staircases (Miller and Houston 1987; Schele and Freidel 1991:290; Cohodas 1991: Fig. 14.1). The activities in these settings were probably sequential, with a contest or "game" played in a formal ballcourt followed by a deeply symbolic ceremony—including sacrifice—played out against steps or a stepped structure.

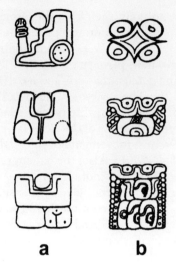

a   b

FIGURE 8.4 Glyphic signs for (a) ballcourts (Krochock and Freidel 1994; Fig.1; (b) "star war" events (after Harris and Stearns 1997:57).

Related to this is a considerable body of iconography, beginning in the Early Classic period (e.g., the Leiden Plate), depicting rulers standing with bound, prone captives. In a study of such figures in Maya art, Dillon (1982:28) interpreted details of how captives are bound, suggesting that the "reverse hog-tie"—prone and with hands tied behind the back—represents a prisoner who is either already dead and a trophy or about to be executed. This position, however, suggests neither decapitation (typically a neck-baring kneeling position) nor heart removal (spread-eagled on the back).

Instead, the "reverse hog-tie" displays a prisoner's vulnerability prior to the second stage of the ballgame played on a staircase. Much of the iconography for this second phase of the ballgame can be found on Yaxchilán's Structure 33, on a series of carved stone blocks making up Hieroglyphic Stair 2 on the structure's plinth (see Schele and Miller 1986:247; Christie 1995:207n5; Freidel, Schele, and Parker 1993:356–362). Here (Fig. 8.5), the staircase ballgame on Panels 7 and 8 is played with a ball that is actually a tightly bound human body—probably the loser of the contest played out in the court and thus a sacrificial victim—with the king attired in ballplayer regalia overseeing the ritual.

Images of the ball in the Yaxchilán and other staircase ballgame scenes show the glyph *nab*, *na'ab*, or *naab'*, prefixed by the numbers 9, 12, 13, or 14. Na'ab is often translated "waterlily," but it is difficult to accept that meaning in this context (Cohodas's [1991] explanation is

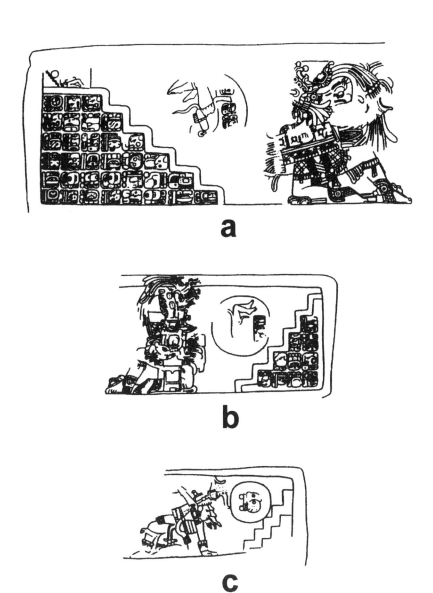

FIGURE 8.5 Steps 7, 8, and 10 of Hieroglyphic Stair 2 on Yaxchilán's Structure 33, showing the staircase version of the ballgame being played with a large "ball" that is a tightly bound human body (after drawings by Ian Graham).

unconvincing). Nab refers to "a measurement, the span of a hand" and naab' refers to a hand span measure of about 8 or 9 inches (Hofling and Tesucun 1998). Perhaps the appearance of a number with this glyph on the ball in the ballgame registers the size, and indirectly the weight, of the ball, hence the rigor of the game.

The hog-tied captive image frequently appears on period-ending monuments at Late and Terminal Classic Tikal and its realm, particularly in Tikal's twin-pyramid complexes, strongly suggesting that the second or staircase version of the ballgame ritual took place in these assemblages. It was already thought that the captive on Altar 8 (see Fig. 5.11), paired with Stela 20 in Twin-Pyramid Complex P (3D-2; A.D. 751), might be an individual who died in a ballgame and the rope-ringed altar itself represents a ball (Miller and Houston 1987:56; Schele and Miller 1986:249). It appears, rather, that this altar displays the individual as he was trussed in preparation for the second phase of the ballgame, his body substituted for the ball in a ritual set against a stairway.

Another example comes from the surviving text on the lower panel of Tikal Stela 21, which refers to the Tikal ruler as kalomte'. Both occurrences of the kalomte' glyph use the head variant, with ba' in the forehead and the expected te' postfix; ba'te' is a word for ballcourt. The accompanying Altar 9 shows a prone, bound captive from Calakmul. These monuments were found near Temple VI rather than in a twin-pyramid group, but as I suggested in Chapter 5, they might have been moved from one of the complexes.

At Tikal, the twin-pyramid staircase ballgame probably would have occurred at the radial pyramid on the west side of the assemblage. This is suggested in part because the eastern structure had a row of stelae and altars in front of it (although these could have been placed subsequently) but also because of the association of west with death. The prone, bound captives shown on stelae and altars in Tikal's twin-pyramid groups would be the vanquished lords of the preceding "real" ballgame, trussed to be used as the ball in the second stage of the ritual. Alternatively, prisoners of actual battles might have been expected to replay their defeat in the cosmically symbolic theater of ballgame ritual. As noted in earlier chapters, the appearance of bound captives on period-ending monuments at Tikal recalls the alternative meaning of k'atun as "combat, battle, warrior," and underscores the popular interpretations of astrally sanctioned warfare in Late Classic Maya society. In addition, the text on Tikal Stela 16 in Twin-Pyramid Group N seems to indicate that these assemblages were metaphorically the chasm and entrance to the Underworld, where the mythical ballgame was played by the Hero Twins.

Tikal's staircase version of the ballgame would have been very public. Eight of the nine twin-pyramid groups at Tikal are located close to causeways (see Fig. 5.16). Similarly, Late Classic ballcourts in northern Yucatán are typically situated at causeway termini (Ringle et al. 2004). This location hints that the activities occurring in twin-pyramid complexes and ballcourts involved ceremonial processions (see also Ashmore 1992:178). At Tikal, three twin-pyramid groups (complexes O, Q, R) are situated on an east-west axis bisected by the north-south Maler Causeway, and five lie at the ends of causeways (primarily the distal ends; two are located at the north end of the Maler Causeway). It may also be significant that along Tikal's Maler Causeway, extending north-south between two clusters of twin-pyramid groups (complexes M and P to the north; O, R, and Q to the south), there is a large (12' × 20') Late Classic rock sculpture showing two bound captives, one seated and one standing (Coe 1988:84). This sculpture records Tikal's "overthrow" of Naranjo in 744 (Grube 2000b:261).

There are additional architectural and other links between ballgame ritual, k'atun celebrations, and twin-pyramid groups at Tikal. In the middle seventh century Tikal's largest ballcourt and "reviewing stand" (a radial temple), in the Gulf Coast (El Tajin) talud-tablero style, were built in the East Plaza, east of the Main Plaza. The ballcourt was placed directly over the earliest twin-pyramid pair at the site, dating to the early sixth century (Jones 1985:51). Thus the East Plaza area, at the southern terminus of the Maler Causeway and the northern terminus of the Méndez Causeway, could have been the stage of calendrical ceremonies for a century or more before the ballcourt and radial temple were built.

In any case, I believe twin-pyramid complexes in Late Classic Tikal and central Petén, beginning in the reign of Jasaw Kan K'awil and used in k'atun-ending celebrations (and perhaps in New Year's celebrations), were also associated with the second stage or staircase version of the ballgame. If this is true, then there is a direct relationship between the ballgame and period-endings as celebrated architecturally by the cities seating the thirteen k'atuns and the 256-year *may*. Such a relationship might explain why there are thirteen panels depicting stairway ballgame scenes on the hieroglyphic step of Yaxchilán's Structure 33. The dates on these panels span the reigns of several rulers over possibly as many as 128 years (half a *may*), indicating that the site's scribes "were assembling on this step a history of famous game rituals performed in the city" (Freidel, Schele, and Parker 1993:357). More precisely, they were recording period-ending ballgame rituals.

Similarly, Seibal Structure A-10, the eastern structure of an E-Group, was a probable site of the stairway ballgame, as suggested by the images of ballplayers on "Stelae" 5 and 7, set on either side of the west-facing stairway. Christie (1995:171) suggests that the game was played against that stairway, and "the sacrificial victims used as balls were offered to the outgoing or 'dying' k'atun" at the changeover of deities occurring on the lajuntun 9.18.10.0.0 10 Ajaw 8 Zak (800). Finally, it is useful to recall that thirteen ballcourts were constructed at Chich'en Itza. Other associations among prisoners, ballgames, and stairways can be seen at Dos Pilas (Miller and Houston 1987:58), where the hieroglyphic stairs show ballplayers on three risers; on one, two teams face each other across two large, tied bundles. At Dzibanché in Calakmul's realm, carved stair risers show bound prisoners, but there is no clear association with a ballgame (Martin and Grube 2000:103). And both El Tajin and Chich'en Itza emphasize the skull, rather than the human body, as ball (see Gillespie 1991 for discussion of the "Rolling Head" and celestial periodicities).

Some intriguing but inconclusive evidence comes from epigraphy. The word b'aat means "ax," and it is also at the root of b'a'te'el (or b'a'ate'el) 'fight; war, combat' and b'ate' 'ballcourt'. In addition, the title kalomte' (see Fig. 4.7) was formerly read as 'b'atab', perhaps "warrior" or "ax fighter." As noted, some head variants of this glyph (new 1125; Ringle and Smith-Stark 1996:331), for example, on Tikal Stela 21, shows the head variant with ba' in the forehead and a te' postfix, recalling b'ate' 'ballcourt'. This prompts speculation that the ax-in-hand element of this glyph might refer to the decapitation before the stairway version of ballgame.

Finally, several pages of the Madrid Codex show decapitated human bodies wrapped and bundled in a shroud, sometimes upside down and other times seated, in what might be an analogue to the bundling of sacrificial victims into a ball for the staircase version of the ballgame. These Postclassic scenes, however, relate to sacrifices carried out during the Wayeb' days and sacrifices as part of New Year's ceremonies (Bricker 1997b:178).

Maya "Warfare"

The Classic Maya world was once romanticized as an idyllic tropical garden of peaceful farmers and benign philosopher-stargazers—the Mesoamerican equivalent of the Old World humanistic Greeks vis-à-vis the militaristic Romanlike Aztecs (Spinden 1917). Today, however, the ancient Maya are widely acknowledged to have been as inclined toward warfare and human sacrifice as any premodern chiefdom or state society. This shift in scholarly thinking is a consequence of many factors, not the least of which are new hieroglyphic decipherments. A direct-historical perspective and insights into calendrical cycling can shed further light on the broader context of political conflict in the Classic period (P. Rice n.d.c).

There is little doubt that Classic lowland Maya polities sustained variable degrees of mutual hostility, but the extent, causes, and consequences are unclear. Interpretations of the nature and causes of hostilities range from highly materialist (population pressure, lack of resources) to highly ideological (celestial activity, particularly movements of Venus). These conflictual relations often have been referred to as "warfare," a term that, like "militarism," carries heavy baggage (Webster 1976:815; 1977:363–364; 1993; 1998): it implies substantial infrastructural investment and organization, including imperialist politics, territorial expansion, standing armies and supply systems, weaponry systems, defensive fortifications, large-scale offensive operations often at long distance, conquest by force, destruction of enemies and property, tribute collection systems, and the ability to maintain control of the defeated society. Yet, as Stuart (1995:293, 329) has pointed out for the Maya, "no event glyph is known that literally reads 'to wage war'," and textual references do not exist until after the sixth century A.D.

Ross Hassig's (1992:70–81, 94–99) study of warfare in Mesoamerica provides a measured overview of lowland Maya data. He notes that among the Classic Maya, warfare was primarily "aristocratic," involving small numbers of soldiers who were probably nobles (to judge from their sumptuous attire), and highly individual or one-on-one, suggested by hand-held rather than long-range weapons. True warfare would have been limited, he believes, by the tropical forest environment hindering massive troop movements, by the lack of easily portable foodstuffs (e.g., tortillas), and by seasonal rainfall cycles making trails impassable for many months. In short, Hassig's observations support the idea that Maya warfare was primarily a matter of quick raids and highly symbolic combat intended for "internal political purposes, such as validating rulers" through acquisition of captives, rather than territorial conquest to gain control over resources. Similarly, Culbert (1991c:335–336), in summarizing the role of warfare in Maya political history, emphasizes that most of the captives are unnamed or "unprovenienced" as to home site, suggesting that they may not have been important individuals.

Insights into Classic lowland Maya warfare come from Late Postclassic and early Colonial period northern Yucatán. Spanish chroniclers inform us that conflict between towns in the region was relatively constant and pervasive. Landa reported "great strifes and enmities" among the major ruling lineages, along with a probably exaggerated reference to the killing of 150,000 men in one unnamed battle and the Mayas' legitimate fears of capture, being sold into slavery, or sacrificed as a result of defeat (Tozzer 1941:40–41, 217). Herrera (Tozzer 1941:217) also reported that after the battles with the Spaniards the Maya "were scattered. And their discords had increased so much that for any little cause they fought. . . . And so they never had peace, especially when the cultivation was over."

Landa (Tozzer 1941:113, 122n562) tells us that wars were led by the nakom, a war captain who was elected to office for three years. Soldiers, or *jolkans*, from each town were headed by its b'atab', who led the warriors into battle. The nakom, who ruled over the month Pax, was treated almost as a god and during his term of office largely withdrew from normal life, having no contact whatsoever with women. All of this points to "the religious significance placed on warfare" by the Maya (Tozzer 1941:123n563).

The reasons for the unrest and skirmishing in postconquest Yucatán are not difficult to comprehend. Among the many causes that can be identified (see Farriss 1984, 1987; Restall 1997; Roys [1943] 1972:65–70), some are specific to the Colonial circumstance and led to rebellions against the new overlords: defense of traditional territorial boundaries; conversion to Christianity versus maintenance of traditional practice; onerous demands of tithes to the Church; labor and tribute payments to both native lords and new Spanish encomenderos; forced resettlements (congregación) and crowding; voluntary flight from Spanish centers into the hinterlands and mixing with long-established groups (Rice and Rice in press); elimination of traditional social and political authority structures; and so on. These new elements were superimposed on historical and internal events and practices, leading to rivalries between towns and lineages such as the taking of captives for sacrifice (nobles) or enslavement (commoners), access to or control of trade goods, and deeply rooted feuds over perceived misdeeds, slights, and crimes.

Carefully hidden from the Spanish rulers but subtly interwoven into the native chronicles is another, deeper reason for some of the belligerence: long-standing antagonisms over specific calendrical matters. According to Edmonson (1986a:99), "katuns not only chronicled the wars of Yucatan but actually caused them." During the Postclassic period, there was considerable inter "ethnic" disagreement between the Xiw and Itza about calendrical issues as well as competition between major towns for the power and prestige of seating the k'atuns and the *may*. In this regard, it again bears recalling that while the word k'atun refers to a period of 7,200 days, it is also a noun and verb meaning fight, combat, battle, war, or warrior. Numerous derivations also exist (Marcus 1992a:416): *k'atun yaj* and *k'atun chuk luum* 'to conquer land'; *aj k'atun* 'warrior'; and *k'atuntaj* 'to fight with someone', apparently referring to one-on-one or hand-to-hand combat. That so many terms for warfare or conflict derive from the calendrical period suggests a deep and inextricable association. Indeed, the so-called k'atun wars (*u k'atun k'atunob*) were waged over the competing calendars, resulting in "a formal bifurcation of the politico-religious system" and adoption of a new calendar in 1539 (Edmonson 1982:xvi–xvii). But calendrical disputes continued, with an attempted later resolution by means of the short-lived Valladolid calendar in 1752.

The books of the chilam b'alams reveal the presence of numerous military orders, among both nobles and peasantry, all given various nicknames. For example, the pro-Xiw *Chumayel* mentions the Flags, Possums, Many Skunks, Hanging Rabbits, and Foxes as peasant orders opposed to the nobility (Edmonson 1986a:209–214). The pro-Itza *Tizimin* mentions the Snakes, Ants, Jaguars, and Silent Leopards, whose members were apparently pro-peasant, Christianized Xiw, as were probably the Locusts, Monsters, and Chiggers, active around Merida in a K'atun 3 Ajaw (Edmonson 1982:37, 113–114). Elsewhere, the Strong Skunks, Masked Deer, and Rabbits were described as being usurpers in the land in a K'atun 7 Ajaw (ending A.D. 1342, 1599) (Edmonson 1982: 62–63).

These books also indicate that K'atuns 11 Ajaw were nicknamed the "flower k'atun," alluding to the "Flowery Wars" (i.e., divine wars) of Aztec central Mexico. The year 1539, date of the calendrical compromise of the Itza and Xiw, was the transition from a K'atun 13 Ajaw to a K'atun 11 Ajaw. K'atuns 7 Ajaw also have associations with war and conflict: in the *Tizimin* K'atun 7 Ajaw is described as one of chaos, usurpation, and "seven-day rule" (Edmonson 1982:62–63). In addition, the day 1 Ajaw is also the preferred ending date of the idealized Venus cycle (Milbrath 1999:170), with its association of star wars. Can the Colonial period prophetic histories be read to suggest k'atuns of conflict during the Classic period?

Here it is useful to return to the discussion in Chapters 4 and 5 concerning Tikal's *may* seatings in the Middle and Late Classic periods. These seatings occurred at 256-year intervals in K'atuns 8 Ajaw, with the kuch, or burden of office, being transferred at the lajuntun, or midpoint, of that k'atun. After their tenure as "guest," Tikal and other cities seating the *may* had different responsibilities during the first and last halves, 130 tuns or 128 years each, of their full cycle. It was proposed that Middle Classic Tikal seated the *may* at the midpoint of the K'atun 8 Ajaw interval of 416 through 435, a lajuntun falling on a day 9 Ajaw 3 Muwan (January 30, 426). Counting forward 128 years or half a *may* brings us to the year 554, which is the ending of a K'atun 9 Ajaw and the beginning of a K'atun 7 Ajaw. Similarly, Tikal's Late Classic *may* seating began in the lajuntun of the K'atun 8 Ajaw dating from 672 to 692, with the midpoint falling on a day 9 Ajaw 18 Sotz' in 682. Counting forward 128 years brings us to 810, another year ending a K'atun 9 Ajaw and initiating a K'atun 7 Ajaw.

If this midpoint of the *may* marked the start of competition for a new *may* seat, or the point where an incoming *may* seat had to display that it was indeed "born of heaven" and sanctioned by cosmic authority, then this could account for K'atuns 7 Ajaw being k'atuns of competition, conflict, and political chaos. In this light, it is perhaps significant that Caracol's "defeat" of Tikal in 562 occurred just before the midpoint of a K'atun 7 Ajaw. Likewise, the twenty-year interval from 810 to 830, often taken as marking the end of the Late Classic or Terminal Classic occupation of the southern lowlands, is a K'atun 7 Ajaw, the k'atun of political competition and change.

This leaves explanation of K'atun 1 Ajaw and its Venus-warfare associations. During the Early Classic period, the k'atun ending of 8.17.0.0.0 1 Ajaw 8 Ch'en fell in 376, which was two years before the arrival of the central Mexican Siyaj K'ak' and the putative introduction of Venus-Tlaloc war imagery into the Maya lowlands. In addition, two star wars involving Calakmul-Caracol against Naranjo occurred around the end of the 9.10.0.0.0 K'atun 1 Ajaw ending in 633, one in 631 and another in 636. We know via the Dresden and Grolier codices that Venus and its observed movements were carefully tracked by the Maya. Corrections given in the Dresden allowed Venus's movements to be tracked for 384 years before new reckonings had to be made (Sharer 1994:578–579). An interval of 384 years is, of course, 128 + 256 years, the full three phases of a *may* cycle. However, there is virtually no direct mention of the planet or star in the *Chumayel* or *Tizimin*. This could be because the authors of these books chose to be cryptic about matters of native cosmology. One also wonders, however, if Venus's importance was severely diminished by the Late Postclassic, perhaps by the fact that warfare was increasingly frequent and "real" rather than largely symbolic or ritualized.

It is appropriate here to return to consideration of representations of captives on Classic period-ending monuments and their poses. As noted previously, prone and bound (hog-tied) captives were commonly depicted on stelae and altars in Tikal's twin-pyramid complexes, which I associate with the stair version of the ballgame. The pose is known from Early Classic times, but in the Late Classic it appears on monuments at sites more widely distributed in time and space (see Dillon 1982: Table 3). Of thirty-four occurrences, sixteen are on k'atun endings beginning in 9.10.0.0.0 (A.D. 633, the ending of a K'atun 1 Ajaw), twelve on lajuntun endings beginning in 9.8.10.0.0, and four on jotun endings. This position continued to be used on k'atun-ending stelae through Tikal's Stela 11, dating 10.2.0.0.0 (869).

Table 8.1. Xiw versus Itza 256-year cycles of named k'atuns.

Xiw	Itza
6 Ajaw	**Begin 13 Ajaw**
4 Ajaw	11 Ajaw
2 Ajaw	9 Ajaw
13 Ajaw	7 Ajaw
11 Ajaw	5 Ajaw
9 Ajaw	3 Ajaw
7 Ajaw	1 Ajaw
5 Ajaw	12 Ajaw
3 Ajaw	10 Ajaw
1 Ajaw	8 Ajaw
12 Ajaw	6 Ajaw
10 Ajaw	4 Ajaw
End 8 Ajaw	2 Ajaw

During the late Late Classic and Terminal Classic periods at Tikal and its realm, captives were somewhat more frequently depicted seated and in multiples rather than as a single prone, bound individual. The transition began around 771, with Altar 10 in Twin-Pyramid Group Q showing five captives, one prone and bound atop the altar and four seated around its circumference. Altar 6 in Twin-Pyramid Group R, dated 790, shows five similarly posed captives. Several recently found (post-1982, date of Dillon's tabulation) altars in the Petén lakes region depict seated captives but are not precisely dated; stylistically they conform to very late Late Classic and Terminal Classic programs.

Edmonson (1982:39n723) noted, without elaboration, that the half-cycle sequence of seven odd-numbered k'atuns—K'atuns 13 Ajaw, 11 Ajaw, 9 Ajaw, 7 Ajaw, 5 Ajaw, 3 Ajaw, and 1 Ajaw—seems to have been a source of *may*-related conflict in Colonial period Yucatán. Perhaps this is because the Xiw counted k'atuns on their terminal dates from 6 Ajaw through 8 Ajaw, while the Itza counted them from their initial dates from 11 Ajaw through 13 Ajaw (Table 8.1). The origin of these different dating systems can be traced to Early Classic Petén. During the

Late Classic period, Tikal's *may* cycles focused on K'atuns 8 Ajaw and terminal dating, the same used by the later Xiw of Yucatán. However, Tikal's traditional "enemy," Calakmul, and its alliance partners such as Caracol, seemed to gain power in K'atuns 2 Ajaw (which precede K'atuns 13 Ajaw; see Table 3.4). For example, on the lajuntun ending on a day 9.9.10.0.0 2 Ajaw 13 Pop (A.D. 623), Calakmul ended its hiatus and erected large numbers of stelae through the K'atun 2 Ajaw ending of 9.16.0.0.0. Similarly, Caracol was particularly aggressive after the same lajuntun in 623. What was the origin of this alternative system?

I believe the changed activity at these sites during this lajuntun could relate in part to the division of the b'ak'tun into quarters. For example, given the Maya fondness for quadripartition, I suspect—although I have not accumulated evidence to satisfactorily demonstrate—that, just as twenty-year k'atuns are divided into four parts of five years each (jotun, lajuntun, jolajuntun), so might the twenty-k'atun b'ak'tun be divided into four parts of five, ten, and fifteen k'atuns. Thus the date 9.9.10.0.0, the lajuntun before the end of the first half of the b'ak'tun (at 9.10.0.0.0), might have been cause for some adjustments in prevailing political arrangements.

With respect to the K'atun 2 Ajaw, I suspect the origin of its importance can be traced to the Early Classic period and the presence of central Mexicans at Tikal. As I have argued above (Chap. 4) and elsewhere (Rice n.d.b), the much-discussed arrival of Teotihuacanos at Tikal on a day 11 Eb' in A.D. 378 has been accorded excessive importance to us today as a sudden and pivotal event in lowland history. But archaeological evidence indicates that central Mexican–style (talud-tablero) architecture was visible at central Tikal considerably earlier, beginning around A.D. 250. One apparent consequence of the A.D. 378 arrival event was the death of the Tikal ruler Chak Tok Ich'ak, who, interestingly enough, might have been preceded by an earlier ruler by that name around 250 and was followed by a later Chak Tok Ich'ak who died in 508. The dates 250 to 378 to 508 represent periods of 128 and 130 years or, combined, a *may* cycle. Furthermore, the years 250 and 508 fall within K'atuns 13 Ajaw if the k'atuns are identified by their terminal day, or in K'atuns 2 Ajaw if they are named by the alternative system, their initial day.

By the middle to late fourth century, there seem to have been two disputatious elite lineage groups at Tikal, one representing the traditional rule of the Jaguar Paw dynasty and the other having ties to central Mexico. The traditional rulers observed calendrico-cosmic cycling based on K'atuns 8 Ajaw, whereas the opposing faction observed those associated with K'atuns 13/2 Ajaw. While the Teotihuacan-supporting faction seems to be implicated in the events of 378, including the death of the ruler and the imposition of a stranger-king, succeeding rulers forcefully reasserted their connections with the names, symbols, and icono-graphic programs of their dynastic predecessors, including celebration of K'atuns 8 Ajaw. This would suggest that the central Mexican–leaning, K'atun 13/2 Ajaw faction had diminished power and might have even-tually been ousted from Tikal. It is not difficult to imagine, then, that this disaffected group or groups opposed to the Jaguar Paw ruling line might have retreated—sans Teotihuacanos—to Calakmul, where they established, in effect, a center for alternative calendrics. Sometime dur-ing the sixth-century hiatus, if not before, proponents were able to ele-vate the importance of K'atun 13/2 Ajaw–based cycling, and thus inter-site conflicts escalated.

That Tikal eventually won these disagreements, in some senses, is evidenced by the fact that there were no further battles with Caracol or Calakmul after Tikal "defeated" the latter site in 695, and the Tikal cal-endar continued in use into the Colonial period. Yet arguments about initial versus terminal naming, and K'atun 8 Ajaw versus K'atun 13/2 Ajaw cycling, continued to rage through the Postclassic period until the calendrical compromise achieved in 1539.

Dual Rulership

It is widely agreed among scholars that Classic kings were sacred, as indicated by their Emblem Glyph titles (holy [place] lord), and the ex-istence of a hierarchy of offices has recently gained considerable ac-ceptance. At the top of the hierarchy is the kalomte' (T1030, previously read as *chak'te'* and *b'atab'*), who ruled over a large domain as a sort of overlord; this title "was of special importance and restricted to only the strongest dynasties during the Classic proper" (Martin and Grube 2000:17). *Lom* or *kalom* means "warrior," and a key element of most of the glyph T1030 variants is an upraised hand holding an ax. Below the kalomte' is the ajaw (king, lord). Ajaws—sublords and local lords—may reside at several towns under the hegemony of a kalomte' and even in his own city. Below ajaws are lesser lords or vassals known in some parts of the lowlands as sahals.

There have been several recent suggestions that the Classic Maya might have had dual rulers and diarchical political organization, an idea raised earlier by Thompson (1970:97). Such a diarchy might have in-volved corulers or divisions based on sacred/secular or internal/external affairs of various sorts. The best-known example of diarchy in Meso-america is that of the Late Postclassic Tenochca (Aztec) in central Mex-ico. There the *tlatoani* 'speaker', who presided over a judicial body of thirteen, plus himself, ruled jointly with the *cihuacoatl* 'serpent-woman', who was also a military leader (Sahagun 1950–1970, bk. 8:55;

Berdan 1982), and they came from different family lines. The principal temple of the Aztec capital, Tenochtitlan, was likewise a dual temple dedicated to their indigenous deity Huitzilopochtli and the long-standing central Mexican storm or war god, Tlaloc (Matos Moctezuma 1987). Recently, it has also been suggested that the Toltecs too had a dual government (Mastache and Cobean 2000:107).

One basis for the suggestion of dual rulership among the Maya is kinship—the possible existence of moieties in lowland Maya social organization, comparable to that in the highlands (Fox 1991), which would require some mechanism for sharing governance and ritual. According to Becker (1983), early sociopolitical structure in the Maya lowlands might have been dominated by moieties. During the Preclassic period, the Maya were at a chiefdom level of organization, with "political" aspects regulated by kin groups (moieties) having different responsibilities: one was "charged with internal affairs (land use, personal conflicts) while the leader of the other group would handle external affairs (warfare, ritual)" (Becker 1983:161). Through time—by the Late Classic—this was transformed by economic wealth into a more formal and less kinship-based, diarchical structure. Furthermore, "the divine origins of the dual rulers are clearly described in the *Popol Vuh* and other origin myths which reify the cognitive processes involved with this kind of political structure" (Becker 1983:174).

Another example comes from Viel (1999), who suggested dual rulership at Late Classic Copán on the basis of the iconography of the pectorals on the rulers portrayed on Altar Q and the Structure 11 Bench. He proposes that "a diarchy was institutionalized in the eighth century that took the form of a ruler/co-ruler (or heir apparent) system" (1999:388; see also Webster, Freter, and Gonlin 2000:178; Schele and Freidel 1990:333–334; Cheek 2003). Within this system at Copán, power was shared between two corporate descent groups, one controlling the appointment of four "ministers" or politico-religious officers and one controlling the four military officers, one of each for each of the four quarters. An "executive branch" consisting of the ruler, coruler, four ministers, and four war captains would have been advised by a council of nine lords. His model is similar to that of the Aztec *tlatoani* and *cihuacoatl* (Viel 1999:392; see also Edmonson 1979:11). The idea of a coruler or heir apparent at a site calls to mind the host-guest arrangement of k'atun lords and *may* seats; also, the deer hoof or *may* glyph has been read as "heir apparent" (Montgomery 2001a:Fig. 9-3).

Another line of reasoning for the suggestion of diarchy is more strictly "political": a functional division based on control of "internal," primarily ritual, affairs versus authority for "external" or intersite affairs including diplomacy and conflict management. The possibility of dual rulership was raised by Coe (1965; also Thompson 1970:97), who cited Landa's comments about the presence of two nakoms in Colonial Yucatán. Landa had reported that the same term, "nakom," was used to refer to two different offices and individuals: one nakom was an elected war chief; the other was in charge of human sacrifices. From this, Coe (1965:103n2) proposed that "we have here a suggestion of dual organization, contrasting military with religious office."

Subsequently, there have been suggestions of dual rulers in Uaxactún (Valdés and Fahsen 1995:205) and at Caracol, where there is strong evidence of preemptive accessions and corule during the latter years of certain rulers as evidenced by stuccoed texts on Structure B19 (Houston 2000:165). Similarly, dual rulership might have been in existence at Tikal, as suggested by the apparent succession of titles from ajaw to kalomte' (Valdés and Fahsen 1995:204–207). After the rule of Jaguar Claw I (Chak Tok Ich'ak) there may have been "two officials who ruled together, kalomte' and ajaw. When the kalomte' died, the reigning ajaw usually succeeded to his title, while another lord, the next in line, moved up into the position of ajaw" (Harrison 1999:79, orthography changed from original). Similar interpretations have been articulated by Laporte and Fialko (1990:58) and Braswell (2003b:26). Again, such a division would accommodate an intrasite successional pattern similar to that of overlapping guest and host k'atun idols and *may* seats. While at Copán the corulers would have been approximately equal and shared the k'ul ajaw title, at Tikal this was a more hierarchical relationship.

Other kinds of evidence could be interpreted in the context of dual rulership. In western Belize, the sites of Buenavista and Cahal Pech apparently were effectively dual capitals, where two separate palaces served a single royal court (Ball and Taschek 2001:187). Similar coruling sites might have existed in the Petexbatun, where Tamarindito and Arroyo de Piedra seem to have been centers of a kingdom before a new capital was established at Dos Pilas. Recent reinterpretation of the latest stelae at Machaquilá (Stelae 5–8) reveals the possibility that Ruler 6 may have been two people, perhaps twins (Myers and Rice n.d.).

There are also numerous instances—particularly in the Pasión-Usumacinta region—of two sites sharing the same Emblem Glyph, or a single site having paired Emblems (Martin and Grube 2000:19, 119). Paired sites sharing Emblem Glyphs include Bonampak and Lacanhá, Cancuen and Machaquilá (?), Tamarindito and Arroyo de Piedra, Dos Pilas and Tikal, Palenque and Tortuguero, Motul de San José and Bejucal, and Quiriguá and Pusilhá. Sites with two-part Emblems are Machaquilá, Yaxchilán, Palenque, Caracol, Sacul, Ucanal, among others. While some of these could be interpreted in terms of dual rulers or ruling lineages of a site, others could indicate the paired succession of *may* seats, as incoming guest or coseat, ruling or host seat, and then out-going with a new guest seat.

There have been several suggestions of triadic organization as well. Laporte and Fialko (1990:45) discussed the possibility of three lineages with respect to the Early Classic rulership of Tikal and linked them to triadic architecture. The well-known Palenque Triad of gods (Lounsbury 1985), along with the three hearthstones of creation, suggest mytho-cosmological bases for such structuring, complemented by David Sedat's (1992:86) observations on the symbolism of triadic dot clusters as they relate to early fire-related ceremonies. More recently, a triadic political organization, with sacred, secular, and military components, has been proposed for Calakmul (Folan, Gunn, and Domínguez Carrasco 2001). Additional support comes from the names of numerous sites that incorporate "three": OxWitza 'Three Hills Water' (Caracol), Ox Te' Tun 'Three Tree Stones' (Calakmul), Ox Tun 'Three Kawak [earth stones]' (Seibal), Ox Witik (Copán), and Uxmal/Ox Mal 'Thrice Built'. It is also useful here to recall one of the types of political organization Quezada (1993) identified in sixteenth-century Yucatán, in which military, religious, and politico-judicial administrative functions were held by three individuals. Similarly, Lincoln (1994) uses what he calls "Dumézilian trifunctional structuralism" to assess the possibility of triadic kingship at Chich'en Itza.

During the Postclassic and Contact periods in the Petén lakes region, the Itza, who had returned to their Classic period ancestral homeland after the fall of Chich'en Itza in the north, appear to have had dual rulership. The supreme ruler of Tayasal and the Itza was Ajaw Kan Ek', who "shared power equally" with his cousin, the high priest Aj K'in Kan Ek' (Jones 1998:94). This joint rule at the highest levels of authority apparently was paralleled in the provinces by a quadripartite system of senior-junior pairs of an ajaw b'atab' and a b'atab' (ibid.:95), each pair associated with one of the four cardinal directions and also the wards or districts of a town or region. In addition, the Itza of Petén recognized thirteen soldier-priests with the title Ach Kat, each of whom "represented the military, religious, and practical interests of his home community" (ibid.:104). They were also the heads of the thirteen k'atun seats under the Itza hegemony of the *may* (ibid.:102).

Further amplification of the possibility of dual rulership comes from Edmonson. In posing a series of provocative questions about Classic Maya organization derived from his studies of the chronicles, Edmonson (1979:10–11) noted that in Postclassic and Colonial Yucatán the lord of the k'atun held the title b'alam (jaguar) and was "the supreme ruler of the entire country during his 20 *tun* term of office." Similarly, the jaguar lords in Yucatán were assisted by a spokesman (chilam) who was a sage, great sun priest (aj noj k'in) of the k'atun, sun priest of the cycle (aj k'in may), and also registrar of lands (aj p'iz te). Edmonson believes the role of spokesman might be "a Postclassic Mexican addition to Mayan culture," specifically that of the Aztecs (and perhaps the Toltecs).

However, a tantalizing bit of evidence for an early "speaker" role among the Maya comes from a Late Classic polychrome vase showing a lord receiving tribute. He and three other individuals are identified as aj k'uhun scribes, one of whom also carries the title "chilam," which Coe (1998:95) translates as "interpreter." Even earlier, Middle Classic Tikal Stela 8 (9.5.2.9.0 1 Ajaw 8 K'ank'in) refers to the main personage as *ti juun* 'mouth [of the] headband' (Guenter 2000:23, 24n4, citing D. Stuart). Guenter interprets this individual as a backer of the female ruler, Lady of Tikal, who was suffering declining power and "needed male support to rule" [*sic*]. Instead, the expression "speaker for the ruler" might indicate a Middle Classic politico-religious role of "spokesman" for the ruler-priest like that of the chilam b'alam in Postclassic and Colonial times in northern Yucatán. It is useful here to recall once again that the literal meaning of ajaw is "he who shouts" (Stuart 1995) or proclaims or announces.

If, as Edmonson suggested, the Maya adopted a diarchical administrative structure during Postclassic times, the roles and responsibilities of secular authorities (jalach winik, b'atab's, etc.) and ritual authorities (both the b'alam and the chilam were priests) were likely to have differed significantly from the Aztec model. In addition, the roles of Classic divine kings, as interpreted through epigraphy and iconography, obviously would have undergone substantial transformation. If, on the other hand, the Maya already maintained a political diarchy during the Classic period (and perhaps earlier?) this would have greatly eased problems of succession from one king to another. The role of intermarriage between royal lineages, with naming practices (and perhaps descent reckoning?) recording both maternal and paternal names ("child of mother, child of father"), similarly could have contributed to resolving transitions of kingship. We know that the late Itza rulers of Petén observed dual descent (see Jones 1998:447), as did nobles in Yucatán (*almehen* 'child of mother, child of father').

How might any of this be recognized archaeologically? It seems virtually unarguable that during the Early, Middle, Late, and Terminal Classic periods the Maya in the southern lowlands regarded their kings as the Jaguar Sun God. Kings are shown on stelae, lintels, and ceramic vessels dressed in jaguar pelts or kilts, wearing jaguar masks or booties, sitting on jaguar skin thrones, or having jaguar protectors looming over them. Kings' bodies were interred covered with jaguar pelts, and their funerary rituals were commemorated with incensarios decorated with the imagery of the JGU or JGIII, the Jaguar God of the Underworld, the god of the night sun as it journeyed back to the east through the Underworld. The rituals carried out by the kings on k'atun endings were most specifically marked by jaguar imagery and costuming. It seems clear from Classic iconography, then, that Classic Maya kings portrayed on stelae and lintels were also b'alams, that is, jaguar priests.

Given this, I propose that Classic period ajaws and kalomte's were predecessors of the jaguar priests in k'atun and *may* ceremonies in the Postclassic and Colonial periods. Their role at the time, judging from depictions on Classic stelae, seems to have been most directly involved in autosacrifice or scattering, probably simultaneously a ritual to ensure earthly fertility, an invocation of ancestral approbation for kingly power and legitimacy, and a reaffirmation of cosmic continuity in the endless cycling of time.

This raises the question, who were the individuals portrayed on Classic stelae, altars, and lintels? The old answer was gods and priests; the current answer is kings and lords. But in light of the Late Postclassic and early Colonial evidence for the important role of jaguar priests, it is not unreasonable to wonder if the Classic personages depicted in grandiose jaguar costuming—heads, paws, robes, kilts, tails—were also priests. Did Classic kings have dual roles and titles as lord-ruler and chief calendar priest–b'alam? Did they also have spokesmen—chilams or ti juuns? Or were jaguar priests and kings separate individuals in the Classic period? Did a Classic title "jaguar priest" exist at all? Answers to these questions await further epigraphic and iconographic study.

Overview

Classic period Maya rulers participated in numerous kinds of rituals, many of which were calendrical. The accumulating inscriptional and iconographic evidence associated with calendrical ceremonies is providing new insights into the nature of rulership and political action among the Maya. In addition, the spatiotemporal distribution of certain ritual-related glyphs and imagery allows inferences as to the changing geopolitical situation in the Late and Terminal Classic lowlands.

For example, the fire sequence glyphs indicating Burner ritual seem to occur in Initial Series inscriptions in two areas of the southern lowlands. One of these is southeastern Petén and Belize, the area later occupied by Mopan Maya speakers and also associated with Late Classic use of E-Groups; the other is along the Pasión and Usumacinta Rivers, at the sites of Piedras Negras, Palenque, Bonakpak, and Yaxchilán. Fire rituals also became very important at Terminal Classic Chich'en Itza, where architectural and iconographic evidence suggests strong ties to the Pasión-Usumacinta area (see Chap. 7). In light of this distribution, it is tempting to link the occurrence of the fire sequence and Burner rituals to the introduction and spread of the Campeche calendar during the seventh century (Edmonson 1988). For example, it is known that of the thirty-five identified days associated with these fire ceremonies, twenty-four were days Ajaw, which is a Burner day. However, five of the remaining identified days are yearbearers associated with the Campeche calendar and the Dresden Codex: Ak'bal' (twice), Lamat (twice), and B'en (once). Another is a day 8 Ok, which also occurs as one of the Burner days in the Dresden Codex (pp. 30, 31) (Bricker 1997a: 5). The presence of fire-drilling iconography and Burner phrases at Naranjo might also correlate with the otherwise unexplained occurrence of the Campeche calendar there.

The new calendars in the western lowlands involved changing the counting system as well as the introduction of terminal naming of the year. The latter practice is characterized as distinctively non-Maya: Edmonson (1988:103) calls it an "intrusive foreign idea" and attributes it to Ch'olan speakers and calendars used in the Gulf Coast or Oaxaca region. As noted above, the practice of terminal dating of years came to be used in the Late Classic at sites in the Usumacinta region (Palenque, Yaxchilán, Bonampak, Piedras Negras) and in the Puuc area of Campeche (Uxmal, Edzná, Jaina, Holactún, and doubtless other sites). Apparently, it was not adopted elsewhere in the eastern or central lowlands (except at Naranjo?), where the so-called Mexican Tlaloc-Venus star wars were most intensely fought (P. Rice n.d.c).

It is not unreasonable to argue that the role of warfare in Late Classic lowland Maya society has been exaggerated in recent assessments. Many of the new glyph decipherments have yielded words that are sufficiently general that they could be interpreted less violently in other arenas of competition or combat, such as the ballgame (P. Rice n.d.c). Also, many of the relationships between supposedly warring sites are difficult to explain in the context of warfare as territorial conquest. According to Quiriguá Stela E, K'ak' Tiliw came to rule Quiriguá in 724 under the supervision of (u kab'iy) the very man he subsequently killed, Copán's ruler Waxaklajun Ub'aj K'awil (Martin and Grube 2000:218). In 738 Quiriguá "defeated" Copán, but none of the Quiriguá accounts of this event refer to it by using a term for war (Martin and Grube 2000:219).

In another example, Schele (Schele and Grube 1995:21) describes the lords of Tikal and Calakmul as "deadly enemies." But there are no recorded wars between these great Classic sites after Tikal's defeat of Calakmul in 695, and their rulers were able to come together—presumably peaceably—with other lords on state occasions, as seen on Copán

Stela A (731). The notion of deep and enduring hostilities between Tikal and Calakmul is belied by the latter site's material culture affiliations. During the Late Classic period, Calakmul's architecture is of Petén style and its pottery complex is a full member of the Tikal-centric Tepeu sphere, ceramic spheres traditionally interpreted as indicative of some degree of economic integration. If the two sites were in protracted wars of conquest, it is hard to imagine why they would share material symbols displaying social identities, as well as let traders bringing such utilitarian goods as pottery pass through embattled territory.

Evidence for destruction of sites and monuments, which has been an important contributor to scenarios of widespread Classic period warfare, could instead represent the termination rituals that accompanied the end of the seating of the *may* in a particular city. As Edmonson comments about the Postclassic Maya in northern Yucatán, they

destroyed the primate city and its road at the end of the *may*. There are indications that this "destruction" may have been largely ritual and symbolic, and that the "abandonment" of the city was an evacuation by the ruling dynasty rather than total depopulation. But since the dynasties (e.g., the Xiu and the Itza) did not necessarily agree on the ending date of the cycle, there was room for maneuver in politics, ideology and warfare. The Postclassic theory did not end the legitimacy or existence of a dynasty, but only its right to rule a particular city. (1979:11)

On the eastern edge of Tikal's Late Classic *may* realm, Naranjo reportedly inflicted numerous "burnings" of its satellites, particularly Ucanal, between 692 and 711, during a K'atun 6 Ajaw, the first k'atun of the traditional Tikal calendar, and spilling over into the first jotun of the succeeding k'atun. The demise and destruction of Late Classic sites attributed to some generalized belligerence may be more specifically tied to calendrics and the real or symbolic destruction—termination ritual—that accompanies the ending of the cycle of seats of the *may* or k'atuns.

At the same time, these Late Classic "wars" could be analogous to the "wars of proof" carried out by Aztec kings in order to seize captives as evidence of cosmic sanction for their rule. As Martin and Grube (2000:14) remark, "[A]lthough blood[line] was their main claim to legitimacy, candidates still had to prove themselves in war. A bout of captive-taking often preceded elevation to office." In this light, the Bonampak raids may have been for the purpose of taking captives in preparation for accession to office (Justeson 1989:106, citing M. Miller

1986). Whatever the proximate or ultimate causes of the Late Classic wars, I see them as forms of ritual conflict designed to demonstrate calendrical-cosmological legitimation of the right to rule, specifically the seating of *mays* and k'atuns. Hassig's (1992) assessment of lowland Maya warfare as being largely ritualized, one-on-one combat, is generally correct in terms of scale, then, but not for all the right reasons.

Much of the vocabulary interpreted as warfare could refer to the ritual conflict symbolized in the ballgame. Throughout Mesoamerica, the ballgame was increasingly politicized and tied to warfare in the Classic period (Santley, Berman, and Alexander 1991; Taladoire and Colsenet 1991; Fox 1991), and this certainly appears to hold true in the central Maya area. The captives displayed on monuments and in ballgame scenes were sometimes among the governing elites of important cities, and the permanent and public display of their defeat on stone monuments seems to be of paramount significance (Miller and Houston 1987). In addition, the texts of Yaxchilán's ballgame panels identify associated sacrifices as "conquests" (Freidel, Schele, and Parker 1993:361). In such cases, the battle of the ballgame might have been the context of conquest (*ajal*) and the bound captive the actual or symbolic vanquished opponent in a ballgame contest, bound for sacrifice. These and other textual references to combat, battle, and conquest could therefore be interpreted in the context of symbolic and ritualized contests between structurally mandated "opponents" rather than as literal warfare. Here the obvious analogy is to the *Popol Vuh,* in which the Hero Twins conquered the evil Lords of the Underworld in a ballgame contest.

Justeson (1989) has pointed out that Venus positions are better associated with blood sacrifice and the ballgame than with warfare among the Classic Maya. I suggest the "combat" and "warfare" mentioned in the Classic inscriptions refer to the taking of captives before, during, or after the ballgame for the purposes of sacrifice, particularly in the staircase version of the ballgame. This also explains the Venus imagery on stelae in some of Tikal's twin-pyramid groups as well as prone captives on the altars, because I believe these architectural complexes were used in the staircase ballgame. It is not a great stretch to move from discussion of ballgame ritual to a broader political interpretation:

[T]he ballgame was used as a substitute and a symbol for war. . . . If the ballgame had acquired a war-like and political meaning, it may have been restricted to prominent sites and capitals. Ballcourts would then be built only at major sites or in communities where political or military activities were especially important. (Taladoire and Colsenet 1991:174)

In this light, the emphasis on the ballgame and ballcourts at the Terminal Classic northern lowlands site of Chich'en Itza is of great interest. This site is now believed, in line with the chronicles, to have been established by agreement among various lineages, including the Itza from central Petén. The founding confederacy appears to have decided to retain, return to, or reemphasize the ballgame as it may have been traditionally played in formal ballcourts as the appropriate setting for rituals—sacrifice and fire ceremonies—at the seating of k'atuns and especially at the seating of the *may*. In this scenario there is a logic to the construction of thirteen ballcourts at Chich'en Itza, one for each k'atun of its *may* seating (see Krochock and Freidel 1994 for alternative views of the political significance of ballgame ritual at Chich'en Itza).

In any case, the situation in the southern lowlands by the end of the Late Classic was highly volatile. It is not difficult to envision that the introduction of new calendars and associated ritual along the western periphery would have disrupted existing alliances and exacerbated existing tensions, not to mention prompting serious cosmological interrogations. An explosion of "wars" and "defeats," whether real or symbolic, among these sites during this interval may be indicative of such disagreements. So too, the increased frequency of Terminal Classic monuments (Chap. 7) showing seated individuals, including captives, conversing or displaying only glyphic texts, might represent attempts to resolve them.

CHAPTER 9

Conclusion

My working definition of political organization has been "the hierarchically structured offices or roles of power and authority existing within, between, and among polities and their elites, whereby goal-oriented decisions about internal/external relations (including relations with the supernatural realm) and allocation of resources (human, material, and ideational) are made and implemented." And my concern has been to determine the nature of the political organization of the Classic lowland Maya: the structure of its power relations and the decision-making functions within that structure.

Several lines of evidence support the proposition that Classic lowland Maya political organization is best explained through direct-historical analogy to arrangements described in the Postclassic and Colonial period indigenous and ethnohistorical literature. The *may*—a 256-year, thirteen-k'atun calendrical cycle—was the key geopolitical device that structured power relations from the Preclassic period onward. The *may* model proposes that during the Classic period there existed multiple "capitals" throughout the Maya lowlands, each a sacred city that seated the *may* and thereby shouldered responsibility for ensuring cosmic continuity, for a period of 256 years. Within the realm dominated by each cycle seat, or *may ku*, were numerous subsidiary sites that had similar responsibilities for seating the k'atun for periods of twenty years within that cycle. *May* cycles—along with shorter temporal cycles folded in them, longer cycles (the b'ak'tun) within which they operated, and the overarching Mesoamerican principle of quadripartition—provided a mytho-religious charter for the structure of regional roles of power and authority.

Acknowledging the imperative of recursive calendrical cycling in Maya geopolitico-ritual organization does not mean retrogression to simplistic early models of the Maya as peaceful farmers ruled by stargazing priests in empty towns. Although calendrical cycles established an underlying structure for political events, they did not determine them mechanistically. Maya kings were individual agents with an impressive arsenal of tools of statecraft, including the ability to muster labor and tribute to construct buildings, plant and harvest crops, conduct trade, wage war, and organize ballgames. They likely had a host of advisers—other nobles, family members, priests, councils of rulers of subordinate cities—to assist in decision making. That some *may* or half-*may* intervals discussed in the preceding chapters were not always precisely 256 or 128 years, but sometimes 236 or 130, demonstrates the administrative flexibility in kings' agency. Similarly, variations in architectural programming, and even in acceptance of which k'atuns mark the beginning and ending of cycles, reveal temporal and regional variability. The *may*, then, was neither a singularly inviolable determinant of kingly action nor a mere ideoritual flourish. Rather, the *may* model acknowledges that cosmic cycling and quadripartition were operational principles that established the deep structure of the Maya world.

Evidence to support the extended duration of this organizational system can be drawn from various sources: epigraphic, linguistic, iconographic, architectural, archaeological, historical, ethnohistorical, and ethnographic. Historical, ethnohistorical, and ethnographic data established the outlines of the calendrico-quadripartite model, traces of which lingered at least into the eighteenth if not the twentieth century. In northern Yucatán, these traces include quadripartite rotation of town leaders and their twenty-year terms and perhaps the jetz' luum ceremony (Thompson 1999).

Bishop Landa's sixteenth-century account is especially illuminating. At one point he noted carved monuments at the Late Postclassic capital of Mayapán, commenting that the "lines of the characters which they use"—their hieroglyphic inscriptions on stelae—were worn away by rain, and the Maya living nearby said they "were accustomed to erect one of these stones every twenty years" (Tozzer 1941:38–39). In other words, Mayapán, with at least thirteen sculptured and twenty-five plain stelae (Morley 1920:574–576; Proskouriakoff 1962b:134–136), had revived the Late Classic k'atun-ending stela cult as part of the public celebrations accompanying its seating of the *may*. (The plaza floor around Structure 162, the Castillo, was reconstructed thirteen times, presumably every k'atun [Pugh 2001b:253], suggesting that such refurbishing was also part of *may* ceremonies.)

Postclassic codices also echo the imagery of Late Classic stelae in the Tikal region: page 34a of the Madrid Codex (see Fig. 8.3), one of the Wayeb' pages, shows the Kawak yearbearer wearing a jaguar pelt and headdress and scattering. A blue-painted ancestor is seated above in a cartouche, surrounded by dots, reminiscent of the dotted scrolls in which the Terminal Classic Paddlers rode. This suggests that by the Postclassic period the rituals accompanying k'atun endings might have been more overtly incorporated into or conflated with New Year's ceremonies.

That calendrical cycling was key to Maya "politics" is not a novel suggestion. Twenty-five years ago, Dennis Puleston (1979:63) high-lighted "the Maya conception of historical repetition [that entailed] a conformance of history to certain underlying, predictable patterns as re-vealed in the katun prophecies." At the same time, Edmonson (1979) raised "some Postclassic questions about the Classic Maya" that hy-pothesized many of the same possibilities pursued here regarding the *may.* Yet the profound implications of the concept of calendrical cycling for illuminating our understanding of the Maya political world have not been adequately pursued.

Much of what can be deduced from the Postclassic and Colonial pe-riod Maya prophetic histories indicates an emphasis on rotating politico-religious offices and responsibilities, suggesting that a cyclical structuring of secular or earthly affairs was modeled on cosmological-calendrical cycles. But the foundations of authority, the roles of priests and kings and subsidiary lords and councils, were not only changing with the imposition of Spanish rule, they were also suborned.

> In many cases priestly and political functions had been combined in such a manner that it was difficult, if not impossible, to differen-tiate them. Consequently the Spaniards regarded the native priests with great suspicion. Moreover, any resurgence of loyalty to the ab-original forms of religion was regarded not only as a serious threat to the missionary program but even as a sign of incipient revolt against Spanish supremacy. (Tozzer 1941:27n149; see also Avendaño y Loyola 1987:39)

Under such circumstances, it was in the best interests of the Maya to hide or disguise the operations of their traditional geopolitico-religious structure. And as it was hidden from the Spaniards, it has remained opaque to us today. Yet some diagnostic components survived the con-quest and, as illustrated by Edmonson (1979) and the preceding chapters, they can be teased out of extant documents and retrodicted into earlier times.

That the Classic lowland Maya observed *may* cycles is most readily evident from the architecture and monuments of Tikal, beginning with the Middle Preclassic E-Group assemblage in Mundo Perdido, later accompanied by k'atun-ending monuments. This architectural grouping became very widespread throughout the lowlands; what came to have more enduring significance, however, is the complex's western structure, a radial platform. The construction of radial platforms in the centers of plazas, often accompanied by monuments recording meetings of regional lords, was later repeated throughout the Classic and Terminal Classic lowlands, as exemplified by Copán Structure 4, Seibal Structure A-3, Dzibilchaltún's Temple of the Dolls, and numerous others at Chich'en Itza and Postclassic Mayapán.

Tikal's twin-pyramid groups are particularly important, in part because the twin east-west temples are radial structures, revealing deep continuities in the ritual significance of this form. More important, the stela-altar pairs in the northern enclosures reveal that the complexes were built to commemorate k'atun endings. Nine of these groups are known at Tikal, and others have been identified at four or five nearby sites. This suggests that these sites—Yaxhá, Ixlú, Zacpetén—would have been k'atun seats within Tikal's Late Classic seating of the *may*. Although these other nearby complexes do not exactly duplicate Tikal's, perhaps by intention or perhaps never completed, their existence suggests that these sites were united by a powerful shared ideology given explicit material form as cosmograms. Similar programs, characterized by multiple iterations of a distinctive structural form with mythocosmic associations (e.g., thirteen ballcourts at Chich'en Itza) or monument style (e.g., Giant Ajaw period-ending altars at Caracol), reveal that *may*-based geopolitico-religious organization was widespread throughout the southern lowlands. They also support Aveni's (2003:160) assertion that "there is little doubt that a state calendar . . . played a role in certain stages of site planning" (see also Ashmore 1989, 1991).

Retrodiction of the Postclassic and Colonial system also has been facilitated over the past few decades by accelerating linguistic and epigraphic analyses of Classic period inscriptions. These analyses have revealed continuities and identities in words and linguistic structures, including calendrical observations and rulers' titles. Supplemented by iconographic studies of the imagery on Classic period monuments, the texts reveal considerable information about the nature and importance of kings' calendrical celebrations. All of this complements what has been long known from the past century of archaeological investigations: certain large lowland Maya sites like Tikal, Calakmul, Seibal, Caracol, Chich'en Itza, Dzibilchaltún, Cobá—and some smaller ones like Copán and Palenque—were the principal cities of sizable territories and capitals of regional realms.

There is considerable evidence to support the proposition that the Maya extended the Mesoamerican concept of a quadripartite cosmos into the terrestrial or geopolitical sphere, with ethnographic and ethnohistoric data on four quarters or wards (Jones 1998) and four roads and entrances into modern towns such as Mama (Thompson 1999:246). In the Late Classic, four regional capitals were associated with the four directions (Morley 1946; Barthel 1968; Marcus 1976); in the Postclassic, *The Chilam Balam of Chumayel* relates that in a K'atun 4 Ajaw, which Edmonson (1986:57–58) dates to the period ending in 11.1.0.0.0 (A.D. 1244), "there occurred the overthrow of Chichen of the Itzas," and four new capitals were named: Kin Colah Peten in the east, Na Cocob in the north, Hol Tun Zuyua in the west, and Can Hek Uitz or Bolon Te Uitz in the south.

Maya rulers and priests might have engaged in some tinkering so that overlapping *may* cycles (128 + 256 = 384 years) were accommodated into b'ak'tuns of 400 tuns or 394.5 years, such that four new capitals were established at the turning of the b'ak'tuns. Thus, around 8.0.0.0.0 in A.D. 41, Late Preclassic capitals such as Cerros and El Mirador were terminated and new capitals or *may* seats put into place; at 9.0.0.0.0 (A.D. 435), the dynasties of the four capitals Tikal, Copán, Palenque, and Calakmul were established; at 10.0.0.0.0 (A.D. 830), new capitals would have included Seibal, Chich'en Itza, and Uxmal, perhaps inaugurated 128 years earlier as "guests." At 11.0.0.0.0 (A.D. 1224), the four capitals named above would have been identified with specific lineages and covered both northern and southern lowlands: Kin Colah Peten being the Kowoj in eastern Yucatán-Belize-Petén; Na Cocob being the Kokom (Itza) of Mayapán in the north; Hol Tun Zuyua as the Xiw (Cetelac or Merida) in the west; and Can Hek Uitz referring to Kan Ek' Witz or the Lake Petén Itzá region in the south. Some variant of this last organization seems to have prevailed through 12.0.0.0.0 (A.D. 1618) but with the introduction of Valladolid as the (north-)eastern capital.

Similarly, quadripartition of the b'ak'tuns could possibly have had some geopolitical significance, although the evidence is weak and, because of the absence of dates, it is difficult to evaluate this in any interval other than B'ak'tun 9. The year 534, or 9.5.0.0.0, a quarter b'ak'tun, for example, is commonly cited as the beginning of the hiatus in monument erection in the lowlands. The year 731, or 9.15.0.0.0, the three-quarter-b'ak'tun marker, is the date of the meeting of four lords recorded on Copán Stela A; another such meeting took place at the next b'ak'tun completion at Seibal in 10.0.0.0.0.

What has heretofore gone unrecognized is the calendrical foundation of the large Classic cities' power in seating the *may* and the role of allied cities as k'atun seats, which was manifested through shared architectural or monument programs.

Origin and Operation of the *May* System

I believe that the calendrical basis for inter- and intrasite relations in the Maya lowlands originated in the Preclassic period, probably by the end of the Middle Preclassic. While the absence of dated texts in the Preclassic period renders verification problematic, it can be postulated on the basis of shared building programs, specifically the E-Group assemblage. These complexes—radial structures centered west of a north-south linear platform supporting three structures—are thought to have initially functioned in observational astronomy, marking sunrise positions on the solstices and equinoxes. They spread widely throughout the southern and central lowlands during the Late Preclassic and Early Classic periods, and in places their active use in connection with k'atun ceremonies extended into the Late and Terminal Classic. Elsewhere, they often continued to be refurbished; perhaps their ritual function changed.

The role of these complexes in establishing the existence of *may*-based political organization in the Preclassic becomes apparent with recognition that the earliest k'atun-ending stelae were erected in front of the linear structure of these putative astronomical complexes, or elsewhere in the plazas, in the late fourth century A.D. It is very likely that these carved stone valedictory monuments had been preceded for centuries by plain wooden or stone markers placed in the same positions. The solar function and symbolism of these structures was appropriated by later rulers and translated into their titles (K'inich 'sun-faced' or perhaps more literally 'sun-facing') and costuming.

If we allow that *may*- and k'atun-based calendrical cycling lay at the foundation of lowland Maya political organization, then it is important to try to understand how it "worked." We can hypothesize, for example, on the basis of analogy to the k'atun ceremonies described by Bishop Landa in the sixteenth century (Tozzer 1941:134–149), that the system was operationalized on the midpoints of 20-year and 256-year cycles. Cities serving as new *may* and k'atun seats would have been decided on in the midpoint of a cycle—10 years for a jetz' k'atun and 128 years for a *may ku*—and their role was initiated as they collaborated during the second half of that cycle as the guest of the current ruler of the period. They then came to full power as seats of authority at the beginning of the relevant cycle and ruled alone for its first half. At the midpoint, new seats were decided for the upcoming k'atun and *may*, and these shared rule as guest of the existing seat for the second half of the cycle. A variant of, or exception to, this procedure would have occurred when k'atun and *may* seats were renewed, as was Tikal for several cycles.

How did certain cities achieve the eminent—indeed, divine—*may* seat status? Founder's history? Genealogies and lineage claims? Strength of marital or military alliances? Cosmological cycling and auguries? Warfare? In the absence of precise information, we can only assume that it might have been some combination of any of the above. Clearly Preclassic first founders and their associated families or lineages—their houses, or naj—would have played fundamental roles in establishing the wealth, power, and ritual sanctity of their villages. The founders of Maya settlements had to establish positive relations with cosmic forces and establish a "ritual *axis mundi*" by constructing a ceremonial structure (McAnany 2001:145; see also McAnany 1995), and it appears that during the Middle and Late Preclassic periods (and into the Early Classic) such facilities included E-Groups.

The sites proposed here as *may* seats reveal variability in their histories before, during, and after they seated the cycle, yet some general elements seem common to them. The critical events, in approximate sequence, are (1) a real or hypothetical dynastic founding date; (2) commemoration of a period ending (usually a k'atun ending and usually with the erection of a stela); (3) display of an Emblem Glyph; (4) the symbolic conquest of the existing *may* seat, apparently through the taking and sacrificing of captives; and (5) at some point, typically in the middle of a k'atun, inauguration of a new ruler who seats the *may* and begins to regularly celebrate k'atun endings while undertaking a massive building or iconographic program. These rulers frequently participated in accession events at other sites or sent members of the royal family to marry into other dynasties. At some sites, there seems to be (6) a pattern of placing a final stela to commemorate the third k'atun after the ending of the *may* seating. For example, Tikal, Uaxactún, Quiriguá, Calakmul, and Toniná erected a carved dated stela in the Terminal Classic, sixty years after their Late Classic *may* seating expired. Sometimes these stelae indicate that the k'atun ending was celebrated by two rulers. The meaning of this ceremony is not known.

An intriguing issue in *may ku* selection concerns the role of cenotes and caves, regarded as openings to the Underworld. Two important Postclassic seats of the *may*, Chich'en Itza and Mayapán, incorporate words for "well" or "cenote" in their names. Might, then, a ch'en or cavelike opening to the watery Underworld have been a requirement for the city seating the *may* in the Postclassic period? Could a similar requirement have existed in the Classic? If it was, this strengthens the arguments advanced by Brady (1997) for site centers being situated over natural caves or for the excavation of artificial caves—or even large reservoirs, as at Tikal and Calakmul (both with thirteen) and Cobá—where cenotes do not exist.

There are hints that caves or cenotes could have been significant features of *may* sites in the Classic period. Numerous inscriptions report that important rituals took place "in the center of" a site or in part of a site identified by glyphs that read *ch'en* 'cave, well' (Montgomery 2001a:236–237). These come from the so-called impinged bone set, one variant of which has been read as *kun* 'seat'. While these references could refer to tombs—human-made caves in the pyramidal "mountains" of temple substructures—their role in calendrical ceremonies merits further attention. Tikal Stela 16 (see Fig. 5.5), for example, refers to Jasaw Kan K'awil ending the k'atun at the "first maw/hole" or first entrance to the Underworld (Harris and Stearns 1997:166–168). Tikal Lintel 3 of Temple 1 includes a reference to an event occurring "in the center of the cave/seat of Tikal," and reference to a ch'en or cave can also be seen on Tikal Stela 5. The main sign of the Emblem Glyph for Piedras Negras is *yokib'*, meaning "cave or entrance," and refers to a large sinkhole near the site (Stuart, Houston, and Robertson 1999:143). Uxmal Stela 14 (see Fig. 7.11) shows the ruler Lord Chak standing over naked captives lying in a cave or cenote. Naranjo Stela 23 refers to *quema la sede*, or burning the seat or ch'en of Yaxhá in A.D. 710 (Grube 2000b:257), but in this context it seems more likely that a seat (of power) rather than a watery well was burned. Coggins (1983:61–63) noted that the base of Dzibilchaltún Structure 1-sub was decorated with a stucco water frieze, providing Underworld associations that she linked to a cenote cult of divination and prophesy.

The *may* model also prompts some speculative interpretations of Emblem Glyphs themselves. As noted in Chapter 3, these glyphs have three parts, one of which, variably present, is *k'ul* 'divine, holy'. Emblem Glyphs are typically read in nonstandard order, that is, as prefix–main sign–superfix (e.g., divine Tikal lord), instead of the standard prefix–superfix–main sign (divine lord [of] Tikal). I suggest that the presence or absence of the *k'ul* prefix in an Emblem might be interpreted in the context of cities as seats of the *may*, following Edmonson's description of those cities seating the *may* as sacred (*siyaj kan* 'heaven born'). Thus if Classic sites with full, tripartite Emblem Glyphs were considered sacred like their later Yucatán counterparts, then the Emblem could be read "divine-Mutul lord" (i.e., lord of divine-Mutul) as easily as "divine Mutul-lord" (i.e., divine-lord of Mutul). After all, it is "the kingship and not the king who is divine" (Feeley-Harnik 1985:276).

Emblem Glyph main signs lacking the k'ul prefix are generally viewed as toponyms, simply indicating the site as a location without reference to its politico-ritual status. However, display of Emblems without this prefix might be a privilege of sites and their lords that are or intend to be k'atun seats (jetz' k'atun) and ultimately, perhaps, eligible to compete to seat the *may* cycle. In addition, the distribution of Emblem Glyphs according to apparent site hierarchies might be a consequence of distribution of these k'atun seats within the various realms of the *may*. How did a city become a k'atun seat? We can only assume that there were criteria and rituals similar to those of a *may* seat.

The Maya recorded relations of political subordination/domination, such as the u kab'iy and yajaw expressions, between major centers or seats of the *may* and lords of lesser cities that would have been k'atun seats. Subordinate relations such as u kab'iy and yahaw likely relate to the *may* seating, such as designation of k'atun seats or *may* seat successors. Through time, as more and more civic-ceremonial centers were established in the Late Classic, erecting monuments and displaying Emblem Glyphs, the process for becoming a k'atun seat might have become more competitive. As noted previously, Colonial period seats of the k'atun held significant power and responsibilities in political and ritual affairs. As the physical k'atun seat, or jetz' k'atun, changed, so did the layers of administrative lordship or priestly oversight of the period.

One implication of the *may* model is that arguments about Classic Maya "political" organization in Western, secular terms, using paradigms such as unitary versus segmentary states or hierarchies of site sizes, are somewhat misguided. Attempts to force the Classic Maya onto political templates extracted from Africa, the Aegean, medieval Europe, and Bali have not been successful. A more appropriate first step is to test the applicability of an existing, indigenous Maya model, one derived from direct-historical analogy, as an explanation of Maya political geography and organization.

At the same time, the notion of large Maya states whose power is explicitly derived from and manifested by control of calendrical cycling and associated *may* and k'atun ritual does not require that all the old models must be discarded. It is in the context of an indigenous model like that of the *may* that some of these concepts become more comprehensible. For example, the *may* model suggests that notions of regal-ritual cities and theater states have considerable relevance to the Maya. These concepts acknowledge, in one way or another, that Classic Maya cities grew as grandiose monuments to sacred elites, deified ancestors, cosmological cycles, and the endlessly repetitive rituals required to maintain all of them.

As places, Maya cities were organized as locations dedicated to ancestor veneration, housing royal courts (in palaces) and god effigies (in temples, or *wayib'*), accommodating the services and people necessary to their maintenance, and performance of political theater, including the reception and display of captives and tribute. (Houston 2000:173)

In addition, the allocation of resources is an important component in the definition of political organization, and the role of the economy—production, consumption, and distribution—needs to be more carefully assessed in the context of the *may* model. For example, Kazuo Aoyama (2001) suggested that Copán's state power derived from a "managerial" function, that is, control of the distribution of Ixtepeque obsidian, and this control faltered by the end of the Yax Kuk' Mo' dynasty.

The Classic Maya: A Theocratic State

Maurice Bloch, in his Malinowski Memorial Lecture, "The Past and the Present in the Present," made two important points concerning social structure that are pertinent to understanding Classic Maya political structure. One is that political-cum-social "structure is only extracted from ritual communication [and] turns out to be a system of classification of human beings linked to other ritual cognitive systems, such as the ritual notion of time" (Bloch 1977:286). The other is that in societies the amount of "social theory expressed in the language of ritual" varies directly with the degree of social hierarchization: that is, "the amount of social structure, of the past in the present, of ritual communication is correlated with the amount of *institutionalized* hierarchy" (Bloch 1977:288–289; emphasis in original).

These concepts are of interest given the changes—the evolution, if you will—of Classic Maya political organization from Preclassic through Postclassic times. Among the Maya, the "sacred" and the "secular" are so deeply intertwined as to be inseparable, and early archaeologists commonly considered the Maya a theocracy or a theocratic state. The latter term has been out of favor for some time, as the recent emphasis among epigraphers and archaeologists has been on relatively continuous warfare among the hithertofore "peaceable" Classic Maya. Yet despite some serious theoretical ambiguities, "theocracy" seems to best describe the Maya geo-socio-politico-religious system and the concept is worth reexamining. The importance to the Maya of ritual and ritual celebrations of time's passage and the clear hierarchy of their society underscores the applicability of the term.

But what is a theocracy? According to David Webster (1976:813, 815), a theocracy represents both a type of society and a stage of sociopolitical evolution that precede "secular" states. When used in a typological sense, à la Thompson and Coe, it carries substantial baggage besides that of supernatural sanctions. The subjective connotations are of peaceful, nonmilitaristic, nonurban, stable societies, as compared to secular states (Webster 1976:814). While these implications of "theocracy" are neither necessary nor necessarily accurate, they became the focal terms structuring debates about Classic lowland Maya political organization in the past two to three decades.

Whether type or stage, leadership in a theocracy is socially validated and legitimized by supernatural sanctions. Leaders come from socially advantaged kin groups and are religious specialists or priest-kings whose power to rule is derived from the power of cosmological sanctions, archaeologically visible through the deployment of labor forces in the construction of large civic-ceremonial buildings. This touches on the delicate problem of "institutional balance."

[T]he fundamental target of bureaucratic elite control is . . . the minor or peripheral leadership (call them local officials, governors, . . .) of localized, or perhaps specialized, segments of the larger society. . . . These are the individuals ultimately responsible for translating central directives into social action [and] are, in other words, potential competitors of the centralized elites. [At the same time, however,] they shared, at least to some degree, a common consensus in the moral or supernatural legitimization of the centralized leadership's claim to high religious status and control of ceremonialism. (Webster 1976:818)

In Webster's (1976:826) view, theocratic societies and the supernatural sanctions at their core developed as part of a larger evolutionary process, as adaptive and stabilizing "responses to the stresses of rapid culture change from hierarchical kin-based societies to class-structured ones." A particular problem in such periods is the transformation of charismatic (or shamanic; Freidel 1992) roles into permanent, institutionalized offices of power, a problem Webster (1976:820–821) resolves by postulating the existence of "charismatic office": institutionalized but with a "supernatural aura." He goes on to note the existence in several archaic states (Egypt, Near East) of "[p]luralistic or dualistic modes of authority structure," whether secular and religious or economic and political, that may be symbolized ideologically (Webster 1976:823; also Webster 2002:129). Finally, he emphasizes that a transition from theocratic to secular modes of social integration does not indicate any inherent instability of theocratic states but rather highlights that "theocratic structures were successful in providing enormously fertile environments for the emergence" of new and more adaptive organizational modes (Webster 1976:824).

To translate some of these concepts to the particular case of the lowland Maya and the *may*, it is evident that Classic Maya rulers were drawn from certain elite kin groups or lineages or houses, whose ancestors or founders were deeply revered. They proclaimed their sanctified power through public texts, regalia, art, and the theater of architecture, referring to the gods and the ancestors as their supernatural patrons and carrying out public and private rituals to sustain that cosmic blessing. During the Late Preclassic, the Jaguar God of the Sun, patron of Maya rulers, was powerfully invoked on the facades of public buildings, some of which were associated with the distinctive and widely shared E-Group assemblages. By the end of the second century A.D., Maya kings had assumed a sacred or divine status as k'ul ajaw and the role of the Jaguar Sun God was transformed with it. Still later, after 475, Tikal royal regalia changed and the Jaguar Sun God was appropriated as a powerful icon of Classic kingly office worn and brandished by rulers (Freidel and Schele 1988b:69) and decorating incense burners used in royal mortuary ritual (Rice 1999).

Another concept that can be reinterpreted in the context of the Maya *may* is that of divine kingship (see Feeley-Harnik 1985 for a review). Like theocracy, the concept of divine kingship carries a heavy theoretical load, but much of it directly opposes that which clings to theocracy. Developed primarily out of early British structural-functionalist studies of postcolonial African descent-based kingdoms, the concept of divine kingship has been associated with instability, tendency toward civil war, and regicide, particularly as these phenomena are associated with royal successions. Freidel and Schele's analyses of the emergence of the k'ul ajaw fit well into the long-recognized anthropological distinction between "achieved" and "ascribed" leadership roles, and also the distinction between an office and the person who holds it. The death of an individual king is not the same as the death of the office (Feeley-Harnik 1985:278).

This brings up two interesting points. First, could the "k'ul" of the Classic period k'ul ajaw title and Emblem Glyphs refer to the holy quality of the office or the site where the ruler is seated and not the ruler himself or herself? Second, what do we know of succession in Classic Maya kingship? The answer to the second question is, surprisingly little, although the deer hoof sign read *may* is also read to indicate heir apparency. The inscriptions typically indicate intervals of a few months to two or more years between the recorded date of death of one king and the recorded accession of another (see, e.g., Martin and Grube 2000). But what happened in the interregnum? Were the Maya lords waiting for their priests to identify a day with a favorable augury for installation? Who ruled during this liminal period: the office of the deceased king? Such questions demand answers.

Underlying the history of transformations in Maya political leadership—from charismatic (or shamanic) leaders to sacred kings—were corresponding changes in their relationship with the cosmos. That is, sometime during the Preclassic period the Maya replaced their relatively simple techniques of observational astronomy with the far more powerful calculus of predictive astronomy. The origins of Mesoamerican observational astronomy cannot be reliably dated (Rice n.d.a), but human interest in the movements of the sun, moon, and stars assuredly can be traced back into Paleolithic times, along with some recognition of their periodicity. Systematic deification of those celestial bodies and the intervals of time they control may have similarly deep antiquity. But such knowledge systems are only recognizable archaeologically by material evidence, and in Mesoamerica formal and imperishable architectural commemoration of the regularity of celestial movements appears to date to the Early Preclassic or Formative period (perhaps ca. 2000–1500 B.C.). This was followed by the development of formal systems for recording observations of astronomical and seasonal cycling: a writing system and a mathematical system, allowing permanent records of time's passage. Available data indicate that ancient Mesoamericans began to make such permanent registers sometime in the first half of the first millennium, perhaps almost simultaneously in the Gulf Coast region and in Oaxaca.

Predictive astronomy, far more complex, could develop only after record-keeping systems were quite advanced. Predictive astronomy had to be based on a large body of recorded observations accumulated over the centuries, allowing recognition of periodicities in the past that could be projected into the future. While observational astronomy was practiced throughout Mesoamerica, and may be traceable to a single, shared, calendrical system—the Calendar Round, correlating the 260-day and 365-day calendars, known from Olmec times—this more esoteric and awe-inspiring system, which allowed prediction of eclipses and other celestial events, was, at least early on, known only to the Maya (and/or their Mixe-Zoque ancestors). Predictive astronomy not only confirmed the divine sanction of the king or k'ul ajaw as the ruler of time, it also authenticated the divine sanction of his city as the operational center through which time was manipulated and controlled. As such, it was an essential tool for maintaining long-term cycles of cosmically based geopolitical authority and the cosmic mandates of prophetic history.

With advances in predictive astronomy, the utilitarian observational functions of the E-Groups probably became obsolete. However in some areas of the lowlands—for example, southeastern Petén—this architectural complex continued into the Late Classic period. Perhaps it endured as a powerful symbol of cosmic order and the supernatural forces— the daily appearance of the Sun God—that oversaw the kingdom. Alternatively, perhaps the astronomical esoterica essential to predicting eclipses, Venus movements, and so on was controlled by an elite priesthood associated with only the most powerful lineages or residing only at the most sacred sites. In such a circumstance, dissenting or out-of-favor lineages, factions, or subsidiary lords and towns would have been denied access to this information and the superior statuses it assured. They might have had little recourse but to continue the "old-fashioned" observatory technology of the E-Groups.

The sacred or divine king or lord known as k'ul ajaw stood at the very heart of Classic Maya political structure. Classic Maya kings commanded a broad range of responsibilities, whether they were lords of the *may* or of the k'atun, and some of these roles are seen in their portrayals on monuments and lintels and in their titles and epithets. They were sovereigns but also ballplayers, sacrificers, dancers, warriors, and captors. They were very likely priests, or at least trained in the arcane knowledge of the priesthood involving calendrics, prophetic histories, and auguries and in maintaining records of these (aj kujun). The multiple, complex roles of Maya kings can be elucidated etymologically, for example, in the case of Tikal. Tikal's dynastic founder was named Yax Eb' Xok 'First Step Shark', but *xok* also means "to count, to read"; one of the meanings of *may* is "to count, to divine." What was being counted or read? Days. The calendar. Time itself.

This suggests that early Maya rulers were also aj k'in, priests called daykeepers, calendric specialists in the sense of the K'iche' (and other highland Maya) indigenous leaders and diviners. In addition, the original name of Tikal comes from *mut* 'prophecy' and the root of ajaw is *aw* 'to shout'. This indicates that early kings also bore the responsibility of shouting or proclaiming the prophecies they divined as keepers of time, particularly at cycles of k'atuns and *mays* based on days Ajaw. There are hints that the role of chilam, "speaker or interpreter" (of the prophecies of the ajaw), might have existed in the Classic period.

Maya divine kings, in other words, were "fulcrums of cosmic order" (Mundy 1998:234). Their powers derived from knowledge—and therefore control, or at least custodianship—of the mysterious forces of the cosmos. As Houston and Stuart note, the rituals portrayed on Maya monuments represent the Classic kings

> in a perpetual state of ritual action. . . . [R]ulers were themselves embodiments of time and its passage—a role that was fundamental to the cosmological underpinnings of divine kingship. We find this expressed most directly by the overt solar symbolism that surrounded the office of Maya kingship. . . . The cyclical reappearance of the Ajaw day at each Period Ending in the Long Count calendar was not only a renewal of cosmological time but also a renewal, in effect, of the institution of kingship—an elaboration of the conceptual equation of the ruler and the sun. (1996:165–167)

In the Classic Maya lowlands, as in so many other early state societies, ideology and power cannot be disarticulated. Nor can ritual and history be decoupled from structures of power (Kelly and Kaplan 1990). Among the Maya, "political" power was embedded in an ideology whose key elements were cyclical time and cosmic quadripartition. The critical aspect of the temporal cycles is not the calendrical interval itself but rather the regular and public ritual celebration of the completion of these cycles by the sacred king. Such rituals, assuming they were conducted efficaciously, reaffirmed social, natural, and dynastic history and communicated cosmic order and continuity.

The significance of the 256-year cycles of the *may* and the 20-year cycles of k'atuns lies in their establishing a cosmological charter for praxis: the pragmatic structuring of history and power vis-à-vis intra- and intersite relations in the Classic period lowlands. The *may* model provides archaeologists with a basis for more parsimonious yet robust explanations of the overwhelming political, social, economic, architectural, iconographic, and material variability in the lowlands area. The hierarchical relations between k'atun seats and the *may* center resulted in a geopolitical system of shared, overlapping, and rotating power among sites in a region. It was this system and its ideology that resolved practical concerns with political legitimation and succession and also provided stability for the Maya through periods of change and transformation over two millennia.

Finally, it is important to recall that the calendrical rituals of the *may* and b'ak'tun recorded in the books of the chilam b'alams are the accumulation of two millennia of elaboration through Preclassic, Classic, and Postclassic periods. During these millennia, ritual practices and paraphernalia—the role of ancestors, the ballgame, New Year's cycles, human sacrifice, fire ceremonies—would have been added, deleted, modified, or otherwise reworked to accommodate particular circumstances.

In consequence, not all the components of Colonial period ceremonies precisely replicate those of the Classic, and we should not expect them to do so. However, the continuities in core elements and key metaphors—maintenance of the Short Count calendar, celebration of k'atun endings, the speaker's prophecy, the ruler's sacrifice, the erection of a monument and its unveiling—cannot be denied. These reveal that the *may*, the multi-k'atun calendrical cycles by which Classic and Postclassic period political organization was structured, also contoured the topography of Classic period political geography. For some two millennia, then, Maya calendrical cycles and their underlying astronomical science provided the basis for Maya "political science."

BIBLIOGRAPHY

Abrams, Eliot M.
1994   *How the Maya Built Their World: Energetics and Ancient Architecture.* Austin: University of Texas Press.
Adams, Richard E. W.
1971   *The Ceramics of Altar de Sacrificios.* Papers of the Peabody Museum of Archaeology and Ethnology, vol. 63, no. 1. Cambridge, Mass.: Peabody Museum.
1981   Settlement Patterns of the Central Yucatan and Southern Campeche Regions. In *Lowland Maya Settlement Patterns,* ed. Wendy Ashmore, pp. 211–257. Albuquerque: School of American Research—University of New Mexico Press.
1986   The Maya City of Rio Azul. *National Geographic* 169(4):420–451.
1990   Archaeological Research at the Lowland Maya Site of Rio Azul. *Latin American Antiquity* 1(1):23–41.
Adams, Richard E. W., and Richard C. Jones
1981   Spatial Patterns and Regional Growth among Classic Maya Cities. *American Antiquity* 46:301–322.
Adams, Richard E. W., and Woodruff D. Smith
1977   Apocalyptic Visions: The Maya Collapse and Mediaeval Europe. *Archaeology* 30(5):292–301.
1981   Feudal Models for Classic Maya Civilization. In *Lowland Maya Settlement Patterns,* ed. Wendy Ashmore, pp. 335–349. Albuquerque: University of New Mexico Press and School of American Research.
Aimers, James John
1993   Messages from the Gods: An Hermeneutic Analysis of the Maya E-Group Complex. M.A. thesis, Trent University, Peterborough, Canada.
Aimers, James John, and Prudence M. Rice
n.d.   The History and Meaning of E-Groups. Manuscript.
Andrews, Anthony P.
1984   The Political Geography of the Sixteenth-Century Yucatan Maya: Comments and Revisions. *Journal of Anthropological Archaeology* 40(4):589–596.

Andrews, Anthony P., and Fernando Robles C.
1985 Chichen Itza and Coba: An Itza-Maya Standoff in Early Postclassic Yucatan. In *The Lowland Maya Postclassic*, ed. Arlen F. Chase and Prudence M. Rice, pp. 62–72. Austin: University of Texas Press.

Andrews, E. Wyllys, V
1981 Dzibilchaltun. In *Archaeology. Supplement to the Handbook of Middle American Indians*, vol. 1, vol. ed. Jeremy A. Sabloff, gen. ed. Victoria Reifler Bricker, pp. 313–341. Austin: University of Texas Press.

1990 Early Ceramic History of the Lowland Maya. In *Vision and Revision in Maya Studies*, ed. Flora S. Clancy and Peter D. Harrison, pp. 1–19. Albuquerque: University of New Mexico Press.

Andrews, E. Wyllys, IV, and E. Wyllys Andrews V
1980 *Excavations at Dzibilchaltun, Yucatan, Mexico*. Middle American Research Institute, Pub. 48. New Orleans: Tulane University.

Aoyama, Kazuo
2001 Classic Maya State, Urbanism, and Exchange: Chipped Stone Evidence from the Copán Valley and Its Hinterland. *American Anthropologist* 103(2):346–360.

Ascher, Robert M.
1961 Analogy in Archaeological Interpretation. *Southwestern Journal of Anthropology* 17:317–325.

Ashmore, Wendy (ed.)
1981 *Lowland Maya Settlement Patterns*. Albuquerque: University of New Mexico Press and School of American Research.

1989 Construction and Cosmology: Politics and Ideology in Lowland Maya Settlement Patterns. In *Word and Image in Maya Culture: Explorations in Language, Writing, and Representation*, ed. William F. Hanks and Don S. Rice, pp. 272–286. Salt Lake City: University of Utah Press.

1991 Site-Planning Principles and Concepts of Directionality among the Ancient Maya. *Latin American Antiquity* 2(3):199–226.

1992 Deciphering Maya Architectural Plans. In *New Theories on the Ancient Maya*, ed. Elin C. Danien and Robert J. Sharer, pp. 173–184. University Museum Symposium Series, vol. 3, University Museum Monograph 77. Philadelphia: The University Museum, University of Pennsylvania.

Avendaño y Loyola, Fray Andrés de
1987 *Relation of Two Trips to Peten, Made for the Conversion of the Heathen Ytzaex and Cehaches*. Trans. Charles P. Bowditch and Guillermo Rivera, ed. and with notes by Frank E. Comparato. Culver City, Calif.: Labyrinthos.

Aveni, Anthony F.
1981 Archaeoastronomy in the Maya Region: A Review of the Past Decade. *Journal for the History of Astronomy* 11(3):S1–S13.

2000 Out of Teotihuacan: Origins of the Celestial Canon in Mesoamerica. In *Mesoamerica's Classic Heritage, from Teotihuacan to the Aztecs*, ed. Davíd Carrasco, Lindsay Jones, and Scott Sessions, pp. 253–268. Boulder: University Press of Colorado.

2003   Archaeoastronomy in the Ancient Americas. *Journal of Archaeological Research* 11(2):149–191.

Aveni, Anthony F., Horst Hartung, and Beth Buckingham

1978   The Pecked Cross Symbol in Ancient Mesoamerica. *Science* 202(4365):267–279.

Ball, Joseph W.

1977   An Hypothetical Outline of Coastal Maya Prehistory: 300 B.C.–A.D. 1200. In *Social Process in Maya Prehistory*, ed. Norman Hammond, pp. 167–196. London: Academic Press.

1979a   Ceramics, Culture History, and the Puuc Tradition: Some Alternative Possibilities. In *The Puuc: New Perspectives*, ed. Lawrence Mills, pp. 18–35. Pella, Iowa: Central College Press.

1979b   The 1977 Central College Symposium on Puuc Archaeology: A Summary View. In *The Puuc: New Perspectives*, ed. Lawrence Mills, pp. 46–51. Pella, Iowa: Central College Press.

1986   Campeche, the Itza, and the Postclassic: A Study in Ethnohistorical Archaeology. In *Late Lowland Maya Civilization, Classic to Postclassic*, ed. Jeremy A. Sabloff and E. Wyllys Andrews V, pp. 379–408. Albuquerque: School of American Research—University of New Mexico Press.

Ball, Joseph W., and Jennifer Taschek

1991   Late Classic Lowland Maya Political Organization and Central-Place Analysis: New Insights from the Upper Belize Valley. *Ancient Mesoamerica* 2(2):149–165.

2001   The Buenavista-Cahal Pech Royal Court: Multi-Palace Court Mobility and Usage in a Petty Lowland Maya Kingdom. In *Royal Courts of the Ancient Maya*, vol. 2: *Data and Case Studies*, ed. Takeshi Inomata and Stephen D. Houston, pp. 165–200. Boulder, Colo.: Westview Press.

Barrera Vásquez, Alfredo, et al.

1980   *Diccionario maya cordemex: Maya-español, español-maya.* Mérida: Ediciones Cordemex.

Barthel, Thomas S.

1968   El complejo "emblema." *Estudios de Cultura Maya* 7:159–193. México, D.F.: Universidad Nacional Autónoma de México.

Baudez, Claude F.

1991   The Cross Pattern at Copán: Forms, Rituals, and Meanings. In *Sixth Palenque Round Table 1986*, ed. Merle Greene Robertson, pp. 81–88. Norman: University of Oklahoma Press.

Becker, Marshall Joseph

1971   The Identification of a Second Plaza Plan at Tikal, Guatemala, and Its Implications for Ancient Maya Social Complexity. Ph.D. dissertation, University of Pennsylvania.

1979   Priests, Peasants, and Ceremonial Centers: The Intellectual History of a Model. In *Maya Archaeology and Ethnohistory*, ed. Norman

Hammond and Gordon R. Willey, pp. 3–20. Austin: University of Texas Press.

1983   Kings and Classicism: Political Change in the Maya Lowlands during the Classic Period. In *Highland-Lowland Interaction in Mesoamerica: Interdisciplinary Approaches,* ed. Arthur G. Miller, pp. 159–200. Washington, D.C.: Dumbarton Oaks.

Bell, Betty

1956   An Appraisal of the Maya Civilization. In *The Ancient Maya,* 3d ed., ed. Sylvanus G. Morley and George W. Brainerd, pp. 424–441. Stanford, Calif.: Stanford University Press.

Bennett, Anne K.

1970   La cruz parlante. *Estudios de Cultura Maya* 8:227–237. México, D.F.: Universidad Nacional Autónoma de México.

Berdan, Frances F.

1982   *The Aztecs of Central Mexico: An Imperial Society.* New York: Holt, Rinehart, and Winston.

Berlin, Heinrich

1958   El glifo "emblema" en las inscripciones mayas. *Journal de la Société des Américanistes* 47:111–119. Paris.

1959   Glifos nominales en el sarcófago de Palenque: Un ensayo. *Humanidades* 2(10):1–8. Guatemala City.

1968   The Tablet of the 96 Glyphs at Palenque, Chiapas, Mexico. *Middle American Research Institute,* Pub. 26, pp. 135–149. New Orleans: Tulane University.

Bey, George J., II, Tara M. Bond, William M. Ringle, Craig A. Hanson, Charles W. Houck, and Carlos Peraza L.

1998   The Ceramic Chronology of Ek Balam, Yucatan, Mexico. *Ancient Mesoamerica* 9:101–120.

Blanton, Richard E., Gary M. Feinman, Stephen A. Kowalewski, and Peter N. Peregrine

1996   A Dual-Processual Theory for the Evolution of Mesoamerican Civilization. *Current Anthropology* 37(1):1–14.

Bloch, Maurice

1977   The Past and the Present in the Present. *Man* 12:278–292.

Blom, Frans

1924   Report on the Preliminary Work at Uaxactun, Guatemala. *Carnegie Institution of Washington Yearbook* 23:217–219.

Boone, Elizabeth Hill

1992   Pictorial Codices of Ancient Mexico. In *The Ancient Americas: Art from Sacred Landscapes,* ed. Richard Townsend, pp. 197–209. Chicago: University of Chicago Press.

Boot, Eric

1995   Kan Ek' at Chich'en Itsa: A Quest into a Possible Itsa Heartland in the Central Peten, Guatemala. *Yumtzilob* 7(4):333–339.

2002   The Dos Pilas–Tikal Wars from the Perspective of Dos Pilas Hieroglyphic Stairway 4. http://www.mesoweb.com/features/boot/DPLHS4.pdf

Borowicz, James
2003 Images of Power and the Power of Images: Early Classic Iconographic Programs of the Carved Monuments of Tikal. In *The Maya
and Teotihuacan: Reinterpreting Early Classic Interaction*, ed.
Geoffrey E. Braswell, pp. 217–234. Austin: University of Texas
Press.
Borremanse, Didier
1998 *Hach Winik: The Lacandon Maya of Chiapas, Southern Mexico.* Institute for Mesoamerican Studies, Monograph 11. Albany: State University of New York at Albany.
Bove, Frederick J.
1981 Trend Surface Analysis and the Lowland Classic Maya Collapse.
American Antiquity 46:93–112.
Brady, James E.
1997 Settlement Configuration and Cosmology: The Role of Caves at Dos
Pilas. *American Anthropologist* 99(3):602–618.
Braswell, Geoffrey
2002 Pusilhá Archaeological Project. www.famsi.org/reports
2003a (ed.) *The Maya and Teotihuacan: Reinterpreting Early Classic Interaction.* Austin: University of Texas Press.
2003b Introduction: Reinterpreting Early Classic Interaction. In *The Maya
and Teotihuacan: Reinterpreting Early Classic Interaction*, ed.
Geoffrey E. Braswell, pp. 1–43. Austin: University of Texas Press.
Braswell, Geoffrey E., Joel D. Gunn, María del Rosario Domínguez Carrasco, William J. Folan, Laraine A. Fletcher, Abel Morales López,
and Michael D. Glascock
2004 Defining the Terminal Classic at Calakmul, Campeche. In *The
Terminal Classic in the Maya Lowlands: Collapse, Transition, and
Transformations*, ed. Arthur A. Demarest, Prudence M. Rice, and
Don S. Rice, pp. 162–194. Boulder: University Press of Colorado.
Braudel, Fernand
1972 *The Mediterranean and the Mediterranean World in the Age of
Philip II.* London: Collins.
Bricker, Victoria R.
1983 Directional Glyphs in Maya Inscriptions and Codices. *American Antiquity* 48:347–353.
1984 Las ceremonías de año nuevo en los monumentos clásicos mayas: Investigaciones recientes en el área maya. *XVII Mesa Redonda 1981*,
vol. 1, pp. 227–245. San Cristóbal de las Casas, Chiapas: Sociedad
Mexicana de Antropología.
1989 The Calendrical Meaning of Ritual among the Maya. In *Ethnographic Encounters in Southern Mesoamerica*, ed. Victoria Bricker
and Gary Gossen, pp. 231–249. Studies in Culture and History, no. 3,
Institute of Mesoamerican Studies. Albany: State University of New
York at Albany.
1997a The Structure of Almanacs in the Madrid Codex. In *Papers on the
Madrid Codex.* Middle American Research Institute, Pub. 64, ed.

Victoria R. Bricker and Gabrielle Vail, pp. 1–25. New Orleans: Tulane University.

1997b The "Calendar-Round" Almanac in the Madrid Codex. In *Papers on the Madrid Codex*. Middle American Research Institute, Pub. 64, ed. Victoria R. Bricker and Gabrielle Vail, pp. 169–180. New Orleans: Tulane University.

Bricker, Victoria R., and Gabrielle Vail (eds.)

1997   *Papers on the Madrid Codex*. Middle American Research Institute, Pub. 64. New Orleans: Tulane University.

Brinton, Daniel G.

[1885] 1969 *Annals of the Cakchiquels*. Brinton's Library of Aboriginal American Literature, no. 6. Philadelphia.

Brotherston, Gordon

1976   Mesoamerican Description of Space 2: Signs for Direction. *Ibero-Amerikanisches Archiv*, n.f. 2:39–62.

1983   The Year 3113 B.C. and the Fifth Sun of Mesoamerica: An Orthodox Reading of the Tepexic Annals (Codex Vindobonensis obverse). In *Calendars in Mesoamerica and Peru: Native American Computations of Time*, ed. Anthony F. Aveni and Gordon Brotherston. Oxford: BAR International Series 174.

Brown, M. Kathryn

1999   Investigations of Middle Preclassic Public Architecture at the site of Blackman Eddy, Belize. www.famsi.org/reports/96052

Bullard, William R., Jr.

1960   Maya Settlement Patterns in Northeast Peten, Guatemala. *American Antiquity* 25(3):355–372.

Burns, Allan F.

1983   *An Epoch of Miracles: Oral Literature of the Yucatec Maya*. Austin: University of Texas Press.

Campbell, Lyle, and Terrence Kaufman

1976   A Linguistic Look at the Olmecs. *American Antiquity* 41(1):80–89.

Carlson, John B.

1981   A Geomantic Model for the Interpretation of Mesoamerican Sites: An Essay in Cross-Cultural Comparison. In *Mesoamerican Sites and World-Views*, ed. Elizabeth P. Benson, pp. 143–215. Washington, D.C.: Dumbarton Oaks.

Carmean, Kelli, Nicholas Dunning, and Jeff Karl Kowalski

2004   High Times in the Hill Country: A Perspective from the Terminal Classic Puuc Region. In *The Terminal Classic in the Maya Lowlands: Collapse, Transition, and Transformations*, ed. Arthur A. Demarest, Prudence M. Rice, and Don S. Rice, pp. 424–449. Boulder: University Press of Colorado.

Carr, Robert F., and James E. Hazard

1961   *Tikal Report no. 11, Map of the Ruins of Tikal, El Peten, Guatemala*. Museum Monographs. Philadelphia: The University Museum, University of Pennsylvania.

Carr, H. Sorayya
1996   Precolumbian Maya Exploitation and Management of Deer Popula-
        tions. In *The Managed Mosaic: Ancient Maya Agriculture and Re-
        source Use*, ed. Scott L. Fedick, pp. 251–261. Salt Lake City: Univer-
        sity of Utah Press.
Carrasco, Ramón, and Silviane Boucher
1987   Las escaleras jeroglíficas del Resbalón, Quintana Roo. In *Primer sim-
        posio mundial sobre epigrafía*, pp. 1–21. Guatemala: Instituto Na-
        cional de Antropología y Historia, and Washington, D.C.: National
        Geographic Society.
Chase, Arlen F.
1983   A Contextual Consideration of the Tayasal-Paxcaman Zone, El Pe-
        ten, Guatemala. Ph.D. dissertation, University of Pennsylvania.
1985   Troubled Times: The Archaeology and Iconography of the Terminal
        Classic Southern Lowland Maya. In *Fifth Palenque Round Table,
        1983*, vol. 7, ed. Merle Greene Robertson, pp. 103–114. San Fran-
        cisco: Pre-Columbian Art Research Institute.
1991   Cycles of Time: Caracol in the Maya Realm. In *Sixth Palenque
        Round Table, 1986*, ed. Merle Greene Robertson, pp. 32–50. Nor-
        man: University of Oklahoma Press.
Chase, Arlen F., and Diane Z. Chase
1992   Mesoamerican Elites: Assumptions, Definitions, and Models. In
        Mesoamerican Elites, an Archaeological Assessment, ed. Diane Z.
        Chase and Arlen F. Chase, pp. 3–17. Norman: University of Okla-
        homa Press.
1995   External Impetus, Internal Synthesis, and Standardization: E-Group
        Assemblages and the Crystallization of Classic Maya Society in the
        Southern Lowlands. In *The Emergence of Maya Civilization: The
        Transition from the Preclassic to the Early Classic*, ed. Nikolai
        Grube, pp. 87–101. Acta Mesoamericana, no. 8. Berlin: Verlag von
        Flemming.
1996   More than Kin and King: Centralized Political Organization among
        the Late Classic Maya. *Current Anthropology* 37(5):803–810.
1998   Late Classic Maya Political Structure, Polity Size, and Warfare Are-
        nas. In *Anatomía de una civilización, aproximaciones interdiscipli-
        narias a la cultura maya*, ed. Andrés Ciudad Ruiz et al., pp. 11–29.
        Madrid: Sociedad Española de Estudios Mayas.
2001   The Royal Court of Caracol, Belize: Its Palaces and People. In *Royal
        Courts of the Ancient Maya*, vol. 2: *Data and Case Studies*, ed.
        Takeshi Inomata and Stephen D. Houston, pp. 102–137. Boulder,
        Colo.: Westview Press.
2004   Terminal Classic Status-Linked Ceramics and the Maya "Collapse":
        De Facto Refuse at Caracol, Belize. In *The Terminal Classic in the
        Maya Lowlands: Collapse, Transition, and Transformations*, ed.
        Arthur A. Demarest, Prudence M. Rice, and Don S. Rice, pp. 342–
        366. Boulder: University Press of Colorado.

Chase, Arlen F., Nikolai Grube, and Diane Z. Chase
1991   Three Terminal Classic Monuments from Caracol, Belize. *Research Reports on Ancient Maya Writing*, no. 36. Washington, D.C.: Center for Maya Research.
Chase, Arlen F., and Prudence M. Rice (eds.)
1985   *The Lowland Maya Postclassic.* Austin: University of Texas Press.
Chase, Diane Z.
1985   Ganned but Not Forgotten: Late Postclassic Archaeology and Ritual at Santa Rita Corozal, Belize. In *The Lowland Maya Postclassic,* ed. Arlen F. Chase and Prudence M. Rice, pp. 104–125. Austin: University of Texas Press.
1992   Postclassic Maya Elites: Ethnohistory and Archaeology. In *Mesoamerican Elites, an Archaeological Assessment,* ed. Diane Z. Chase and Arlen F. Chase, pp. 118–134. Norman: University of Oklahoma Press.
Cheek, Charles D.
2003   Maya Community Buildings: Two Late Classic *Popol Nahs* at Copan, Honduras. *Ancient Mesoamerica* 14(1):131–138.
Christie, Jessica Joyce
1995   Maya Period Ending Ceremonies: Restarting Time and Rebuilding the Cosmos to Assure Survival of the Maya World. Ph.D. dissertation, University of Texas.
Clark, John E.
1997   The Arts of Government in Early Mesoamerica. *Annual Review of Anthropology* 26:211–234.
Clark, John E., and Richard D. Hansen
2001   The Architecture of Early Kingship: Comparative Perspectives on the Origins of the Maya Royal Court. In *Royal Courts of the Ancient Maya,* vol. 2: *Data and Case Studies,* ed. Takeshi Inomata and Stephen D. Houston, pp. 1–45. Boulder, Colo.: Westview Press.
Cobos Palma, Rafael
2004   Chich'en Itza: Settlement and Hegemony during the Terminal Classic Period. In *The Terminal Classic in the Maya Lowlands: Collapse, Transition, and Transformations,* ed. Arthur A. Demarest, Prudence M. Rice, and Don S. Rice, pp. 517–544. Boulder: University Press of Colorado.
Coe, Michael D.
1965   A Model of Ancient Community Structure in the Maya Lowlands. *Southwestern Journal of Anthropology* 21(2):97–114.
1968   *America's First Civilization.* New York: American Heritage.
1973   *The Maya Scribe and His World.* New York: Grolier Club.
1978   *Lords of the Underworld.* Princeton, NJ: Princeton University Press.
1989   The Hero Twins: Myth and Image. In *The Maya Vase Book, Vol. 1,* ed. Justin Kerr, pp. 161–184. New York: Kerr Associates.
Coe, Michael D., and Richard A. Diehl
1980   *In the Land of the Olmec.* 2 vols. Austin: University of Texas Press.

Coe, Michael D., and Justin Kerr
1998   *The Art of the Maya Scribe.* New York: Harry N. Abrams.
Coe, William R.
1988   *Tikal. Guide to the Ancient Maya Ruins.* Philadelphia: The University Museum, University of Pennsylvania.
1990a   Excavations in the Great Plaza, North Terrace and North Acropolis of Tikal. *Tikal Report no. 14,* vol. II, series ed. William R. Coe and William A. Haviland. University Museum Monograph 61. Philadelphia: The University Museum, University of Pennsylvania.
1990b   Excavations in the Great Plaza, North Terrace and North Acropolis of Tikal. *Tikal Report no. 14,* vol. 3, series ed. William R. Coe and William A. Haviland. University Museum Monograph 61. Philadelphia: The University Museum, University of Pennsylvania.
Coggins, Clemency C.
1970   Displaced Mayan Sculpture. *Estudios de Cultura Maya* 8:15–24. México, D.F.: Universidad Nacional Autónoma de México.
1975   *Painting and Drawing Styles at Tikal: An Historical and Iconographic Reconstruction.* Ph.D. dissertation, Harvard University. Ann Arbor: University Microfilms.
1979   A New Order and the Role of the Calendar: Some Characteristics of the Middle Classic Period at Tikal. In *Maya Archaeology and Ethnohistory,* ed. Norman Hammond and Gordon R. Willey, pp. 38–50. Austin: University of Texas Press.
1980   The Shape of Time: Some Political Implications of a Four-Part Figure. *American Antiquity* 45(4):727–739.
1983   *The Stucco Decoration and Architectural Assemblage of Structure 1-sub, Dzibilchaltun, Yucatan, Mexico.* Middle American Research Institute Publication 49. New Orleans: Tulane University.
1987   The Names of Tikal. In *Primer simposio mundial sobre epigrafía maya,* pp. 23–45. Guatemala: Instituto Nacional de Antropología y Historia; Washington, D.C.: National Geographic Society.
1990   The Birth of the Baktun at Tikal and Seibal. In *Vision and Revision in Maya Studies,* ed. Flora S. Clancy and Peter D. Harrison, pp. 79–97. Albuquerque: University of New Mexico Press.
1992   Pure Language and Lapidary Prose. In *New Theories on the Ancient Maya,* ed. Elin C. Danien and Robert J. Sharer, pp. 99–107. University Museum Symposium Series, vol. 3. University Museum Monograph 77. Philadelphia: The University Museum, University of Pennsylvania.
1996   Creation Religion and the Numbers at Teotihuacan and Izapa. *RES* 29–30:17–38.
Coggins, Clemency C., and R. David Drucker
1988   The Observatory at Dzibilchaltun. In *New Directions in American Archaeoastronomy,* ed. Anthony F. Aveni, pp. 17–56. Proceedings of the 46th International Congress of Americanists. Oxford: BAR International Series 454.

Cohen, Ronald, and John Middleton
1967   Introduction. In *Comparative Political Systems: Studies in the Politics of Pre-industrial Societies*, ed. Ronald Cohen and John Middleton, pp. ix–xiv. Garden City, N.Y.: Natural History Press.
Cohodas, Marvin
1980   Radial Pyramids and Radial-Associated Assemblages of the Central Maya Area. *Journal of the Society of Architectural Historians* 39(3):208–223.
1991   Ballgame Imagery of the Maya Lowlands: History and Iconography. In *The Mesoamerican Ballgame*, ed. Vernon L. Scarborough and David R. Wilcox, pp. 251–288. Tucson: University of Arizona Press.
Corzo, Lilian A., Marco Tulio Alvarado, and Juan Pedro Laporte
1998   Ucanal: Un sitio asociado a la cuenca media del Río Mopan. In *XI simposio de investigaciones arqueológicas en Guatemala, 1997*, ed. Juan Pedro Laporte and Héctor L. Escobedo, pp. 191–214. Guatemala City: Museo Nacional de Arqueología y Etnología and Asociación Tikal.
Covarrubias, Miguel
1966   *Indian Art of Mexico and Central America*. New York: Alfred A. Knopf.
Cowgill, George L.
2003   Teotihuacan and Early Classic Interaction: A Perspective from Outside the Maya Region. In *The Maya and Teotihuacan: Reinterpreting Early Classic Interaction*, ed. Geoffrey E. Braswell, pp. 315–335. Austin: University of Texas Press.
Culbert, T. Patrick
1973   (ed.) *The Classic Maya Collapse*. Albuquerque: University of New Mexico Press.
1988   Political History and the Decipherment of Maya Glyphs. *Antiquity* 62(234):135–152.
1991a   Preface. In *Classic Maya Political History: Hieroglyphic and Archaeological Evidence*, ed. T. Patrick Culbert, pp. xv–xviii. Cambridge: Cambridge University Press.
1991b   (ed.) *Classic Maya Political History. Hieroglyphic and Archaeological Evidence*. Cambridge: Cambridge University Press.
1991c   Maya Political History and Elite Interaction: A Summary View. In *Classic Maya Political History: Hieroglyphic and Archaeological Evidence*, ed. T. Patrick Culbert, pp. 311–346. Cambridge: Cambridge University Press.
1993   The Ceramics of Tikal: Vessels from the Burials, Caches and Problematical Deposits. *Tikal Report no. 25*, series ed. William R. Coe and William A. Haviland. University Museum Monograph 81. Philadelphia: The University Museum, University of Pennsylvania.
Culbert, T. Patrick, and Don S. Rice (eds.)
1990   *Precolumbian Population History in the Maya Lowlands*. Albuquerque: University of New Mexico Press.

Dahlin, Bruce H.
2000   The Barricade and Abandonment of Chunchucmil: Implications
        for Northern Maya Warfare. *Latin American Antiquity* 11(3):283–
        298.
Davies, Paul
2002   That Mysterious Flow. *Scientific American* 287(3):40–47.
Demarest, Arthur A.
1992   Ideology in Ancient Maya Cultural Evolution: The Dynamics of
        Galactic Polities. In *Ideology and Pre-Columbian Civilizations*, ed.
        Arthur A. Demarest and Geoffrey W. Conrad, pp. 135–157. Albu-
        querque: University of New Mexico Press.
2004   After the Maelstrom: Collapse of the Classic Maya Kingdoms and
        the Terminal Classic in Western Petén. In *The Terminal Classic in
        the Maya Lowlands: Collapse, Transition, and Transformations*, ed.
        Arthur A. Demarest, Prudence M. Rice, and Don S. Rice, pp. 102–
        124. Boulder: University Press of Colorado.
Demarest, Arthur A., Prudence M. Rice, and Don S. Rice (eds.)
2004   *The Terminal Classic in the Maya Lowlands: Collapse, Transition,
        and Transformations.* Boulder: University Press of Colorado.
de Montmollin, Olivier
1989   *The Archaeology of Political Structure: Settlement Analysis in a
        Classic Maya Polity.* Cambridge: Cambridge University Press.
Dillon, Brian D.
1982   Bound Prisoners in Maya Art. *Journal of New World Archaeology*
        5(1):24–45.
Duby, Gertrude, and Frans Blom
1969   The Lacandon. In *Ethnology, Part I*, vol. ed., Evon Z. Vogt, pp. 276–
        297. *Handbook of Middle American Indians*, vol. 7, gen. ed. Robert
        Wauchope. Austin: University of Texas Press.
Dunham, Peter S.
1990   Coming Apart at the Seams: The Classic Development and Demise
        of Maya Civilization (A Segmentary View from Xnaheb, Belize).
        Ph.D. dissertation, State University of New York at Albany.
Earle, Duncan, and Dean Snow
1985   The Origin of the 260-Day Calendar: The Gestation Hypothesis Re-
        considered in Light of Its Use among the Quiche People. In *Fifth
        Palenque Round Table, 1983*, ed. Virginia M. Fields, gen. ed. Merle
        Greene Robertson, pp. 241–244. San Francisco: Pre-Columbian Art
        Research Institute.
Edmonson, Munro S.
1979   Some Postclassic Questions about the Classic Maya. In *Tercera
        Mesa Redonda de Palenque*, vol. 4, ed. Merle Greene Robertson and
        Donnan Call Jeffers, pp. 9–18. Palenque, Chiapas, Mexico: Pre-
        Columbian Art Research Center. (Reprinted in *Ancient Meso-
        america, Selected Readings*, 2d ed. [1981], ed. John A. Graham,
        pp. 221–228. Palo Alto, Calif.: Peek Publications.)

1982   *The Ancient Future of the Itza: The Book of Chilam Balam of Tiz-imin.* Austin: University of Texas Press.
1985   The Baktun Ceremonial of 1618. *Fourth Palenque Round Table, 1980,* vol. 6, ed. Merle Greene Robertson and Elizabeth P. Benson, pp. 261–265. San Francisco: Pre-Columbian Art Research Institute.
1986a   *Heaven Born Merida and Its Destiny: The Book of Chilam Balam of Chumayel.* Austin: University of Texas Press.
1986b   The Olmec Calendar Round. In *Research and Reflections in Archaeology and History: Essays in Honor of Doris Stone,* ed. E. Wyllys Andrews V, pp. 81–86. Middle American Research Institute, Publication 57. New Orleans: Tulane University.
1988   *The Book of the Year: Middle American Calendrical Systems.* Salt Lake City: University of Utah Press.
Eliade, Mircea
1954   *The Myth of the Eternal Return, or Cosmos and History.* Princeton, N.J.: Princeton University Press.
1979   *Tratado de historia de las religiones.* México, D.F.: Biblioteca Era.
Fahsen, Federico
1984   Notes for a Sequence of Rulers of Machaquilá. *American Antiquity* 49(1):94–104.
2002   Rescuing the Origins of Dos Pilas Dynasty: A Salvage of Hieroglyphic Stairway #2, Structure L5-49. www.famsi.org/reports/01098
Farriss, Nancy M.
1984   *Maya Society under Colonial Rule: The Collective Enterprise of Survival.* Princeton, N.J.: Princeton University Press.
1987   Remembering the Future, Anticipating the Past: History, Time, and Cosmology among the Maya of Yucatan. *Comparative Studies in Society and History* 29:566–593.
Fash, Barbara W.
1992   Late Classic Architectural Sculpture Themes in Copán. *Ancient Mesoamerica* 3(1):89–104.
Fash, Barbara W., William Fash, Sheree Lane, Rudy Larios, Linda Schele, Jeffrey Stomper, and David Stuart
1992   Investigations of a Classic Maya Council House at Copán, Honduras. *Journal of Field Archaeology* 19(4):419–442.
Fash, William L.
1991   *Scribes, Warriors and Kings: The City of Copán and the Ancient Maya.* London: Thames and Hudson.
Fash, William L, E. Wyllys Andrews, and T. Kam Manahan
2004   Political Decentralization, Dynastic Collapse, and the Early Postclassic in the Urban Center of Copán, Honduras. In *The Terminal Classic in the Maya Lowlands: Collapse, Transition, and Transformations,* ed. Arthur A. Demarest, Prudence M. Rice, and Don S. Rice, pp. 260–287. Boulder: University Press of Colorado.
Fash, William L., and Barbara W. Fash
2000   Teotihuacan and the Maya: A Classic Heritage. In *Mesoamerica's*

Classic Heritage: From Teotihuacan to the Aztecs, ed. Davíd Carrasco, Lindsay Jones, and Scott Sessions, pp. 433–463. Boulder: University Press of Colorado.

Fash, William L., and David S. Stuart
1991   Dynastic History and Cultural Evolution at Copán, Honduras. In *Classic Maya Political History: Hieroglyphic and Archaeological Evidence,* ed. T. Patrick Culbert, pp. 147–179. Cambridge: Cambridge University Press and School of American Research.

Feeley-Harnik, Gillian
1985   Issues in Divine Kingship. *Annual Review of Anthropology* 14:273–313.

Feinman, Gary M., and Joyce Marcus (eds.)
1998   *Archaic States.* Albuquerque, New Mex.: School of American Research Press.

Flannery, Kent V.
1977   Review of *Mesoamerican Archaeology: New Approaches* (ed. Norman Hammond). *American Antiquity* 42(4):659–661.

Flores Gutiérrez, Daniel
1989   260: Un período astronómico. In *Memorias del segundo coloquio internacional de mayistas,* vol. 1. México, D.F.: Universidad Nacional Autónoma de México.

Folan, William J.
1983   The Ruins of Coba. In *Coba: A Classic Maya Metropolis,* by William J. Folan, Ellen R. Kintz, and Laraine A. Fletcher, pp. 65–87. New York: Academic Press.

Folan, William J., Laraine A. Fletcher, Jacinto May Hau, and Lynda Florey Folan (coord.)
2001   *Las ruinas de Calakmul, Campeche, México: Un lugar central y su paisaje cultural.* Campeche, México: Universidad Autónoma de Campeche.

Folan, William J., Joel D. Gunn, and María del Rosario Domínguez Carrasco
2001   Triadic Temples, Central Plazas, and Dynastic Palaces: A Diachronic Analysis of the Royal Court Complex, Calakmul, Campeche, Mexico. In *Royal Courts of the Ancient Maya,* vol. 2: *Data and Case Studies,* ed. Takeshi Inomata and Stephen D. Houston, pp. 223–265. Boulder, Colo.: Westview Press.

Folan, William J., Ellen R. Kintz, and Laraine A. Fletcher
1983   *Coba: A Classic Maya Metropolis.* New York: Academic Press.

Folan, William J., Joyce Marcus, Sophia Pincemin, et al.
1995   Calakmul: New Data from an Ancient Maya Capital in Campeche, Mexico. *Latin American Antiquity* 6(4):310–334.

Fought, John
1985   Cyclical Patterns in Chorti (Mayan) Literature. In *Literatures,* ed. Munro S. Edmonson, Supplement to the *Handbook of Middle American Indians,* vol. 3, gen. ed. Victoria Reifler Bricker, pp. 133–146. Austin: University of Texas Press.

Fox, James A., and John S. Justeson
1984   Polyvalence in Mayan Hieroglyphic Writing. In *Phoneticism in Mayan Hieroglyphic Writing*, ed. John S. Justeson and Lyle Campbell, pp. 17–76. Institute for Mesoamerican Studies, Publication 9. Albany: State University of New York at Albany.

Fox, John Gerard
1996   Playing with Power: Ballcourts and Political Ritual in Southern Mesoamerica. *Current Anthropology* 37(3):483–496.

Fox, John W.
1991   The Lords of Light versus the Lords of Dark: The Postclassic Highland Maya Ballgame. In *The Mesoamerican Ballgame*, ed. Vernon L. Scarborough and David R. Wilcox, pp. 213–238. Tucson: University of Arizona Press.

Fox, John W., Garrett W. Cook, Arlen F. Chase, and Diane Z. Chase
1996   Questions of Political and Economic Integration: Segmentary Versus Centralized States among the Ancient Maya. *Current Anthropology* 37(5):795–801.

Fox, Richard G.
1977   *Urban Anthropology: Cities in Their Cultural Settings.* Englewood Cliffs, N.J.: Prentice-Hall.

Freidel, David A.
1986   Maya Warfare: An Example of Peer Polity Interaction. In *Peer Polity Interaction and Socio-Political Change*, ed. Colin Renfrew and John F. Cherry, pp. 93–108. Cambridge: Cambridge University Press.
1992   The Trees of Life: *Ahau* as Idea and Artifact in Classic Lowland Maya Civilization. In *Ideology and Pre-Columbian Civilizations*, ed. Arthur A. Demarest and Geoffrey W. Conrad, pp. 115–133. Santa Fe, New Mex.: School of American Research Press.

Freidel, David A., and Linda Schele
1988a   Kingship in the Late Preclassic Lowlands: The Instruments and Places of Ritual Power. *American Anthropologist* 90(3):547–567.
1988b   Symbol and Power: A History of the Lowland Maya Cosmogram. In *Maya Iconography*, ed. Elizabeth P. Benson and Gillett G. Griffin, pp. 44–93. Princeton, N.J.: Princeton University Press.

Freidel, David A., Linda Schele, and Joy Parker
1993   *Maya Cosmos: Three Thousand Years on the Shaman's Path.* New York: Morrow.

Freter, AnnCorinne
1992   Chronological Research at Copán: Methods and Implications. *Ancient Mesoamerica* 3(1):117–133.

Fritz, John M., and Fred Plog
1970   The Nature of Archaeological Explanation. *American Antiquity* 35:405–412.

Gann, Thomas, and J. Eric S. Thompson
1935   *The History of the Maya, from the Earliest Times to the Present Day.* New York: Charles Scribner's Sons.

Geertz, Clifford

1973   Person, Time, and Conduct in Bali. In *The Interpretation of Cultures: Selected Essays by Clifford Geertz*, pp. 360–411. New York: Basic Books.

1980   *Negara: The Theatre State in Nineteenth-Century Bali.* Princeton, N.J.: Princeton University Press.

Gendrop, Paul

1980   Dragon-Mouth Entrances: Zoomorphic Portals in the Architecture of Central Yucatán. In *Third Palenque Round Table, 1978*, Part 2, ed. Merle Greene Robertson, pp. 138–150. Austin: University of Texas Press.

Gillespie, Susan D.

1991   Ballgames and Boundaries. In *The Mesoamerican Ballgame*, ed. Vernon L. Scarborough and David R. Wilcox, pp. 317–345. Tucson: University of Arizona Press.

2000a   Maya "Nested Houses": The Ritual Construction of Place. In *Beyond Kinship: Social and Material Reproduction in House Societies*, ed. Rosemary A. Joyce and Susan D. Gillespie, pp. 135–160. Philadelphia: University of Pennsylvania Press.

2000b   Rethinking Ancient Maya Social Organization: Replacing Lineage with House. *American Anthropologist* 102(3):467–484.

Girard, Rafael

1962   *Los mayas eternos.* México, D.F.: Antigua Librería Robredo.

Gossen, Gary H.

1974   *Chamulas in the World of the Sun: Time and Space in a Maya Oral Tradition.* Cambridge, Mass.: Harvard University Press.

Gossen, Gary H., and Richard M. Leventhal

1993   The Topography of Ancient Maya Religious Pluralism: A Dialogue with the Present. In *Lowland Maya Civilization in the Eighth Century A.D.*, ed. Jeremy A. Sabloff and John S. Henderson, pp. 185–217. Washington, D.C.: Dumbarton Oaks.

Gould, Richard A., and Patty Jo Watson

1982   A Dialogue on the Meaning and Use of Analogy in Ethnoarchaeological Reasoning. *Journal of Anthropological Archaeology* 1(4):355–381.

Graff, Donald H.

1997   Dating a Section of the Madrid Codex: Astronomical and Iconographic Evidence. In *Papers on the Madrid Codex.* Middle American Research Institute Publication 64, ed. Victoria R. Bricker and Gabrielle Vail, pp. 147–167. New Orleans: Tulane University

Graham, Ian

1967   *Archaeological Explorations in El Petén, Guatemala.* Middle American Research Institute Publication 33. New Orleans: Tulane University.

Graham, John

1973   Aspects of Non-Classic Presences in the Inscriptions and Sculptural Art of Seibal. In *The Classic Maya Collapse*, ed. T. Patrick Culbert, pp. 207–219. Albuquerque: University of New Mexico Press.

1990   Monumental Sculpture and Hieroglyphic Inscriptions. *Excavations at Seibal, Department of Peten, Guatemala.* No. 1. Memoirs vol. 17. Cambridge, Mass. Peabody Museum of Archaeology and Ethnology, Harvard University.

Grazioso Sierra, Liwy
1995   Cruz punteada en el Grupo 5 de Teotihuacan. In *II Simposio de investigaciones arqueológicas en Guatemala,* ed. Juan Pedro Laporte and Héctor L. Escobedo, pp. 447–459. Guatemala City: Instituto de Antropología e Historia and Asociación Tikal.

Grazioso Sierra, Liwy, T. Patrick Culbert, Vilma Fialko, et al.
2001   Arqueología en el Bajo La Justa, Petén, Guatemala. In *XV Simposio de investigaciones arqueológicas en Guatemala,* ed. Juan Pedro Laporte and Héctor L. Escobedo, pp. 205–209. Guatemala City: Instituto de Antropología e Historia and Asociación Tikal.

Grube, Nikolai
1991   An Investigation of the Primary Standard Sequence on Classic Maya Ceramics. In *Sixth Palenque Round Table, 1986,* ed. Merle Greene Robertson, pp. 223–232. Norman: University of Oklahoma Press.
1994   Hieroglyphic Sources for the History of Northwest Yucatan. In *Hidden among the Hills: Maya Archaeology of the Northwest Yucatan Peninsula,* ed. Hanns J. Prem, pp. 316–358. First Maler Symposium, Bonn 1989. Acta Mesoamericana, vol. 7. Möckmühl: Verlag von Flemming.
2000a The City-States of the Maya. In *A Comparative Study of Thirty City-State Cultures: An Investigation Conducted by the Copenhagen Polis Centre,* ed. Mogens Herman Hansen, pp. 547–565. Copenhagen: Royal Danish Academy of Sciences and Letters.
2000b Monumentos esculpidos e inscripciones jeroglíficas en el triángulo Yaxhá-Nakum-Naranjo. In *El sitio maya de Topoxté: Investigaciones en una isla del Lago Yaxhá, Petén, Guatemala,* ed. Wolfgang W. Wurster, pp. 249–268. Mainz am Rhein: Verlag Philipp von Zabern.
2000c Fire rituals in the context of Classic Maya initial series. In *The Sacred and the Profane: Architecture and Identity in the Maya Lowlands,* ed. Pierre R. Colas, Kai Delvendahl, Marcus Kuhnert, and Annette Schubart, pp. 93–110. Acta Mesoamericana 10. Berlin: Verlag Anton Saurwein Markt Schwaben.

Grube, Nikolai, and Simon Martin
1998   Deciphering Maya Politics: The Proceedings of the Maya Hieroglyphic Workshop, March 14–15, 1998. Transcr. and ed. Phil Wanyerka. Department of Art History, University of Texas, Austin.
2000   The Dynastic History of the Maya. In *Maya: Divine Kings of the Rain Forest,* ed. Nikolai Grube, pp. 149–171. Cologne: Könemann.

Guenter, Stanley
2000   The Murder of the Queen of Tikal? *PARI Journal* 1(2):22–24.

Guillemin, George F.
1968   Development and Function of the Tikal Ceremonial Center. *Ethnos* 33:1–35.

Haggett, Peter
1966   *Locational Analysis in Human Geography.* New York: St. Martin's Press.
Hamblin, Nancy L.
1984   *Animal Use by the Cozumel Maya.* Tucson: University of Arizona Press.
Hammond, Norman
1972   Locational Models and the Site of Lubaantun: A Classic Maya Centre. In *Models in Archaeology,* ed. David L. Clarke, pp. 757–800. London: Methuen.
1974   The Distribution of Late Classic Maya Major Ceremonial Centers in the Central Area. In *Mesoamerican Archaeology: New Approaches,* ed. Norman Hammond, pp. 313–334. Austin: University of Texas Press.
1975   *Lubaantun, a Classic Maya Realm.* Peabody Museum of Archaeology and Ethnology Monograph 2. Cambridge, Mass.: Harvard University.
1982   A Late Formative Period Stela in the Maya Lowlands. *American Antiquity* 47(2):396–403.
1991   Introduction. In *Classic Maya Political History: Hieroglyphic and Archaeological Evidence,* ed. T. Patrick Culbert, pp. 1–18. Cambridge: Cambridge University Press and School of American Research.
Hanks, William F.
1989   Elements of Maya Style. In *Word and Image in Maya Culture: Explorations in Language, Writing, and Representation,* ed. William F. Hanks and Don S. Rice, pp. 92–111. Salt Lake City: University of Utah Press.
Hansen, Richard D.
1992   El proceso cultural de Nakbe y el área del Petén nor-central: Las épocas tempranas. In *V simposio de investigaciones arqueológicas en Guatemala, 1991,* ed. Juan Pedro Laporte, Héctor L. Escobedo A., and Sandra Villagrán de Brady, pp. 81–96. Guatemala City: Museo Nacional de Arqueología y Etnología and Asociación Tikal.
2000   The First Cities: The Beginnings of Urbanization and State Formation in the Maya Lowlands. In *Maya: Divine Kings of the Rain Forest,* ed. Nikolai Grube, pp. 51–65. Cologne: Könemann.
Hanson, Craig A.
1995   The Hispanic Horizon in Yucatan: A Model of Franciscan Missionization. *Ancient Mesoamerica* 6:15–28.
Harris, John F., and Stephen K. Stearns
1997   *Understanding Maya Inscriptions: A Hieroglyph Handbook,* 2d rev. ed. Philadelphia: The University Museum, University of Pennsylvania.
Harrison, Peter D.
1999   *The Lords of Tikal: Rulers of an Ancient Maya City.* London: Thames and Hudson.

Hassig, Ross
1992   *War and Society in Ancient Mesoamerica.* Berkeley: University of California Press.
Haviland, William A.
1970   Tikal, Guatemala, and Mesoamerican Urbanism. *World Archaeology* 2:186–198.
1972   A New Look at Classic Maya Social Organization at Tikal. *Ceramica de Cultura Maya* 8:1–16.
1981   Dower Houses and Minor Centers at Tikal, Guatemala: An Investigation into the Identification of Valid Units in Settlement Hierarchies. In *Lowland Maya Settlement Patterns,* ed. Wendy Ashmore, pp. 89–117. Albuquerque: University of New Mexico Press and School of American Research.
1992   From Double Bird to Ah Cacao: Dynastic Troubles and the Cycle of Katuns at Tikal, Guatemala. In *New Theories on the Ancient Maya,* ed. Elin C. Danien and Robert J. Sharer, pp. 71–80. University Museum Symposium Series, vol. 3. Philadelphia: The University Museum, University of Pennsylvania.
Hawking, Stephen
1996   *The Illustrated A Brief History of Time.* New York: Bantam Books.
Healy, Paul F.
1990   Excavations at Pacbitun, Belize: Preliminary Report on the 1986 and 1987 Investigations. *Journal of Field Archaeology* 17:247–262.
Hellmuth, Nicholas M.
1976   *Tikal, Copan Travel Guide: A General Introduction to Maya Art, Architecture, and Archaeology.* St. Louis: Foundation for Latin American Anthropological Research.
Hill, James N. (ed.)
1977   *The Explanation of Prehistoric Change.* Albuquerque: University of New Mexico Press.
Hill, Warren D., and John E. Clark
2001   Sports, Gambling, and Government: America's First Social Compact? *American Anthropologist* 103(2):331–345.
Hill, Warren D., T. Michael Blake, and John E. Clark
1998   Ball Court Design Dates Back 3400 Years. *Nature* 392:878–879.
Hofling, Charles Andrew, and Francisco Tesucún
1998   *Itzaj Maya-Spanish-English Dictionary.* Salt Lake City: University of Utah Press.
Houston, Stephen D.
1987   The Inscriptions and Monumental Art of Dos Pilas, Guatemala: A Study of Classic Maya History and Politics. Ph.D. dissertation, Yale University.
1991   Appendix: Caracol Altar 21. In *Sixth Palenque Round Table, 1986,* ed. Virginia M. Fields, pp. 38–42. Norman: University of Oklahoma Press.
1992   Classic Maya Politics. In *New Theories on the Ancient Maya,* ed.

Elin C. Danien and Robert J. Sharer, pp. 65–69. University Museum Symposium Series, vol. 3. Philadelphia: The University Museum, University of Pennsylvania.

1993   *Hieroglyphs and History at Dos Pilas: Dynastic Politics of the Classic Maya.* Austin: University of Texas Press.

2000   Into the Minds of Ancients: Advances in Maya Glyph Studies. *Journal of World Prehistory* 14(2):121–201.

Houston, Stephen, Oswaldo Chinchilla Mazariegos, and David Stuart (eds.)

2001   *The Decipherment of Ancient Maya Writing.* Norman: University of Oklahoma Press.

Houston, Stephen D., and Peter Mathews

1985   *The Dynastic Sequence of Dos Pilas, Guatemala.* Monograph 1. San Francisco: Pre-Columbian Art Research Institute.

Houston, Stephen D., John Robertson, and David Stuart

2000   The Language of Classic Maya Inscriptions. *Current Anthropology* 41(3):321–356.

Iannone, Gyles

2002   Annales History and the Ancient Maya State: Some Observations on the "Dynamic Model." *American Anthropologist* 104(1):68–78.

Jackson, Sarah, and David Stuart

2001   The *Aj K'uhun* Title: Deciphering a Classic Maya Term of Rank. *Ancient Mesoamerica* 12(2):217–218.

Jones, Christopher

1969   The Twin-Pyramid Group Pattern: A Classic Maya Architectural Assemblage at Tikal, Guatemala. Ph.D. dissertation, University of Pennsylvania.

1985   The Rubber Ball Game, a Universal Mesoamerican Sport. *Expedition* 27(2):44–52.

1991   Cycles of Growth at Tikal. In *Classic Maya Political History: Hieroglyphic and Archaeological Evidence,* ed. T. Patrick Culbert, pp. 102–127. Cambridge: Cambridge University Press and School of American Research.

2003   The Tikal Renaissance and the East Plaza Ball Court. In *Tikal: Dynasties, Foreigners, & Affairs of State: Advancing Maya Archaeology,* ed. Jeremy A. Sabloff, pp. 207–225. School of American Research Advanced Seminar Series. Santa Fe, New Mex.: School of American Research Press; Oxford: James Currey.

Jones, Christopher, and Linton Satterthwaite

1982   *The Monuments and Inscriptions of Tikal: The Carved Monuments.* Tikal Report no. 33, Part A. University Museum Monograph 44. Philadelphia: The University Museum, University of Pennsylvania.

Jones, Grant D.

1998   *The Conquest of the Last Maya Kingdom.* Stanford, Calif.: Stanford University Press.

Joyce, Rosemary A.

2000   *Gender and Power in Prehispanic Mesoamerica.* Austin: University of Texas Press.

Justeson, John S.
1986   The Origin of Writing Systems: Preclassic Mesoamerica. *World Archaeology* 17(3):437–457.
1989   Ancient Maya Ethnoastronomy: An Overview of Hieroglyphic Sources. In *World Archaeoastronomy*, ed. Anthony Aveni, pp. 76–129. Cambridge: Cambridge University Press.
Justeson, John S., and Lyle Campbell
1997   The Linguistic Background of Maya Hieroglyphic Writing: Arguments about a "Highland Mayan" Role. In *The Language of Maya Hieroglyphs*, ed. Martha J. Macri and Anabel Ford, pp. 41–67. San Francisco, Calif.: Pre-Columbian Art Research Institute.
Justeson, John S., and Terrence Kaufman
1993   A Decipherment of Epi-Olmec Hieroglyphic Writing. *Science* 259:1703–1711.
Justeson, John S., and Peter Mathews
1983   The Seating of the *tun:* Further Evidence Concerning a Late Preclassic Lowland Maya Stela Cult. *American Antiquity* 48(3):586–593.
Justeson, John S., William M. Norman, and Norman Hammond
1988   The Pomona Flare: A Preclassic Maya Hieroglyphic Text. In *Maya Iconography*, ed. Elizabeth P. Benson and Gillett G. Griffin, pp. 94–151. Princeton, N.J.: Princeton University Press.
Kappelman, Julia Guernsey
2001   Sacred Geography at Izapa and the Performance of Rulership. In *Landscape and Power in Ancient Mesoamerica*, ed. Rex Koontz, Kathryn Reese-Taylor, and Annabeth Headrick, pp. 81–111. Boulder, Colo.: Westview Press.
Kaufman, Terrence, and John Justeson
2001   Epi-Olmec Hieroglyphic Writing and Texts. Mesoamerican Languages Documentation Project. [http://www.albany.edu/anthro/maldp]
Kelley, David H.
1962   A History of the Decipherment of Maya Script. *Anthropological Linguistics* 4(8):1–48.
1968a   Kakupacal and the Itzás. *Estudios de Cultura Maya* 7:255–268. México, D.F.: Universidad Nacional Autónoma de México.
1968b   Mayan Fire Glyphs. *Estudios de Cultura Maya* 7:141–157. México, D.F.: Universidad Nacional Autónoma de México.
1982   Notes on Puuc Inscriptions and History. In *The Puuc: New Perspectives: Papers Presented at the Puuc Symposium, Central College*, ed. Lawrence Mills. Pella, Iowa: Central College Press.
Kelly, John D., and Martha Kaplan
1990   History, Structure, and Ritual. *Annual Review of Anthropology* 19:119–150.
Kidder, Alfred V., Jesse Jennings, and Edwin Shook
1946   *Excavations at Kaminaljuyu, Guatemala.* Pub. 501. Washington, D.C.: Carnegie Institution of Washington.
Kowalski, Jeff Karl
1994   The Puuc as Seen from Uxmal. In *Hidden among the Hills: Maya Ar-*

chaeology of the Northwest Yucatan Peninsula, ed. Hanns J. Prem, pp. 93–120. First Maler Symposium, Bonn 1989. Acta Mesoamericana, vol. 7. Möckmühl: Verlag von Flemming.

Kremer, Jürgen
1994   The Putun Hypothesis Reconsidered. In *Hidden among the Hills: Maya Archaeology of the Northwest Yucatán Peninsula,* ed. Hanns J. Prem, pp. 289–307. First Maler Symposium, Bonn 1989. *Acta Mesoamericana,* vol. 7. Möckmühl: Verlag von Flemming.

Krochock, Ruth
1991   Dedication Ceremonies at Chichén Itzá: The Glyphic Evidence. In *Sixth Palenque Round Table, 1986,* ed. Merle Greene Robertson, pp. 43–50. Norman: University of Oklahoma Press.
1997   The Chich'en Itza Ballcourt Stone. Presentation at the UCLA Archaeological Institute's Maya Weekend on "The Maya Terminal Classic." Los Angeles: University of California, Los Angeles.
1998   The Development of Political Rhetoric at Chichen Itza, Yucatan, Mexico. Ph.D. dissertation, Southern Methodist University.

Krochock, Ruth, and David A. Freidel
1994   Ballcourts and the Evolution of Political Rhetoric at Chichén Itzá. In *Hidden among the Hills: Maya Archaeology of the Northwest Yucatán Peninsula,* ed. Hanns J. Prem, pp. 359–375. First Maler Symposium, Bonn 1989. Acta Mesoamericana, vol. 7. Möckmühl: Verlag von Flemming.

Krupp, E. C.
1997   *Skywatchers, Shamans & Kings.* New York: John Wiley and Sons.

Kubler, George
1977   The Initial Series Vase from Uaxactún Reconsidered. In *Aspects of Classic Maya Rulership on Two Inscribed Vessels,* by George Kubler. Studies in Pre-Columbian Art and Archaeology, no. 18. Washington, D.C.: Dumbarton Oaks.

Kurjack, Edward B., Rubén Maldonado C., and Merle Greene Robertson
1991   Ballcourts of the Northern Maya Lowlands. In *The Mesoamerican Ballgame,* ed. Vernon L. Scarborough and David R. Wilcox, pp. 145–159. Tucson: University of Arizona Press.

Kurtz, Donald V.
2001   *Political Anthropology: Paradigms and Power.* Boulder, Colo.: Westview Press.

Lacadena García-Gallo, Alfonso
n.d.   Letter circulated to epigraphers about glyph T174.

Lacadena García-Gallo, Alfonso, and Andrés Ciudad Ruíz
1998   Reflexiones sobre la estructura política maya clásica. In *Anatomía de una civilización, aproximaciones interdisciplinarias a la cultura maya,* ed. Andrés Ciudad Ruíz et al., pp. 31–64. Madrid: Sociedad Española de Estudios Mayas.

Laporte, Juan Pedro
1996   La cuenca del Río Mopan-Belice: Una sub-región cultural de las tierras bajas maya central. In *IX simposio de investigaciones arqueológicas en Guatemala, 1995,* ed. Juan Pedro Laporte and Héctor

Escobedo, pp. 253–279. Guatemala City: Museo Nacional de Arqueología y Etnología and Asociación Tikal.

2003   Architectural Aspects of Interaction between Tikal and Teotihuacan during the Early Classic Period. In *The Maya and Teotihuacan: Reinterpreting Early Classic Interaction*, ed. Geoffrey E. Braswell, pp. 199–216. Austin: University of Texas Press.

2004   Terminal Classic Settlement and Polity in the Mapan Valley, Petén, Guatemala. In *The Terminal Classic in the Maya Lowlands: Collapse, Transition, and Transformations*, ed. Arthur A. Demerest, Prudence M. Rice, and Don S. Rice, pp. 195–230. Boulder: University Press of Colorado.

Laporte, Juan Pedro, and Vilma Fialko C.

1990   New Perspectives on Old Problems: Dynastic References for the Early Classic at Tikal. In *Vision and Revision in Maya Studies*, ed. Flora S. Clancy and Peter D. Harrison, pp. 33–66. Albuquerque: University of New Mexico Press.

1995   Un reëncuentro con Mundo Perdido, Tikal, Guatemala. *Ancient Mesoamerica* 6:41–94.

Laporte, Juan Pedro, and Héctor E. Mejía

2002   Ucanal: Una ciudad del Río Mopan en Petén, Guatemala. *U tz'ib* 1(2). Guatemala City: Asociación Tikal.

León-Portilla, Miguel

1988   *Time and Reality in the Thought of the Maya*, 2d ed. Norman: University of Oklahoma Press.

Leventhal, Richard M.

1990   Southern Belize: An Ancient Maya Region. In *Vision and Revision in Maya Studies*, ed. Flora S. Clancy and Peter D. Harrison, pp. 125–141. Albuquerque: University of New Mexico Press.

1992   Development of a Regional Tradition in Southern Belize. In *New Theories on the Ancient Maya*, ed. Elin C. Danien and Robert J. Sharer, pp. 145–153. University Museum Symposium Series, vol. 3, University Museum Monograph 77. Philadelphia: The University Museum, University of Pennsylvania.

Lincoln, Charles E.

1994   Structural and Philological Evidence for Divine Kingship at Chichén Itzá, Yucatán, México. In *Hidden among the Hills: Maya Archaeology of the Northwest Yucatán Peninsula*, ed. Hanns J. Prem, pp. 164–196. First Maler Symposium, Bonn 1989. Acta Mesoamericana, vol. 7 Möckmühl: Verlag von Flemming.

Little, Barbara J. (ed.)

1992   *Text-aided Archaeology*. Boca Raton, Fla.: CRC Press.

Long, R. C. E.

1923   The Burner Period of the Mayas. *Man* 23(108):173–176.

Lounsbury, Floyd G.

1973   On the Derivation and Reading of the 'ben-ich' Prefix. In *Mesoamerican Writing Systems*, ed. Elizabeth P. Benson, pp. 99–143. Washington, D.C.: Dumbarton Oaks.

1978   Maya Numeration, Computation, and Calendrical Astronomy. *Dic-*

tionary of Scientific Biography, vol. 15, suppl. 1, ed. Charles Coulston-Gillispie, pp. 757–818. New York: Charles Scribner's Sons.

1985 The Identities of the Mythological Figures in the Cross Group Inscriptions of Palenque. *Fourth Palenque Round Table, 1980*, vol. 6, ed. Merle Greene Robertson and Elizabeth P. Benson, pp. 45–58. San Francisco: Pre-Columbian Art Research Institute.

Love, Bruce

1994 *The Paris Codex: Handbook for a Maya Priest.* Austin: University of Texas Press.

Lowe, Gareth W.

1982 Izapa Religion, Cosmology, and Ritual. In *Izapa: An Introduction to the Ruins and Monuments*, ed. Gareth W. Lowe, Thomas A. Lee Jr., and Eduardo Martínez Espinosa, pp. 269–306. New World Archaeological Foundation Paper 31. Provo, Utah: Brigham Young University.

Lowe, Gareth W., Thomas A. Lee Jr., and Eduardo Martínez Espinosa (eds.)

1982 *Izapa: An Introduction to the Ruins and Monuments.* New World Archaeological Foundation Paper 31. Provo, Utah: Brigham Young.

Lucero, Lisa J.

1999 Classic Lowland Maya Political Organization: A Review. *Journal of World Prehistory* 13(2):211–263.

Lundell, Cyrus L.

1934 *Ruins of Polol and Other Archaeological Discoveries in the Department of Petén, Guatemala.* Publication 436, Contributions to American Archaeology No. 8, pp. 175–186. Washington, D.C.: Carnegie Institution of Washington.

Lyman, R. Lee, and Michael J. O'Brien

2001 The Direct Historical Approach, Analogical Reasoning, and Theory in Americanist Archaeology. *Journal of Archaeological Method and Theory* 8(4):303–342.

Macri, Martha J.

2000 Mutal, a Possible Mixe-Zoque Toponym. *Glyph Dwellers*, Report 12. Maya Hieroglyphic Database Project, University of California, Davis.

In press A Lunar Origin for the Mesoamerican Calendars of 20, 13, 9, and 7 days. In *Proceedings of the Oxford V Conference: Cultural Aspects of Astronomy.* Santa Fe, New Mex.: School of American Research.

Maler, Teobert

1911 *Explorations in the Department of Peten, Guatemala. Tikal.* Memoirs of the Peabody Museum of American Archaeology and Ethnology. Cambridge, Mass.: Harvard University.

Malmström, Vincent H.

1973 Origins of the Mesoamerican 260-Day Calendar. *Science* 181:939–941.

1978 A Reconstruction of the Chronology of Mesoamerican Calendrical Systems. *Journal for the History of Astronomy*, ed. M. A. Hoskin, 9:105–116.

Manahan, T. Kam

2002 La fase Ejar de Copán, Honduras, y el fin de la dinastía clásica maya. In *XV simposio de investigaciones arqueológicas en Guatemala*,

2001, ed. Juan Pedro Laporte, Héctor Escobedo, and Bárbara Arroyo, pp. 33–40. Guatemala City: Museo Nacional de Arqueología y Etnología and Asociación Tikal.

Marcus, Joyce

1973 Territorial Organization of the Lowland Classic Maya. *Science* 180:911–916.

1976 *Emblem and State in the Classic Maya Lowlands: An Epigraphic Approach to Territorial Organization.* Washington, D.C.: Dumbarton Oaks.

1983 On the Nature of the Mesoamerican City. In *Prehistoric Settlement Patterns: Essays in Honor of Gordon R. Willey,* ed. Evon Z. Vogt and Richard M. Leventhal, pp. 195–242. Cambridge, Mass.: Peabody Museum of Archaeology and Ethnology; Albuquerque: University of New Mexico Press.

1987 *The Inscriptions of Calakmul: Royal Marriage at a Maya City in Campeche, Mexico.* Museum of Anthropology, Technical Report 21. Ann Arbor: University of Michigan.

1992a *Mesoamerican Writing Systems: Propaganda, Myth, and History in Four Ancient Civilizations.* Princeton, N.J.: Princeton University Press.

1992b Political Fluctuations in Mesoamerica. *National Geographic Research and Exploration* 8(4):392–411.

1993 Ancient Maya Political Organization. In *Lowland Maya Civilization in the Eighth Century A.D.,* ed. Jeremy A. Sabloff and John S. Henderson, pp. 111–183. Washington, D.C.: Dumbarton Oaks.

1995 Where Is Lowland Maya Archaeology Headed? *Journal of Archaeological Research* 3:3–53.

1998 The Peaks and Valleys of Ancient States: An Extension of the Dynamic Model. In *Archaic States,* ed. Gary M. Feinman and Joyce Marcus, pp. 59–94. Santa Fe, New Mex.: School of American Research.

2001 Textos dinásticos. In *Las ruinas de Calakmul, Campeche, México: Un lugar central y su paisaje cultural,* coord. William J. Folan, Laraine A. Fletcher, Jacinto May Hau, and Lynda Florey Folan, pp. 37–42. Campeche, México: Universidad Autónoma de Campeche.

Marcus, Joyce, and Gary M. Feinman

1998 Introduction. In *Archaic States,* ed. Gary M. Feinman and Joyce Marcus, pp. 3–13. Santa Fe, New Mex.: School of American Research.

Marcus, Joyce, Kent V. Flannery, and Ronald Spores

1983 The Cultural Legacy of the Oaxacan Preceramic. In *The Cloud People. Divergent Evolution of the Zapotec and Mixtec Civilizations,* ed. Kent V. Flannery and Joyce Marcus, pp. 36–39. New York: Academic Press.

Martin, Simon

2003 In Line of the Founder: A View of Dynastic Politics and Tikal. In *Tikal: Dynasties, Foreigners, & Affairs of State: Advancing Maya Archaeology,* ed. Jeremy A. Sabloff, pp. 3–45. School of American Research Advanced Seminar Series. Santa Fe, New Mex.: School of American Research Press; Oxford: James Currey.

Martin, Simon, and Nikolai Grube

1995 Maya Superstates: How a Few Powerful Kingdoms Vied for Control of the Maya Lowlands during the Classic Period (A.D. 300–900). *Archaeology* 48:41–46.

2000 *Chronicle of the Maya Kings and Queens: Deciphering the Dynasties of the Ancient Maya.* London: Thames and Hudson.

Martínez Hernández, Antonio

[1585] 1929 *Diccionario de Motul: Maya-español.* México.

Mastache, Alba Guadalupe, and Robert H. Cobean

2000 Ancient Tollan, the Sacred Precinct. *RES* 38:101–133.

Matheny, Ray T.

1987 An Early Maya Metropolis. *National Geographic* 172(3):316–339.

Mathews, Peter

1985 Maya Early Classic Monuments and Inscriptions. In *A Consideration of the Early Classic Period in the Maya Lowlands,* ed. Gordon R. Willey and Peter Mathews, pp. 5–54. Institute of Mesoamerican Studies, Publication 10. Albany: State University of New York.

1991 Classic Maya Emblem Glyphs. In *Classic Maya Political History: Hieroglyphic and Archaeological Evidence,* ed. T. Patrick Culbert, pp. 19–29. Cambridge: Cambridge University Press and School of American Research.

2001 The Dates of Toniná and a Dark Horse in Its History. *PARI Journal* 2(1):1–6. www.mesoweb.com/pari/publications/journal/201/Tonina.pdf

Mathews, Peter, and Gordon R. Willey

1991 Prehistoric Polities of the Pasion Region: Hieroglyphic Texts and Their Archaeological Settings. In *Classic Maya Political History: Hieroglyphic and Archaeological Evidence,* ed. T. Patrick Culbert, pp. 30–71. Cambridge: Cambridge University Press and School of American Research.

Matos Moctezuma, Eduardo

1987 Symbolism of the Templo Mayor. In *The Aztec Templo Mayor,* ed. Elizabeth P. Boone, pp. 185–209. Washington, D.C.: Dumbarton Oaks.

McAnany, Patricia A.

1995 *Living with the Ancestors: Kinship and Kingship in Ancient Maya Society.* Austin: University of Texas Press.

2001 Cosmology and the Institutionalization of Hierarchy in the Maya Region. In *From Leaders to Rulers,* ed. Jonathan Haas, pp. 125–148. New York: Kluwer Academic/Plenum.

McGee, R. Jon

1990 *Life, Ritual, and Religion among the Lacandon Maya.* Belmont, Calif.: Wadsworth.

Mejía Amaya, Héctor E., Heidy Quezada, and Jorge E. Chocón
1998   Un límite político territorial en el sureste de Petén. In *XI simposio de investigaciones arqueológicas en Guatemala, 1997*, ed. Juan Pedro Laporte and Héctor L. Escobedo, pp. 171–190. Guatemala City: Museo Nacional de Arqueología y Etnología and Asociación Tikal.

Milbrath, Susan
1999   *Star Gods of the Maya: Astronomy in Art, Folklore, and Calendars.* Austin: University of Texas Press.
2002   New Questions Concerning the Authenticity of the Grolier Codex. *Latin American Literatures Journal: A Review of American Indian Texts and Studies* 18(1): 50–83.

Miller, Arthur G.
1977   "Captains of the Itzá": Unpublished Mural Evidence from Chichén Itzá. In *Social Process in Maya Prehistory: Studies in Honour of Sir Eric Thompson*, ed. Norman Hammond, pp. 197–225. London: Academic Press.
1982   *On the Edge of the Sea: Mural Painting at Tancah-Tulum.* Washington, D.C.: Dumbarton Oaks.
1986   *Maya Rulers of Time/Los soberanos mayas del tiempo.* Philadelphia: The University Museum, University of Pennsylvania.

Miller, Mary Ellen
1986   *The Murals of Bonampak.* Princeton, N.J.: Princeton University Press.
1993   On the Eve of the Collapse: Maya Art of the Eighth Century. In *Lowland Maya Civilization in the Eighth Century A.D.*, ed. Jeremy A. Sabloff and John S. Henderson, pp. 355–413. Washington, D.C.: Dumbarton Oaks.

Miller, Mary Ellen, and Stephen D. Houston
1987   Stairways and Ballcourt Glyphs: New Perspectives on the Classic Maya Ballgame. *RES* 14: 47–66.

Miller, Mary Ellen, and Karl Taube
1993   *The Gods and Symbols of Ancient Mexico and the Maya: An Illustrated Dictionary of Mesoamerican Religion.* London: Thames and Hudson.

Montgomery, John
2001a   *How to Read Maya Hieroglyphs.* New York: Hippocrene Books.
2001b   *Tikal: An Illustrated History of the Ancient Maya Capital.* New York: Hippocrene Books.
2002   *Dictionary of Maya Hieroglyphs.* New York: Hippocrene Books.

Morley, Sylvanus G.
1915   *An Introduction to the Study of the Maya Hieroglyphs.* Bureau of American Ethnology, Bulletin 57. Washington, D.C.: Smithsonian Institution.
1917   The Historical Value of the Books of Chilam Balam. *Journal of the Archaeological Institute of America* 15(2): 195–214.

1920   *The Inscriptions at Copan.* 2 vols. Washington, D.C.: Carnegie Institution of Washington, Department of Archaeology.

1935   *Guide Book to the Ruins of Quirigua.* Supplemental Publication 16. Washington, D.C.: Carnegie Institution of Washington.

1937–1938 *The Inscriptions of Peten,* vol. 3. CIW Publication 437. Washington, D.C.: Carnegie Institution of Washington.

1946   *The Ancient Maya* [2d ed. 1947]. Stanford, Calif.: Stanford University Press.

Morley, Sylvanus G., and George W. Brainerd

1956   *The Ancient Maya,* 3d ed. Stanford, Calif.: Stanford University Press.

Morley, Sylvanus G., George W. Brainerd, and Robert J. Sharer

1983   *The Ancient Maya,* 4th ed. Stanford, Calif.: Stanford University Press.

Mundy, Barbara E.

1998   Mesoamerican Cartography. In *Cartography in the Traditional African, American, Arctic, Australian, and Pacific Societies,* ed. David Woodward and G. Malcolm Lewis, pp. 183–256. History of Cartography, vol. 2, bk. 3. Chicago: University of Chicago Press.

Myers, Bethany, and Prudence M. Rice

n.d.   Dual Rulership at Machaquilá? Manuscript.

Nash, Manning

1958   *Machine Age Maya: The Industrialization of a Guatemalan Community.* American Anthropological Association, Memoir 87.

Navarrete, Carlos

1988   Acotaciones a dos estelas de Flores, El Petén. *Mayab* 4:9–12. Madrid: Sociedad Española de Estudios Mayas, Universidad Complutense.

Nuttall, Zelia

1928   Nouvelles Lumières sur les Civilizations Américaines et le Système du Calendrier. In *Proceedings of the Twenty-second International Congress of Americanists,* pp. 119–128. Rome.

O'Mansky, Matt, and Nicholas P. Dunning

2004   Settlement and Late Classic Political Disintegration in the Petexbatun Region, Guatemala. In *The Terminal Classic in the Maya Lowlands: Collapse, Transition, and Transformations,* ed. Arthur A. Demarest, Prudence M. Rice, and Don S. Rice, pp. 83–101. Boulder: University Press of Colorado.

Pahl, Gary W.

1982   A Possible Cycle 7 Monument from Polol, El Petén, Guatemala. In *Pre-Columbian Art History: Selected Readings,* ed. Alana Cordy-Collins, pp. 23–31. Palo Alto, Calif.: Peek Publications.

Paxton, Merideth

1986   Codex Dresden: Stylistic and Iconographic Analysis of a Maya Manuscript. Ph.D. dissertation, University of New Mexico.

Perry, Richard, and Rosalind Perry

1988   *Maya Missions: Exploring the Spanish Colonial Churches of Yucatan.* Santa Barbara, Calif.: Espadana Press.

Pincemin, Sonia, Joyce Marcus, Lynda Florey Folan, et al.
1998   Extending the Calakmul Dynasty Back in Time: A New Stela from a Maya Capital in Campeche, Mexico. *Latin American Antiquity* 9(4):310–327.
Pohl, Mary D.
1981   Ritual Continuity and Transformation in Mesoamerica: Reconstructing the Ancient Maya *cuch* Ritual. *American Antiquity* 46:513–529.
Pohl, Mary D., and John D. Pohl
1994   Cycles of Conflict: Political Factionalism in the Maya Lowlands. In *Factional Competition and Political Development in the New World*, ed. Elizabeth M. Brumfiel and John W. Fox, pp. 138–157. Cambridge: Cambridge University Press.
Pohl, Mary E. D., Kevin O. Pope, and Christopher von Nagy
2002   Olmec Origins of Mesoamerican Writing. *Science* 293:1984–1987.
Pollock, H. E. D.
1980   *The Puuc, an Archaeological Survey of the Hill Country of Yucatan and Northern Campeche, Mexico.* Peabody Museum of Archaeology and Ethnology, Memoirs 19. Cambridge, Mass.: Harvard University.
Proskouriakoff, Tatiana
1950   *A Study of Classic Maya Sculpture.* Publication 593. Washington, D.C.: Carnegie Institution of Washington.
1960   Historical Implications of a Pattern of Dates at Piedras Negras. *American Antiquity* 25:454–475.
1962a   The Artifacts of Mayapan. In *Mayapan, Yucatan, Mexico,* by H. E. D. Pollock, Ralph L. Roys, Tatiana Proskouriakoff, and A. Ledyard Smith, pp. 321–442. Pub. 619. Washington, D.C.: Carnegie Institution of Washington.
1962b   Civic and Religious Structures of Mayapan. In *Mayapan, Yucatan, Mexico,* by H. E. D. Pollock, Ralph L. Roys, Tatiana Proskouriakoff, and A. Ledyard Smith, pp. 87–163. Publication 619. Washington, D.C.: Carnegie Institution of Washington.
1993   *Maya History.* Ed. Rosemary A. Joyce. Austin: University of Texas Press.
Puleston, Dennis E.
1979   An Epistemological Pathology and the Collapse, or Why the Maya Kept the Short Count. In *Maya Archaeology and Ethnohistory,* ed. Norman Hammond and Gordon R. Willey, pp. 63–74. Austin: University of Texas Press.
Pugh, Timothy W.
1999   Cycle 10 Monuments in the Central Petén and the Pasión Regions. Paper prepared for ANTH 420, Department of Anthropology, Southern Illinois University Carbondale.
2001a   Architecture, Ritual, and Social Identity at Late Postclassic Zacpetén, Petén, Guatemala: Identification of the Kowoj. Ph.D. dissertation, Southern Illinois University Carbondale.

2001b   Flood Reptiles, Serpent Temples, and the Quadripartite Universe: The *Imago Mundi* of Late Postclassic Mayapan. *Ancient Mesoamerica* 12:247–258.

Quezada, Sergio
1993   *Pueblos y caciques yucatecos, 1550–1580.* México, D.F.: El Colegio de México.

Radcliffe-Brown, A. R.
1940   Preface. In *African Political Systems,* ed. Meyer Fortes and E. E. Evans-Pritchard, pp. xi–xxiii. London: Oxford University Press.

Rands, Robert L.
1973   The Classic Maya Collapse in the Southern Maya Lowlands: Chronology. In *The Classic Maya Collapse,* ed. T. Patrick Culbert, pp. 43–62. Albuquerque: University of New Mexico Press.

Recinos, Adrián, and Delia Goetz (trans.)
1953   *The Annals of the Cakchiquels.* Norman: University of Oklahoma Press.

Redfield, Robert, and Alfonso Villa Rojas
1934   *Chan Kom: A Maya Village.* Chicago: University of Chicago Press.

Reents-Budet, Dorie
1994   *Painting the Maya Universe: Royal Ceramics of the Classic Period.* Durham, N.C.: Duke University Press.

Reents-Budet, Dorie J., Ronald L. Bishop, and Barbara MacLeod
1994   Painting styles, workshop locations and pottery production. In *Painting the Maya Universe: Royal Ceramics of the Classic Period,* ed. Dorie Reents-Budet, pp. 164–233. Durham, N.C.: Duke University Press.

Relaciones de Yucatán
1898–1900 Incluidas en la colección de documentos inéditos relativos al descubrimiento, conquista y organización de las antiguas posesiones españoles de ultramar. 2d series, vols. 11, 13. Madrid.

Renfrew, Colin (ed.)
1973   *The Explanation of Culture Change: Models in Prehistory.* London: Duckworth.

Renfrew, Colin, and John F. Cherry (eds.)
1986   *Peer Polity Interaction and Socio-Political Change.* Cambridge: Cambridge University Press.

Restall, Matthew
1997   *The Maya World: Yucatec Culture and Society, 1550–1850.* Stanford, Calif.: Stanford University Press.
2001   The People of the Patio: Ethnohistorical Evidence of Yucatec Maya Royal Courts. In *Royal Courts of the Ancient Maya,* vol. 2: *Data and Case Studies,* ed. Takeshi Inomata and Stephen D. Houston, pp. 335–390. Boulder, Colo.: Westview Press.

Rice, Don S.
In press Late Classic Maya Populations: Characteristics and Implications. In *Urban Populations,* ed. Glen Storey. Tuscaloosa: University of Alabama Press.

Rice, Don S., and T. Patrick Culbert
1990   Historical Contexts for Population Reconstruction in the Maya Low-
        lands. In *Precolumbian Population History in the Maya Lowlands*,
        ed. T. Patrick Culbert and Don S. Rice, pp. 1–36. Albuquerque: Uni-
        versity of New Mexico Press.
Rice, Don S., and Prudence M. Rice
In press Seventeenth-Century Maya Political Geography and Resistance in
        Central Petén, Guatemala. In *The Postclassic- to Spanish-Era Transi-
        tion in Mesoamerica: Archaeological Perspectives*, ed. Rani Alexan-
        der and Susan Kepecs. Albuquerque: University of New Mexico Press.
Rice, Prudence M.
1987   *Macanché Island, El Petén, Guatemala: Excavations, Pottery, and
        Artifacts.* Gainesville: University of Florida Press.
1996   La cerámica del Proyecto Maya-Colonial. In Proyecto Maya-
        Colonial: Geografía política del siglo XVII en el centro del Petén,
        Guatemala. Informe preliminar al Instituto de Antropología e His-
        toria de Guatemala sobre investigaciones del campo en los años 1994
        y 1995, ed. Don S. Rice, Prudence M. Rice, Rómulo Sánchez Polo,
        and Grant D. Jones, pp. 247–318. Carbondale, Ill.
1997   Late Stelae in the Central Petén Lakes Region. Paper presented at the
        62d annual meeting of the Society for American Archaeology,
        Nashville, Tenn.
1999   Rethinking Classic Lowland Maya Pottery Censers. *Ancient Meso-
        america* 10(1):25–50.
n.d.a   The Isthmian Origins of Maya Calendrical Ritual. Manuscript.
n.d.b   States, Stelae, and "Stranger-Kings": Rethinking Teotihuacan-Tikal
        Contacts in Mesoamerica. Manuscript.
n.d.c   The Classic "Collapse" and Its Causes: The Role of Warfare.
        Manuscript.
Rice, Prudence M., and Donald W. Forsyth
2004   Terminal Classic-Period Lowland Ceramics. In *The Terminal Classic
        in the Maya Lowlands: Collapse, Transition, and Transformations*,
        ed. Arthur A. Demarest, Prudence M. Rice, and Don S. Rice, pp. 28–
        59. Boulder: University Press of Colorado.
Rice, Prudence M., and Don S. Rice
2004   Late Classic to Postclassic Transformations in the Petén Lakes Re-
        gion, Guatemala. In *The Terminal Classic in the Maya Lowlands:
        Collapse, Transition, and Transformations*, ed. Arthur A. Demarest,
        Prudence M. Rice, and Don S. Rice, pp. 125–139. Boulder: University
        Press of Colorado.
Rice, Prudence M., Don S. Rice, and Grant D. Jones
1996   Development of 17th-Century Political Geography of Central Petén,
        Guatemala. Paper presented at the annual meeting of the American
        Anthropological Association, San Francisco.
Ricketson, Oliver G.
1928   Notes on Two Maya Astronomic Observatories. *American Anthro-
        pologist* 30:434–444.

Ricketson, Oliver G., and Edith B. Ricketson
1937   *Uaxactun, Guatemala, Group E, 1926–1931. Part 1: The Excavations; Part II: The Artifacts.* Pub. 477. Washington, D.C.: Carnegie Institution of Washington.

Riese, Berthold
1984   *Hel* Hieroglyphs. In *Phoneticism in Mayan Hieroglyphic Writing,* ed. John S. Justeson and Lyle Campbell, pp. 263–286. Institute for Mesoamerican Studies. Albany: State University of New York at Albany.

Ringle, William M., George J. Bey III, Tara Bond Freeman, Craig A. Hanson, Charles W. Houck, and J. Gregory Smith
2004   The Decline of the East: The Classic to Postclassic Transition at Ek Balam, Yucatán. In *The Terminal Classic in the Maya Lowlands: Collapse, Transition, and Transformations,* ed. Arthur A. Demarest, Prudence M. Rice, and Don S. Rice, pp. 485–516. Boulder: University Press of Colorado.

Ringle, William M., and Thomas C. Smith-Stark
1996   *A Concordance to the Inscriptions of Palenque, Chiapas, Mexico.* Middle American Research Institute, Publication 62. New Orleans: Tulane University.

Robertson, Merle Greene
1972   Monument Thievery in Mesoamerica. *American Antiquity* 37(2): 147–155.

Robicsek, Francis
1975   *A Study in Maya Art and History: The Mat Symbol.* New York: Museum of the American Indian, Heye Foundation.

Robles Castellanos, Fernando, and Anthony P. Andrews
1986   A Review and Synthesis of Recent Postclassic Archaeology in Northern Yucatan. In *Late Lowland Maya Civilization, Classic to Postclassic,* ed. Jeremy A. Sabloff and E. Wyllys Andrews V, pp. 53–98. Albuquerque: University of New Mexico Press and School of American Research.

Rockmore, Matthew
1998   The Social Development of the Itzá Maya: A Reassessment of the Multiple Lines of Evidence. M.A. thesis, Southern Illinois University Carbondale.

Roscoe, Paul B.
1993   Practice and Political Centralisation: A New Approach to Political Evolution. *Current Anthropology* 34(2):111–140.

Roys, Ralph L.
1957   *The Political Geography of the Yucatan Maya.* Publication 613. Washington, D.C.: Carnegie Institution of Washington.
[1933] 1967   *The Book of Chilam Balam of Chumayel.* Norman: University of Oklahoma Press.
[1943] 1972   *The Indian Background of Colonial Yucatan.* Norman: University of Oklahoma Press.

Ruppert, Karl J.
[1940] 1977 A Special Assemblage of Maya Structures. In *The Maya and Their Neighbors: Essays on Middle American Anthropology and Archaeology*, ed. Clarence L. Hay, Ralph L. Linton, et al., pp. 222–231. New York: Dover Publications.

Sabloff, Jeremy A.
1986 Interaction among Maya Polities: A Preliminary Examination. In *Peer Polity Interaction and Socio-political Change*, ed. Colin Renfrew and John F. Cherry, pp. 109–116. Cambridge: Cambridge University Press.

Sabloff, Jeremy A., and E. Wyllys Andrews V. (eds.)
1986 *Late Lowland Maya Civilization, Classic to Postclassic*. Albuquerque: School of American Research—University of New Mexico Press.

Sahagún, Bernardino de
1950–1970 *Florentine Codex: General History of the Things of New Spain*. Trans. and ed. A. J. O. Anderson and C. E. Dibble. 12 bks., in 13 vols. Santa Fe, New Mex.: School of American Research and University of Utah Press.

Sahlins, Marshall
1983 Other Times, Other Customs: The Anthropology of History. *American Anthropologist* 85:517–544.

Salmon, Merilee H.
1982 *Philosophy and Archaeology*. New York: Academic Press.

Sanders, William T., and Barbara Price
1968 *Mesoamerica: The Evolution of a Civilization*. New York: Random House.

Sanders, William T., and David Webster
1988 The Mesoamerican Urban Tradition. *American Anthropologist* 90(3):521–546.

Santley, Robert S., Michael J. Berman, and Rani T. Alexander
1991 The Politicization of the Mesoamerican Ballgame and Its Implications for the Interpretation of the Distribution of Ballcourts in Central Mexico. In *The Mesoamerican Ballgame*, ed. Vernon L. Scarborough and David R. Wilcox, pp. 3–44. Tucson: University of Arizona Press.

Scarborough, Vernon L.
1998 Ecology and Ritual: Water Management and the Maya. *Latin American Antiquity* 9(2):135–159.

Scarborough, Vernon L., and David Wilcox (eds.)
1991 *The Mesoamerican Ballgame*. Tucson: University of Arizona Press.

Schele, Linda, and David Freidel
1990 *A Forest of Kings: The Untold Story of the Ancient Maya*. New York: William Morrow.
1991 The Courts of Creation: Ballcourts, Ballgames, and Portals to the Maya Otherworld. In *The Mesoamerican Ballgame*, ed. Vernon L.

Scarborough and David R. Wilcox, pp. 289–315. Tucson: University of Arizona Press.

Schele, Linda, and Nikolai Grube

1995   The Proceedings of the Maya Hieroglyphic Workshop. Late Classic and Terminal Classic Warfare, March 11–12, 1995. Transcr. and ed. Phil Wanyerka. Department of Art History, University of Texas, Austin.

Schele, Linda, Nikolai Grube, and Erik Boot

1995   Some Suggestions on the K'atun Prophecies in the Books of Chilam Balam in Light of Classic-Period History. *Texas Notes on Precolumbian Art, Writing, and Culture*, no. 72.

Schele, Linda, and Peter Mathews

1991   Royal Visits and Other Intersite Relationships among the Classic Maya. In *Classic Maya Political History*, ed. T. Patrick Culbert, pp. 226–252. Cambridge: Cambridge University Press.

1998   *The Code of Kings: The Language of Seven Sacred Maya Temples and Tombs.* New York: Scribner's.

Schele, Linda, and Mary Miller

1986   *The Blood of Kings: Dynasty and Ritual in Maya Art.* Fort Worth, Tex.: Kimbell Art Museum.

Scholes, France V., and Robert L. Roys

1968   *The Maya Chontal Indians of Acalan-Tixchel: A Contribution to the History and Ethnography of the Yucatan Peninsula,* 2d ed. Norman: University of Oklahoma Press.

Schuster, A. M. H.

1999   Redating the Madrid Codex. *Archaeology* 52(1):26–27.

Sedat, David

1992   Preclassic Notation and the Development of Maya Writing. In *New Theories on the Ancient Maya*, ed. Elin C. Danien and Robert J. Sharer, pp. 81–90. University Museum Symposium Series, vol. 3. Philadelphia: The University Museum, University of Pennsylvania.

Seler, Edouard

1904   *The Mexican Chronology with Special Reference to the Zapotec Calendar.* Bureau of American Ethnology, Bulletin 28, pp. 11–55. Washington, D.C.: Bureau of American Ethnology.

Sharer, Robert J.

1990   *Quirigua, a Classic Maya Center and Its Sculptures.* Durham, N.C.: Carolina Academic Press.

1991   Diversity and Continuity in Maya Civilization: Quirigua as a Case Study. In *Classic Maya Political History*, ed. T. Patrick Culbert, pp. 180–198. Cambridge: Cambridge University Press.

1992   The Preclassic Origin of Lowland Maya States. In *New Theories on the Ancient Maya*, ed. Elin C. Danien and Robert J. Sharer, pp. 131–136. University Museum Symposium Series, vol. 3. Philadelphia: The University Museum, University of Pennsylvania.

1994   *The Ancient Maya,* 5th ed. Stanford, Calif.: Stanford University Press.
2003   Tikal and the Copan Dynastic Founding. In *Tikal: Dynasties, Foreigners, & Affairs of State: Advancing Maya Archaeology,* ed. Jeremy A. Sabloff, pp. 319–353. School of American Research Advanced Seminar Series. Santa Fe, New Mex.: School of American Research Press; Oxford: James Currey.

Smith, A. Ledyard
1950   *Uaxactun, Guatemala: Excavations of 1931–37.* Pub. 588. Washington, D.C.: Carnegie Institution of Washington.

Smith, M. G.
1960   *Government in Zazzau: 1890–1950.* London: Oxford University Press.
1968   Political Anthropology: Political Organization. In *International Encyclopedia of the Social Sciences,* ed. David Sills, pp. 192–202. New York: Macmillan/Free Press.

Smith, Robert E.
1971   *The Pottery of Mayapan.* 2 vols. Peabody Museum of Archaeology and Ethnology Papers 66. Cambridge, Mass.: Harvard University.

Solís Alcalá, Ermilo
1949a   *Diccionario español-maya.* Mérida.
1949b   (trans.) *Códice Pérez.* Mérida: Liga de Acción Social.

Southall, Aidan W.
1956   *Alur Society: A Study in Processes and Types of Domination.* Cambridge: Heffer.
1988   The Segmentary State in Africa and Asia. *Comparative Studies in Society and History* 30:52–82.

Spinden, Herbert J.
1917   *Ancient Civilizations of Mexico and Central America.* New York: American Museum of Natural History.

Šprajc, Ivan
2000   Astronomical Alignments at Teotihuacan. *Latin American Antiquity* 11(4):403–415.

Steggerda, M.
1941   *Maya Indians of Yucatan.* Publication 531. Washington, D.C.: Carnegie Institution of Washington.

Stross, Brian
1988   The Burden of Office: A Reading. *Mexicon* 10:118–121.

Stuart, David
1984   A Note on the "Hand-scattering" Glyph. In *Phoneticism I Mayan Hieroglyphic Writing,* ed. John S. Justeson and Lyle Campbell, pp. 307–310. Albany: Institute for Mesoamerican Studies, State University of New York at Albany.
1988   Blood Symbolism in Maya Iconography. In *Maya Iconography,* ed. Elizabeth P. Benson and Gillette Griffin, pp. 175–221. Princeton, N.J.: Princeton University Press.
1995   A Study of Maya Inscriptions. Ph.D. dissertation, Vanderbilt University.

1996 Kings of Stone: A Consideration of Stelae in Ancient Maya Ritual and Representations. *RES* 29/30:148–171.

2000 "The Arrival of Strangers": Teotihuacan and Tollan in Classic Maya History. In *Mesoamerica's Classic Heritage, From Teotihuacan to the Aztecs*, ed. Davíd Carrasco, Lindsay Jones, and Scott Sessions, pp. 465–513. Boulder: University Press of Colorado.

n.d. An Unusual Calendar Cycle at Toniná. *PARI Journal.*

Stuart, David, and Stephen Houston

1994 Classic Maya Place Names. *Studies in Pre-Columbian Art and Archaeology*, no. 33. Washington, D.C.: Dumbarton Oaks.

Stuart, David, Stephen Houston, and John Robertson

1999 Classic Mayan Language and Classic Maya Gods: The Proceedings of The Maya Hieroglyphic Workshop, March 13–14. Transcr. and ed. Phil Wanyerka. Department of Art History, University of Texas, Austin.

Stuart, George E.

1992 Quest for Decipherment: A Historical and Biographical Survey of Maya Hieroglyphic Investigation. In *New Theories on the Ancient Maya*, ed. Elin C. Danien and Robert J. Sharer, pp. 1–63. University Museum Symposium Series, vol. 3. Philadelphia: The University Museum, University of Pennsylvania.

1997 The Royal Crypts of Copan. *National Geographic* 192(6):68–93.

Sugiyama, Saburo

1998 Termination Programs and Prehispanic Looting at the Feathered Serpent Pyramid in Teotihuacan, Mexico. In *The Sowing and the Dawning: Termination, Dedication, and Transformation in the Archaeological and Ethnographic Record of Mesoamerica*, ed. Shirley Boteler Mock, pp. 147–164. Albuquerque: University of New Mexico Press.

Suhler, Charles, Traci Ardren, David Freidel, and Dave Johnstone

2004 The Rise and Fall of Terminal Classic Yaxuna, Yucatán, Mexico. In *The Terminal Classic in the Maya Lowlands: Collapse, Transition, and Transformations*, ed. Arthur A. Demarest, Prudence M. Rice, and Don S. Rice, pp. 450–484. Boulder: University Press of Colorado.

Taladoire, Eric, and Benoit Colsenet

1991 "Bois Ton Sang, Beaumanoir": The Political and Conflictual Aspects of the Ballgame in the Northern Chiapas Area. In *The Mesoamerican Ballgame*, ed. Vernon L. Scarborough and David R. Wilcox, pp. 161–174. Tucson: University of Arizona Press.

Tambiah, Stanley

1977 The Galactic Polity: The Structure of Traditional Kingdoms in Southeast Asia. *Annals of the New York Academy of Sciences* 293:69–97.

Taube, Karl A.

1992 The Major Gods of Ancient Yucatan. *Studies in Pre-Columbian Art and Archaeology*, no. 32. Washington, D.C.: Dumbarton Oaks.

1998 The Jade Hearth: Centrality, Rulership, and the Classic Maya Temple. In *Function and Meaning in Classic Maya Architecture*, ed.

Stephen D. Houston, pp. 427–478. Washington, D.C.: Dumbarton Oaks.

Tax, Sol
1937   The Municipios of the Midwestern Highlands of Guatemala. *American Anthropologist* 39(3):423–444.

Tax, Sol, and Robert Hinshaw
1969   The Maya of the Midwestern Highlands. In *Ethnology, Part One,* vol. ed. Evon Z. Vogt, pp. 69–100. *Handbook of Middle American Indians,* vol. 7, gen. ed. Robert Wauchope. Austin: University of Texas Press.

Tedlock, Barbara
1992   *Time and the Highland Maya,* rev. ed. Albuquerque: University of New Mexico Press.

Tedlock, Dennis
1985   *Popol Vuh: The Definitive Edition of the Mayan Book of the Dawn of Life and the Glories of Gods and Kings.* New York: Simon and Schuster.
1992   The Popol Vuh as a Hieroglyphic Book. In *New Theories on the Ancient Maya,* ed. Elin Danien and Robert J. Sharer, pp. 229–240. University Museum Symposium Series, vol. 3. University Museum Monograph 77. Philadelphia: The University Museum, University of Pennsylvania.

Thomas, Cyrus
1882   *A Study of the Manuscript Troano.* Washington, D.C.: Government Printing Office.

Thompson, J. Eric S.
1930a   On the Origin of the 260-Day calendar. In *Archaeological Investigations in British Honduras, Appendix IV,* pp. 349–353. Field Museum of Natural History, Anthropological Series, vol. 17, no. 3. Chicago: Field Museum of Natural History.
1930b   *Ethnology of the Mayas of Southern and Central British Honduras.* Anthropological Series 2. Chicago: Field Museum of Natural History.
1931   *Archaeological Investigations in the Southern Cayo District, British Honduras.* Anthropological Series, vol. 17, no. 3. Chicago: Field Museum of Natural History.
1934   *Sky Bearers, Colors and Directions in Maya and Mexican Religion.* Pub. 436, Contrib. 10. Washington, D.C.: Carnegie Institution of Washington.
1942   The Civilization of the Mayas. *Anthropology Leaflet* 25 (4th ed.). Chicago: Field Museum of Natural History.
1960   *Maya Hieroglyphic Writing: An Introduction.* Norman: University of Oklahoma Press.
1962   *A Catalog of Maya Hieroglyphs.* Norman: University of Oklahoma Press.
1970   *Maya History and Religion.* Norman: University of Oklahoma Press.
1972   A Commentary on the Dresden Codex: A Maya Hieroglyphic Book.

Memoirs of the American Philosophical Society, no. 93. Philadelphia, Pa.

Thompson, Philip C.
1999   *Tekanto, a Maya Town in Colonial Yucatán.* Middle American Research Institute Publication 67. New Orleans: Tulane University.

Tichy, Franz
1981   Order and Relationship of Space and Time in Mesoamerica: Myth or Reality? In *Mesoamerican Sites and World-Views,* ed. Elizabeth P. Benson, pp. 217–245. Washington, D.C.: Dumbarton Oaks.

Tolstoy, Paul
1989   Coapexco and Tlatilco: Sites with Olmec Materials in the Basin of Mexico. In *Regional Perspectives on the Olmec,* ed. Robert J. Sharer and David C. Grove, pp. 85–121. Cambridge: Cambridge University Press and School of American Research.

Tourtellot, Gair, and Jason González
2004   The Last Hurrah: Continuity and Transformation at Seibal. In *The Terminal Classic in the Maya Lowlands: Collapse, Transition, and Transformations,* ed. Arthur A. Demarest, Prudence M. Rice, and Don S. Rice, pp. 60–82. Boulder: University Press of Colorado.

Tourtellot, Gair, and Jeremy A. Sabloff
1994   Community Structure at Sayil: A Case Study of Puuc Settlement. In *Hidden among the Hills: Maya Archaeology of the Northwest Yucatan Peninsula,* ed. Hanns J. Prem, pp. 71–92. First Maler Symposium, Bonn 1989. Acta Mesoamericana, vol. 7. Möckmühl: Verlag von Flemming.

Tozzer, Alfred M. (ed.)
1941   *Landa's Relación de las cosas de Yucatan: A Translation.* Papers of the Peabody Museum of Archaeology and Ethnology, no. 28. Cambridge, Mass.: Peabody Museum, Harvard University. [New York: Kraus Reprint Co., 1966]

Turner, E. S., N. I. Turner, and Richard E. W. Adams
1981   Volumetric Assessment, Rank Ordering, and Maya Civic Centers. In *Lowland Maya Settlement Patterns,* ed. Wendy Ashmore, pp. 71–88. Albuquerque: School of American Research—University of New Mexico Press.

Vail, Gabrielle
1996   The Gods in the Madrid Codex: An Iconographic and Glyphic Analysis. Ph.D. dissertation, Tulane University.
1997   The Deer-Trapping Almanacs in the Madrid Codex. In *Papers on the Madrid Codex.* Middle American Research Institute, Publication 64, ed. Victoria R. Bricker and Gabrielle Vail, pp. 73–110. New Orleans: Tulane University.

Valdés, Juan Antonio
1997   El Proyecto Miraflores II dentro del marco preclásico en Kaminaljuyu. In *X simposio de investigaciones arqueológicas en Guatemala 1996,* ed. Juan Pedro Laporte and Héctor L. Escobedo, pp. 81–

91. Guatemala City: Museo Nacional de Arqueología y Etnología and Asociación Tikal.

Valdés, Juan Antonio, and Federico Fahsen

1995   The Reigning Dynasty of Uaxactun During the Early Classic. *Ancient Mesoamerica* 6(2):197–219.

2004   Disaster in Sight: The Terminal Classic at Tikal and Uaxactun. In *The Terminal Classic in the Maya Lowlands: Collapse, Transition, and Transformations*, ed. Arthur A. Demarest, Prudence M. Rice, and Don S. Rice, pp. 140–161. Boulder: University Press of Colorado.

Viel, René H.

1999   The Pectorals of Altar Q and Structure 11: An Interpretation of the Political Organization at Copán, Honduras. *Latin American Antiquity* 10(4):377–399.

Villacorta, Carlos A., and J. Antonio Villacorta C.

[1930] 1989 *The Dresden Codex: Drawings of the Pages and Commentary in Spanish*. Mayan Studies 3. Laguna Hills, Calif.: Aegean Park Press.

Villacorta C., J. Antonio, and Carlos A. Villacorta

1976   *Códices mayas*, 2d ed. Guatemala: Tipografía Nacional.

Villa Rojas, Alfonso

1945   *The Maya of East Central Quintana Roo*. Pub. 559. Washington, D.C.: Carnegie Institution of Washington.

1969   The Maya of Yucatan. In *Ethnology, Part I*, vol. ed. Evon Z. Vogt, pp. 244–275. *Handbook of Middle American Indians*, vol. 7, gen. ed. Robert Wauchope. Austin: University of Texas Press.

Vogt, Evon Z.

1961   Some Aspects of Zinacantan Settlement Patterns and Ceremonial Organization. *Estudios de Cultura Maya* 1:131–145. México, D.F.: Universidad Nacional Autónoma de México.

1964   The Genetic Model and Maya Cultural Development. In *Desarrollo Cultural de los Mayas*, ed. Evon Z. Vogt and Alberto Ruz, Seminario de Cultura Maya, pp. 9–48. México. D.F.: Universidad Nacional Autónoma de México.

1969   Introduction. In *Ethnology, Part I*, vol. ed. Evon Z. Vogt, pp. 3–17. *Handbook of Middle American Indians*, vol. 7, gen. ed. Robert Wauchope. Austin: University of Texas Press.

1981   Some Aspects of the Sacred Geography of Highland Chiapas. In *Mesoamerican Sites and World Views*, ed. Elizabeth P. Benson, pp. 119–142. Washington, D.C.: Dumbarton Oaks.

Von Euw, Eric, and Ian Graham

1984   *Corpus of Maya Hieroglyphic Inscriptions*, vol. 5, part 2, *Xultun, La Honradez, Uaxactun*. Peabody Museum of Archaeology and History. Cambridge, Mass.: Harvard University.

von Nagy, Christopher L.

1997   Some Comments on the Madrid Deer-Hunting Almanacs. In *Papers on the Madrid Codex*. Middle American Research Institute, Publication 64, ed. Victoria R. Bricker and Gabrielle Vail, pp. 27–71. New Orleans: Tulane University.

Wagley, Charles
1941   Economics of a Guatemalan Village. *Memoirs of the American Anthropological Association*, no. 58.
1969   The Maya of Northwestern Guatemala. In *Ethnology, Part I*, vol. ed. Evon Z. Vogt, pp. 46–68. *Handbook of Middle American Indians*, vol. 7, gen. ed. Robert Wauchope. Austin: University of Texas Press.

Wanyerka, Phil
1996a   The Carved Monuments of Uxbenká, Toledo District, Belize. *Mexicon* 28(2):29–35.
1996b   A Fresh Look at a Maya Masterpiece. *Cleveland Studies in the History of Art* 1:72–97.
1999   Pecked Cross and Patolli Petroglyphs of the Lagarto Ruins, Stann Creek District, Belize. *Mexicon* 21:108–112.
2002   Classic Maya Political Organization: Epigraphic Evidence for Macro-Political Organization in Southern Belize. Presentation to Department of Anthropology, Southern Illinois University Carbondale, October 25.

Watson, Patty Jo, Steven A. LeBlanc, and Charles L. Redman
1971   *Explanation in Archeology. An Explicitly Scientific Approach.* New York: Columbia University Press.

Waugh, Alexander
1999   *Time: Its Origin, Its Enigma, Its History.* New York: Carroll and Graf.

Webster, David
1976   On Theocracies. *American Anthropologist* 78(4):812–827.
1977   Warfare and the Evolution of Maya Civilization. In *The Origins of Maya Civilization*, ed. Richard E. W. Adams, pp. 335–372. Albuquerque: School of American Research and University of New Mexico Press.
1992   Mesoamerican Elites: The View from Copán. In *Mesoamerican Elites: An Archaeological Assessment*, ed. Diane Z. Chase and Arlen F. Chase, pp. 135–156. Norman: University of Oklahoma Press.
1993   The Study of Maya Warfare: What It Tells Us about the Maya and about Maya Archaeology. In *Lowland Maya Civilization in the Eighth Century A.D.*, ed. Jeremy A. Sabloff and John S. Henderson, pp. 415–444. Washington, D.C.: Dumbarton Oaks.
1997   City-States of the Maya. In *The Archaeology of City-States: Cross-Cultural Approaches*, ed. Deborah Nichols, D. Charlton, and Thomas Charlton, pp. 135–154. Washington, D.C.: Smithsonian Institution Press.
1998   Warfare and Status Rivalry: Lowland Maya and Polynesian Comparison. In *Archaic States*, ed. Gary M. Feinman and Joyce Marcus, pp. 311–351. Santa Fe, New Mex.: School of American Research.
2002   *The Fall of the Ancient Maya: Solving the Mystery of the Maya Collapse.* London: Thames and Hudson.

Webster, David, AnnCorinne Freter, and Nancy Gonlin
2000 *Copán: The Rise and Fall of an Ancient Maya Kingdom*. Fort Worth, Tex.: Harcourt College Publishers.

Webster, David, AnnCorinne Freter, and Rebecca Storey
2004 Dating Copán Culture History: Implications for the Terminal Classic and the Collapse. In *The Terminal Classic in the Maya Lowlands: Collapse, Transition, and Transformations*, ed. Arthur A. Demarest, Prudence M. Rice, and Don S. Rice, pp. 231–259. Boulder: University Press of Colorado.

Wilkerson, S. Jeffrey K.
1991 And Then They Were Sacrificed: The Ritual Ballgame of Northeastern Mesoamerica through Time and Space. In *The Mesoamerican Ballgame*, ed. Vernon L. Scarborough and David R. Wilcox, pp. 45–71. Tucson: University of Arizona Press.

Willey, Gordon R.
1974 The Classic Maya Hiatus: A Rehearsal for the Collapse? In *Mesoamerican Archaeology: New Approaches*, ed. Norman Hammond, pp. 417–444. Austin: University of Texas Press.

1986 The Classic Maya Sociopolitical Order: A Study in Coherence and Instability. In *Research and Reflections in Archaeology and History: Essays in Honor of Doris Stone*, ed. E. Wyllys Andrews V, pp. 189–198. M.A.R.I. Publication 57. New Orleans: Tulane University.

1990 General Summary and Conclusions. *Excavations at Seibal, Department of Peten, Guatemala*. Peabody Museum of Archaeology and Ethnology, *Memoirs*, vol. 17, no. 4. Cambridge, Mass.: Harvard University.

Willey, Gordon R., William R. Bullard, John B. Glass, and James C. Gifford
1965 Prehistoric Maya Settlement in the Belize Valley. *Papers of the Peabody Museum*, vol. 54. Cambridge, Mass.: Harvard University.

Willey, Gordon R., A. Ledyard Smith, Gair Tourtellot III, and Ian Graham
1975 Introduction: The Site and Its Setting. *Excavations at Seibal, Department of Peten, Guatemala*. Peabody Museum of Archaeology and Ethnology, Memoirs, vol. 13. Cambridge, Mass.: Harvard University.

Willey, Gordon R., and Jeremy A. Sabloff
1974 *A History of American Archaeology*, 2d ed. San Francisco: W. H. Freeman.

Wobst, H. Martin
1977 Stylistic Behavior and Information Exchange. In *For the Director: Research Essays in Honor of James B. Griffin*, ed. Charles E. Cleland, pp. 317–342. Anthropological Papers, no. 61. Ann Arbor: Museum of Anthropology, University of Michigan.

1978 The Archaeo-Ethnology of Hunter-Gatherers or the Tyranny of the Ethnographic Record in Archaeology. *American Antiquity* 43(2): 303–309.

Worthy, Morgan, and Roy S. Dickens Jr.

1983   The Mesoamerican Pecked Cross as a Calendrical Device. *American Antiquity* 48(3): 573–576.

Wren, Linnea H.

1991   The Great Ball Court Stone from Chichén Itzá. In *Sixth Palenque Round Table, 1986*, ed. Merle Greene Robertson, pp. 51–58. Norman: University of Oklahoma Press.

Wren, Linnea H., and Peter Schmidt

1991   Elite Interaction during the Terminal Classic Period: New Evidence from Chichen Itza. In *Classic Maya Political History: Hieroglyphic and Archaeological Evidence*, ed. T. Patrick Culbert, pp. 199–225. Cambridge: Cambridge University Press and School of American Research.

Wylie, Alison

1985   Between Philosophy and Archaeology. *American Antiquity* 50(2): 478–490.

Yoffee, Norman

1991   Maya Elite Interaction: Through a Glass, Sideways. In *Classic Maya Political History: Hieroglyphic and Archaeological Evidence*, ed. T. Patrick Culbert, pp. 285–310. Cambridge: Cambridge University Press.

INDEX

Page numbers in italics refer to figures and tables.

cargo system, 30, 81
Carnegie Institution of Washington, 23, 226
Catholic religion, 18, 28, 29, 30. See also cargo system; Christianity; cofradía
causeway, 147 (see specific sites); and ballcourts, 257
cave, 192, 222, 282. See also cenote; ch'en
Cehpech, 26
ceiba (tree), 20, 78
cenote: cult, 235; role in may seat selection, 281–282
Cenote (site), 166
centralized (political organization), 23, 25, 28, 47, 48, 49–51, 52 (see also "overkingship"); Barthel-Marcus model of, 49 (see also Barthel, Thomas; Marcus, Joyce)
central Mexico(-an). See Teotihuacan
central place theory, 32–33, 34
ceremonial bar, 106, 127, 128, 136, 141, 144, 147, 152, 154, 159, 184, 185, 192, 218, 249; serpent, 94, 106, 172, 175, 211, 213; staff-like, 128, 133, 147, 162; as surveying stick, 147. See also stelae, staff
ceremonial center, 29
ceremonial circuit. See processions
Cerros, 279; Preclassic occupation of, 85; Str. 5C-2, 90
ch'a chak (ritual), 28, 29
Chak, 21, 38, 80, 164, 165, 246
Chakan (province), 26
Chalcatzingo, 72
Chalpate, 166; as k'atun seat, 125, 126, 167
Champoton, 26
Chamula, 133, 251
chan kaj, 26
charisma (of rulers), 38, 46, 285
Chase, Arlen F., 51, 53
Chase, Diane Z., 51
ch'en, 78, 281–282
Chi, Gaspar Antonio, 16
Chiapa de Corzo, Stela 2, 73
Chiapas, 14
ch'ib'al, 7, 42
Chich'en Itza, 11, 24, 228; Atlantean figures, 229, 230; ballcourts, 228,

230–231, 232–233, 258, 278; ballgame at, 233, 258, 274; Casa Colorada, 228, 233, 248; ceramic complexes of, 226–227, 232; dates at, 227, 231; Emblem Glyph lacking, 227; fire ritual (see fire ritual); founding of, 227; Great Ballcourt Stone, 230; Hakawitzil, 214; High Priest's Grave, 228, 232, 234; K'ak'upacal, 227, 230, 232; and k'atun lords, 229; Las Monjas, 228, 232; lintel dedication ceremony, 231–232; as may seat, 227, 229, 231, 233–234, 236; and meeting of lords, 239; and multepal, 232; overthrow of, 279; and Petén, 227, 231; as pilgrimage site, 234; radial structures, 228, 278; sacrifice at, 81, 230; Temple of the Hieroglyphic Jambs, 232; Temple of the Initial Series, 231; Temple of the Jaguar, Lower, 229; Temple of the Jaguar, Upper, 229–230; as Terminal Classic capital, 278, 279; and Toltecs, 226, 227, 228, 231; and triadic kingship, 268 (see also above, founding of); and Usumacinta region, 271; Venus Platform, 248; walled precincts, 227–228
Chichicastanango, 29
chief (-dom), 26, 47, 266
Chikinchel (province), 26
chilam (spokesman, speaker), 12, 39, 78–79, 241, 268, 269; in Classic period, 39, 288 (see also aj kuhun); glyphic sign for, 37; proclaiming k'atun prophecy, 81, 83, 290; writing history of k'atun, 112–113. See also books of the chilam balams
Chimaltenango, 29
Chiman Nam (title), 30
Chinkultic, as regional state, 35
Ch'olan language, 8; speakers of, 74, 271
Ch'olti'an language, 8
Chontal region, 13, 239
Christianity, 12. See also Catholic religion
Chronicle of the Maya Kings and Queens, 168. See also Grube, Nikolai; Martin, Simon
Chumayel, (book of the) Chilam Balam of, 20; and calendar origins, 67; and Chich'en Itza, 227; and may/k'atun